Transportation
and Economic Policy

Transportation and Economic Policy

John B. Lansing

THE FREE PRESS, NEW YORK

COLLIER-MACMILLAN LIMITED, LONDON

Fp

Preface

IT IS THE PURPOSE of this book to use fundamental economic concepts in an analytic approach to problems of economic policy in the field of transportation. The manuscript has been developed in a course in the economics of transportation and it is intended to be used as a textbook. The book may also be helpful in other courses in economics, including courses in the field of industrial organization and courses concerned with economic problems. Anyone seriously concerned with one or another of the problems of transportation policy also may find the discussion relevant.

The theoretical framework for the volume is set forth in Part I. The treatment assumes a previous knowledge of economics such as may be gained in a basic elementary course. The approach taken grows out of the author's twin convictions that economic theory is essential to a grasp of economic problems and that economic theory is most meaningful when closely tied to economic reality. Problems of the role of transportation in economic development are considered in Part II and current problems of transportation policy in the United States in Part III in the context of the theory set forth in Part I. The treatment is designed to give to students a grasp of the manner in which statistical investigations can be used in the analysis of these problems.

Although the discussion emphasizes public economic policy, much of

v

the analysis is also relevant to private economic policy. Furthermore, although the emphasis is on economic policy, the treatment is intended to give to the student a sense of the connections between economic policy and its political environment.

The author of a textbook has many intellectual debts. An attempt has been made in the footnotes to give recognition to the sources of the ideas discussed. In a sense, the number of these debts is too few. The literature in the field of transportation is very extensive, and there are undoubtedly many examples of important works relevant to the subject matter treated which are not mentioned. Some of these omissions no doubt are the result of ignorance. It is the intent of this volume, however, to provide a framework for study, to get the reader beyond a superficial level of understanding, and to stimulate him to raise questions about the subject, rather than to provide an exhaustive treatment of the topics raised.

This volume has greatly benefited from critical review of the manuscript by Shorey Peterson. The author also wishes especially to acknowledge the comments he has received from W. Geoffrey Shepherd and Dwight M. Blood. He owes a large debt to his students and to people concerned with transportation both in public agencies and in private business who have contributed to his understanding of the subject. The librarians of the Engineering and Transportation Library of the University of Michigan have been most helpful. He has been fortunate in the quality of the secretarial assistance provided by Laura Gunnarson and Anita Grob. Finally, he is indebted for financial support to a Ford Foundation Faculty Research Fellowship and to the Institute for Social Research for special duty assignment that made it possible for him to spend the time necessary to complete this book.

JOHN B. LANSING

Contents

III

Modern Transportation in the United States   165

LIST OF DIAGRAMS

LIST OF TABLES

Introduction

THERE HAS BEEN EVIDENCE in recent years of a revival of interest in the economics of transportation. Leading economic theorists such as Taussig, Pigou, and J. M. Clark turned their attention to problems of transportation in the 1920s and earlier, and distinguished economists such as William Z. Ripley and I. L. Sharfman specialized in the subject. In the decades of the Great Depression and World War II, however, while some important work was done on transportation the attention of the profession was directed mainly elsewhere.

This situation has been changing. Since the late 1950s and the early 1960s more has been done about transportation, more research carried out, and more books and articles have been appearing. The interest in the subject is not by any means confined to professional economists. Social scientists with other academic backgrounds are interested, as well as others with backgrounds ranging from engineering to law, mathematics, and business administration. One of the interesting aspects of the intellectual ferment is the widespread sense of a need for cooperation among people of different backgrounds.

What are the causes of all this interest? The sheer size of the transportation system is impressive. The cost of the transportation of commodities has been estimated at 9.2 per cent of the gross national product in 1960.[1] In addition, the typical urban family allocates about one-eighth of its income to purchasing transportation for its members. Total expenses for transportation may exceed 20 per cent of the gross national product.[2]

In part the problems of transportation capture the public imagination because of the romantic interest of moving vehicles, an interest which finds expression not only in the antiquarian's delight in models of clipper ships and antique steam locomotives but also in popular interest in the possibilities of dramatically new forms of transportation like monorails, supersonic aircraft, automatic highways, high speed railroads, or hydrofoil ships. Popular interest is important because it may find expression in people's willingness to spend their own money to buy tickets individually, and, even more important, in willingness to have their elected representatives spend their money collectively on new forms of transportation.

Interest by professional economists in the field, however, has another explanation. It is possible to rely mainly on the forces of competition and the workings of markets to control the functioning of most of the American economy. Government plays a role in such sectors of the economy as manufacturing, it is true, but it is a strictly limited role. Ownership is private, and the basic economic decisions about investment, products to be produced, and prices are private. In transportation, however, the role of competition as a regulator, while important, is more limited, and the government is directly involved in many of the basic economic decisions. The government itself owns important parts of the nation's transportation system, such as the highways; it closely regulates others, such as the railroads; it subsidizes others, such as the merchant marine; and it directly operates still others, such as many local transit companies. As a consequence a large share of the basic economic decisions in transportation is made directly by public officials or is subject to their influence, either through direct regulation and review or through indirect control of the structure of the situation in which private businesses make the choices.

There are few who would argue that American national transportation policy is coherent or that, viewed as a whole, the economic decisions taken in transportation meet the highest standards. The late President Kennedy in his Message to Congress on Transportation de-

1. J. L. Heskett, "Macroeconomic Cost of Physical Distribution," *Papers, Third Annual Meeting, American Transportation Research Forum, December 1962,* pp. 169–189.
2. Ernest W. Williams, Jr., and David W. Bluestone, *Rationale of Federal Transportation Policy,* United States Department of Commerce, 1960.

scribed the development of federal transportation policy in these words: "A chaotic patchwork of inconsistent and often obsolete legislation has evolved from a history of specific actions addressed to specific problems of specific industries at specific times." Similar comments would apply equally to state policy and to the policy of the multitude of political agencies concerned with transportation within urban areas. No basic changes have been made since the late President's Message.

Recent developments in the economics of transportation may be regarded as an attempt to respond to this situation. There are contributions being made to the analysis of economic problems of transportation by men working within many different intellectual traditions. The attempt is made in the chapters which follow to give to the reader at least some elementary understanding of these different methods of thought.

One group of scholars has focussed attention directly upon the economic analysis of government policy toward transportation, including in their analysis actual and proposed legislation, activities of the regulatory commissions and the executive branch of the government, and court decisions. A related body of work is concerned with the history of the development of government policy. This type of analysis has influenced especially the chapter on railroads.

Recently, some economic historians have shown renewed interest in transportation. They attempt to apply modern statistical tools or theoretical formulations or both to the study of the causes and the consequences of economic policy in the past. The discussion of the Union Pacific Railroad in Chapter 7 is a summary of an investigation by a modern economic historian.

Economic theorists in varying degree for many years have been interested in transportation and have developed theoretical tools which are relevant to its problems. Much of microeconomic theory is directly relevant. In recent years there has been an elaboration of the theory of public enterprise economics which has been applied in other contexts, primarily problems of the use of water resources, as well as to problems of transportation. The chapter on rates and especially the chapter on the theory of investment make use of these theoretical developments as well as the older theory.

Another tradition of economic thought useful in the field of transportation is that developed by specialists in public finance. Discussions of economic policy with respect to highways have been written by specialists in public finance. This work has influenced especially the chapter on highways.

Location theory is an important branch of economic theory with direct relevance to transportation policy. Location theory is closely related to transportation since the decision to place a firm or a household in a particular location is in effect a decision to use transportation facilities which serve that site. A special section is devoted to a brief introduction to the place of transportation in location theory.

Parallel with these approaches to transportation has been the development of engineering economics. This intellectual tradition has been developed by men who typically have been closely concerned with practical problems, notably in the highway field. The introductory discussion of investment in the chapter on that subject has been to some degree influenced by this approach, but it is more clearly in evidence in the discussion in the chapter on highways of the costs and gains of new roads. Systems analysis is a related approach; it is exemplified by the treatment of the cost of marine transportation in Chapter 17.

Within economics there also has developed since the late 1930s a group of specialists in industrial organization. These writers have developed a systematic approach to the analysis of individual industries which has been applied recently to transportation. While the influence of this work may be found elsewhere, it is strongest in the chapter on air transportation.

Econometric techniques of analysis have developed rapidly in the last few decades. They are being applied with increasing sophistication to such problems as the analysis of the costs of transportation. Some of the results of this work are briefly discussed in the chapter on railroads. Many of the results, unfortunately, cannot be understood without knowledge of the techniques employed.

There has been a series of attempts to apply modern sample survey techniques to the analysis of the demand for transportation. Some results are introduced in the chapter on urban transportation and the discussion of competition among modes of transport.

Progress in all these directions has been uneven. The intellectual traditions have not all been fully reconciled with each other. The conceptual frameworks and analytical tools have not been applied systematically to all of the problems to which they are applicable. For many purposes the basic statistical information about transportation which is now assembled is incomplete or otherwise inadequate. Economics as a discipline is sufficiently well developed, however, so that there is a similarity of approach in the work of competent economists which leads to a degree of consensus about economic policy, or, in the absence of such agreement, to a consensus as to the nature of the unresolved issues. The uneven and irregular state of development may in itself be taken as evidence of the vitality of the field.

While the focus of the discussion which follows is economic policy, much of the analysis is concerned with the economics of the transportation industry. Issues of economic policy can be best formulated and analyzed in the light of analysis of the situations in which they arise. The point of departure, however, is a general statement of the objectives toward which transportation policy is directed.

*Transportation
and Economic Policy*

Economic Theory
Applied to Transportation

1

Objectives of Policy

IN A SYSTEMATIC CONSIDERATION of policy a logical point of departure is an explicit statement of the objectives toward which it is proposed to proceed. To an economist, and to most people who live in an economic society, economic objectives deserve a high priority. Public policy toward transportation, however, in the United States and in other nations, is by no means exclusively motivated by economic considerations. Following a discussion of economic objectives, therefore, is a discussion of political and social objectives of transportation policy.

Economic Objectives

There is a reasonable degree of consensus among economists as to the general goals of economic policy. Among these goals are economic efficiency, economic growth, a high level of employment and freedom from pronounced cyclical fluctuations, and a degree of equity in the distribution of the products of economic activity which avoids the juxtaposition of extreme poverty and extreme wealth. The transportation industry is directly involved in the attainment of these objectives.

It is, perhaps, possible to imagine a perfectly functioning market economy which would proceed automatically toward these goals, guided

3

by the impersonal processes of the market place. In transportation, however, public intervention has been frequent. The reasons for public involvement will be reviewed in Chapter 5, which concerns the organization of the industry. The historical development of public intervention will be one of the themes of Parts II and III. Assuming, for the moment, the necessity of public intervention, it becomes appropriate to review and to make explicit the general goals of policy with special reference to transportation. The questions of the nature and specific purposes of public intervention may then be considered essentially as questions of the choice of means to achieve desired ends.

EFFICIENCY—An allocation of productive resources is efficient if, for a given set of productive resources, no increase in the value of total output can be obtained by transfer of any part of the resources from one use to another. In other words, of two arrangements of a given set of productive resources, that arrangement is to be preferred which yields the output with the greater value. In the production of an output of a given value, of two sets of productive resources, that set is to be preferred which costs the less.

The criterion of efficiency as stated requires the use of prices to estimate values. It is also assumed that the relative market prices of the factors of production reflect the relative cost to society of those factors. When there is reason to question this assumption, the criterion must be modified accordingly. The price of transportation by one method may be artificially depressed in some manner, for example, by a subsidy. The price of transportation by an alternative method may be artificially raised, for example, by a tax or by a monopolistic price policy. The prices of these methods to potential shippers will not reflect the relative cost to society of the two methods. The price system will be giving false signals. Shippers, in seeking to minimize their own costs, will be led to decisions which are wasteful from the point of view of society. They may select a method of transportation which requires more inputs of the factors of production than an alternative method of production. In order to prevent inefficient use of the factors of production prices should reflect costs. The development of this proposition plays an important part in analysis of the pricing of transportation services, as will be further discussed in connection with policy in setting rates.

GROWTH—A second major objective of economic policy is the objective of economic growth or economic development. Logically, the objective of growth is related to the objective of efficiency but the two are distinct. Efficiency refers to the use of given, fixed resources at a particular time. Growth refers to increase in the available resources

over time and improvement in the technique of using them. There is a
connection between the two in the sense that a gain in efficiency at
any time makes possible more output, some of which can be used to
increase the stock of capital. It is possible to imagine an efficient
economy, however, in which the entire output of goods and services is
consumed. The consumers in such an economy might even prefer present consumption over future consumption so strongly that they consume
part of the capital stock of the economy. At the same time, they might
be allocating the resources available for production in an efficient manner. The objective of growth, on the other hand, is to increase the
total value of goods and services to be produced by the economy in
the future. While increased production of goods and services is desirable
from an economic point of view, economic growth may be desired for
reasons which are essentially political such as increasing the relative
productive capacity and, hence, military strength of one country in
contrast to other countries. The contribution which transportation can
make to the attainment of a high rate of economic growth is frequently
advanced as a reason for developing new methods of transportation or
expanding or improving the service offered by existing methods.

FULL EMPLOYMENT AND STABILITY—The objective of maintaining a
high level of employment is not ordinarily thought of as a goal of policy
toward the transportation industry. This objective is prominent in discussions of fiscal policy and monetary policy. Yet, on occasion there
may be important repercussions of public policy toward transportation
on the level of economic activity and these repercussions may be considered in the formulation of transportation policy. Expenditures on
highway construction may be increased, for example, as a way of stimulating the economy when the level of economic activity is believed by
the responsible public authorities to be too low. Also, considerations
having to do with the general movement of prices in the economy may
influence public policy when what is at issue is a general increase in
rates for transportation services. The control of inflation is an important part of the maintenance of stability in the economy.

EQUITY—Considerations of equity lie on the boundary between economics and politics. Economists have tended to accept criteria of fairness
as relevant to economic affairs but it is not agreed in the profession
that economists have a special contribution to make to the definition
of what is equitable. Judgments as to what is equitable rest ultimately
upon the moral sense of the community and tend to be expressed in
the development of the law. But economists generally tend to prefer

to move toward more equality in the distribution of goods and services rather than less equality.

Economists, speaking strictly as economists, tend to base their positions on other foundations, notably the criterion of efficiency. They argue that if any adjustment can be made in the economy which makes one or more persons better off without injury to others, the action should be taken. There is, for example, an economic argument against monopoly which rests essentially on the ground that monopoly tends to interfere with the allocation of resources by restricting output and raising the price of a commodity or service which is monopolized. Thus, monopoly leads to economic inefficiency. There is a corresponding objection to monopoly profits. Excessive returns to capital invested in some economic activity may arise because of artificial monopolistic restrictions on the amount of capital invested in that activity. Monopoly may lead to inequality in incomes, and, by preventing change, to rigidity in the distribution of incomes.

Equity may be a consideration in two contexts, equity in the distribution of goods and services, and equity in treatment of competing producers. A policy may be attacked, for example, because it places a burden upon the poor or the aged, or an alternative policy may be proposed as desirable because it assists these elements in the population. Thus, proponents of programs to assist local bus companies seek to show that the services are needed by people who are physically or financially unable to operate automobiles.

Considerations of fairness among producers, or the avoidance of unreasonable differences in treatment between different geographical areas or different people, have played an important part in the development of transportation policy, especially in the development of rate structures. For example, regulation of railroads in the United States in the nineteenth century had its origin in part in the deep sense of injustice of western farmers who shared a conviction that they were being exploited by eastern railroad barons. As another example, owners of coal mines in Pennsylvania have been deeply concerned about whether the rates they paid for the movement of coal were fair in relation to the rates paid by coal from mines in Kentucky. Considerations of equity, like considerations of the general level of economic activity in the economy, thus, do play a part in analysis of problems of transportation.

AREAS OF DIFFICULTY—It is not always easy to state any goal of economic policy in a way to which everyone will agree. Even when there is agreement as to a general criterion, there is frequently room for disagreement as to how that criterion should be applied to a given situation. The relevant facts may not be known or may be in dispute. Perhaps the hardest choices arise when there is a conflict of basic goals. A desire for economic efficiency, especially efficiency in the short run, may conflict with the desire for economic growth. A policy of subsidy of a new method of transportation, for example, is likely to be attacked by the people associated with the older method with which it competes. For example, the managers of railroad passenger services in the late 1940s and 1950s were less than enthusiastic about federal aids to aviation. Why subsidize a new mode, they asked, when the efficient solution is to use our existing facilities? Let the price of an air ticket reflect its costs! Proponents of a subsidy, however, may turn to considerations of growth and argue that subsidy now is necessary to develop a method of transportation which in the future will become efficient.

There are no easy resolutions of conflicts of objectives. The disinterested analyst can offer only his best judgment as to where the public interest lies. He can at least attempt to make clear in as detailed a manner as possible the extent to which one objective conflicts with another. The conflicts as far as transportation is concerned are usually resolved in the end by the political process. Political objectives, thus, have more than abstract relevance to transportation policy.

Political and Social Objectives

Political considerations arise in connection with transportation policy in several ways. Economic objectives may be reached by private businesses acting with a minimum of political intervention, but in transportation, as noted earlier, political intervention is inevitably important. The achievement of economic objectives then must be sought through political means. In addition, there are political objectives, both military and nonmilitary, which may be important independent considerations in policy toward transportation. The nonmilitary purposes shade off into social considerations. These objectives, which are discussed below, may be thought of as parallel to the economic objectives just considered. It would be an error, however, to think of all political considerations as parallel in importance to the economic. Any developed economic system requires the maintenance of order: it must have a political framework. We turn first to the implications for transportation of this imperative.

POLITICAL PRE-REQUISITES AND POLITICAL RISKS—The development of a transport system cannot proceed without a minimum of political security. The owners of goods to be transported must have reasonable assurance that the goods will reach their destination. People will insist even more strongly upon safe arrival if it is their own persons which are to be transported. Organized piracy sporadically appeared as a problem until the nineteenth century. It is often forgotten that the United States was compelled to mount an expedition against the pirates of the Barbary Coast.

Modern political requirements, however, are concerned primarily with the activities of national states. Each nation is ordinarily in a position to guarantee reasonable security within its borders. International boundaries frequently serve as limits on trade. For a nation to rely upon trade beyond its boundaries implies a political risk that the necessary degree of international friendship for the continuance of that trade may not persist. If the nation meanwhile has developed a division of labor with other nations built upon that trade, interruption of the trade may have serious consequences. This type of interruption may be illustrated by the drastic reduction of commercial interchange between the United States and Cuba in 1960. A similar but more serious interruption threatened Great Britain with a severance from her sources of food and raw materials during World Wars I and II.

Within their own frontiers nations cannot tolerate any private action to disrupt transportation except on a limited and partial basis. There were no national railroad strikes in the United States in the days when the railroads dominated transportation; if one is ever permitted it will be an indication of the decline of the railroads to relative unimportance. A nation which relies on its transportation system for the distribution of food must prevent interruption to that service as a matter of political as well as economic necessity.

MILITARY USES OF TRANSPORT SYSTEMS—National states rely on their military power. Transport systems may be of direct military usefulness for the movement of troops and their supplies. Early transportation systems such as the road systems of the Incas in Peru were developed primarily for this purpose and illustrate the point clearly. The Incas engaged in an active policy of enlarging their empire by military conquest. The first step in such a conquest was the construction of a road in the direction in which the attack was to be delivered. The road made it possible for them to assemble tens of thousands of men, one account states as many as a hundred thousand, for a particular assault. These roads were primitive by modern standards. No wheeled vehicles were used. Yet they involved bridges over mountain streams, paving in some places, the use of culverts for drainage, and a system

of rest houses and stations for runners.[1] Without the road it would not
have been possible to deliver a concentrated attack on such a scale. The
underlying objective is exactly the same as in the provision of a fleet
of jet transports for the movement of troops by air.

A related objective is to provide for flexibility of movement of a
military force in time of war. The ability to mount a massive thrust
at a given point is less than the ability to move the striking force from
place to place within the combat area. This use of a transport network
is also ancient; it may be illustrated by the defense developed by the
Germans in East Prussia in the early part of World War I. The German railroad network was planned and built for war and its personnel
trained to a high level of efficiency in the movement of troops. The
Russian railroads were built for defense; they were constructed with
a broad gauge to make invasion difficult from the west. The Russians
attacked, however, in 1914 and ran into difficulties of mobility because
of the change in gauge at the frontier. The Germans used their superior
mobility to inflict a decisive defeat.[2] The ability of the United States
to move a large striking force into position quickly in Florida was a
consideration in the late President Kennedy's confrontation with the
Soviet Union over the matter of missiles in Cuba. In general the possibility that defensive forces, concentrated in one place, will be caught
"off balance" while an attack occurs elsewhere can be minimized by
a transport network. The same type of system, of course, may lend
flexibility to an attacking force as well as to a force on the defensive.

An important indirect military use of transport systems at present
is in economic activity in support of a military effort in a total conflict.
Excess capacity in the system may prove extremely convenient to provide for direct military use as discussed above plus serving the needs
of the wartime economy.

In a country under attack, such as a nuclear attack, transport may
be of importance for the repair of damage, including the movement of
resources to any area in which damage has been inflicted. Such movement may be essential for the provision of supplies to the population,
the repair of factories, and the like. Transport may be required to
evacuate the civilian population from an area. The greater the carrying
capacity of the transport facilities available, and the less vulnerable
these facilities to interruption, the better the position of the nation in
resisting the attack.

1. Victor W. Von Hagen, *Highway of the Sun,* Duell, Sloan and Pearce and Little
Brown, 1955, pp. 170–1.
2. Barbara Tuchman, *The Guns of August,* Macmillan, Chapter 15.

The preceding consideration may influence public policy with regard to the development and maintenance of transport systems themselves, including road, water, rail, pipeline, air networks, and an ocean shipping industry. They have been urged both for the speedier development of new systems and for the maintenance in operation of obsolescent systems on a stand-by basis. These same considerations may also influence policy with regard to the industries which supply the transport industry, the shipbuilding industry, the aircraft construction industry, and the manufacture of railroad equipment.

OTHER POLITICAL OBJECTIVES—The development of transport systems may be urged for nonmilitary political purposes. An improved system of transportation may promote the political unity of a nation. Increased trade and the increased movement of persons which result from lower transport costs will make a country more homogeneous and less subject to regional dissension. In the eighteenth century the risk of loss of the Mississippi drainage basin to the Spanish, who held New Orleans, was one of the considerations which led George Washington to take an active interest in the development of a canal up the Potomac River to penetrate the Appalachian Mountains to the Ohio. Lesser figures have urged the same arguments. They were put forward before the Civil War by Senator Stephen Douglas as reasons for the construction of the Illinois Central Railroad, uniting North and South.

Transportation systems may also be included in politics in another sense. The particular private objectives of a politician may be of value locally but of doubtful value or no value at all from the point of view of the interests of the general public. Appropriations of federal funds for improvements of rivers and harbors are commonly believed to serve such private objectives more often than they meet economic needs. Desire to prevent the use of a particular project for such purposes may be a consideration in the choice of a form of organization for that project.

Prestige has been an important consideration in public policy toward the transportation industry. Motives of conspicuous consumption or status influence people in their collective consumption patterns as well as their individual consumption. National prestige may be involved in the development of international carriers. Each of the major powers maintains its own international airline and commonly includes the name of the country in the name of the airline (Air France, British Overseas Airways Corporation). Smaller powers seek to achieve the same mark of status.

Prestige also may play its role in the provision of terminals. American cities a few decades ago felt called upon to erect monumental railroad stations which were felt to be gateways appropriate to the dignity and opulence of the metropolises which erected them. More recently what is required is a suitable air terminal. The air terminal in Brussels, for example, which was erected at the time of the International Exposition in 1959, seems to have been constructed with a view to the dignity of the city and the nation more than to any immediate requirements of air traffic. It is not here argued, nor is it intended to imply, that such considerations are unworthy. From a merely economic point of view, however, the expenditures on these structures were not justified.

SOCIAL OBJECTIVES—Finally, objectives of social well-being may play a part in public policy: improved transport may make possible development of public institutions which can be operated efficiently only if they can take advantage of economies of large size. For example, the development of rural roads was related to the development of consolidated rural schools. Also, it may be urged that a particular investment in a transportation facility will contribute to the beauty of a city, or to the amenities enjoyed by the citizens. This is essentially an argument in favor of what may be called public or social consumption as opposed to private consumption. People may prefer to appropriate funds to the public authorities for facilities to be enjoyed collectively rather than to retain the money to spend individually.

CONCLUSION—In discussions of transportation policy it is possible to proceed systematically only when the goals of policy have been made explicit. The variety of goals which are relevant, both political and economic, complicates discussions of transportation policy and produces conflicts between groups and between objectives. Intelligent development of transportation policy, however, requires understanding of the choices which must be made and of their consequences and the evaluation of these consequences in the light of the goals of policy.

It is the purpose of Chapters 2, 3, and 4 to develop the connection between the economic goals of transportation policy and the specific issues which arise. Chapter 2 is devoted to a general discussion of the economic function of transportation. Chapters 3 and 4 consider the areas of investment and rate policy, respectively, and take up questions of criteria for the evaluation of proposed investments and rates in the light of the general objectives of policy. Chapter 5 concerns problems of choice among methods of organization of transportation, these methods being viewed essentially as instruments for achieving desired outcomes with the properties outlined in the preceding chapters.

2

Economic Functions of Transportation

FROM AN ECONOMIC POINT of view transportation has two functions. The transportation of people for vacations or pleasure or for personal affairs is a "final" service. In the national accounts it is entered as a part of total purchases of goods and services by consumers. To the economic theorist the demand for such services should be approached through the theory of the household.

That part of the transportation of people which is in connection with their work, however, plus virtually the whole of the transportation of goods are "intermediate" services. In the national accounts the value of the services is not entered as a part of consumption. To the economic theorist the demand for such services should be approached through the theory of the firm or the theory of production. Outlay for such transportation is analytically comparable to outlay for other factors of production.

It might be argued that the transportation of goods owned by consumers for purposes of vacations or pleasure should be considered a part of final consumption. For example, a charge for shipping a yacht overland from one body of water to another might be so classified. Such exceptions are trivial in magnitude compared to the total volume of freight movements. The distinction between transportation as a final good and transportation as a factor of production thus cuts the transportation of people into two parts but leaves the transportation of goods in the one category.

Most economic analysis of transportation has been concerned with transportation as a factor of production, and the remainder of this chapter will be concerned primarily with this topic. The connection between this discussion and the basic objective of economic efficiency stated in Chapter 1 should become increasingly apparent as the discussion progresses. The discussion of transportation as an input to the productive process in the first half of this chapter will lead to a discussion of location decisions in the second main division. It is to a large extent in his choice of location that a businessman decides how much and what kind of transportation he will require. In Chapter 3 we will consider investments in transportation.

Transport Costs in Relation to Other Costs of Production

Viewed analytically, there is no difference between inputs of transportation and inputs of other factors. Enterprises which seek to minimize their costs will combine inputs of transportation with inputs of whatever they purchase—raw materials, semiprocessed goods, land, labor, machines, in whatever forms they require—in such a way as to minimize their total cost for any given level of output. There may well be technical possibilities of substitution between transport inputs and other inputs, particularly if a long enough period is allowed for readjustment of the location of production. Entrepreneurs in these circumstances may be expected to choose transport-intensive methods of production or transport-minimizing methods of production depending on relative cost of transport inputs and other inputs. Only if there are no technical possibilities of substitution between transport inputs and other inputs will entrepreneurs have no choice as to the quantity of transportation in the mix of factors they use.

These abstract generalizations can be made more concrete by discussing the reasons why the movement of goods takes place and why people travel on business. The reasons for the movement of goods are the same as the reasons why there is geographic specialization of communities and trade among them. People may be more accustomed to thinking of geographic specialization than of inputs of transportation. The approach which will be taken here, therefore, is to review the reasons for specialization of areas and consider in this context what are the possibilities of substitution open to individual firms.

GEOGRAPHICAL SPECIALIZATION BASED ON NATURAL RESOURCES— The simplest type of geographical specialization arises from the differences in climate and natural resources from place to place. Such differences have led to the transportation of agricultural and forest products over substantial distances from the earliest times to the present day. In about 3000 B.C. an Egyptian monarch named Snefru is known to have sent a fleet of 40 ships to Lebanon to bring back cedar.[1] For thousands of years Lebanon was famed for its cedar trees, while Egypt has never been able to grow timber. The economic reason for that movement is the same as for the movement of citrus fruits from Florida to New York or the movement of orchids from Hawaii to New York by air. Commodities which can be grown easily in one location are desired for use in another location where it is difficult or impossible to grow them in commercial quantities. This phenomenon has been well understood for many years. Adam Smith's example is the movement of wine from France to Scotland.

King Snefru had no choice as to the method of production. He could not obtain cedar wood in Egypt since it does not grow there. The only possible method of production was the use of the required number of transport inputs.

The seller of orchids in New York, however, may have a choice. He can grow orchids in hothouses in New York, or fly them in from Hawaii, whichever is cheaper. He, thus, chooses between a method of production which is transport intensive and one which involves little outlay for transportation.

We may illustrate the situation of the flower merchant with a table containing hypothetical numbers. There are two columns to allow for the two methods of obtaining the flowers:

| METHOD I | | METHOD II | |
Grow the flowers in New York		Transport the flowers by air from Hawaii	
Production cost in New York	$C	Cost in Hawaii	$A
		Air freight	$B
Total cost	$C	Total Cost	$A + $B

Obviously the choice will rest on whether $C is larger than $A + $B. Since flowers can be grown cheaply in Hawaii, the cost of importing them will be largely the cost of transportation; it is this cost which

---

1. C. Ernest Fayle, *A Short History of the World's Shipping Industry*, G. Allen and Unwin Ltd., 1933, p. 35.

will be compared with the cost of production in New York. Essentially, the competition is between greenhouses and airplanes.

Minerals are distributed unevenly over the surface of the earth. Large volumes of transportation result from the assembly of mineral products for fabrication into consumer goods and services. Iron ore moves from Labrador to steel mills in the United States. Coal moves from mines to primitive brick plants in Indian villages. Oil moves from the Middle East to European power plants. Each of these industries is unable to rely on local materials. An industry may have a choice between two or more geographically separated sources of supply. The selection will depend upon the cost of material at its source plus the cost of transport to the place of use. In a word, it is the delivered cost which counts. One source, say, of oil, with low cost at the oil well plus a long haul may compete with another source which is closer but has a higher cost at the well. The price of transportation will be one element in the choice. Perhaps it is a question of pumping oil to the surface at a nearby well in a field which has been depleted or bringing oil in by tanker from a new field. Then, it is not too farfetched to say: tankers compete with pumps.

Geographical differences in resources may give rise to trade in finished goods as well as in raw materials. Thus, in the colonial period in North America the extensive forests along the Atlantic seaboard led both to the shipment of ship timbers to Great Britain and to the production of wooden sailing vessels for sale to British merchants. In deciding how to procure a ship, an English merchant would compare the two methods of production and decide whether to import lumber or the complete vessel to England. He would decide between the two methods of obtaining the ship which involved different transport requirements.

GEOGRAPHICAL SPECIALIZATION BASED ON ECONOMIES OF THE CONCENTRATION OF ACTIVITY—Geographical specialization may arise and flourish in the absence of differences in climate or in natural resources from one place to another. Specialization which originally was based on geographical advantage may continue after the original advantage has become irrelevant for reasons of technological change. A fundamental reason for this phenomenon is that there are economies in concentrating economic activity. These economies are of two kinds. Some economies, referred to as economies of scale, are internal to a firm. They arise to the extent that cost per unit output for the firm is less if it produces on a large scale, say, in a large factory rather than a small one. External economies, the second category, do not depend on the scale of operations of a single enterprise. They are the economies which arise because of the clustering together in a limited area of two or more economic activities. For example, it may be more economical for one large power plant to serve several factories than for each to have its own source of power. A power plant can be built to minimum efficient size to serve many small factories as well as one giant factory. It should be clear that whether a particular economy is external or internal to a firm depends on the extent of the activities of the firm. To continue the example, if the small factories were all to become part of one giant enterprise which also acquired the power plant, what were external economies to the small firms would be internal economies to the new colossus. Both internal economies of scale and external economies are important reasons for geographic specialization and require further discussion. External economies will also be discussed in the chapter on urban transportation since, as there explained, external economies are the basic economic reason for urban development.

Economies of scale in economic activity are common. In most manufacturing industries as the size of the individual plant increases the average cost of production per unit of output tends to fall. This decline is ordinarily at a diminishing rate, but in the initial stages the decline may be substantial. In the distribution of goods and services, also, economies of scale are important, as the rise of the supermarket has brought to everyone's attention.

The extreme condition of no economies of scale would mean that each household could construct a complete modern economy with its own steel mill, automobile factory, glass factory, cement mill, petroleum refinery, and so forth, provided only that the household possessed the necessary raw materials. It is the efficiency of the division of labor and modern techniques as well as the uneven distribution of raw materials that make such a possibility seem ridiculous.

A more realistic choice may be described by extending the preceding analysis of transport costs to allow for two markets. Consider a situation in which there is a single "mine" which produces the raw material for some single product, and a single manufacturer who sells in two equal markets, city A and city B. The mine is midway between the markets which are joined by a single transportation route:

```
_____|_____

A                     Mine                      B
```

Suppose that the manufacturer faces equal processing costs at each location on the route—there is no variation, for example, in the price of labor. Suppose, however, that the technology of this industry is such that the average total cost per unit output is a declining function of size of plant, as shown in Figure 2.1.

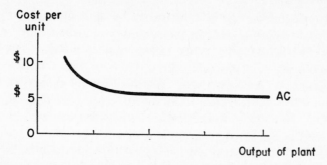

Figure 2.1   Average Cost as a Function of Plant Size

It is the long run average cost curve of the theorist which is relevant here. The long run curve shows the effect of different sizes of plant, other things equal. Assume, for example, the following demand conditions and transport costs:

Total sales	1000 units per year, 500 at each city
Cost of shipment	$1 for raw materials per unit final output
	$2 per unit for finished goods

The manufacturer will have a choice between two plants, one at each city, and a single plant at the mine. His comparative costs will be as follows:

Single plant solution		Two plant solution	
Manufacturing cost at $7		Manufacturing cost at $10	
$7 × 1000 units	$7,000	$10 × 1000	$10,000
Cost of shipping finished		Cost of shipping finished	
goods at $2		goods	nil
$2 × 1000	2,000		
		Cost of shipping raw	
Cost of shipping		materials at $1	
raw materials	nil	$1 × 1000	1,000
Total	$9,000	Total	$11,000

Economies of scale in manufacturing in the above example more than offset the extra transportation cost required by the single large plant. Note, however, that the result would be changed if the cost of shipping finished goods were very high, say, $5 each instead of $2. Such an increase in transport rates would lead to a cost increase for the single plant solution so great that the two plant solution would become the more economical. If transport costs were the same for finished goods as for raw materials, the single plant solution would become more attractive.[2]

These principles may be illustrated by the automobile industry. There are economies of scale in the assembly of automobiles, and there are economies in shipping parts rather than complete vehicles. The decision as to where to assemble cars must take both sets of considerations into account. A decline in the cost of shipping assembled vehicles, other costs constant, will lead to increased geographic concentration of the industry. An increase in the economies of scale, other costs constant, will also lead to increased geographic concentration.

External economies also are important to an understanding of geographic specialization. As an industry expands it frequently becomes profitable for firms to develop that specialize in the provision of services to that industry. There may be a number of industries that are closely related. Consumers who build their own houses are introduced to the variety of enterprises concerned with construction, such as general contractors, sub-contractors, and suppliers of different types of building materials. There are diverse enterprises whose activities are related to the export trade, such as shipping lines, ship chandlers, dealers in foreign exchange, marine insurance, custom house brokers, freight forwarders, and specialists in packing goods for overseas shipment. External economies tend to be more important for industries comprised of small firms than large firms. The large firm may provide for itself many of the functions provided externally for small firms.

Many of these economies external to a firm are more readily accessible if the firm selects a location near other firms. Such economies are important in highly developed industrial areas. Once an area has been developed it will have available basic services such as a transport network, low cost electric power, and oil and gas supplies. In such an area a firm may be able to purchase the factors of production that it requires at lower cost than elsewhere. While the area may have some underlying geographical advantages, these advantages need not be directly relevant to a particular enterprise.

FURTHER EFFECTS OF BROADENING A MARKET—Transport has one important economic function that does not arise from the development of geographic specialization. A developed transportation system has the advantage of broadening the market for any commodities that can be

---

2. If we allow a more complex rate structure, with rates tapering with distance, there is another possibility. The single plant might be at A or B, eliminating cost in one market of shipping the finished product.

moved by the system. The effect is to reduce the power of local monopolies, to minimize the importance in the enlarged market of local fluctuations in supplies, and to limit the fluctuation of prices. There is an averaging over a broader area of the effects of such factors as variations in weather. Wheat, for example, is exported by several countries and the total supply in any period represents the sums of the supplies offered from the several areas. World supplies of wheat are less subject to the vagaries of the weather than supplies in any one country; within a country, supplies for a whole country are less subject to fluctuation than supplies for a region.

The stabilization of the supply of wheat in an area from one harvest to the next might also be achieved by the provision of storage facilities. Storage capacity, thus, can be used to substitute for transportation facilities. The point is general in the sense that it applies to efforts to cope with fluctuating demands for any good that can be stored regardless of the reason for the fluctuation. A chain store, for example, may maintain a single warehouse to serve its stores in a certain area and rely on rapid transportation from the central depot; or it may maintain more warehouses and reduce the need for fast transport. Thus, trucks and airplanes are substitutes for warehouses.

SUMMARY—Geographic specialization may arise for several reasons. It may be the result of the unequal distribution of natural resources. It may arise out of economies from the geographic concentration of economic activity either from economies of scale internal to the firm or from economies external to the firm. Even without geographic specialization there are benefits from the broadening of markets arising out of the pooling of reserves and the minimizing of local fluctuations in supply and from reduction in the power of local monopolies.

Location Decisions as Determinants of Use of Transportation

Geographic specialization results from the interplay of economic decisions taken by two sets of people on the two sides of the market for transportation, the shippers and the transportation companies. The choices made by the shippers concern what they will produce or the economic activity in which they will engage, where they will carry on this activity, and by what technology. The choices made by the suppliers of transportation concern what transportation service they will provide and what prices or rates they will charge.

What is done on either side of the market has its effects upon the other. Decisions to produce certain goods at certain locations by certain technology will influence the demand for transportation between those locations and other locations. Decisions to establish certain transportation facilities that will provide service of a particular quality at a particular set of charges will influence decisions concerning the location of economic activity. It is as a result of the working of the economic principles just discussed that the result of the interaction between the two is often the development of geographic specialization of production with associated development of transportation.

Before turning to Chapters 3 and 4 concerning investment in transportation and transportation rates, some discussion of location decisions is appropriate. A full discussion of location theory would far exceed the limits of this chapter. What follows is simply a brief introduction to the subject intended to provide some further insight into the demand for transportation.

Location decisions by private individuals include both the decisions concerning the location of their homes, that is, their places of residence, and the decisions of businessmen concerning the location of economic activity. The location of residences is a matter of importance within urban areas. Whether people live near the center of a city or in remote suburbs has direct implications for their requirements of local transportation. This subject will be considered in Chapter 15 on urban transportation. There are also, of course, decisions by government agencies as to location of different branches of the government and different functions of these agencies. While these public decisions are not analyzed here, it should at least be recognized that they have economic importance. The present discussion will focus attention on the location decisions of producers.

PRODUCERS' LOCATIONAL CHOICES—In analyzing producers' choices of location, it is useful to distinguish three activities that are involved in the production of goods: procurement, processing, and distribution.[3] In evaluating a location as a possible site an entrepreneur will consider the differences in cost between that location and other locations with regard to each of these three activities.

Procurement costs differ when the prices of inputs delivered to the site under consideration differ from the prices of inputs at some other site. The delivered prices of inputs, of course, will include the cost of transportation to the site.

3. This distinction is developed by E. M. Hoover in *The Location of Economic Activity,* McGraw-Hill, 1948. The discussion that follows has been influenced by Hoover's analysis.

Distribution costs may also vary. That is, one site may differ from another in the cost of the shipment of the output of the establishment to the point or points where it is to be sold or consumed. The entrepreneur will be interested in the realized price at a site, net of the cost of shipment. If the location of his customers and their requirements are taken as fixed, we may say that he will tend to prefer that site at which the cost of shipment of the finished product is the least.

Processing costs may also be different from one location to another. In this context "processing" should be understood to include in addition to physical processing such functions as storage. Sites may differ in that there is variation in the quantities needed of factors of production in order to produce a required change in the purchased inputs. An obvious example is variation in the cost of heating a plant, which certainly will be greater in a cold climate than in a warm climate. In cotton textile manufacturing there may be differences in the required expenditure for humidifiers in moist and in dry regions. The availability of an assured supply of necessary inputs in adequate quantity is a vital consideration in location of many types of economic activity. A firm may have important requirements of certain characteristics, for water, for electricity, for labor, etc. Only sites can be considered where these requirements for production are available. Furthermore, there may be variations from one location to another in the prices of inputs which are purchased locally. For example, wage rates may vary. Those sites will tend to be preferred where the local prices are lowest for inputs of given quality.

It is, therefore, with reference to processing costs that external economies come to the attention of the entrepreneur. As noted in the previous section, there often are economies in locating an economic activity in an area where other economic activities are being carried on nearby. It is also with reference to processing costs that economies of scale are relevant in the entrepreneur's calculations.

Though these topics have been discussed in the previous section, further analysis of the more limited problem of minimizing transport costs is needed. A comparison of the economic advantages of locations to an entrepreneur can be reduced to a comparison of transportation costs if several prior requirements have been met. First, there is the technical requirement: that there is an adequate supply of factors of production at the sites considered. Second, the demand must be assumed not to depend on location except as differences in transportation costs are associated with differences in location. (This assumption may be true for some industries but not for others. For example, in the manufacture of women's dresses speed of delivery to the markets which are located at style centers may be important.) Finally, there must be no important differences in processing costs between the sites.

We may proceed under these assumptions to the problem of minimizing transfer costs. To simplify still further, consider a situation with one producer, one source of raw materials, one market, and one single product. The accompanying diagram, Figure 2.2, shows on the horizontal axis two locations. The source of the single raw material is A; B is the single market, with distance between them representing physical distance in miles between the two points. The vertical axis measures money.

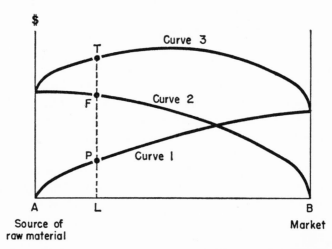

Figure 2.2   Transport Costs and Choice of Location

The problem is where to locate the plant, at A, at B, or in between. Curve 1 shows for different locations the cost of shipping to the plant the raw material needed to produce a given number of units of product. In other words it shows an element in procurement costs. Curve 1 starts at the level of 0 at location A, since there will be no cost of moving the raw material from its source to the point of processing if processing is carried on at the source. Curve 1 rises from A to B showing the increase in costs of procurement of the commodity as one shifts the plant from A to B. The increase is at a decreasing rate in the diagram, reflecting the fact that freight rates are usually not calculated as a fixed charge per mile but increase with distance at a decreasing rate.

Curve 2 shows for different plant locations the transfer cost of finished goods produced from the same volume of raw material considered in the construction of Curve 1. At location B there will be no transfer cost of *finished* goods since a location of the processing plant at B implies a location at the market. For locations at different points from B back to the source of material at A, however, there will be some transfer costs for moving the finished goods to market at B. The farther one is from B and the closer to A in locating this plant, the greater will be the cost of distribution.

At a particular point, such as the point L, then, procurement costs are indicated by the distance LP and distribution costs by the interval LF. It is possible to construct an estimate of total transfer costs at location L by adding together LP and LF. This addition has been performed not only for the location L but for all locations and the result appears in Curve 3. In deciding where transfer cost is a minimum, the entrepreneur will study Curve 3. He may find that its lowest point is at the source of material, A, at the market, B, or at some point in between.

Even this simple model captures some of the basic relationships between transportation and location. Note in particular that it is the transport costs associated with a site that the entrepreneur considers. Physical distance is not in itself a consideration. It becomes relevant through its influence upon the cost of transportation.

These locations correspond to different orientations actually found in different industries. That is, some industries are oriented to materials, some exhibit orientation to markets, and some, location at intermediate points. In what situation does one tend to find each of these different orientations?

ORIENTATION TO MATERIALS—Transportation rates must be applied to the relevant quantities. It is necessary to consider not only the rate for a given weight of raw material and the rate for a given weight of product, but the relative quantity of raw material in comparison to the relative quantity of product to be shipped. If there is a large loss of weight in processing a particular raw material, there will be reason to locate the processing near the source of the material. This consideration is important frequently in the first stage of processing. It is found, for example, in agriculture. Wheat is threshed on the farm. Sugar cane is crushed near the sugar cane fields. Similarly, ore smelting plants tend to be located near mines. In recent years there has been increasing use of the taconite ores in the Lake Superior region. These ores are concentrated into pellets of much greater iron content than is found in the original ore itself before they are fed into furnaces for the production of iron and steel. The plants in which this first stage processing occurs are located near the mines; it is the *concentrated* ore which is shipped.

Industrial processes with very large fuel requirements tend to be located near a source of fuel. The classic example is the tendency for steel mills to be located near supplies of coking coal. Here, again, what is involved is an early stage in an industrial process.

While it is necessary to consider the weights of the materials to be transported, ease of transportation and cost of transportation are not exclusively matters of weight. Bulk will also be important. For example, cotton gins tend to be located near the places where cotton is produced. The baled cotton which has been pressed into compact form is more economical to transport than the product which comes from the field.

For many industries the pull toward location close to the source of materials is powerful. For example, only about one-sixth of the weight of a sugar beet emerges as refined sugar. The economic forces which tend to determine the location of sugar factories, therefore, are not likely to lead to locations remote from the areas of production and close to areas where sugar is finally consumed.

ORIENTATION TO MARKETS—Orientation to markets may be the result of a weight gain. Some products gain weight rather than lose weight in the course of processing, usually because of the addition of water, which is available in all populous areas. Perhaps the most familiar example is the bottling plant for beverages. Soft drinks are not shipped bottled all over the United States; they are shipped in concentrated form and bottled locally.

Orientation to markets may also be the result of higher transfer costs for the finished products. Especially at intermediate and later stages of production the weight of transported materials may be about equal to the weight of the final product. Processing, however, can make goods more fragile, more difficult to pack for shipment, bulkier in relation to weight, and even more perishable. Grain, for example, is less perishable than bread. The baking industry, therefore, tends to be distributed in the same manner as the population. Another product which becomes bulky in the final stages of processing is an automobile. A finished automobile is essentially an empty container for people. It is far bulkier in relation to its weight than an equal number of pounds of sheet metal, glass, rubber, etc. There is an economic reason, therefore, for automobile assembly plants to be dispersed toward the centers of population where automobiles are sold. (This tendency, as discussed above, is opposed by other tendencies, and the actual location of automobile assembly plants represents a compromise between two sets of forces.)

There is a tendency for freight rates to be based on value per pound, for reasons to be discussed in a later chapter. Freight charges per pound for finished goods, therefore, tend to be higher than those for raw materials by amounts even larger than would be required to reflect the added cost of shipping the goods in finished form. To the extent that this situation exists it tends to make it economical to locate plants close to markets.

LOCATION AT INTERMEDIATE POINTS—Total transfer costs may be lowest for a location at an intermediate point, not for a location at the market or at the source of materials. Such a point may occur where two methods of transportation meet, for example, rail transportation and water transportation. Transshipment from one mode of transportation to another may be necessary at such a point. In terms of the type of diagram used above (Figure 2.2), the transshipment point may be the minimum in the curve of total transfer costs. The point of transshipment may be the most efficient location for a processing activity.

An example is flour milling. Both the raw material, grain, and the product, flour, are bulky. The expense of transshipment is important. Flour mills may be located at points such as Buffalo where grain must be removed from lake steamers before it can be shipped on to the eastern United States by rail. It is more economical to do the milling at Buffalo than to interrupt the rail journey for milling at, say, a city in the Mohawk Valley. It is more economical, that is, from a social point of view. What is economical for the shipper of grain will depend on the rate structure, which may offer him the privilege of milling the grain "in transit" without charge.

Commercial activities which involve no physical transformation of the product also may be located at intermediate points. Distribution centers may develop where commodities are received in bulk, stored in warehouses, and shipped out to a network of local markets. Similarly, collection centers may develop where materials are assembled for initial processing.

ZONE OF INDIFFERENCE—In recent years there have been a number of studies of how location decisions are actually made, especially location decisions of manufacturers. These studies suggest that for many entrepreneurs there may be a zone of indifference with respect to where they locate their activity. That is, there may be compelling reasons for them to locate within a particular geographic area, but these reasons may not dictate location at a unique point. There may be a considerable region in which the net balance of advantages and disadvantages is about the same. In terms of Figure 2.2, the curve of total transfer costs may be flat for a considerable range. Processing costs and demand considerations also may be the same within a considerable area. Within such a region the choice of location may be determined by any of a variety of minor factors. The personal preferences of the entrepreneur himself (or his wife) may be decisive. He will be free to select the location nearest the town with the best golf course or the biggest shade trees.

From the point of view of the entrepreneur, thus, the choice may be a matter of little importance. From the point of view of others concerned with his decision, the choice may be a matter of critical importance. There may be two small towns involved, each concerned with local unemployment that would be relieved by the new activity. There may be two railroads, each with excess capacity, and the plant may locate on the route of one or the other. In such situations there may be economic pressure arising out of competition among communities or among carriers to adjust transportation rates.

The entrepreneur, finally, may locate at a site selected for its closeness to markets or to materials, or at an intermediate point. Whatever his decision, once he has made it he has gone far toward committing himself as to the transportation he will require for the operation of his activity as long as it remains at that site. Changes in his sources of supply or markets or reorganization of his productive process are the only remaining ways of changing his transportation requirements.

CONCLUSION—In part, the transportation of people is for their vacations and pleasure and to that degree transportation is a consumer service. Most of transportation, however, is for the production of intermediate rather than final services. The economic usefulness of this part of transportation arises from the economic advantages of geographic specialization and the broadening of markets. The decisions which determine the volume of transportation involve interplay between the shippers on the one side of the market and the suppliers of transportation on the other. The shippers largely determine their requirements for transportation when they select the sites at which they will carry on their activities and the methods of production they will use. Locational choices are, therefore, closely related to the demand for transportation. These choices are influenced by differences in processing costs from site to site and by differences in transfer costs associated with different locations.

3

Introduction to the Theory of Investment

TRANSPORT SYSTEMS almost always require substantial capital investment. The first decision to be taken with respect to any transportation facility is the decision whether or not to make the necessary investment to build it with the implied further commitment of resources to operate the facility. The initial questions are essentially whether any scarce resources should be devoted to the construction of the proposed facility, and, if so, how much should be invested in it. Subsequently, if a start is made, periodically there will be additional questions: Should further resources be invested? In what amounts? Should the plant or some part of it be scrapped? The discussion that follows is an introduction to the theory of investment in transport, which is concerned with the answers to the above questions. At an abstract level, the economic theory of investment is general and much of what is said would apply to investment in other parts of the economy; but the emphasis here is on the special difficulties of investment decisions in transportation. As far as possible the discussion of the pricing of transportation services is postponed until Chapter 4.

It should be kept in mind that there is a large number of possible investments in transportation including investments in vehicles (and in terminals), for any of the transport systems including highways and railroads, as well as systems of transportation by air and by water. Examples have been selected primarily from the highway field in which the largest investments have been made in recent years in the United States.

Framework for Analysis of Investment

The starting point for the analysis of the question of whether a particular investment should be made is the need to compare the costs of the investment with the benefits or gains. The point of view taken here as a starting point is the point of view of society as a whole. Hence, the gains from the project to any member of society should be taken into account, as should the costs to any member of society. Answers to two questions are needed. Are the costs larger than the gains? If so, the project should be abandoned. If, however, the gains exceed the costs, a second question must be answered. How does the excess of gains over costs for this investment compare with the gains for other possible projects?

The necessity for selecting among alternative investments arises from the limitation that funds for investment are never unlimited. For any proposed investment it is appropriate to ask, what is society giving up for this project? The *opportunity cost* of an investment is the cost of giving up alternative uses of the resources required. This type of problem is common, for example, in the planning of highway systems. The institutional arrangements are that highway departments may be given fixed budgets. Given a limited budget for the construction of new roads, and a list of highways whose gains exceed their costs, the problem is to decide which ones should be built. The choices which must be made include both choices among entirely separate projects and choices among alternative ways of designing a particular project.

Private businesses, like public enterprises, face the basic questions of how much to invest altogether and how to allocate resources among alternative projects. The only difference is that the private enterprise may take a narrow view of costs and gains and consider only those which are reflected in its private accounts to the exclusion of costs and gains, if any, to others. This difference may be a matter of importance and may lead, for example, to subsidies by government agencies of private enterprise. Thus, the gains to the defense of the United States from its merchant marine do not appear as part of the commercial receipts of the shipping companies but are justification for subsidies to investment in American ships. In this discussion the more inclusive, social point of view is generally taken.

Both the estimation of gains and the estimation of costs present difficulties which require discussion. In thinking about problems of investment decisions it may be helpful to keep in mind as a specific example of the general principles the problem of whether to construct a particular bridge. The use of a bridge as an example has a venerable tradition in economics, and most of the theoretical points can be illustrated with this example. Consider, first, the estimation of costs.

INCLUSION OF COSTS OF OPERATION—The calculation of the cost associated with an investment will require both an estimate of the original cost of the facility, for example, the bridge, and an estimate of the costs of operation and maintenance over the life of the facility. The entire expected economic life of the facility should be taken into account since it will presumably yield valuable services for that length of time. Costs of operation and maintenance can properly be omitted from consideration only if they are very small.

DISCOUNTING FUTURE COSTS—Since future costs must be considered as well as the initial investment, the need arises to combine future and present costs. Since in an economy with a positive interest rate, money now and money in the future are not the same; it is necessary to discount the future costs.[1] Investment decisions in transportation frequently involve the consideration of costs for many years into the future since the capital equipment is long lived. For example, the Brooklyn Bridge has been with us since 1884. A correct procedure in computing the cost of providing a service under a proposed investment plan is to discount the series of future costs over the economic life of the project back to present costs by applying an appropriate rate of interest. What rate of interest should be used for the discounting is a difficult and on occasion a controversial question, which is discussed below, but there is no question that some rate of interest should be used.

1. To understand the reason for this difference, one has only to ask, would he rather be compelled to pay 1000 dollars today or 1000 dollars a year from today? If one has the 1000 dollars in hand, he can earn interest on it for a year if he need not pay until then. To compute what sum today is equivalent to 1000 dollars a year from now when the going interest rate is, say R per cent, one has only to calculate what amount of money must be invested at R per cent interest to yield 1000 dollars a year from now. (For a recent discussion of the theory of investment with special reference to transportation see: Tillo E. Kuhn, *Public Enterprise Economics and Transport Problems,* University of California Press, 1962.)

The formula for converting a series of costs in the future to a single present cost is as follows:

If: C equals present value of the series of costs to be incurred over the life of a project

t equals number of time units in the economic life of the project (if annual periods are considered, and the project has a life of T years, t will have values $t = 0, 1, 2, \ldots, T$).

r equals rate of interest per period

Then

$$C = C_0 + \frac{C_1}{(1+r)} + \frac{C_2}{(1+r)^2} + \cdots + \frac{C_T}{(1+r)^T}$$

That is, the total present value of the stream of costs will be equal to the sum of the costs to be incurred in each period. The cost in each period after the first must be discounted. For example, an initial investment of $100,000 would contribute $100,000 to the total. A cost of $1000 in period 1 would contribute $1000/[(1 + r)^1]$; if $r = 0.05$, the contribution would be $1000/[(1 + 0.05)^1]$ or $952.

Note that the importance of a given outlay declines as the time of the outlay is postponed. The future is discounted. Note also that the amount of the discount depends directly on the rate of interest employed. A high value of r will reduce the size of the later terms in the series, especially if the series is long.

The analysis need not be in periods of one year. Calculations could be made on a quarterly or monthly basis. A given project, of course, will have a life of four times as many quarterly periods as annual periods, and the number of terms in the series will be four times as great. If the calculation is made on a quarterly basis, the interest rate must be converted into interest per quarter.

RESTORING THE SITE—There is an additional entry which may be necessary at the end of the series of costs depending on the anticipated ultimate fate of the project. It may be that the project will be of no value to society at the end of the period. It may even be that the installation will be a nuisance which will have to be cleared away. The cost of restoring the site to its original condition should then be taken into account, and may be included as the last term in the series of costs. It will be discounted by $(1 + r)^T$. If either r or T is large, or the cost of restoring the site is small, this term will be unimportant. Many but not all investments for transportation purposes are sufficiently long lived so that the cost of restoring the site should be ignored. To take an extreme example, it would have been an error for the Romans to include such a term in calculations of the cost of highways which are still used today. The cost of restoring the site should be included, however, when the facility is built to meet a temporary need: transportation to the site of a special event such as a fair.

SUNK COSTS—Once an initial investment has been made, in deciding on a course of action for the future it is important to be clear about which costs should be ignored as well as about which costs should be considered in analysis of proposals for additional investments. The rule to follow with respect to sunk costs is simple: ignore them! All expenditures made in the past or committed in the past should be treated as sunk costs. The only question for decision is, what costs shall be incurred in the future?

This prescription sometimes seems unreasonable on first examination. The difficulty may be that it gives the impression that the analyst is turning his back on the past. The contrary is true. For example, consider a situation in which two plans are proposed to develop a bridge that will handle the expected traffic on a certain crossing. The first plan involves reconstruction of an existing bridge; the second, the scrapping of the old bridge and the building of an entirely new facility on the site. The problem is, which will be cheaper? In this calculation all costs incurred to date on the existing bridge should be ignored. Given the full benefit of the improvements made to date with that money, the question is whether the future cost of increasing the capacity of the existing bridge exceeds the total cost of a new bridge. As he faces the future, the analyst regards work done in the past as if it were a free gift to be gratefully accepted to the extent that it can reduce future expenditure. When it is cheaper to pay the full cost of a new installation disregarding sunk costs, the economic life of the old installation is over.

It may be that in some sense the old bridge is not fully paid for. It may have been financed by bonds which are still outstanding. The decision to be made, however, has nothing to do with these bonds. They must be paid off regardless of what is done about the bridge. The commitment to pay them should be met, of course, but it is irrelevant to the choice between the two methods of meeting the need to handle a future flow of traffic. No need to make it hard to meet the claims of the bondholders by spending more than one must! The comparison of the cost of the alternatives is: how much more must be spent under the two plans.

DISCOUNTING FUTURE GAINS—Consider, now, the gains from the

proposed investment. These gains will include any cash receipts plus other possible benefits either to the enterprise in question or to society at large. Exactly what should be included under gains will depend on the type of project. Some investments are made to reduce costs. For example, a railroad may construct a bridge to shorten its line. The reduction in operating costs would be a gain from the bridge. Highway bridges may be toll bridges: the gains to the bridge authority would include the resulting revenue.

Many of the observations that apply to the measurement of costs also apply to gains. Just as future costs must be considered as well as present costs, future gains must be considered. The gains from the toll bridge, for example, would include the revenues over its entire economic life. The future income should be discounted, in the same manner as future costs should be discounted, and for the same reasons.

The formula is exactly analogous to the formula for the discounting of costs. It is as follows:

If: G equals present value of a series of gains to be expected from the project, with G_0 the gain in the first period, G_1 the gain in the second period, and so forth

t equals number of time units in the life of the project

r equals rate of interest per period

$$\text{Then } G = G_0 + \frac{G_1}{(1+r)^1} + \frac{G_2}{(1+r)^2} + \cdots + \frac{G_T}{(1+r)^T}$$

The total value of the gains is equal to the sum of the gains to be received in each period over the life of the project.

SCRAP VALUE—If there is any scrap value of the project which may be realized at the end of its useful life, that value should be taken into account with the appropriate discount rate. Estimates of scrap value, like estimates of cost of restoring a site, may be unimportant if the life of the project is expected to be long. If the investment under consideration is an investment in vehicles (in trucks, for example), the life span of which is not long and where there is known to be a scrap value, the entry of that value is a necessary part of the calculation.

ALTERNATIVE, EQUIVALENT CALCULATIONS—There are alternative procedures that have the same effect as the use of the formulas given above. For example, it is possible to subtract the costs from the gains in each future year and discount the series of net gains. It is possible to solve for the rate of interest instead of the present value and compute an expected rate of return on an initial investment. This rate can then be compared to a yardstick rate. The conclusion reached should be the same as by the calculation proposed above. The calculations may be complex, but it is easy to understand the idea that the higher the prospective rate of return on an investment, the more attractive the investment.

THE SELECTION OF AN INTEREST RATE—The selection of the interest rate to be used in the calculations themselves or as a yardstick to compare with an estimated rate of return is a matter of obvious importance. A high interest rate may lead to a decision not to proceed with a project. A high interest rate also will lead to a tendency to prefer projects that have a short useful life. If two projects are to be compared, one of which involves a high initial investment and low operating costs while the other involves low initial investment and high operating costs, the rate of interest chosen may very well be decisive. A high rate means that the high operating costs of the low investment alternative will be given little weight in the estimate of C. The initial investment, which is not discounted, will be relatively more important. Conversely, a low rate of interest increases the importance of future costs in the calculation of C.

There is agreement among economists that a zero rate of interest is not correct, but there is not always full agreement as to what rate should be used in particular situations. The usual starting point of economic discussion is the conception of a market rate of interest. The market rate of interest provides a mechanism for bringing consistency into the decisions of separate economic units. It provides the link between analysis of individual projects and general equilibrium analysis for the country as a whole. Suppose rates of return were computed by all economic agencies, public and private, that consider making investments in a given country in a given year. Some economists argue that all should use the same yardstick rate of return, the general interest rate. Then all projects that will not yield this rate of return or better will be rejected, and all that will pay at this rate or above will be accepted.

In consideration of an individual project, it does not matter whether the market rate of interest is used to discount the future, or an internal rate of return is computed and compared to the market rate. If the market rate is used for discounting and the project yields a net excess of gains over costs, it should be adopted. If the internal rate of return is computed, compared to the market rate, and found to exceed the market rate, the project should be adopted. The market rate serves as a measure of the opportunity cost of the project. If a project will yield less than the market rate, then it is inferior to other projects that will yield that level of return. If a project yields more, then it is superior to the alternatives.

It may be there are a great many proposed investments that appear advantageous when the return is compared to the market rate. There may be so many at that rate the demand for investment capital will exceed the market rate. Then the appropriate adjustment is an increase in the market rate. This adjustment is appropriate whether it is made by the market or by some public agency that influences the market.

It is an abstraction, of course, to speak of a single, general, market interest rate. What should be considered is the cost of capital for the project in question or similar projects. Allowance should be made, for private enterprises, for a reasonable division between financing from the sale of stock and from borrowed money. If an enterprise is not in a position to rely only on bonds to raise money, the required rate of return must allow for the actual mix between bonds and other financing. The market may be expected to require a higher average rate of return for projects involving greater risk. Rates for long and short term borrowing may well be different. No fundamental difficulty, however, results. Each project should be evaluated by that rate of interest that applies in the market for debt to mature in a period equal to its economic life.

Interest rates also vary according to whether the borrower is a private enterprise, or the federal government, or some other public agency. There is variation among rates paid according to the credit rating of the borrower. Some economists would prefer to have all public investment planning agencies use as a rate a low risk rate for private borrowers. Others would prefer the rate actually paid by the public agency. The Bureau of the Budget has taken the latter view, and has used the average rate being paid by the government on bonds with maturity of five or more years. What is at issue is the question of how much investment should be undertaken by public agencies. The lower the rate, the more projects will be acceptable.

Private enterprises are not likely to use for investment analysis a rate less than they themselves must pay for money. In fact, it is typical for business enterprises to use a much higher rate of return in evaluating proposed investments, such as fifteen per cent.[2] Such rates, however, represent in part a way of allowing for the uncertainty of the

2. See Vincent J. Roggeven, "Engineering-Economics Planning of Transport Systems," *Papers, Fourth Annual Meeting, Transportation Research Forum, 1963*, pp. 275–288.

estimates. Future costs may be underestimated and benefits may be overestimated. One way to allow for any such bias is to use a high interest rate for purposes of analysis. Any businessman who could freely borrow money at a given rate, say five per cent, and *knew* he could earn more, say six per cent, by investing it in a certain project, would certainly undertake the project. He would hesitate only if he could not freely borrow as much as he wished at that rate, or if he had doubts as to whether he could earn the six per cent.

EXTERNAL VS INTERNAL COSTS AND GAINS—It has been mentioned already that from the point of view of society as a whole both costs and gains to everyone should be included in the calculations. If a private enterprise constructs a facility, such as a bridge, it will take into account only the costs it must pay and the gains it will reap. A public enterprise may be set up with a mandate that makes it similar to a private enterprise in this respect. Internal costs are those the enterprise must pay itself, external costs are those paid by others.

It is useful to divide society into three groups according to gains to be received from a new facility. First, there will be those users of the new facility who now use an alternative service. For example, they may be using an old bridge that is parallel to the new bridge. They will benefit from any reduction in the cost of service that is associated with the improvement—tolls may be less on the new bridge, or the route may be shortened to their desired destination—with resulting reduction in their costs of operation. They will also benefit if a superior service is provided that has some extra value to them in excess to the value of the prior facilities. For example, their travel time may be less. Second, there may be new users who do not now use the present service. They will gain by being given the opportunity to use the new facility. It is also possible, thirdly, for people who never use the facility to benefit indirectly from it, i.e., those who continue to use the old bridge may find it less congested. Also, an individual who owns land that becomes more accessible as the result of the construction of the new bridge will benefit from an increase in the capitalized value of his land whether or not he himself ever crosses the bridge.

In a comparable way some people may be put at a disadvantage by the construction of the new facility. They may incur losses, and these losses should be included in the reckoning of the total value of the bridge from the point of view of society. It may be social policy to compensate them for their losses and if so the compensation should be included directly in the calculations as a cost. The loss will be real, of course, regardless of whether it is compensated. For example, the construction of a bridge may involve building approaching roads through a residential district to the disadvantage of the residents of the area. (There was opposition for this reason to the construction of the Verrazano-Narrows Bridge in New York.)

It is characteristic of transportation systems that the gains and benefits that are indirect—the external ones if the facility is privately owned and operated—are likely to be important. The estimation of these effects is a particularly difficult part of the analysis of proposed investments in transportation. Some systems of organizing transportation projects leave them entirely out of consideration, in effect sacrificing completeness in the calculation of gains and benefits but gaining precision. These problems will be discussed further in later chapters, especially in the discussion of highways.

Practical Methods to Approximate Theoretical Calculations

To understand the implications of the theoretical discussion in the preceding section it may be helpful to consider several choices of practical methods to make investment decisions. These methods may then be compared with theoretical calculations. Three methods will be considered: a voters' referendum, as might be taken on an issue of bonds for improved streets; issuing a franchise to a private company that is empowered to make investments provided it can finance them from charges to users; and a direct calculation of social costs and gains as might be made by a state highway department that is considering a particular road construction project. Other methods also exist for making investment decisions, such as a decision by the elected representatives of the voters in Congress—say, on an appropriation to build a new canal from the Atlantic to the Pacific.

VOTERS' REFERENDUM—One way to proceed on a public project would be to go through the following steps: (1) Compute the cost. (2) Select a proposed scheme of financing so that each individual voter can estimate the cost to himself of the undertaking. (3) Make the information about costs and gains available to the voting public. (4) Take a vote, and let the majority decide whether the project is to be carried forward. Such referenda are in fact carried out. The citizens of San Francisco, for example, decided for a proposal to construct a new rapid transit system.

What are the objections to such a referendum and what difficulties would be encountered? There is the basic question: who should be allowed to vote. Who is involved? Continuing the example of the bridge from the preceding discussion, it may be that some of the people who cross the bridge do not live in the immediate neighborhood of the project. (This is true, for example, of the bridge at the Straits of Mackinac.) On the other hand, most people who live at a distance will never use the bridge. It is not easy as a practical matter to define a population that will coincide with the prospective group of users of the facility for purposes of deciding either who will be taxed or who will vote. If several bridges in different parts of the country are lumped together in a single project by some broad political authority, the sharp focus of public attention on the merits of individual projects will be lost.

A second difficulty with the referendum is that the proposed method of counting one vote for each man may not adequately take into account the complexities of the situation. The magnitude of the net gain for one individual may be very different from the net gain or the net loss from the proposed project for other individuals. It is possible, for example, that the majority may be indifferent while a small group of individuals would be greatly advantaged. If a system of adjusting the burden of paying for the facility could be devised according to which these individuals would make a larger contribution, then it might be that the project would get a majority of the vote. Failing such a scheme, the referendum might lead to the "wrong" (i.e., socially inefficient) decision.

A SYSTEM OF TOLL CHARGES—Another scheme to make investment decisions and to operate facilities after construction is to rely upon private enterprise, or a public enterprise that must cover its expenses from its revenues. A private enterprise will make an investment if it can cover its costs with at least a normal rate of return on the funds it commits. A public enterprise can be instructed to behave like a private enterprise. The steps would be as follows: (1) Establish an agency for the purpose of constructing projects of a certain type. (2) Give to this authority the right to collect tolls. (3) Instruct the authority to go forward with those projects and only those projects that can be financed by bonds to be repaid from future tolls.

Such an arrangement might provide a better match of charges and benefits than the referendum. Benefits from use of the facility will be paid for at the time when they are received. The more often an individual crosses a bridge, the more often he will contribute to the cost of its construction and maintenance. It will yet remain true that there will be some users of the bridge who would have paid even higher tolls if necessary. The match of charges paid with benefits received by users may be improved, but will remain imperfect.

As previously noted, there will also remain some benefits (or losses) to people who are not users of the facility that will not be taken into account even by this arrangement. It is small comfort to the owner of residential property adjoining a new toll road whose scenic view is lost to reflect as he listens to the traffic that he need not pay for the privilege of using the road if he chooses not to drive on it. Part of the social cost of the project may remain external to the authority and uncompensated.

The advantages and limitations of tolls as a method of paying for investment will be discussed further in Chapter 4. There is one advantage of a financial criterion for investment decisions, however, that should be stressed here. It is that the criterion is definite. Everyone understands it. No manager of an enterprise who is expected to make money likes to be in the position of losing money!

DIRECT CALCULATION OF SOCIAL GAINS AND BENEFITS—A third system for making investment decisions is to assign the responsibility to a public agency that does not have to cover its costs from charges for use of each facility. Such an agency may make explicitly a calculation of social gains and losses for each project. Such attempts are made, for example, by public agencies concerned with decisions as to the construction of highways. A common problem in highway planning is to review all possible schemes for highway construction in a given area such as a state and select the projects to be carried out.

The objections to having social calculations made by a public agency are not matters of economic theory. The public agency, in principle, can make the calculations correctly and it can make a complete list of all social gains and benefits. There are still theoretical problems relating to how the calculations are made. On the cost side of the calculation, for example, the problem of the interest rate has been mentioned. On the benefit side, each benefit should be counted once—and only once. The possibilities of double counting are numerous, and sometimes subtle. To take a simple example, it would be an error to count for a toll bridge both the estimated value of time saved by the users and the tolls paid. The problems will vary according to the type of investment under analysis.

Regardless of the method of reaching an investment decision there are difficulties arising out of errors of estimate and problems of measurement. It is to these topics that attention will now be turned. Before doing so, it may be appropriate to note that each of the three systems of making investment decisions is in use; and each system has both advantages and disadvantages. There is no consensus that any one of these methods should be abandoned or should be used in general in preference to the others. As a practical matter the method of making *investment* decisions depends on the *general* choice of organizational arrangement for the transportation system in question.

Problems of Estimation in Investment Decisions

Difficulties of estimation may be expected in any major investment decision. The importance of particular problems, of course, will vary from one investment decision to another. The brief discussion that follows will concern the "lumpiness" of investment decisions, the problems of financial estimates both of costs and gains, the difficulties of measuring nonfinancial consequences of investments, and the consequences of broad margins of error in the estimates.

"LUMPINESS"—It is characteristic of many investments in transportation that they are "lumpy," that is, the investment must be made in large units. This difficulty is especially important for investments in the way. An intercity highway, at least in the United States, is not likely to be built one-lane wide, and the construction of three-lane highways also has been abandoned. The choice is to build two lanes, four lanes, or more than four. Nice adjustment of capacity to expected demand by adding 0.1 more lanes is not possible.

There is another, broader sense in which investment is "lumpy" that arises out of the unity of transportation networks. Incomplete transportation systems may be of little or no value. In the 1860s a railroad half way across the Rocky Mountains would have been of little more value than a canal half way across the Isthmus of Panama some years later. The St. Lawrence Seaway could not hope to become profitable until the necessary channel was complete *both* at the Welland Canal and at the rapids in the St. Lawrence *plus* all the necessary port installations, docks, and marine terminals.

Each part of a complete transportation system makes a contribution to the entire operation. The transportation services produced are a joint product of the system as a whole. To plan and install a system as a whole, however, may involve the commitment of very large sums of money. A recent example of a decision to proceed with a system of transportation was the decision to build the 41,000 mile system of Interstate and Defense Highways in the United States. These roads were planned and are being built to form a single network; they will be especially useful because they are planned to a single set of specifications and they connect! To proceed involved a decision to spend in excess of 40 billion dollars. A national network of highways might have been built, of course, to other specifications, but any national network of modern highways will represent a major investment.

A system can be built in stages, one piece here and another there, but, since roads to nowhere are not very useful, there are strong reasons to make a single decision to proceed or not to proceed with a complete system. Hence, what will be required if the decision is to be based on rational analysis is an estimate of the costs and gains of the system.

ERRORS IN FINANCIAL ESTIMATES—It is a matter of practical experience in transportation that estimates of the cost of a proposed investment may be substantially in error. The margin of error tends to be particularly wide when what is proposed is something dramatically new or different. It was particularly large, for example, in the cost estimates made in connection with the construction of the early railroads. The control and reduction of such errors is more a matter of engineering than of economics.

Attention usually tends to be focused on errors that arise when a project is undertaken on the basis of a particular cost estimate and in the event actual costs exceed the estimates. Errors in the conservative direction are also possible, however. Excessively pessimistic cost estimates may lead to the postponement or abandonment of projects that ought to be undertaken.

The greatest difficulties in making cost estimates are to be expected when there is only one project of a kind and also something dramatically new is being undertaken. Past experience provided little guidance as to the cost of the construction of the first transcontinental railroad and not until the first was successful were other railroads to the Pacific commenced. At present the costs of the proposed supersonic air transport are uncertain. The problem becomes essentially one of how to reach decisions and how to organize the activity in the absence of solid cost estimates.

If one were to hazard a comparison between the two, however, it would be that in financial projections errors in estimates of revenues are likely to be greater than errors in estimates of costs. In attempting to estimate the cost of an investment, at least one has the advantage that one is talking about expenditures that will reach their peak in the immediately coming period when the facility is to be constructed.

As a rule, however, the use of a transportation facility tends to increase with the passage of time. Estimates of revenues, therefore, require attempts to foresee the future years ahead, and it is notoriously difficult to foresee the distant future.

The history of the development of highways in the 1950s provides classic illustrations of the difficulty of forecasting traffic. An example of an underestimate of benefits occurred in the construction of the Hollywood Freeway in Los Angeles. This highway was built with a designed capacity of 100,000 vehicles per day and opened in 1954. In one year the rate of use reached 168,000 vehicles per day. On the New Jersey Turnpike, also opened in 1954, the traffic volume was about three times the estimates. In 1955 the traffic exceeded the estimates made for the 1980s.

A classic example of a miscalculation in the opposite direction is the West Virginia Turnpike, which has attained notoriety as "the turnpike to nowhere." This highway was built across difficult terrain at heavy expense, and, as matters worked out, without satisfactory connections with other through roads. The extent of the miscalculation may be indicated by the fact that in 1958 the net operating revenue from the turnpike was 2.9 million dollars, while the interest on the revenue bonds was 5.1 million. It may be argued that benefits from the turnpike not reflected on the books of the turnpike authority justified its construction; for example, reduced unemployment during construction. A case might have been made for planning to subsidize this project as a contribution to the development of the area. The project, however, was not set up on such a basis. The intent was to meet the costs from the revenues. A gross miscalculation was made!

When a proposed investment is small relative to the economy of the area involved, it is possible to ignore its effect on the rest of the economy. Projections of gross national product, for example, need not be made separately with and without the proposed project. When the investment is large, however, as may be true in an underdeveloped country, its effects on the rest of the economy must be considered. As discussed in Chapter 2, transportation systems may have effects on prices, on the availability of natural resources, on the development of large scale industry, and on the location of economic activity. Thus, the analysis of investment decisions which are large relative to the economy as a whole logically requires analysis of the effects on the economy as a whole. Adequate techniques for carrying out such analysis are not easy to develop and apply.

PROBLEMS OF MEASUREMENT—When nonfinancial gains and benefits are taken into account, problems of measurement are added to the problems of errors in forecasting. The cash receipts of an investment can eventually be counted, and money spent can be counted. Nonmonetary consequences of some investments, however, must be considered.

Two classes of nonmonetary benefits are especially important. First, a new facility may involve savings of time to those who use it. It takes less time, for example, to cross a river on a bridge than by ferry. Should this saving in time be converted into cash equivalent? If the individuals involved are being paid for their time because they are engaged in business as employees of a business enterprise, no difficulty arises, at least no difficulty in principle. One can estimate the value of their time at the rate at which they are being paid for their services. For people not engaged in business the solution is less clear. One may be driven to such expedients as adopting the legal minimum wage as an arbitrary estimate of the value of time. More sophisticated approaches have started from the idea that some people would prefer more income to more leisure, and others, the reverse. Some analysts are inclined to be skeptical of any attempts to put a monetary value on time.

Second, if the new facility is safer than the old, the question arises of how to evaluate the saving in the number of accidents and the reduced death toll. These problems have arisen especially in connection with proposed investments in new highway facilities. The valuation problems are both complex and controversial. There are some parts of the loss due to accidents that can be reduced to financial terms, such as the property damage and medical bills. Other items to cover loss of income, and pain and suffering, range from difficult to nearly impossible to evaluate. It is not clear that the studies made to date in this field exhaust the possibilities of rational analysis, but it may always be with an uneasy feeling that an analyst assigns a dollar value per life saved.

CONSEQUENCES OF BROAD MARGINS OF ERROR—In investment decisions where the margin of error in estimates of costs, gains, or both is very broad there is a tendency for decisions to be influenced by nonrational factors. One promoter of the St. Lawrence Seaway, for example, had people singing songs about being "Rocked in the Seaway to the Deep." People may become enthusiastic about the possibilities and evaluate the investment possibilities positively, or they may become pessimistic about them, and make negative evaluations. Climates of opinion tend to develop. In the absence of a rational basis for making a final evaluation of the situation people support their beliefs and opinions by reference to the beliefs and opinions of others. Sudden changes may occur in the

climate of opinion. The history of the subject is full of such shifts—
from the canal mania in eighteenth-century England onwards.

More deliberate consideration may lead to strategies that range from
extreme conservatism to extreme willingness to assume risks. A conservative policy with respect to investment in transportation will lead
to building only those transportation facilities for which, on any calculation, there is certain to be an excess of gains over costs. The opposite
strategy is to take a favorable view of the prospects and go ahead and
build. The cautious approach also is characterized by a tendency to
consider as benefits only those that are more direct and immediate. An
expansionist approach will emphasize the indirect and future benefits.
The history of investment policy in transportation, as will be developed
more fully below, is in large part the history of choices of this type.

In the present stage of intellectual development it is not possible to
base the major transportation investment decisions entirely on precise
scientific calculations. There may never be a time when all the political
considerations and human considerations can be reduced to a single
calculation with the economic. Analytic progress in developing the tools
of rational decision making, however, is pushing back the frontier of
knowledge and reducing the elements in these decisions that must be
imponderable.

4

Introduction to the Theory of Rate-Making

In the economics of transportation the problems of rate-making rank in importance with the problems of investment decisions. The setting of rates is necessary in any transportation enterprise that meets its costs in whole or in part from fees paid by users of the service whether the enterprise is publicly owned, an unregulated private enterprise, or a private enterprise subject to regulation.

The starting point of analysis of rates from the point of view of society is the development of criteria for the evaluation of existing or proposed rates. Considerations of efficiency in the allocation of resources lead to the criterion that rates should be based on cost, as is more fully discussed below. The argument is that if transportation rates are based on costs, shippers who try to minimize their own costs will choose as between competing modes of transportation the mode that can perform transportation for them at the lowest cost to society. Shippers also will be making the socially correct choice between transport-intensive and transport-minimizing methods of production. Furthermore, the competition among shippers at different geographic locations will be on the correct basis since each shipper will be paying the cost of the inputs of transportation that he uses in the conduct of his activities.

44

Transportation rates, however, are not based exclusively on considerations of cost. Private enterprises seek to maximize their net revenue taking into account both their costs and the demand curves confronting them. Publicly owned enterprises may proceed in the same manner. Only by taking demand into account in the setting of the rates charged for the use of a facility may it be possible to meet the full cost of the facility.

The discussion of rates which follows is divided into two principal sections that concern, respectively, rate determination and the analysis of costs, and pricing to maximize net revenues taking demand as well as costs into account. A summary statement with emphasis on public policy concludes this Chapter.

Rate Determination and the Analysis of Costs

If the criterion for the setting of price is the efficient allocation of resources, then the price should be set equal to the marginal cost. Economists ordinarily urge that price be equated to *long* run marginal cost, but sometimes they propose that price be equal to *short* run marginal cost. The discussion that follows begins with long run marginal cost and then considers the question of when short run marginal cost is the more relevant criterion.

By short run marginal cost, it will be recalled, is meant marginal cost when plant and equipment are taken as fixed. Short run marginal cost per unit necessarily rises with output when an enterprise is straining at the limits of its capacity. By long run marginal cost is meant, not cost in the future, but marginal cost when plant and equipment can be freely expanded. Long run marginal cost per unit will depend on economies of scale. If there are neither economies nor diseconomies of scale, long run marginal cost will be constant.

PRICE EQUAL TO LONG RUN MARGINAL COST—To set price equal to the long run marginal cost of a given unit of service is to set price equal to the value of the resources that must be used to provide the service into the future. Long run marginal cost ordinarily will be the same as full average cost, including the cost of facilities that have to be repaired or replaced. (The two differ only under special circumstances, as will be discussed below.)

To understand the application of this criterion, consider a common problem, a situation in which two methods of transportation compete for a particular type of traffic in circumstances where both expect to remain in business. The question is, which method will haul commodity

X over a particular route for the foreseeable future? Under these circumstances the efficient solution from a social point of view is, again, that the commodity should move by the method that requires the least extra expenditure of scarce resources.

For these calculations costs should be estimated on the basis, not of past expenditures, but of prospective future expenditures. Commonly, in talking about costs one speaks about past costs because it is about past costs that information is most likely to be available. But it is only future costs that are relevant to establishing future policy. Sunk costs must always be disregarded, and the relevant question is, in the present situation, how can society provide the transportation services in the future with the minimum additional outlay of scarce resources? If the rates charged reflect correctly these costs to society, shippers may be expected to make the right choices in their own interests. This result will be achieved if rates are based on long run marginal costs.

There is one uncomfortable possibility that has concerned economic theorists probably more than it has practical administrators: if the long run average cost curve is falling (if there are continuing economies of scale), the long run marginal cost curve will be less than average cost and a price equal to long run marginal cost will imply chronic losses. A rising curve would imply chronic excess returns. When such situations do appear, a remedy such as a subsidy or a tax may be considered as required.

PRICE EQUAL TO SHORT RUN MARGINAL COST—The question of whether price should be equated to short run rather than long run marginal cost arises when the two are substantially different. There are two possibilities: short run marginal cost may be very low when a facility is operating with excess capacity, and it may be very high when a facility is being heavily used.

As an example of a situation in which short run marginal cost is very low, consider the Bridge across the Straits of Mackinac. This facility seems to have excess capacity, and the marginal cost of permitting an additional vehicle to pass over the bridge must be very close to zero. The price, therefore, should be set at zero according to this rule. At the time of writing, the toll for a passenger car is $3.75—from this point of view, $3.75 too much.

To understand the logic behind this rule, consider in general the situation when the price is set higher than zero by some amount. Then there will be some individuals who will be deterred from using the bridge because they are unable or unwilling to pay that amount. They would have crossed, however, if passage were free. The imposition of the price has caused them to be worse off. If their objective had been business, they would have been influenced to produce the same goods in a different manner, or to produce different goods. If pleasure, they would have been deprived of some enjoyment that could have been theirs *at no social cost*. Thus, the imposition of the price interfered with the most efficient use of productive resources.

Some other method of paying for the bridge must be found, of course. The problem to be faced is whether the best alternative method has disadvantages as serious as the loss from charging a price in excess of short run marginal cost.

CONGESTION COSTS—A different problem arises when a fixed facility is becoming crowded. A facility such as a bridge is not crowded when vehicles move freely without interfering with each other. But there will come a point as the number of vehicles is increased when each added vehicle slows down other vehicles to some degree. The delay is a cost to the other vehicles. There will be monetary costs of congestion for vehicles that are delayed, in the form of increased gasoline consumption per mile traveled, increased wear and tear on the vehicle due to stopping and starting, and the like. And there will be the value of the time lost.

Under such circumstances, the rule that price should be set equal to the marginal cost should be understood to mean social marginal cost including the congestion cost. Price, thus, should be used as a rationing device to limit the use of a scarce resource. As the price rises, some potential users of the facility will be discouraged. Total revenue of the operators of the facility will also rise, and profits may well result. The argument is exactly analogous to the argument for price equal to marginal cost in money when no congestion costs are involved. If the price does not cover full social marginal costs, people will consume too much of the transportation service.

Following the principle suggested here, it would be possible to use price to control peak loads on transportation systems. Toll roads might raise their rates on the Labor Day weekend. Higher tolls would prevent some travel entirely, but the more important effect probably would be to shift some of the traffic to off-peak periods. Some people would do their driving earlier or later. Others, who were unable or unwilling to shift, would pay the premium for travel at the time of peak demand, and would benefit by being able to drive on roads free of congestion.

Some economists are impressed with the social gains to be realized by using the price system to ration facilities in short supply in this manner. Other economists argue that the main emphasis in situations where needs for transportation are expanding should be on the expansion of the transportation system and that the short run gains from adjustments in price are likely to be of secondary importance. They may prefer to set price on the basis of long run rather than short run marginal cost.

What is the best policy in any situation will depend on the facts of that situation, specifically, on the probable permanence of the increased need, the price elasticity of demand, the cost of collection, and the strength of the objection to fluctuating prices by users of the service. In the ordinary conduct of business enterprises outside of transportation, say, in manufacturing, where prices can be set by the enterprises concerned, prices often are set at average cost at a specified level of operations. Capacity is adjusted as required without resort to short run adjustments in price. This solution may approximate setting price equal to long run marginal cost.

PROBLEMS OF ASSIGNMENT OF COSTS—Suppose that the officials responsible for the rate policy of an enterprise are agreed that their charges should be based on the principle that the price of each service should equal its long run marginal cost. Will they then know what rates to set? Would it be easy to obtain agreements that X cents per 100 lbs. was the right rate? Far from it! The problem would remain of how to allocate the costs of the transportation enterprise to the particular category of traffic. The problem arises for all modes of transport.

The nature of the difficulty may be grasped by considering the three components of any transportation system, the vehicle, the power plant, and the way. Costs are incurred to construct and maintain the way, to provide the power plant and its fuel, including the associated labor and other materials for operation and maintenance, and to provide and maintain the vehicles for the movement of passengers and freight. No shipment could be made without the existence of all components, but the same facilities that provide for a single shipment are also likely to be used to provide for many other shipments. How, then, should the costs be divided?

For the way, the problem of allocation always arises, since whether it is a highway, railway, canal, or airway, a way will be used for many separate vehicle movements. When a single movement of a vehicle and its associated power plant is entirely devoted to a single shipment, as in the movement of a shipload of grain or a trainload of coal, the problem is somewhat simplified since there is no problem of allocation of the costs of that movement though there is still the common cost of the way. What must be done is to determine the cost of the movement. But it is frequently true that movements such as a train journey or a ship voyage are not undertaken to handle a single large shipment. Freight customarily moves by rail in carload lots, and the cost of the journey must somehow be allocated among the cars if the costs of the individual shipments are to be estimated. For less than carload shipments, or, in general, less than vehicle load shipments, there will be a problem of allocating the cost of the vehicle movement. As some economists have put the matter, the unit of supply is not the same as the unit sold.[1]

In considering these problems economists have found it useful to distinguish two types of costs, *common costs* and *joint costs*. Common costs arise whenever an expenditure is made that is useful for two or more shipments.

Joint costs arise if a transportation company in producing certain services also necessarily produces certain other services. For example, if a railroad produces services by moving goods or people in one direction on its line, it must also produce services by the reverse movement of its equipment. There must be a back haul. The allocation of cost as between the haul in one direction and that in the other is necessarily arbitrary. Hence, an arbitrary element enters the rate structure. Low rates may be charged for travel in the direction of the lesser movement, or the same rates may be charged as in the direction of the greater movement. From the cost point of view there is no criterion for preferring one of these policies to the other. (The actual solution will depend on demand as is discussed in the next section.)

Consider also an airline that moves people from the United States to Europe in the early summer. The eastward flow is much larger than the westward at this season. The airline must bring its planes back for more loads, however, even if they return empty, or nearly empty. How should the costs be allocated? Should the total cost of the round trip be charged to the eastward flight? Or should the costs be evenly divided? What would be a rate based on cost to charge to the westbound traffic? To these questions there is no single answer. There is no unique correct solution to the allocation of joint costs. If an airline asserted that a transatlantic fare of 10 dollars in the direction opposite the peak flow was sufficient to cover its costs, it would be impossible to prove the assertion was incorrect—unless the airline provided meals and extra passenger service costing more than that amount.

Common costs, however, are more frequently found than joint costs.

1. See the discussion by George Wilson, *Essays on Some Unsettled Questions in Transportation,* Foundation for Economic and Business Studies, Indiana University, 1962.

The problem of allocating common costs may be reduced by segregating costs that are directly associated with a shipment. It may be possible to allocate other costs, if not to individual shipments, at least to classes of shipments. One may think of a hierarchy of costs ranked by degree of specificity. Some are allocable to individual shipments, others to classes of shipments somehow defined, while still others are not easily allocable to any services provided.

The crucial question is, what is the marginal cost of the service? What would we save if we did not provide this service, or this type of service? For example, the extra wear on a freight car from making a certain trip is allocable as cost of that shipment. The cost of maintaining a passenger station is allocable to passenger service generally in contrast to freight service. Neither the cost of the top management of the company nor the cost of the roadway is easily allocable to any class of service.

Much can be done by diligent effort to allocate common costs, and much effort has been expended in this direction in recent years; for example, in the *Highway Cost Allocation* study of the Bureau of Public Roads, and in studies of the cost of railroad passenger service. Do trucks pay their fair share of the cost of highways? How much do railroads "really" lose on passenger service? The criterion of efficiency leads to the yardstick that each category of service should pay at least all costs that would not be incurred if that class of service were abandoned. It does not lead to a clear rule about what should be done with those costs that cannot thus be allocated. There is no simple, unique solution to the question of how these remaining costs should be allocated once the other costs have been, as it were, peeled away. Reasonable allocations, however, are possible, and are achieved. In practice, considerations of the elasticity of demand are commonly taken into account, and rates based on calculations of demand as well as of cost—as will be discussed in the next section.

The most general allocation of costs that is possible is an allocation by type of transportation service. It has been urged with increasing vigor in recent years that each mode of transportation should pay for itself. Costs of vehicles and their operation in general are borne by those for whom the service is provided. What is urged is the extension of this principle to cover the cost of the way. These costs should be met by *user charges*. Thus, the total costs of highways should be met by highway users, of airways by the users of airways, of railroads by the users of railroads, etc. Public assistance to any mode should be covered by taxes, rates, or tolls paid by users of that mode.

Pricing to Maximize Net Revenue

As previously noted, considerations of demand enter the determination of rates charged for transportation. The discussion that follows will look at the subject of rate determination from the point of view of an enterprise that seeks to maximize its returns. The economic theory of price discrimination will be introduced for this purpose. Following this discussion is a brief consideration of the social desirability of policies of price discrimination.

THEORY OF PRICE DISCRIMINATION—The economic theory of price discrimination received its classic statement three decades ago in *The Economics of Imperfect Competition* by the English economist, Joan Robinson. It is extremely useful as a succinct way of describing the methods that profit-seeking companies will use to set rates—to the extent that they are free to do so.

It is unfortunate that the word "discrimination" is used in this context. In ordinary usage "discrimination" is used in an unpleasant sense. We are accustomed to deplore discrimination among persons based on their race, religion, or natural origin. The law is concerned with unjust discrimination in price. The word discrimination is also used in a second way. Discrimination means making a distinction, for example, in discriminating between two flavors; one should approach the economic theory of price discrimination with this neutral meaning of the word in mind.

In the theory of monopoly, it will be recalled, a monopolist without price discrimination is thought of as producing a single commodity. He equates the marginal revenue and marginal cost for that type of output, and in this manner maximizes his net revenue. Price is determined by the intersection of his marginal revenue and marginal cost curves. Price discrimination is said to exist if there is a difference in price with no difference in cost. The term is also used in situations where there are differences in cost between markets but no differences in price, or only small differences in price that fail to reflect the full differences in cost.

Price discrimination will occur if, and only if, three conditions are met: (1) the firm must sell in two or more separate markets. (2) There must be differences in the price elasticity of demand between these two markets. (3) The firm must have monopolistic control of price in one or both markets. Under these conditions it will be profitable for the firm to sell the same service or the same product at different prices in the two markets; that is, it will be profitable to discriminate in price between the two markets.

The essential logic of this situation may be seen most easily in the special case in which the marginal cost per unit output of the firm is constant over the entire relevant range of output. (Constant marginal cost implies, it will be recalled, only that the total cost curve is a straight line in the relevant range.) In this situation the firm will equate its marginal cost to the marginal revenue in each market. Since the elasticity of demand differs in the two markets, the demand curves or average revenue curves will differ between the markets, and the marginal revenue curves will also differ. The firm, by setting price and marginal cost equal to marginal revenue in each market separately, will charge separate prices in the two markets. This result is illustrated in Figure 4.1.

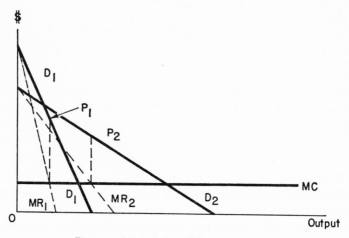

Figure 4.1   Price Discrimination

In this diagram D_1 is the demand curve in one market, and D_2 in a second market. Straight lines are used for simplicity. MR_1 is the marginal revenue curve corresponding to D_1, and MR_2, to D_2. MC is marginal cost, which is shown as a horizontal line over the relevant range of output. The firm equates MC and MR_1 in market 1, and charges P_1. It equates MC and MR_2 in market 2, and charges P_2, which is not equal to P_1.

There is no doubt that the monopolist will make more money in this situation by discriminating between the markets than by charging the same price in the two markets. Since private enterprises are motivated by the profit motive, it is not remarkable that many companies in the transportation agencies spend much of their time trying to devise successful schemes of price discrimination. Success, however, depends on the three conditions previously mentioned, each of which is important.

KEEPING MARKETS SEPARATE—First, any proposed scheme of price discrimination will certainly fail if it is not possible to keep the markets separate. For example, the airlines would like to split the market for business travel from the market for nonbusiness travel, for the reason that the demand for business travel is undoubtedly more price inelastic than the demand for nonbusiness, vacation travel. There is no way, or at least no way has been found, by which these markets can be kept separate. When a passenger boards an aircraft there is no way for the ticket agent to know what the passenger will do when he reaches his destination.

Discrimination among freight shipments is less familiar to most people, but more important to the economy. It is often based on the type of goods. There is no problem of distinguishing refrigerators from wheat. Discrimination may also be based on differences in the place of origin and destination of shipment. The carrier will know where it picked up and where it discharged each shipment. Goods moving in one direction cannot masquerade as goods proceeding in the opposite direction.

ELASTICITY RELATED TO VALUE—Even if differences between markets can be distinguished, however, only differences in elasticity of demand will make differences in price worthwhile. What, then, makes for differences in elasticity? Three factors are important, value, actual competition, and potential entry. The value per pound of a commodity being shipped is commonly taken as a rough approximation of the price elasticity of the demand for shipping that commodity. Goods high in value are charged high prices for this reason. Since the cost of shipment is a small fraction of the total value of the product, it is argued, the rate will be less important to the shipper or to his customers.

ELASTICITY RELATED TO COMPETITION—Differences in the elasticity of the demand curve confronting a seller will also arise depending on the availability of substitute services. Other things being equal, the demand will be more elastic where there are more competing services available. The demand is elastic because if the transportation company raises its rates it will lose its customers to the competition.

A historical example of price discrimination based on differences in competition may be found in the railroad rate structures across the American continent. Traditionally the rates charged from points such as Chicago to west coast ports have been lower *in absolute amount* than the rates charged to some intermediate points. Competition from marine transport is possible for shipments from New York to San Francisco, but obviously ocean going vessels cannot dock at Salt Lake City.

A more modern example of the relation between price elasticity and competition is the relation between trucking and the price elasticity of the demand for railroad freight. When trucks become available to him, the situation of a shipper changes. He will become less willing to pay "high" prices for rail shipment, and prices in excess of truck rates will come to seem "high." An increase in the price of rail freight over the rate offered by truck may even lead a shipper to switch his entire business to the trucks. The demand for rail service thus becomes more elastic, more sensitive to price changes, because of increased competition.

ELASTICITY AND POTENTIAL ENTRY—The demand curve confronting a seller will become price elastic whenever the possibility exists that there may be new sellers in the market. It is not necessary for these sellers actually to enter. The threat of entry may influence the price policy of the sellers already in the market. The threat of entry by the shipper into private carriage of his own goods may have a similar influence.

PRODUCT DIFFERENTIATION IN THE MARKET FOR TRANSPORTATION —The theory of price discrimination has been presented using the assumption that the output of the transportation industry is a single, standard product. The horizontal axis is scaled to measure homogeneous units of transportation provided. Reality is more complex. The measure of transportation service in most common use is the ton-mile. On close inspection, however, ton-miles are far from homogeneous. They differ in part because of inherent variation in the service being provided and in part because of deliberate attempts by sellers of transportation to make their service distinguishable from that of other sellers. The latter may be referred to as product differentiation. All expenditures for customer services, advertising, and public relations may be grouped under this heading.

In passenger service the possibilities of product differentiation are extensive. In recent years the airlines have done the most to develop variations in quality of service. A few years ago overseas carriers agreed to serve only sandwiches to a certain class of passengers, but left what was a sandwich undefined; the resulting competition among the chefs has been referred to as the "Battle of the Sandwiches."

In freight service there are also possibilities of product differentiation. Services differ, for example, with respect to speed, special handling of perishable or fragile merchandise, special attention to the exact time and place requirements of a shipper, and the like.

Ton-miles also differ in cost for reasons quite apart from any special efforts by sellers to differentiate their products. The cost per ton-mile for a given shipment is greater for short than for long distances by any means of transportation. Costs depend upon the bulk as well as the weight of a shipment. The existence of variations in rates based upon differences in costs is by no means evidence of price discrimination. Indeed, the absence of variations in rates when costs differ constitutes discrimination.

Such a system of rates as the actual railroad rate structure in the United States constitutes an elaborate system of price discrimination. The price discrimination, however, is not easy to disentangle from variations in rates based on variations in the cost of service provided, associated with differences in what is being shipped, under what circumstances, and between what points.

COUNTERVAILING POWER IN THE MARKET FOR TRANSPORTATION— The theory of price discrimination also needs to be supplemented in another way to provide a more complete account of events in actual markets. The model of price discrimination applies to markets in which a single seller or a small group of sellers enjoy some degree of monopoly power but the buyers are numerous and too small individually to influence the price. While some markets for transportation are of this type, in others there are large buyers of transportation. For example, the market for the transportation of assembled automobiles from points of assembly to dealers is a market with large buyers. Almost any giant corporation is a large buyer of transportation. In those markets where large buyers confront large sellers, the price is determined by a bargaining process that may be dominated by either party. The price may be more advantageous to the buyer than to the transportation company. The model of a discriminating monopolist is not applicable to these situations. A closer approximation to economic reality may be to think of a bargaining situation.

Buyers of transportation may be able to bargain from positions of strength even if they are individually weak. The classic example of development of a strong position by an atomised industry is the history of the application of political pressure by farmers to obtain low freight rates for the shipment of bulk agricultural commodities. Pressure of this kind exerted on Congress and through Congress on the I.C.C. has been one of the forces which has determined the structure of freight rates in the United States.

Concluding Comments on Public Policy Toward Rates

In the first part of this chapter it was proposed that the standard basis for determining the price of any transportation services should be the cost of the service, with departures from rates based on cost requiring justification. The ordinary standard of cost proposed is the long run marginal cost of the service. Departures may be of two kinds, the average level of rates may exceed average costs, and, even if these average levels are the same, individual rates may be out of line with the cost of the corresponding service.

MONOPOLY RETURNS AND RATE REGULATION—In this discussion, which follows the usual economic convention, cost should be understood to include a normal return on invested capital on the average over good and bad years. The yardstick as to what constitutes a normal return on invested capital for any enterprise is the market rate of return or the average rate of return on comparable investments, due allowance being made for any unusual degree of risk, and for reward for innovation or outstanding economic performance. There are situations in which monopoly returns in excess of any reasonable yardstick can be earned by transportation enterprises. At one time the I.C.C. was concerned with excess, monopoly returns by railroads, but this problem has not greatly burdened the Commission in recent years. Chronic excess returns have not been a general problem in the recent past for any of the major methods of transportation in the United States, the only exception being the special case of the companies engaged in the movement of petroleum by pipeline. When chronic excess returns do persist, remedial action becomes appropriate, either by direct regulation of the rate level, or by indirect means, if that is possible, such as the removal of obstacles to entry of additional enterprises into the activity in question.

SOCIAL DESIRABILITY OF PRICE DISCRIMINATION—In recent years price discrimination as it is practiced in transportation has been under attack. The attack has been of two sorts. The first attack was directed, not at the idea of a rate structure based on price discrimination, but at the existing structure of discriminatory prices. It is argued that this system has become obsolete. The original estimates of the price elasticity of demand no longer apply. The change has come in large part with the development of new methods of transportation that have confronted the elaborate rate system originally set up by the railroads. From the railroad point of view the advent of new competition automatically changed the elasticity of the demand curves confronting them in every market where it appeared. The complaint is that the rate structure has not changed fast enough to take these changes into account. This topic will be considered in more detail in the discussion of railroads in Chapter 13.

The second school of thought attacked the system itself. Rates, it is argued, ought to be based as nearly as possible on costs. This proposal would amount, if carried through, to a drastic reorganization of transportation pricing. It raises directly the question, is there a justification for price discrimination? This question may be considered both in connection with proposed investments and the use of existing facilities.

PRICE DISCRIMINATION AND INVESTMENT DECISIONS—Consider a situation in which it is proposed to make an investment to be paid for entirely out of income from charges to users of the new facility. Whether the revenue will cover the costs may well depend on whether a system of price discrimination is used. In order to understand the logic of this argument it may be helpful to consider the Marshallian doctrine of consumer surplus. In Figure 4.2, the line BD represents an ordinary demand curve with a single price indicated by P and the quantity being used by the distance OQ on the horizontal axis.

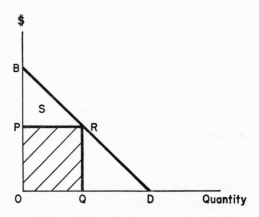

Figure 4.2   Consumers' Surplus

The total revenue, to be realized by the operating authorities if the facility is constructed and there is no price discrimination, may be indicated by the rectangle marked off by OP and OQ. There is a portion of the demand curve, however, that extends above the price P. The meaning of this part of the curve is that there are people who would be willing to pay more than the price P rather than give up entirely the use of the facility. If they obtain the use of the bridge at the price P, they will receive a surplus in excess of the price. For example, a consumer who would have paid OB if necessary receives a surplus of PB if he pays only P. He would have been willing to give up other uses of his money to the extent necessary to pay *OB*. As a first approximation this surplus for all consumers collectively may be measured by the area of the triangle marked with the letter *S* on the diagram.

A perfectly discriminating monopolist could extract from the users of the facility as revenue all of the area *S* as well as the rectangle. It is unlikely that the authority will be able to carry out such a policy of perfect discrimination. Its decision will be based on the revenue that it can realize, and that revenue will be less than the total social benefit, but, with discrimination the authority can appropriate some part of the triangular area.

It should be emphasized that this argument is an approximate one. The demand curve of economic theory is drawn on strict *ceteris paribus* assumptions, that is, it is assumed that all other prices and quantities remain equal. As one moves farther away from the actual equilibrium position of price and output, this assumption becomes increasingly unrealistic. When the demand is highly inelastic, as it often is for transportation, the meaning of the demand curve in the vicinity of the vertical axis becomes doubtful. These difficulties in the measurement of consumer surplus, however, do not destroy the validity of the fundamental point: that the total benefit to the users may substantially exceed the revenue to the operators of the facility without a system of price discrimination. (Indeed, even with price discrimination the social gain from development of new transport facilities may far exceed the revenue realizable by the agency operating the transportation facility.)

PRICE DISCRIMINATION AND EXCESS CAPACITY—A similar argument may be developed for existing facilities with excess capacity. There may be some potential users who would not be willing to pay the going price for the facility, but would pay something. They might be willing to pay more than the marginal cost of providing the extra increment of service needed to accommodate them. The operator of the facility would be better off to accept their patronage than to reject it. The other customers have nothing to lose by the arrangement and even something to gain by the improved financial position of the carrier.

These arguments in favor of discrimination do not destroy the case against it and in favor of prices based on costs. There may be distortions in the allocation of resources as a result of any discrimination, and there also may be unfairness. These considerations lead many economists to believe that rates should not depart too far from costs. Although they may believe that the rate structure should move in the direction of rates closer to costs, few economists would urge that considerations of demand should play no part in rate determination.

5

Introduction to Problems of Organization

THE PRECEDING CHAPTERS have indicated the broad objectives of economic policy toward transportation and what would constitute criteria that should govern decisions about investments in transportation and about transportation rates. It remains to discuss the choice of institutional arrangements for getting the decisions made. The broad question is one of choice of instruments of social control.

Some of the most difficult problems in economic policy in the transportation industry have to do with the organization of the industry. The purpose of this preliminary discussion is to indicate what the issues are and to suggest some of the main considerations. The approach to these topics taken in this introductory discussion is to discuss the need for public intervention in transportation and the reasons why complete reliance on competitive markets is impossible. Different policies are appropriate, however, for different segments of the total industry. It is necessary, therefore, to consider the principles on which all of transportation may be classified into meaningful divisions. For this purpose both technical and economic systems of classification will be considered. The final section of this chapter will take up current issues of organizational policy, indicating where are the margins of choice of organizational arrangements now under discussion in the United States.

The Need for Public Intervention in Transportation

That public intervention in transportation is necessary is not a matter of political controversy. On the record, public agencies have been and continue to be involved in transportation in all kinds of ways. Public agencies subsidize ocean shipping, build highways, plan urban transportation systems, regulate railroads, develop supersonic aircraft, and set limits on the profits of interstate pipelines. All this activity is the joint result of the strategic importance of transportation in the economy and the impossibility of complete reliance on competitive markets as instruments of social control. Each requires elaboration.

STRATEGIC IMPORTANCE OF TRANSPORTATION IN THE ECONOMY— That transportation is essential to a modern economy hardly requires elaborate proof. The discussion of economic functions of transportation in Chapter 2 already has indicated the ways in which transportation is crucial. Geographic specialization requires it. The whole development of modern technology rests upon the division of labor that in turn rests upon the broadening of the market made possible by modern transportation. Transportation makes possible organization of the economy on a national and international rather than a local scale. Illustrated in Part II is the development of transportation as a necessary part of the development of an industrial economy. The sheer volume of transportation required in a modern economy is enormous. As noted in the Introduction, in the United States at present total outlays on public and private transportation amount to one-fifth of the gross national product.

IMPOSSIBILITY OF COMPLETE RELIANCE ON COMPETITIVE MARKETS —It is not possible to rely upon competitive markets for the social control of transportation for several reasons. First, as set out in Chapter 1, some of the objectives of policy are not economic. There is no question of relying on the marketplace for the provision of national defense. Second, competitive markets are possible only in industries where competition is possible. In transportation there are possibilities of competition, and much of the subsequent discussion in this chapter and in the analysis of specific industries in Part III is concerned with consideration of the extent to which competition exists or may be encouraged. Yet there are broad portions of the field in which there are no possibilities or strictly limited possibilities of competition. The underlying reason why the possibilities of competition are restricted is that there are important economies of scale in transportation. The provision of the way is a natural monopoly in many branches of transportation. There can be only one national system of highways, airways, or waterways. Some competition among railways is possible, but the economies of scale are such that the number of railways between any pair of points must be strictly limited. Even the pipelines are characterized by very large economies of scale. The result is that any consideration of social control of transportation must start from recognition of the fact that in the provision of the way, at least, the possibilities of reliance on competition are limited at best.

PUBLIC INTERVENTION TO CONTROL A NATURAL MONOPOLY—Public intervention in the form of economic regulation (or public ownership) may, then, be necessary. It may be necessary for more than one purpose. One basic economic objective of public intervention in transportation is to control monopoly power in those parts of the transportation industry where there is a tendency to natural monopoly. Shippers need protection from the unrestrained exercise of such power. Shippers as a group need protection against an excessively high general level of rates such as a private monopolist might impose to maximize his profits. Small shippers or shippers in a weak bargaining position need protection against a system of rates which discriminates against them because of their economic weakness.

PUBLIC INTERVENTION TO ENSURE THE PROVISION OF NECESSARY AND DEPENDABLE SERVICE—A second basic economic objective of public intervention is to ensure that necessary transportation services be provided in a dependable manner. To this end it often has been urged that certain carriers, usually those already established, must be protected against excessive or destructive competition. Only if they are thus protected, it is argued, can they provide the required services. A responsible enterprise must have a secure position so that it can achieve socially desirable standards of efficiency and continuous service. Note the contrast between this reason for intervention and the first, which is concerned with the direct protection of the shipper rather than the carrier.[1]

This second argument is one which many economists would use cautiously. It is commonly advanced to support public control over the entry of new firms into some form of transportation. It implies that

1. See the discussion of the economic purposes of regulation in Shorey Peterson, "Motor-Carrier Regulation and Its Economic Bases," *Quarterly Journal of Economics*, August 1929, pp. 604–647. The above discussion has been strongly influenced by this article.

without some form of control there would be ill-advised entrants into the service in question, who would cut into the revenue of the existing carriers, thereby weakening them, but the new entrants would be unable to survive. Entry of firms into a market may be a mistake, of course. Yet, since businessmen as a group do not have tendencies toward economic suicide, it seems unlikely that as a general proposition ill-advised entry is a frequent and persistent danger.

A more complex situation arises when an existing carrier provides two types of service and is faced with new competition for one of the two types of business. It is possible that a new entrant may be able to compete effectively for the first class of business but not for the second. The existing carrier may be unable to continue to offer the second type of service if it loses the revenue from the first. Theoretically, in this situation the existing carrier should be allowed freedom to adjust its pricing structure on the basis of its costs. If those costs could not be covered, it should cease to offer both kinds of service. The community might be faced with the loss of the second type of service—a prospect which it might or might not be prepared to accept.

Public intervention in transportation is sometimes proposed for other reasons. It may be urged in order to protect the private interests of existing carriers. Neither the advancement of the private interests of investors and employees of transportation companies nor their protection from the normal hazards of the marketplace is in itself a proper objective of public policy in a competitive economy. Intervention may be urged in order to enforce standards of safe operation, prevent the pollution of the atmosphere from exhaust fumes, control noise levels, and the like. The present discussion is concerned only with intervention undertaken for economic reasons.

A fundamental question in any discussion of public intervention is the extent to which it is possible to rely on the workings of competitive markets. Analysis of this question is facilitated by the classification of the transportation industry into meaningful divisions.

Technical Components of Transportation Systems

THREE ELEMENTS IN TRANSPORTATION SYSTEMS—As already indicated, it is useful to distinguish three elements in a transportation system, the motive power, the vehicle, and the way. The three elements can be found in any transportation system but in some systems the motive power and the vehicle are physically combined while in others they can be separated. For example, the internal combustion engine that provides the motive power for an automobile is attached to the vehicle, while on a railroad the motive power is provided by a separate loco-motive. In the technical development of a transportation system the critical stage is typically the development of the power plant. The airplane, for example, could not be built until a power plant was in existence that provided the necessary output of energy in relation to its weight. In the early development of canals, however, it was not the barges that presented the problems but the locks and the supply of water to the canals.

There is a tendency in popular discussion to underestimate the im-portance of thinking of complete systems of transportation. The de-velopment of transportation by automobile, for example, might be said to have reached maturity in the late 1930s if attention were restricted to the technical characteristics of the vehicle. By that time a vehicle with satisfactory speed, reliability, and comfort could be built at a moderate price. The development of the way, however, came later than the development of the vehicles. The development of limited access highways designed for safe and efficient operation of a vehicle capable of the sustained speed of the motor cars of the late 1930s had barely begun before World War II and is yet to be completed in the United States.

THREE TYPES OF MOVEMENT—It is also useful to distinguish three types of movement that are involved in any transportation system: collection, main line movement, and distribution. These functions are frequently performed by different parts of the system. In a mass trans-portation system in a large city, for example, in the movement of people to work, one may distinguish the collection of people, movement on the main line to the central business district, and the distribution of people from the end of the main line to their several places of work. There is a popular tendency to focus attention on the central part of a trans-portation system, the main line movement, ignoring the importance of the other two functions. Consider the importance of the collection that must take place to permit the movement, for example, of a ship carry-ing 10,000 tons of general cargo. Again, consider the collection and distribution implied by the movement of a freight train with 100 car-loads of merchandise.

EXAMPLES OF THE IMPORTANCE OF KEEPING ALL THREE TYPES OF MOVEMENT IN MIND—Advocates of particular methods of transporta-tion naturally tend to focus attention on the movement that their system performs best. For example, the advocates of urban railways have a good deal to say about the efficiency of rail rapid transit for main line movement. They point out that it is possible to move 40,000 persons per hour on one track. They have less to say about the efficiency of rail transit in collecting people from suburban homes built, say, four houses to the acre, and concentrating them to the point where there will be 40,000 people to move on one track in one hour. Advocates of the automobile emphasize the efficiency of the auto in collecting people from their separate homes and moving them at exactly the time they wish to diverse destinations. Advocates of railroad freight talk about the low coefficient of friction of a steel wheel on a steel rail, leaving to the salesmen for the trucking companies the discussion of what can be done overnight in moving truckload lots from loading dock to loading dock.

The manager of a business enterprise engaged in transportation, for example a railroad, may take the view that his firm makes money on main line movement and should, therefore, concentrate on that function and lop off both the collection and distribution ends. Such a proposal makes sense, but only if it is proposed to rely on some other type of transportation to perform these functions. Analysis of the problem of whether to abandon a length of line used as a feeder to a railroad system requires recognition of the fact that benefits to the system from continued operation of a feeder line fall into two parts: additional revenue received for the movement of freight over the feeder line, and the additional revenue from the movement over other parts of the system of freight that would be lost to the system if the feeder were discontinued. Both freight originating at points on the feeder for distribution to other parts of the system and freight originating elsewhere for distribution to points on the feeder line will be involved. The error should be avoided of thinking of the feeder line as the source of only those ton-miles of traffic that are represented by the actual movement on the feeder line itself.

TERMINALS AND STORAGE FACILITIES—A complete transportation system involves more than the three types of movement of commodities and people. There are also requirements for assembly of the load prior to movement and break-up of the load subsequent to movement. These requirements can be avoided by reducing the scale of the vehicle, but become increasingly important as the vehicle becomes larger in capacity. They are unimportant or nonexistent for private automobiles, but the reverse for ocean liners; they may be unimportant for light trucks, but not for ocean going freighters. Physically, terminals and associated warehouse facilities are required. (For people, the "storage" facilities take the form of waiting rooms and hotels.) Such facilities are not perhaps what one first thinks of when one thinks of a transportation system, but they may be essential for the efficiency of the system. Even private transportation by automobile has a terminal problem that takes the form of need for garage space and parking spaces.

The problem of the organization of the transportation industry, then, is the problem of providing for and organizing the relationships among the three components: vehicle, motive power, and way; the three types of movement: collection, main line movement, and distribution; and terminals and storage facilities as may be required. When there is separation of ownership, provision must somehow be made for the consistency of policy needed for efficient operation of what is technically a single system.

Economic Classification of All Transportation into Industries

The problem of how to classify economic activity into meaningful divisions is a general problem in the study of industrial organization. As previously mentioned, the question, what is an industry? is particularly troublesome in the study of transportation. There are two main approaches to the problem.

DEFINITION OF AN INDUSTRY ON THE BASIS OF TECHNOLOGY— Those firms may be regarded as belonging to the same industry which most closely resemble each other in the technical methods which they employ. When we speak of the railroad industry, for example, it is this definition of an industry that we have in mind. Essentially, the classification is by the type of way that is used. Thus, the railroad industry comprises those firms that are engaged in the movement of people or freight in vehicles drawn by locomotives on pairs of steel rails. This definition is customarily modified to exclude some firms at the fringes of the industry, such as those that are solely engaged in the transport of people by rails located in subways within urban areas. The same technical similarity distinguishes the firms engaged in the movement of liquids through pipelines, those engaged in the movement of people and goods by air, those engaged in the movement of people and freight in motor vehicles over public highways, etc. The regulatory agencies of the federal government have been set up essentially on the basis of industries thus defined. For example, the Civil Aeronautics Board regulates airlines, but the Interstate Commerce Commission regulates the railroads.

MARKET-ORIENTED DEFINITION OF AN INDUSTRY—Economists,

however, customarily define an industry in a different manner. Their approach to the problem of classifying a firm by industry is through analysis of the market in which goods or services produced by the firm are sold. An industry, according to this view, consists of all those firms which sell in the same market. Those firms sell in the same market that sell, to a common group of buyers, goods or services that either are identical or are close substitutes, from the buyers' point of view. It is in terms of such a market oriented approach that monopoly and competition are defined. A monopolist is a firm that has complete control over the entire supply of a particular good or service available to a group of buyers. As the number of firms offering the same or very similar goods or services to a group of buyers increases, the industry becomes more competitive. Whether the services offered by one firm are sold in the same market as the services offered by another firm is essentially a question of whether the services of the two firms are close substitutes in the minds of the people who may buy them.

From this point of view, the transportation industry should be defined in terms of a series of markets for particular services associated with particular geographic points. For example, all firms engaged in the transportation of people from Chicago to New York are said to be in the same industry even though some firms might perform this service by rail and others by air. A firm engaged in the transport of people from Chicago to New York but not from Chicago to Los Angeles would not be in the same industry as another firm in the latter market. A railroad, for example, that carried people from Chicago to the West Coast would not be in the same industry as a railroad that carried people from Chicago to the East Coast.

The recent fierce competition for business between different modes of transportation has emphasized the practical importance of this second approach to the definition of an industry. The airlines that offer service between New York and Chicago have demonstrated in the most forceful manner possible that they *are* in the same industry as the railroads that transport people from New York to Chicago by taking away from the railroads the lion's share of the business.

Carried to its logical extreme, this approach to the definition of an industry would lead to definitions of a large number of overlapping industries. Each pair of origins and destinations for traffic in the United States would become a separate market. Each of the possible classes of commodities to be transported may also be kept separate; a monopolist with a developed policy of price discrimination would certainly keep them separate. For example, the market for the movement of coal is separate from that for the movement of completed automobiles from the point of view of buyers of transportation. The total number of markets would be the product of the number of services *times* the number of pairs of origins and destinations.

On the supply side of the market, however, facilities that can be used for movement of one type of goods usually can be adapted to the movement of other goods or people. Even if vehicles are specialized, power plant and way are not specialized. On a railroad, for example, the same rails serve passenger trains as well as freight trains, and the same freight train commonly includes cars intended for several destinations. Thus, the technical connections among some of the markets are so close that the firms that sell in them may reasonably be regarded as members of the same industry.

Even on the demand side there are important connections among markets for transportation. The price charged by a firm in the transportation industry in one market cannot be considered independently of the prices charged by it in all other markets. For example, the price for the movement of people from Chicago to Buffalo cannot be fixed with no regard for the price from Chicago to New York. There is a powerful argument, thus, for the grouping of markets geographically. Firms may be regarded as belonging to the same industry if they sell in closely related markets.

What is difficult to defend from a market-oriented point of view is not the grouping of similar markets but the attempt to divide markets that are otherwise similar on the basis of differences in technique of production. If two firms produce services that they sell to a common group of buyers, and if the buyers regard those services as close substitutes, then the firms are in the same industry. A situation in which a public regulatory agency establishes rates for some of the firms in an industry but others are unregulated is bound to lead to anomalies. Similarly, a situation in which one agency regulates some of the firms in an industry while another agency regulates others is likely to lead to unintended consequences. Such situations do exist in transportation; for example, both the C.A.B. and the I.C.C. regulate passenger transportation from New York to Chicago.

It is not meant to argue that the use of market-oriented definitions should supplant use of the classification on the basis of technical similarity. Exclusive preoccupation with the definitions based on technology, however, will lead to a tendency to overlook the economic realities of increasing competition among technically dissimilar methods of transportation.

Current Issues of Organizational Policy

The central question in the organization of the transportation industry is to what extent reliance should be placed on competition and to what extent on direction by public authority, whether through regulation or through public ownership. The record as to what policy has developed on this question must be examined in detail industry by industry. It may be mentioned at this stage, however, that the direction of policy has not always been consistent. Competition has been carefully nurtured and protected in some respects, for example, by strict controls over entry of companies which were powerful in one branch of the industry into other branches. No railroad owns a major airline, for example. Yet competition has been limited by controls over entry of new firms that have been enforced by public agencies, for example, in the airline industry, and in the interstate carriage of freight by motor truck.

ALTERNATIVE DIRECTIONS FOR POLICY—According to one viewpoint held by a considerable group of economists, the proper direction for future public policy is to place increasing reliance on competition. Workable competition is held to be attainable in increasing areas in transportation. The technical variety of methods of providing transportation, it is argued, now makes possible reliance on competition to a much greater extent than was possible when the railroads enjoyed a large degree of monopoly power. This position implies strict control over mergers to prevent the formation of monopolies. It implies removal of barriers to entry into transportation. It implies greatly reduced reliance on direct regulation; such matters as the determination of rates would be left to market forces to an increased extent—in the extreme market forces would be relied upon entirely. It also requires equalization of competitive conditions across methods of transportation through the uniform application to all methods of the user charge principle.

The opposite view is that increasing reliance on competition is not possible in transportation. The number of sellers is too small; the risk of arbitrary or unreasonable price discrimination is too large; the public interest is too closely involved. The proper direction of policy is to improve and rationalize the system of public intervention. A more extreme position is that competition is already excessive and should be reduced. Economies may be realized by merger of competing firms, and the resulting savings would represent a major improvement in efficiency.

While this division in direction of emphasis serves to divide two approaches to the problems, it fails to do justice to the intricacies of the specific issues that arise. Consider the classification proposed above for each mode of transportation into vehicle, power plant, and way, plus associated terminals. The question of how much to rely on competition among private enterprises, public regulation, or public ownership arises for each of these elements for transport by air, rail, highway, pipeline, and water, as well as for urban transport systems. A decision with regard to public ownership of marine terminals need hardly imply a decision as to railways.

In practice, in the United States an extraordinary variety of arrangements are in use (let alone the variations in other countries). The terminals, way, plant, and vehicles may be owned by the same agency. The railroad companies own all of these elements. From time to time proposals are made, however, that the way should become public property leaving the vehicles in the hands of the roads. In transportation by air in this country the vehicles are owned privately, the way is owned publicly, and the terminals are primarily public but with substantial private investment. Highways are publicly owned and motor vehicles privately owned; most but not all terminals for trucks are also private. The exact boundary between the spheres of public ownership and private ownership tends to shift constantly with new developments in the field of transportation but the shifts that have taken place in the United States have been at the margin. The development of the division between public and private and the development of regulation will be considered below in their historical context. We may indicate here what are the areas of current controversy.

CONTROVERSY OVER ENTRY—One of the specific areas of frequent controversy has to do with whether freedom of entry should be allowed to a particular branch of transportation. Entry into a market may be of several types. A newly created firm or one not hitherto engaged in transportation may become a common carrier. A firm that is a common carrier may enter new markets, either by serving more markets with the same mode of transportation, as an airline adds service to more cities, or by adding facilities of another type, as when a railroad seeks to enter the trucking business. While it has been public policy in this country to limit all of these types of entry and especially to prevent the same business enterprise from engaging in the provision of transportation by two or more modes, these policies are controversial.

CONTROVERSY OVER MERGERS—Since the number of sellers in a market will also be influenced by mergers that may take place among existing firms, policy towards mergers is a second area of special concern. A basic question is, how many carriers is it necessary to have to insure a satisfactory, workable degree of competition? The practical choice is usually one of monopoly or concentrated oligopoly, that is, should there be one, two, or three sellers in a market? In transportation it is unusual to find a market where more than eight sellers must be included to cover half the market. Mergers, thus, ordinarily increase further what is already a high degree of concentration. Policy toward mergers is currently under much discussion, especially as it involves mergers among airlines and among railroads.

CONTROVERSY OVER THE SCOPE OF REGULATION—A third set of questions of organization arise in branches of transportation in which private carriers are publicly regulated. They concern the limits of regulation and the questions of exactly what areas of competition exist among the regulated firms. What freedom do the private firms have to set prices? Do they charge the same prices by agreement sanctioned by public authority? If so, what forms of nonprice competition exist among them? What forms of product differentiation are permitted or encouraged? Should regulation cover minimum as well as maximum rates?

Taken together, the decisions as to ownership of each branch of the industry, and the decisions that determine the number of sellers, the conditions of entry, and the degree of product differentiation determine the market structure of the industry. They set the stage, as it were, on which will be acted out the rivalries among sellers and on which will be determined what will be sold and the prices at which it will be offered for sale to the buyers of transportation. Another way of stating the problem is to contrast direct controls and indirect controls over transportation. Direct controls, such as specifying the rates to be charged, the equipment to be used, and the service to be offered, lead to more detailed government action than indirect controls over the number of sellers in an industry, and the possibility of new entry. The question is one concerned with the extent to which it is possible to rely on indirect controls to achieve the objectives of public policy toward transportation.

II

Transportation
in Economic Development

6

Transportation and Economic Development: Great Britain 1700-1850

IN THE OPINION of many economists, the most pressing economic problems in the world today are the problems of economic development. The goal of economic growth is more in the center of their attention than the efficient allocation of existing resources or improvement in equity in distribution. Among American economists this sense of urgency arises in part from the international competition in which the United States is now engaged with the nations of Communist ideology and from the need to devote American resources to the assistance of countries all over the world. It also arises from devotion to the objective of raising the standard of living of the people of the United States. Similar concerns occupy the minds of economists in other countries.

In any major effort to raise the productive capacity of an economy, public policy toward transportation is almost certain to be involved. No economy has developed to a high level of productivity without heavy investment in transportation facilities, nor does it seem likely that any economy will be able to progress without transportation. To some degree the decisions as to transportation policy may be made by the market mechanism, but to a large extent the organization of transportation is

such that the decisions involve public policy. The degree to which reliance will be placed on the market in contrast to governmental mecha-
nisms and the other questions of organizational form must be made by
each country in the course of its development.

Perhaps the most important area in which decisions must be made,
whichever organizational form is selected, is the area of investment
policy. Two questions are fundamental. How much investment shall
there be in transportation? In what specific forms of transportation shall
the investment be made?

As has been indicated, investment decisions are inherently difficult.
Difficulties arise because there is a wide range of error in forecasts of
requirements for transportation. There are penalties both for too much
investment in transportation and for too little. Too much investment
means a waste of resources, while too little means that transportation
may become a bottleneck that will prevent the development of the rest
of the economy. Waste may be involved in investment in the wrong
method of transportation, in the wrong location, or in investment in
part but not all, of a facility that cannot be completely used unless
the entire system is made ready.

A variety of strategies have been adopted in different times and
places in attempts to solve the problems of investment decisions in transportation. These arrangements have met with varying degrees of success. The succeeding chapters will take up a series of countries at
periods in which the main emphasis in economic policy toward transportation has been on achieving economic growth. At no time and place
has economic policy been directed exclusively to the achievement of
economic growth to the complete disregard of other objectives. Other
goals of policy, therefore, necessarily will be involved in the discussion.
The main emphasis, however, is on problems of investment.

The countries to be discussed, and the diversity of situations they
represent, may be indicated briefly. Great Britain in the period from
1700 to 1850 was, of course, the first country to achieve modern industrial development. The United States in the nineteenth century
achieved a high level of economic development in an environment where,
in contrast to the situation in Great Britain, the country could not be
settled without investment in transportation. Canada in the same period
was presented with problems similar to those in the United States but
aggravated by extreme difficulties arising out of the geography of the
country. The Soviet Union is of interest because of the differences from
the other countries discussed in the basic organization of the economy
and the implications of these basic differences for policy toward trans-

portation. In the discussion of the Soviet Union the emphasis is on the period of forced industrialization, which came when the country was beyond the early stages of industrialization. India is different from the other nations discussed both as an Asian society with a different political and economic history, and as a nation that at the present time remains in the early stages of economic development.

A comprehensive study of transportation policy in different countries would require the systematic development of a typology of characteristics of countries that might then be related to their policy toward transportation. The discussion here, however, has the modest goal of exploring possible differences in strategy in economic policy toward the development of transportation facilities. The possible strategies seem to be limited, as will become apparent as the discussion progresses. The final chapter of Part II summarizes some of the modern problems of transportation policy in developing countries.

The theme of Part II, then, is the development of transportation and the interconnections between the development of transportation and the general economic development of the countries considered. Often these connections cannot be traced with the particularity that would be desirable if material were available. Yet something can be learned of the role of transportation in the processes of economic development in diverse times and places and of the issues of economic policy toward transportation that have arisen and how they have been resolved.

We turn, then, to Great Britain, since in any discussion of economic development, a treatment of the development of Great Britain has the historical claim to priority. Since economic development is a continuous process, the selection of a historical period for discussion must be in part arbitrary. The present treatment will cover roughly the period from the beginning of the eighteenth century, when the country was still organized as a peasant society, to the middle of the nineteenth century, by which time over 5000 miles of railroad line were in service and the events that ordinarily are thought of as comprising the Industrial Revolution were complete. The discussion will be organized chronologically in the sense that the different modes of transportation will be treated in the order in which they developed.

Two features of British economic development may be mentioned at the outset by way of introduction. In the first place, the economic development of Great Britain was slow by modern standards. The period under consideration here extended for a century and a half. This comparatively slow rate of growth is not a surprising characteristic of the history of the first country to go through the sequence. Other nations benefited from the British experience. The gradualness of development made some of the problems easier. In particular it permitted the gradual accumulation of capital, as will be indicated in more detail below.

A second feature of the history of the development of Great Britain is that for the most part the financing was from private sources. There was no major public effort to promote the development of the internal transportation network. Efforts were made to stimulate ocean transport near the end of the period under discussion, notably through an active policy of subsidizing the development of steamship lines offering regular service on long ocean routes. The policy toward marine transport, however, was the exception. To the extent the public authorities played a part in the development of inland transportation it was primarily with purposes that may be classified as regulatory. The public concern was that the development should take proper forms, and, especially toward the close of the period, the rate structure should be developed in a satisfactory manner.

Conditions at the Beginning of the Eighteenth Century

To understand the extent of the changes in transportation in the eighteenth and nineteenth centuries in Great Britain, it is necessary to have some understanding of what the situation was about the year 1700.[1] At that time internal commerce within the country by land depended upon traveling merchants and peddlers. These men carried their goods on the backs of pack animals, either horses or mules. A small scale peddler might carry his own inventory. There were shops in the towns, and the merchants dealt with these shops, but in the villages there were no shops until the later part of the eighteenth century. The villagers, to the extent the village was not self-sufficient, relied on the peddlers or on trips for trading purposes.

Fairs, temporary gatherings at which buyers and sellers from a distance came together, were an early form of trade that persisted into the eighteenth century. The fairs tended to specialize in the staple products of the region in which they were held.[2]

1. The description of the situation at that period draws on the account in J. L. Hammond and Barbara Hammond, *The Rise of Modern Industry,* Harcourt Brace, Seventh edition, 1947, Chapter V.

2. T. S. Ashton, *An Economic History of England: the Eighteenth Century,* Methuen, 1955, p. 64.

A large part of the food supply of large cities, such as London, moved to town under its own power. Droves of cattle, sheep, pigs, geese, and turkeys were a common sight on the rural roads. In the middle of the eighteenth century an estimate was made of 40,000 cattle a year walking to the meadows of Norfolk from the Highlands. They were rested and fattened in Norfolk, and sent to walk the remaining distance to London in a regular weekly supply.[3]

The reason for the scarcity of wheeled vehicles was the condition of the roads, which was terrible. Many seem to have been tracks rather than roads as we understand them. No roads with hard surfaces had been constructed in Britain since the days of the Roman occupation, a period of a millenium and a half.

The arrangements for the maintenance of the roads are of interest viewed as an approach to what would now be regarded as a problem of public finance. The question, viewed in this light, is one of who benefits from the expenditures on road maintenance, and who pays for them. In the Middle Ages maintenance of roads had been considered a religious duty. In 1412 A.D., for example, indulgences were granted for bridge building. There is also record of hermits who piously occupied themselves with maintaining the road in the vicinity of their retreat.[4] This religious approach to the problem was no longer feasible in the eighteenth century.

In the eighteenth century the obligation to maintain the roads was a common law obligation of the inhabitants of the parishes in which the roads were found. The local people were obligated to spend a certain number of days each year, for example, six days, working under the local surveyor. The general impression is that they made a holiday of the period and did not do a very satisfactory piece of work on the roads.

To the extent that heavy commodities moved at all, they moved by sea. The most conspicuous example was coal, which moved by sea from Newcastle to London. This traffic must have been considerable. It is known, for example, that in a great storm in 1692 more than 200 ships, most of them carrying coal, were wrecked off the coast of Norfolk in a single night. Most of these vessels were small, but even so, they must have carried a considerable quantity of coal.[5]

A considerable volume of merchandise also moved by sea in the

3. Beatrice and Sidney Webb, *English Local Government,* Vol. 5, *The Story of the King's Highway,* Oxford University Press, first published 1913, reprinted 1963, pp. 67–68.
4. C. W. Scott-Giles, *The Road Goes On,* The Epworth Press, 1946, pp. 55–58.
5. Gilbert Slater, *The Growth of Modern England,* Houghton & Mifflin Company, 1932, p. 63.

external trade of the country. The commodities that moved were primarily those that were high in value in relation to their weight, but some bulky commodities also moved. There was an active trade with Constantinople and Smyrna, which involved exports of cloth and other manufactured goods and imports of raw cotton and raw silk. There was the trade of the Hudson Bay Company, which exchanged firearms and metal cooking pots for skins and furs. There was the trade of the East India Company, which imported spices, drugs and saltpetre (a necessary constituent for gun powder), as well as silk and cotton manufactures from India. The exports were silver bullion, metal goods, English woolens, and other manufactures. Finally, there was trade with the "plantations," which involved exports of cloth to Africa and imports from the American colonies of tobacco, cotton, sugar, and the like.

Ocean trade, therefore, was comparatively well developed at the beginning of the eighteenth century and it was not until well into the nineteenth century that there were dramatic changes in the character of marine transport with the development of iron hulls and steam power plants for ships. Ocean transport permitted geographic specialization based on differences in natural resources. Internal transport, however, was in very poor condition and improvements were essential before any substantial industrial development could take place. Geographic specialization based on economies of large enterprise was in its infancy.

Turnpikes and Inland Waterways in the Eighteenth Century

During the eighteenth century two major improvements took place, the development of turnpikes and the development of canals. Since the major development of turnpikes was somewhat earlier than the development of canals, the turnpikes will be discussed first. The development of improved transport by road and by water overlapped, however, especially if the early development of river improvements is taken into consideration.

TURNPIKES—The turnpikes represented essentially a new solution to the problem of financing road construction and maintenance. The method was the establishment of turnpike trusts, each trust being set up by a private act of Parliament with the duty of constructing and maintaining a specified length of road and with the rights to raise a loan to finance the undertaking and to collect tolls. These turnpike trusts became common in the middle of the eighteenth century, although the earliest ones go back to the early years of the century and even before.

The motivation for improving the roads was not entirely economic. As is commonly true in the development of improved methods of transportation, political considerations played a part. The raid from Scotland in 1745 by Prince Charles ("Bonnie Prince Charlie"), the Pretender to the throne, made it necessary to move troops to the north, and the difficulty of doing so turned attention to the poor conditions of the roads.

From an economic point of view, the turnpike movement was a success in increasing the amount of money invested in road construction. It shifted the burden of building and maintaining the principal roads from the local population, who obtained little if any benefit from them, to the people who used the roads and were willing to pay for improvement.

These successes, however, were not achieved without a struggle. When first constructed, the turnpikes were extremely unpopular. There were riots over the turnpikes for a number of years. The rioters destroyed the toll gates, and when attempts were made to prevent them from doing so, in some instances the struggle was so violent that lives were lost.[6]

What was the nature of the objections? In part they came from users of the roads who were now compelled to pay but found little or no improvement in the highways. In part they came from farmers who feared the competition of products that would be moved over the turnpikes. As noted earlier, improvements in transportation do destroy local monopolies. It seems probable that some people were in fact made worse off by the institution of the turnpikes.

Nevertheless, after the middle of the century the opposition died out. The new trusts were careful to include the influential local interests in the trust, and made such rules as that there should be no toll for foot travel. In 1838, which was about the peak of the movement, there were 1116 turnpike companies with a debt of seven million pounds and an annual revenue of a million and a half from 22,000 miles of road.[7]

The turnpike system was never planned as a whole, and developed unevenly, reflecting the results of local pressures and local initiative. It led to a great improvement in the technique of road construction, especially as a result of the work of Thomas Telford and J. L. McAdam, who revolutionized the construction of roads in the early part of the nineteenth century. Their methods, which need not detain us here, were especially concerned with the proper use of layers of stones of different sizes with a small size on top.

6. For contemporary accounts of the riots see Scott-Giles, *op. cit.,* pp. 111–116.
7. Sidney and Beatrice Webb, *op. cit.,* pp. 224–225.

Concurrently with improved roads there was development of regular passenger service. Stagecoach service on a regular and frequent basis developed among the leading towns. No doubt the existence of this service had important consequences for economic activity resulting from the increase in business travel. At the same time goods began to move by wagon rather than by pack horse and wagon services from one town to another were organized on a basis comparable to that of the stagecoaches. Heavy freight, however, does not seem to have moved in large volume by road. Until the development of the railroads it continued to move by water, first on the coastal waterways and rivers, and then, by canal.

The turnpikes continued to exist parallel to the canals, to some extent competing with them and to some extent complementing them, until the development of the railroad system put an end to the turnpikes.

From a modern point of view, the shifting of the burden of maintaining the main roads from a group who derived little or no benefit from them—the inhabitants of the parishes through which the roads happened to pass—to a group who derived benefit from using the roads, represented a major improvement. So long as the roads essentially represented a means of access to the local villages, their expense might reasonably be borne locally, but when a road became essentially a connection between two major towns, it could no longer be reasonably regarded as existing for the benefit of the countryfolk who lived along its route.

RIVERS AND CANALS—Canals in Great Britain have properly been called the arteries of the Industrial Revolution. A central feature of the Industrial Revolution was the development and application of mechanical power. That power was steam power, and the steam was generated by the burning of coal. The coal moved to the boilers by water: by sea, by river, and by canal. There were no railroads until the Stockton and Darlington opened in 1825, but some historians regard the Manchester and Liverpool Railway, which opened in 1830, as the first true railway. By that time the Industrial Revolution in the textile industry was well advanced. For example, in 1829 there were 50,000 power looms in England. It was primarily the canals that brought the raw materials to those looms and took their products to market. The extent of the development of the cotton industry may be inferred from the number of persons employed, which by 1831 was perhaps 375,000 to 400,000.[8] The industry was geographically concentrated in Lancashire and Cheshire. The

---

8. J. H. Clapham, *An Economic History of Modern Britain, Vol. 1, The Early Railway Age, 1820–1850,* Cambridge University Press, 1926–38, vol. 1, reprinted 1950, p. 72.

development of this industry is the classic example of geographic spe-cialization based upon economies of scale—the economies of mechanized production of textiles in factories. We must note, however, that it was later the workers were brought into mills.

The first phase in the development of inland waterways in Great Britain was the improvement of the rivers. Even before the eighteenth century there were some installations of pound-locks and flash-locks. A pound-lock was a kind of lock that was set up in the river. It could be used to raise the vessel to a higher level. A flash-lock was simply a movable portion in the center of a weir. It could be raised to permit a large volume of water to move downstream floating a vessel with it. It is interesting to note that conflicts of interest arose over these installations. The improvement in navigation in a river might very well supplant a town that had as its economic justification a location at the head of navigation. Such a town would tend to resist the installation.[9] These conflicts of interest provide still another example of the frequency with which an improvement in transportation that benefits one group of persons may be of little benefit, or even do actual harm, to another group.

Improvements in rivers were made gradually over a period of many years. From 1660 to 1724, for example, the number of miles of English rivers open to navigation increased from 685 to 1,160 as a result of river improvements.[10] The development of canals in Great Britain, however, came later. It is customarily dated from the Act of Parliament obtained by the Duke of Bridgewater in 1759 for the construction of a canal. The Duke of Bridgewater had seen canals in successful operation on the Continent. He was one of a group of landowners who possessed coal fields, which they were anxious to develop. It is indicative of the state of the technology of canal building at the time that the man whom the Duke of Bridgewater engaged to build his canal was nearly illiterate. He was, however, a genius in engineering. His name, James Brindley, was made famous by his initial success in carrying the Bridgewater Canal by an aqueduct across the River Irwell. That river had to be crossed in order to convey the Canal from the Duke's mine to the market in Man-chester. The Canal was a brilliant success. It halved the price of coal in Manchester, and at the same time made a substantial profit for its owner.

The profitability of this enterprise and other early canals led to a burst of enthusiasm for canal building. The "canal mania," as it was

9. Charles Hadfield, *British Canals,* Phoenix House, 1959, Ch. 1.
10. *Ibid.,* p. 26.

called by contemporaries, led to the passage of no less than twenty acts
of Parliament authorizing the construction of new canals in the single
year 1793! The history of the mania is summarized in the following
tabulation:[11]

Year	Number of New Canals Authorized by Parliament	Capital Authorized (pounds)
1789	2	131,000
1790	1	90,000
1791	6	663,000
1792	6	941,100
1793	20	2,914,300
1794	10	2,037,900
1795	4	375,900
1796	3	585,000
1797	1	18,000

From 1790 to 1793 to 1797 it was not the objective situation that changed
so drastically, but men's assessments of the future of canals. This experience has already been cited as an example of a short burst of enthusiasm followed by pessimism such as may happen when investment
decisions are based largely on a climate of opinion.

Was the investment in canals too much or too little? What was the
contribution to the economic development of the country? Could that
contribution have been made more efficiently? To these questions at
least partial answers can be given. In one respect the development was
inefficient: the gauge of the canals. In any transportation system there
are economies of scale in the construction and operation of large vehicles. Canal boats are no exception. The width of a boat that can be used
on a canal necessarily depends on the width of the canal, and the width
of the canal is the decision of the individual promoters. The length of a
canal boat is limited by the length of the locks through which it must
pass. The main outlines of the problem are the same as those that have
received more attention in connection with the gauge of the railroads.
Economies of scale from the use of larger canal boats must be purchased
at the expense of the construction of a wider and deeper canal and
longer locks. In difficult terrain, for example, in hilly country, the extra
expense of construction will mean that the optimum size will be different
from that in easy terrain. From the point of view of the system as a
whole, however, there are obvious advantages in standardization.

11. *Ibid.*, p. 97.

Lack of standardization of the dimensions of canals plagued their development in eighteenth-century Britain. For example, consider the Leeds and Liverpool Canal. From Liverpool to Wigan a seventy-six foot canal boat could be used. From Wigan to Leeds only a sixty-six foot boat was feasible. At Leeds the canal met the Aire and Calder Navigation, whose locks would accept no boat longer than fifty-three feet. Shippers, thus, were forced to use small, relatively inefficient canal boats for movements of freight or to accept the expense of transhipment from one boat to another. Such situations were by no means unusual.[12] A price was exacted from society for failure to recognize the technical unity of the canal system in time to prevent piecemeal construction.

The question of whether there was overbuilding may be approached through study of the financial returns on the investments in the canals. Clapham has assembled data on the rate of return paid by canals in 1825, the year the construction of the Stockton and Darlington foreshadowed the development of the railroads. He cites one estimate of an average return paid to investors of 5.75 per cent in that year for eighty canals. This average, however, conceals wide variation in results for individual canals. The least successful tended to be those with gauge problems, and those with difficulties in construction and operation because they crossed watersheds. Of eighteen successful canals, fourteen paid over ten per cent, with a maximum of seventy-five per cent plus a bonus.[13] Of thirteen unsuccessful canals which he lists, six paid nothing. The existence of substantial numbers of canals that paid nothing suggests that there was some overbuilding.

The type of data that exist as to the economic impact of the canals and their relation to the economic development of Great Britain are incomplete. There is evidence, however, of the effect of canal construction on prices. The reductions in the price of coal are particularly important; for example, the construction of a canal reduced the price of coal in Birmingham from thirteen shillings a ton to seven shillings a ton in 1772.

It is possible to trace the connection between specific important manufacturing enterprises and the associated transport. For example, Wedgwood, the celebrated potter, in 1765–1766 was treasurer of the company that built the Mersey to Trent canal, which brought Cornish clay cheaply to the potteries. Wedgwood campaigned actively for the construction of the canal, and bought land along its route on which

12. *Ibid.*, pp. 54–56. Above example from J. H. Clapham, *An Economic History of Great Britain, The Early Railway Age, 1820–1850,* 1964, p. 83.
13. Clapham, *ibid.*, p. 81.

he shortly built a factory. A spur of the canal brought coal as well as clay into the factory yard and finished products were shipped out by canal.[14]

One of the side effects of the development of canals was the development of the profession of civil engineering. The technical difficulties of canal construction were not so formidable as to present an insuperable obstacle to a man like Brindley. But as canals ventured into increasingly difficult terrain, problems of considerable complexity were encountered —and solved. A body of skills developed which became very much in demand as owners discovered that able and experienced men were less likely to get into serious technical trouble than men of lesser ability and knowledge.

Public policy, it will be noted, was not of crucial importance in the financing of the canals. It is true that each canal could be constructed only after an act of Parliament had been passed providing the necessary authorization to the promoters, and there are examples of public aid to canals. But there was no systematic attempt to stimulate the development of canals with public funds.

With the development of the railway system there was a gradual shift from reliance on the canals to reliance on the railroads. New factories tended to be constructed near the railroads, or with a railroad siding, rather than with access to a canal. Nevertheless, the canals played an essential part in the growth of the economy in the period when the railroads had yet to develop.

Railroad Construction

There were two essential new elements in the development of the railway, the prepared roadbed, and the steam engine. As has been mentioned these elements were first combined in the Stockton and Darlington, which was constructed under the supervision of George Stephenson. This road was constructed along a route that had been considered for a canal. Some parts of the line were constructed in a manner that made the grades too steep for a locomotive and they were powered by stationary engines. The line was intended primarily for the movement of freight, and separate concessions were planned for operators of passenger coaches, which were drawn by horses. The first true railway, operated entirely by locomotives, ran from Liverpool to Manchester.

---

14. Paul Mantoux, *The Industrial Revolution in the Eighteenth Century,* Harcourt Brace, revised edition, 1961, pp. 128–129.

It was constructed in 1830, with George Stephenson as engineer. Stephenson had conducted experiments that were concerned with the amount of force required to move wagons on grades of different elevation. These experiments impressed upon him the importance of keeping the grade as low as possible in order to reduce operating expenses. He constructed the Liverpool and Manchester with a deep cut to keep the grade down. The Olive-Mount cutting is two miles long and as much as one hundred feet deep. It is indicative of the level of technical accomplishment obtained from the start that the first train covered the line at an average rate of twenty-seven miles per hour in 1830. The advantage in speed over the canals was impressive.

There was active opposition to the early railways for reasons with which the modern reader may feel some sympathy. The townsfolk of Woolwich, for example, drew up a protest against their town being cut in two by a deep and broad trench for the passage of dirty, noisy, and malodorous steam engines.[15] There was objection also from the proprietors of existing transportation companies, the turnpikes, and the canals. If the existing capital facilities in the form of their transportation systems would carry the traffic, why should a new system be constructed? Here, again, we may concur that there was a private loss incurred by the owners of these companies. It is harder to see any reason why that loss should have been borne by the public, or why the canal companies should have been protected from competition any more than any private enterprise.

The financing of the British railroads did not present as formidable difficulties as those that were being experienced by contemporaries in the United States. The early railroads were profitable. They also were short, so that the total absolute volume of capital required was not large. To the end of 1847 the average length of the lines authorized by Parliament was only fifteen miles.[16] Funds for such short lines could be found in Britain.

This system of organizing and financing led to inefficiencies remarkably similar to those in the development of the canals. The short railroad lines were not planned as railroad systems in the modern spirit and, hence, their integration into a national network presented difficulties. The Great Western Railway was the first to be planned as a complete system with the expectation that it would enjoy the monopoly of the traffic of a local region. This plan was developed in 1838 by the cele-

15. Slater, *op. cit.*, p. 341.
16. Slater, *op. cit.*, p. 340.

brated engineer, Isambard Kingdom Brunel, who among other achieve-
ments designed the most advanced ship of the day, the *Great Eastern.*

In contrast to its disinterest in the gauge of canals, Parliament took
an active role in the standardization of railway gauges with the creation
of a *Gauge Commission* in 1845. Some 274 miles of seven foot gauge
and 1,901 miles of four-foot 8.5 inch gauge had been built. The latter
gauge had been adopted by Stephenson for his first lines; its origins go
back to the gauge of the carts used by the Romans. The broader gauge
was introduced by Brunel for the Great Western Railway.

It was obvious by 1845 that there should be a national policy with
respect to the railroad gauge. But which gauge was better? Brunel suggested comparative tests, and his suggestion was adopted. The tests
were enlivened by a series of devices introduced by the advocates of
the narrow gauge to advance their cause. They used pre-warmed boiler
water, and a flying start—arrangements not consistent with normal
operations. On one occasion the axleboxes of vehicles used on the broad
gauge line were found to have had the grease replaced by sand!

The operating performance of the broad gauge line, however, was
clearly superior. Their locomotives attained higher speed with equal
loads, and equal speed with higher loads. One of the narrow gauge
locomotives left the track and then turned over on the second day of
the trials. Even under such strain the narrow gauge locomotives could
not equal the average speed of fifty to fifty-four miles an hour drawing
six ten-ton carriages set by their rivals. Inadvertently, the accident drove
home the point that the broad gauge vehicles were more stable and less
dangerous in operation.

The Commission, however, recommended the adoption of a single
gauge, the four-foot 8.5 inch gauge. The Commission was influenced by
the cost of converting the 1,901 miles of narrow gauge line then in
existence against 274 miles of broad, and was more impressed by the
additional first cost of the broad gauge than by its advantage in speed.
The broad gauge party argued that their system led to savings in the
cost of the rolling stock, both freight carriages and locomotives, and to
savings in operating costs—but their arguments were not successful.
The *Gauge Act* of 1846 forbade the construction of other than four-
foot 8.5 inch gauge in Great Britain except in the territory served by
the Great Western, which was allowed to keep its broad gauge line.[17]

17. The account of the *Gauge Commission's* activities is based on Cuthbert Hamilton
Ellis, *British Railway History,* Vol. 1, 1830–1876, Allen and Unwin Ltd., 1954, pp. 100–
107; and E. T. MacDermott, *History of the Great Western Railway,* Vol. 1, 1833–1863,
Great Western Railroad Company, 1927, pp. 229–247.

In retrospect it seems clear that the decision to insist upon a single gauge was correct. The Commission recognized the necessity of thinking of the railroads as a system, rather than as short isolated lengths of line. It seems probable that the wrong gauge was selected, and that this decision had consequences that still lessen the efficiency of the British railways a century and more later. It seems improbable that the gauge will be changed in the future. The *Gauge Act* of 1846 was decisive for Great Britain, and influenced events in the United States and elsewhere in the world.

The history of the financing of the railroads is a repetition of the history of the financing of the canals. The profits made by many of the promoters of the early railroads led to a "railway mania," comparable to the canal mania half a century earlier. This mania reached its peak in 1846 when no less than 270 bills passed Parliament authorizing 4,538 route miles; while an estimated 200,000 laborers were at work on the construction of railways in that year. By 1860 there were altogether only a little more than 10,000 miles of railway in Great Britain. The bank crisis of 1847 brought an end to the mania. The 4,538 route miles in 1846 provided for in 270 bills implies an average length of line in that year of a little less than seventeen miles. Note that this rapid development in 1846 took place after passage of the *Gauge Act*. Thus, the British experience showed that the problem of gauges that do not match was not an inevitable consequence of separate financing of short sections of line. Strong regulatory action imposed uniformity on the railroads.

From an economic point of view the development of the railway network in Great Britain forms an interesting contrast to that in the United States. They proceed at the same time, and in some ways at a comparable rate, although the absolute mileage of railroads in the United States by 1860 was about three times that in Great Britain. This difference, however, may be regarded essentially as an effort by the Americans to cope with the much greater distances involved in the transportation network. The main difference, however, was that the American railroads were built, for the most part, from existing centers into undeveloped territory. The British railroads were built between existing centers with the immediate prospect of a substantial business. In this way the British railroads were comparable to what might be expected to develop in a modern country when a new transportation network is added to existing networks.

Is it possible to estimate the magnitude of the contribution of the British railroads to the economic development of the country? The available evidence is broadly similar to that for canals. There were substantial reductions in rates. W. Stanford Reid, for example, concluded that in many cases costs of shipment were reduced by fifty per cent or more.[18] The lower rates by rail are known to have forced cuts in rates by canal. For example, Clapham cites a reduction from fifteen shillings a ton to ten shillings for light goods on the important route between Liverpool and Manchester. No doubt the effect of railroads on rates for heavy goods was less dramatic.

The greatest competitive advantage of the railroads in the early period, however, was in increased speed. As noted, even in 1830 a speed of twenty-seven m.p.h. was possible. Speed is at a premium in the movement of people. In 1845 nearly two-thirds of the gross receipts of the British railroads were revenues from passengers.[19] This fraction gradually declined with the passage of time. The movement of people does have important economic advantages, but it was only gradually that the railroads took over from the canals the basic function of moving heavy freight. Hence, it is difficult to find examples of completely new forms of economic activity made possible by the railroads that would not have been possible with the canals. The improvement in freight service undoubtedly had major consequences; it is their timing and magnitude that is difficult to trace. The connections between the improvements in service and the resulting economic development have not been worked out in detail.

CONCLUSION—What, then, are the central features of the history of the development of the British transportation system in the period 1700–1850? How were the problems of investment policy solved? What were the consequences of the solutions adopted?

The organization of the transportation industry was in the form of private enterprise on a small scale. There were large numbers of turnpike companies, canal companies, and railroads.

These organizational arrangements made it possible to proceed with the construction of individual sections of the turnpike system, the canal system, and the railroad system with amounts of capital much smaller than would have been required if the systems had been planned and constructed on a national scale. The problem of raising adequate capital for sections of a few miles at a time was soluble because of the prospect of large profits. Some of the early investments were extremely profitable. Men who saw a hope of substantial profit were eager to invest. That

18. W. Stanford Reid, *Economic History of Great Britain*, Ronald Press (1954), Ch. 13, p. 252.
19. Clapham, *op. cit.*, pp. 397, 400.

their expectations were not always met is beside the point. They invested because, at the time they made their decision to invest, they expected large returns.

While the system of piecemeal construction by private enterprises proved to be workable, it had its defects. Perhaps the most serious weakness was in the waste of resources arising from failure to plan the transportation systems as complete entities. The difficulties were most acute in connection with the problems of the gauge of the canals. The gauge problem arose also in the development of the railroads, and was handled by the adoption of a standard gauge at a relatively early date, although in retrospect it appears probable that the wrong gauge was chosen. Even for the railroads, however, substantial outlays had to be made to correct the early development of lengths of road of different gauges.

The organization of the industry led also to spurts of energetic effort in the "manias" for canals and railroads followed by periods of little new investment. The manias were a natural consequence of a situation in which reliance was placed on the optimism of a large number of individual investors. Optimism, which in the nature of the situation was not likely to be based on accurate forecasts of costs and of demand, rested on the hopes of individuals reinforced by their observation of the sentiments of others. Some enterprises conceived in such periods of enthusiasm should never have been undertaken for they led to the waste of some or all of the resources invested in them. In retrospect, it is possible to point to specific companies that were financial failures from the point of view of the investors.

A broader calculation of social benefits and social costs for individual enterprises is much more difficult. A range of uncertainty is likely to persist as to which individual undertakings in this period made a sufficient contribution to the economy so that on balance they benefited society even though they lost money for the private promoters and investors involved. Thus, the amount of inefficiency in the use of resources remains unknown.

The connection between improved transport and the exploitation of economies of scale in factories is not easy to trace in detail. In general, in the early days, industrialization did not involve establishments we would regard as large. But changes did take place. Clapham cites statistics on employment from the Census of 1851 for 677 English "engine and machine makers."[20]

20. Clapham, *op. cit.*, pp. 447–448.

Number of Employees	Number of Firms
Under 10	457
10–39	147
40–99	39
100–199	9
200–299	8
300–349	3
350 or more	14

He also notes that in 1851, 113 cotton firms and 34 woolen or worsted firms employed over 350 persons. Even today a plant with 350 employees is a substantial establishment. The basic connections between transport and factories are clear enough. Perhaps the single most important connection is that factories are based on power, power increasingly meant coal during the Industrial Revolution, and coal had to be moved. The coal barges loading in the Duke of Bridgewater's mines are the symbol of the change. Gaps in knowledge should not obscure the general social benefits that arose from the fact that the transportation system in Great Britain did improve, and thereby made available one prerequisite to the development of the economy as a whole.

7

Transportation in the Economic Development of the United States in the Nineteenth Century

For the analysis of the relation between transportation and economic growth, the history of the United States in the nineteenth century is of special interest. The growth of the American economy during this period is one of the outstanding successes in the history of the world's economy. Extensive research has been done on American economic history in the nineteenth century, and the painstaking assembly of data by many investigators makes possible a reasonably satisfactory account of what happened.

The Nature of the Problems at the Beginning of the Period

THE GEOGRAPHIC PROBLEM—The central problems of American economic development were in some respects similar to those in British development in the period just discussed, but there were important differences. The United States in 1800, like Britain in 1700, was an agricultural and trading country. Great Britain, however, was a settled country relying on natural waterways, which were then the principal means of bulk shipment. The American settlements were primarily along the Atlantic seaboard with a few outposts on the western side of the Appalachian Range. Transportation was primarily by ship along the seaboard or along the rivers of the coastal region. Some country roads existed, but these were primarily roads to tidewater, and the principal means of transportation was by small sailing vessels.[1]

Trade on the Mississippi system was also beginning, but for the most part economic penetration of the interior of the continent had been restricted to the fur trade, which depended on expensive water transportation capable of moving only a small volume of highly valued goods. Guns, knives, cooking pots, and other metal products were of great value to the Indians, as were furs to the settlers. Trade, therefore, could take place and had done so for centuries, but the transportation system that supported it was incapable of bulk movements of heavy commodities. There are limits to what can be carried in a canoe!

There were two main geographic barriers to the westward expansion of the economy. First, the Appalachian Mountains, extending from the northern boundary of the country 1,200 miles to the south. The system was too long to be outflanked: it had to be pierced. The width of the belt of mountains varies, and not all parts of the ranges are equally precipitous, but on most of the potential routes some hundreds of miles of difficult country had somehow to be gotten through.

Beyond the Appalachians, central United States presented no major obstacles to the development of a transportation system or to the settlement of the country. In the West, however, the Rocky Mountains, the desert, and the Sierras presented another series of even more formidable barriers. Here again the difficult country could not be outflanked.

The basic facts of the geography of the country had major economic consequences. A repetition in the United States of the British solution of piecemeal financing of a series of small transportation companies, which could later be stitched together into systems, was not everywhere possible. There were situations in the settled areas where between pairs of established communities short segments of way could be developed. In the less developed parts of the country, however, transportation was needed in advance of demand. What was needed especially was

1. This chapter relies extensively on two volumes: George Rogers Taylor, *The Transportation Revolution 1815–1860,* Holt, Rinehart and Winston, 1951; Carter Goodrich, *Government Promotion of American Canals and Railroads 1800–1890,* Columbia University Press, 1960.

penetration of the major barriers. A canal half-way through the Appalachians or a railroad half-way through the Rockies would be inadequate. In other words, there was a problem of the unusually great "lumpiness" of the required investments. Large sums of money, therefore, had to be committed at one time by an economy in a primitive state of development with a general scarcity of capital and in situations where the technical engineering difficulties were formidable.

The future value of the transportation system to be developed in the new regions, furthermore, was in the nature of the situation uncertain. The future revenues of the transportation system would necessarily depend on the general economic future of the new regions, which it was hardly possible to foresee except in the most general way. The country was bound to develop sooner or later, no doubt, but would it develop fast enough that interest and principal could be paid on time on a particular issue of bonds? The history of the role of transportation in the development of the United States is in large part the history of how these difficulties were faced.

Public Policy

THE SPIRIT OF PUBLIC SERVICE—It was widely understood that there would be an excess of total economic benefit to be derived from a transportation facility over the private revenue that would accrue to the owners of the facility in the form of tolls or charges. The contemporary discussion, however, did not use modern terminology to refer to consumers' surplus received by shippers on the transportation facilities or to external economies or other benefits received by nonusers. Nevertheless, from the early years of the republic the question of internal improvements was approached in a spirit of public service by the leading figures of the country. The example was set by President Washington himself who was well aware of the potential importance of the West to the country, and was a leading advocate of internal improvements. He served at one time as President of the Potomac Company, which was interested in the development of a canal extending up the Potomac River. In 1784 he had urged development of communication with the West, "by one or both of the rivers of this state [Virginia] which have their sources in the Appalachian Mountains."[2] In 1812 Chief Justice John Marshall served as chairman of a commission

2. Goodrich, *ibid.*, p. 87.

appointed by the Virginia legislature to examine that state's problems and recommend improvements. The report ranked close to "the enjoyment of civil liberty itself" the advantages that governments should secure to the people "by good roads, navigable rivers and canals."[3] Goodrich cites other examples of the same philosophy. Among the members of Congress who voted for the *Pacific Railroad Act* of 1864 there were several who did not expect the government's loan ever to be repaid. The railroad was justified, in their eyes, on other grounds. The legislature of Virginia decided to build a tunnel through the Blue Ridge as a means of insuring the progress of the Virginia Central Railroad. The legislators took this action, not because they expected a profit, but precisely because they believed that this development, though necessary, would be unprofitable. It could not, therefore, be left to private enterprise. The very extensive efforts to develop transportation by the cities of Baltimore, Cincinnati, and Portland, Maine, were based on the belief of the citizens that development of transportation lines would redound to the general prosperity of their cities.

NATIONAL PLAN REJECTED—In the situation as it existed in the early part of the century there was no choice as to whether governmental support would be committed to the development of the transportation system. Private resources were inadequate. There were choices, however, as to the nature and extent of public involvement. A basic political question was, to what extent should the effort be made by the national government rather than by the states and local governmental bodies? A national approach was seriously considered.

In 1807 the Senate of the United States directed the then Secretary of the Treasury, Albert Gallatin, to prepare a report that would compromise a general plan of road, canal, and railroad improvements. Gallatin responded with a celebrated report on roads and canals, which was submitted in 1808. It was a remarkable document. Gallatin summarized the problem of coastal navigation, recommending the development of artificial waterways crossing four necks of land. Eventually all four of the proposed waterways were constructed, namely the Cape Cod Canal, the Delaware and Raritan Canal in New Jersey, the Delaware and Chesapeake Bay Canal, and the Dismal Swamp Canal from Chesapeake Bay to Albemarle Sound. Gallatin proposed penetration of the mountain barrier by development of the route up the Hudson to Lake Champlain and down the Mohawk to Lakes Ontario and Erie. He further proposed the exploitation of four pairs of rivers for additional

3. Goodrich, *ibid.*, p. 89.

crossings of the Appalachian Mountains: the Allegheny and the Juniata or Susquehanna; the Monongahela and Potomac; the Kanawha and James; and the Tennessee and the Savannah or Santee.

A start was made on some of these projects under federal auspices, but with the election of Andrew Jackson to the Presidency the federal government largely withdrew from the field. The main improvements during the early half of the nineteenth century were made under the auspices and with the assistance of state and local governments with limited amounts of federal participation. While the federal government did take important steps to assist the development of transportation especially in the second half of the century, the idea of a comprehensive national plan was abandoned.

STATE AND LOCAL POLICY—The decision to rely on state and local efforts had important consequences. It meant that the history of public efforts to assist transportation in the first half of the century would be in large part the history of the rivalry of different states and cities.

The State of New York for reasons of geological history was in the best position to construct a system of transportation capable of moving heavy volumes of freight between the region west of the mountains and the eastern seaboard. The Hudson-Mohawk river system served for a time as the drainage for the region now occupied by the Great Lakes when the St. Lawrence valley was blocked by glacial ice. As a consequence these river valleys constitute a break in the mountain chain and offer a route through the entire Appalachian system to Lake Erie without the necessity of rising over 650 feet above sea level. The Erie Canal was constructed by the State of New York to take advantage of this route. It was completed in 1825 to a depth of four feet.

The Erie Canal was a brilliant success by any criterion. The contemporary verdict was: "They have built the longest canal in the world in the least time, with the least experience, for the least money, and to the greatest public benefit."[4] This opinion was justified. The canal was 363 miles long, longer than anything existing in Western Europe or elsewhere in the United States. It had taken about eight years to construct. The two principal engineers were men who had been trained as lawyers, judges, and surveyors. They devised methods of canal building as they went. The total cost of 7 million dollars is low in comparison to the cost of other projects of the period. By the conservative criterion of financial success the canal had earned enough by 1836 to pay for its entire cost. While half of the surplus used for this purpose came from

4. Quoted by Goodrich, *ibid.*, p. 53 (from Noble E. Whitford, *History of the Canal System of the State of New York,* 2 Volumes, Brandow Printing Company, 1906).

a subsidy, after the debt was paid there was an annual excess of tolls over expenditures of a million dollars a year, some of which was used to pay general expenses of the State of New York.

The American development was characterized by the same alternation of periods of optimism and pessimism that have been described for Great Britain. The fact that these sentiments were felt by voters as well as by investors did not change the importance of the climate of opinion nor did it reduce the uncertainty of estimates of costs and benefits. Decisions to invest or not to invest were not made in an atmosphere of cold blooded, rational calculation. On the contrary, the history of the period is one of an alternation between periods of enthusiasm and energetic construction and periods of pessimism during which no new projects would be inaugurated and work often ceased on projects already started.

The first great burst of enthusiasm dates from the success of the Erie Canal. The advantages to the City of New York were a matter of concern to rival ports. A leading example of a transportation route developed in response to the Erie was the Main Line of Pennsylvania. This system is commonly regarded as a moderate success. It was built across difficult terrain and used a remarkable combination of modes of transportation. From Philadelphia there was a railroad 82 miles to the Susquehanna River at Columbia. Thence, the Main Line Canal worked its way west along the Susquehanna and Juniata Rivers for 172 miles until it reached the backbone of the mountains. Here a special railroad was built that consisted of a series of inclined planes up which the canal boats were hauled on cable cars on one side of the ridge to be lowered down to the western section of 105 miles of canal on the other side of the ridge. The total route was nearly 400 miles long and cost over 12 million dollars.

From its completion in 1834 until the Pennsylvania Railroad reached Pittsburgh in 1855, the Main Line did a considerable business with operating revenues in excess of operating costs. The development of the railroad, however, effectively ended its usefulness as a major transportation route. It would be unreasonable to be too critical of the failure to foresee the effect of the railroad. The world's first railroad, the Stockton and Darlington in Great Britain, was constructed in 1825, and the first "true" railroad, the Liverpool and Manchester, in 1830. When the Main Line was planned the Erie Canal had just been completed with great success and the usual method of movement of bulk commodities in Great Britain, leading industrial nation in the world, was by canal. There was, however, a keen controversy between advocates of a railroad versus a canal in Pennsylvania when the Main Line was being planned. There was also a controversy between those who advocated immediate action and those in favor of delay and a more deliberate response to the Erie. It is clear in retrospect that the wrong decision was taken. The Main Line must stand as an example of a transportation system made obsolete by technological innovation as a result of a mistaken choice of method of transportation.[5]

Gallatin had realized that his program had a chance of political success only if it made provision for a variety of projects that would assist different localities other than those in which the main works were to be constructed. This problem of obtaining political consent from all of the elected representatives of the population, or at least of a working majority, was transferred to the state level by the change from emphasis on the nation to emphasis on state programs. States for which an effort was required to construct a single major work, such as the effort required by the State of Pennsylvania to construct the Main Line, might be forced also to develop a series of projects designed to "do justice" to the interests of the various parts of the state. The State of Pennsylvania, to continue the example, constructed by 1834 a total mileage of canals approximately twice that necessary for the through route to Pittsburgh. Further construction for the satisfaction of additional sections of the state continued until 1842. In retrospect it seems clear that many of these subordinate projects had less economic justification than the Main Line, and very probably many of them should not have been built. There is no doubt as to the financial failure of the total effort. By August 1842 Pennsylvania had incurred a debt of 33 million dollars for public works and the state was forced into bankruptcy.

The difficulty in satisfying the electorate in all parts of Pennsylvania may result from use of the type of process of making an investment decision described in Chapter 3 as a "voters' referendum." When a group of people, such as those in one part of a state, feel they are not likely to benefit from a project to be paid for from the general revenue, they may insist on additional projects designed to redress the balance. In Pennsylvania in this period these projects were ill-advised, and the results were disastrous. If the Main Line could have been financed entirely from tolls, there would have been less of a case for public subsidy of projects elsewhere in the state.

If Pennsylvania's record indicates a program pushed to the limit of

5. See the account by Julius Rubin, "An Imitative Public Improvement: The Pennsylvania Mainline," in Goodrich, *Canals and American Economic Development*, Columbia University Press, 1961.

the resources of the state, not every state went as far. The years following the panic of 1837 saw a major shift in the opposite direction. An
example of the change in sentiment is the history of Michigan in this
regard. Michigan became a state in 1837 at the height of enthusiasm
for railroad building. Michigan's first constitution stated: "that internal
improvements shall be encouraged by the government of the state." A
new constitution adopted five years later included a prohibition against
public works by the state and against participation by the state in mixed
enterprise with private investors. The reversal of opinion came even
more rapidly than these dates suggest. The legislature in 1837 adopted
an extensive program of State Works. In the four years 1837–1840 the
state spent 1.5 million dollars on railroad construction.[6] In 1840 op-
ponents of internal improvements won the election. The program was
abandoned except for continuing work on two railroads. In 1846 these
two railroads were sold and the state was completely out of the transportation business. High costs, technical difficulties, charges of misman-
agement and corruption, and especially difficulties in obtaining funds
all played their part in this reversal of sentiment, which was paralleled
by developments taking place at the same time in other parts of the
country.

FEDERAL POLICY—In spite of the failure to adopt Gallatin's plan
the federal government participated directly in the construction of a
number of projects in the early years of the century. The most notable
was the National Road, originally known as the Cumberland Road,
which ran from Cumberland, Maryland to Wheeling, Virginia on the
Ohio River by 1818. This road was gradually extended to Columbus,
Ohio in 1833 and to Vandalia, Illinois about the middle of the century.

The other major project that received important direct support from
the federal government was the Union Pacific Railroad, the first railroad to pierce the Western barrier, in 1869. The construction of the
railway to the Pacific came in a surprisingly short time after the penetration of the Appalachians by the railroads. It was not until 1853 that
the New York Central was formed completing the combination of a
series of small companies that owned segments of line between New
York and Buffalo. The Pennsylvania reached Pittsburgh about the same
time. Without public assistance a transcontinental railroad in 1869
would have been impossible.

6. E. R. Wicker, "Railroad Investment Before the Civil War," in *Trends in the
American Economy in the Nineteenth Century, Studies in Income and Wealth,* Volume
24, Princeton University Press, 1960, p. 523. See also the account in Goodrich, *Government Promotion of American Canals and Railroads, 1800–1890.*

From 1850 onward the principal assistance to the construction of transportation networks by the federal government was grants of land. This idea had been popularized by Asa Whitney who proposed to build a transcontinental railroad that would be financed entirely through this method. From an economic point of view the system is of interest because it is a device for appropriating to the benefit of the builders of the road the gains in the value of land along the route. What could be more natural than that the increase in the value of the land should be used to defray the expense of construction of the transportation system? Where private lands were involved, ordinarily there did not seem to be any method of appropriating the windfall gain received by the owners of the land, though frequently these, individually or through governmental units, might make some contribution to the costs of the railroad. But there was nothing to prevent Congress from appropriating the public lands to this purpose and the total volume of land grants made to the railroads in the end amounted to approximately 129 million acres, which works out to about 200,000 square miles.[7] In addition to the federal grants, large tracts of land were donated by states; notably by the State of Texas, which in the latter part of the century was the only state with large tracts of public land it was in a position to donate to such a purpose.

This system of subsidy amounted, in effect, to the offering of special inducements to private capitalists to put their resources into the development of railroads. It could be effective only to the extent that private capital existed that could be tempted into this employment. Hence, it is not remarkable that this device enjoyed greater popularity in the second half of the nineteenth century when such capital existed in the country in large amounts. A limitation of the method was that it did not provide cash when liquid resources were required for the advancement of a project. The funds from the sale of the land were available only when the land had become valuable as a result of the successful conclusion of the developmental construction.

SUMMARY OF PUBLIC AID—Estimates have been compiled by Goodrich of the total investment in canals and railroads and of the amount of public funds contributed.[8] From 1815 to 1860 the total sum invested in canals he estimates at 195 million dollars. Of that amount seventy per cent was public money. Cranmer in discussing this period has made a distinction between "developmental" and "exploitative" canals. The

7. Goodrich, *ibid.*, p. 197.
8. Goodrich, *ibid.*, Ch. 8.

former were intended to stimulate the economic life of a region, and, he finds, were almost always public enterprises in the period. Virtually all (ninety-four per cent) of the investment in canals east of the Alleghenies, in the settled part of the country, was by private enterprise. West of the mountains the reverse was true, eighty-nine per cent was by state governments.[9]

Before 1860 the total capitalization of the railroads was 1,145,-000,000 dollars by Goodrich's estimate. Public aid amounted to 280,-000,000 dollars plus land grants. From 1861 to 1890 the total capital increased to 10 billion dollars. Public aid in this period was 350 million dollars plus the land grants. These estimates no doubt are subject to error and to adjustment for changes in prices. The main sequence of events, however, is one of a major public effort in the early part of the century with an increasing share of private investment as development proceeded.

Both public and private securities, of course, could be offered for sale either in the United States or in foreign capital markets. The record seems to be incomplete, but foreign investment was undoubtedly substantial. For example, bonds issued by New York State for the construction of the Erie Canal were held by foreign investors to the amount of half the total debt by the time the canal was completed. Before 1840 about 200 million dollars of American railroad securities were held abroad. In 1899 the total of American securities abroad is estimated to have been 3 billion dollars, primarily railroad securities.

To the extent that securities secured by the credit of public agencies were sold abroad, the effect was to use the public credit to attract foreign capital for American investments. This device was particularly appropriate in the early period when few American private enterprises could have been large enough to enjoy an international reputation.

Evaluation

The problem of evaluation of the investments in transportation in the nineteenth century in the United States may be treated at two levels. We shall consider, first, the evaluation of individual projects with special attention to the Union Pacific Railroad, and second, the more general problem of evaluating the total effects of the canals and railroads.

EVALUATION OF INDIVIDUAL PROJECTS—Of the multitude of indi-

9. H. Jerome Cranmer, "Canal Investment, 1815–1860" in *Studies in Income and Wealth,* Volume 24, Princeton University Press, 1960, p. 559.

vidual projects that were undertaken, which should be regarded in retrospect as successes and which as failures? From a theoretical point of view this question could be answered precisely if given adequate information, as indicated earlier. What is required is a calculation of costs, a calculation of gains, and a comparison of the two. In the actual state of our knowledge, however, even today it is in some cases impossible to reach any firm conclusion as to the desirability of some of the improvements that were made. It is possible at least to rank the projects on a continuum from the obvious successes to those which were complete failures. There can be no question of the economic wisdom of the Erie Canal, at one extreme. The Erie paid for itself and at the same time made a major contribution to the development of the country.

At the other extreme are projects that were incomplete and never were utilized. Perhaps the most dramatic example was the effort by the State of South Carolina to build a through railroad to the West. The project required the digging of a tunnel 6,000 feet through solid granite in Stump House Mountain. It had been carried about two-thirds of the way through with great effort by the time the Civil War broke out in 1861. After the War the project was never carried to conclusion. The money spent on that enterprise was clearly wasted.

But there are many enterprises that fall between. One possible criterion is to consider as failures those projects that were not able to cover operating expenses, let alone any return on the capital invested. The logic here is not too clear since there were social gains not taken into account in the calculation of the financial returns. Use of this criterion implies that these gains were not large enough to offset the costs of the projects.

The central difficulty is in the estimation of the social benefit in excess of the amounts paid to the proprietors as tolls or rates. There will be the net gains to the users of the facility in excess of the tolls they pay. There will be economic gains to nonusers, their nature depending on the type of project. A successful developmental project may lead to important external economies from the growth of economic activity, such as the gains to the shipping industry from the increased level of activity in the port of New York in the decades after the completion of the Erie Canal. There may be political gains from increased unity of the country. The more general and indirect the benefits, as a rule, the harder they are to evaluate.

The usual data, which are available for the evaluation of the social contribution of a transportation project, are of two sorts: prices of transportation before and after the inauguration of service on the new system; and the volume of tonnage that moved over the system during its lifetime. There may also be estimates of the proportion of the total traffic which originated in a particular transportation system and estimates of improvements of the quality of service, especially in speed. An example of the type of information frequently available about price is the celebrated set of statistics for the Erie Canal. Before it was constructed the expense of transportation from Buffalo to New York City was 100 dollars a ton. From 1830 to 1850 tolls averaged $8.81 a ton. Taylor has converted these figures into costs per ton-mile.[10] They work out to about 19.1 cents per ton-mile in 1817, and an average of 1.7 cents for the period 1830 to 1850. In 1857–1860 the average rate was 0.82 cents per ton-mile.

The gain by the development of rail transportation during this period was not in price but in speed. The average speed of freight trains in New York State in 1858 was about 11 miles an hour, including stops, while the average speed for through flour shipments on the Erie Canal was about 1.8 miles per hour. Freight rates in cents per ton-mile on the New York Central in 1853 were about 3.4 cents. This average rate was about the same as that charged on the Pennsylvania but somewhat higher than the Erie, which averaged 2.4 cents per ton-mile at that date.

As an example of statistics of tonnage we may mention the shipments of flour, plus wheat reduced to equivalent barrels of flour, on the Erie Canal. These shipments amounted to 268,000 barrels in 1835 and by 1860 totaled 4,344,000 barrels.[11] Similar statistics are available for other major transportation routes. Through freight moving eastward on the Erie Canal in 1860, for example, was about twice as great as that on the three competing railroads combined: the New York Central, the Erie, and the Pennsylvania. Thus, this Canal, up to 1860, was the principal outlet to the East for the agricultural produce of the area it served: that part of the northwest whose commerce did not go down the Mississippi River to New Orleans. Such information is persuasive as to the social usefulness of the Erie even though it does not permit an estimate of the dollar value to society.

A more difficult case from the point of view of evaluation is the James River Canal in Virginia. This Canal carried the bulk of the produce of the Shenandoah Valley to market for a considerable period. It also lost money all of its life. Was the investment justified? Did the benefits not appropriated by the operators of the Canal in tolls offset the capital loss? If settlers had not gone into the Shenandoah

10. Taylor, *op. cit.*, p. 137.
11. Taylor, *op. cit.*, p. 161, 167.

Valley presumably they would have settled elsewhere. It would be in-correct to assign to the James River Canal the full value of the produce of the area it opened to settlement. The proper comparison would be between the actual value of the product of the Shenandoah Valley and the value that would have been produced had the resources of labor and capital devoted to the exploitation of the Valley been utilized else-where. A method of estimating this magnitude was developed by Robert W. Fogel and is discussed below.

EVALUATION OF THE UNION PACIFIC—Perhaps the most ambitious attempt that has been made to evaluate an investment in a specific transportation facility in the United States in this period is a study made by Robert W. Fogel of the Union Pacific Railroad.[12] The study is of interest both as an exercise in methodology and as a study of the first transportation system to penetrate the mountains and deserts to the West—constituting the second major barrier to American expansion to the Pacific.

The main facts concerning the railroad can be outlined briefly. The Union Pacific was built as a result of legislation passed by Congress in 1862 and 1864 that was intended to provide sufficient public assist-ance to entice private capital to undertake the construction of the road. The government offered a land grant of 20,000,000 acres and a loan of 60,000,000 dollars. Construction proceeded from Omaha west, while the Central Pacific was built east from Sacramento, 1800 miles away; the Central Pacific eventually met the Union Pacific at Promontory Point in Utah in 1869. Attention here will focus on the Union Pacific, for which the financial information is more complete.

The investing public at first took a pessimistic view of the prospects of successful completion of the road and the company's bonds sold at a heavy discount. As a consequence, the road when completed was overcapitalized and financially unstable. The debt to the government proved a heavy burden. The road finally was unable to meet its obli-gations and went into receivership in 1893.

From an engineering point of view the Union Pacific was an un-doubted success. It was built in a five-year period, 1864–1869, across unsettled country including the Rocky Mountains. From a political point of view it led to the *Credit Mobilier* scandal, which figured in the 1872 election and involved charges of bribery against members of the House of Representatives who were implicated in dealings with the construction company that built the line. The present concern, how-ever, is with economic analysis of the investment.

12. Robert William Fogel, *The Union Pacific Railroad, A Case in Premature Enter-prise,* Johns Hopkins Press, 1960.

As usual, the problem resolves into two parts, the estimation of costs and benefits. The estimation of the costs of the road can rely primarily on the costs as they appeared on the books of the company. In retrospect these costs are known. The amount spent on the actual construction of the road to completion was 57 million dollars. The total cost of the project, however, must also include the profits to the promoters of the road, which had to be sufficient to induce them to undertake the enterprise. The amount necessary in this instance (not the amount actually paid) was 11 million dollars. Finally, it was necessary to pay a premium to other private investors to induce them to lend money to the Union Pacific. This premium on borrowed funds Fogel estimates at 7 million dollars, bringing the total necessary cost of the railroad to 75 million dollars by his estimate.

Fogel carried out an interesting calculation in arriving at the above estimates, which involves an estimate of the subjective probability of the failure of the project in the minds of private investors implied by their behavior. He notes that government bonds paid about 6.02 per cent during the relevant period in 1867. This rate may be taken as indicating the rate of return on riskless securities. The price that private investors would pay for the bonds of the company fluctuated. Fogel takes "40" as representative of the market price during the crucial period.

If the project failed, there would be no return on the bonds. If the project succeeded, the bonds would be paid.

Let p = probability of failure of the railroad.
Let q = probability of success of railroad.
Then $p + q = 1$, since the road must either succeed or fail.

The weighted sum of the rate of return in the event of failure and the return in the event of success should equal the rate for riskless investment. At a price of 40 an income stream of the amount specified on the face of the bonds would yield to an investor a return of 21.3 per cent.

Then:
$$0 \times p + 21.3 \times q = 6.02$$
Or,
$$0 \times p + 21.3 \ (1\text{-}p) = 6.02$$
Solving,
$$p = .717 \quad q = .283$$

Investors presumably were indifferent to a rate of return of 6.02 with certainty and a rate of return of 21.3 with a probability of 0.283. Thus, a price of 40 implied an estimate that the chances were 0.717 out of 1,000 that the road would fail, and 0.283 that it would succeed.

Fogel observes that the need to pay premiums to investors and promoters would have been removed if Congress had acted in such a manner as to guarantee the successful completion of the project. Congress, however, by offering aid only in the forms of a loan and a land grant, failed to remove this risk, and risk premiums became a necessary part of the cost of the undertaking.

Was there any social cost incurred in the construction of the Union Pacific not taken into account in the above calculation? The answer appears to be, "no," apart from the cost to the Indians, whose way of life was destroyed. If the cost to them is not included, the figure of 75 million dollars seems a complete estimate of the social cost of the project. The actual construction expenditure was only 59 million dollars accumulated through 1879.

What were the benefits? First, the net earnings of the road must be included. Fogel estimates net earnings in constant dollars of 1869. He also adjusts the company's financial reports to deduct larger depreciation charges from earnings—the reported figures took account of only part of the actual depreciation. He then finds earnings yielded an average rate of return on construction expenditure of 11.6 per cent for 1869–1879. (Note that this calculation is *not* an estimate of the actual return in current dollars to the actual investors.)

Second, the construction of the Union Pacific led to the opening of settlement of the lands along its route. Fogel has been able to estimate the amount of the increase in the value of the land on the route on the basis of data from the United States Census. He concerns himself with a strip of land eighty miles wide, extending forty miles on either side of the right-of-way, between the terminals at Omaha, Nebraska, and Ogden City, Utah. In 1860 this land was worth only about 4,370,000 dollars (measured in 1869 dollars). Land values generally increased in the United States by about one-third between 1860 and 1880; but even after allowing for such an increase, the land along the Union Pacific would have had a value of only about 5.8 million dollars in 1880. The actual value of the land, net of improvements, Fogel estimates at 158.5 million dollars, and he attributed the difference, or 152.7 million dollars, to the construction of the railroad. The value of the land in 1880, as he observes, represents essentially the capitalized value of the amount by which the annual product of labor and capital on this land exceeded their value on marginal lands. He converts the capital back into an annual flow using the average mortgage rates of 1880 in the states involved. After carrying out these calculations Fogel estimates the sum of the net earnings of the company plus the increase in land values to have yielded a social rate of return equal to 30 per cent on the expenditure on construction over the decade 1870–1879.

Third, the construction of the Union Pacific led to other unpaid benefits whose magnitudes remain unknown. There were benefits to shippers who made use of the railroad that were not offset in full by the payments made by them to the company. The reason for belief in the existence of such benefits has been developed above. Both public and private shippers are involved. Consider, for example, the situation of the government. The government made shipments of supplies to outposts in the West prior to the building of the railroad by the primitive and expensive means of transportation then existing. It was a savings to be able to ship by railroad. The whole situation changed so completely with the settlement of the country, however, that it is not enlightening to estimate what it would have cost in 1880 to ship freight to the frontier posts of 1860 if they had continued to exist unchanged. The same type of difficulty applies to estimating benefits to private shippers.

There remains one major social benefit of the Union Pacific, which might be called its "demonstration effect." The successful completion of this project transformed the situation confronting potential promoters of other railroads to the West. If the barrier of the mountains and deserts could be breached once, it could be breached again. Private capital could be interested in the development of new railroads without the necessity of paying heavy premiums for risk and without the necessity of large loans from the United States Government. The policy of land grants to promoters of railroads continued as long as there were large tracts of undeveloped land, but became of decreasing importance as the country became settled. These grants were more attractive once it had been proven that a transcontinental railroad could succeed. The demonstration effect of the Union Pacific is not easily quantified but one can speculate that few of the later western railroads would have been constructed if their promoters had been under the necessity of paying 21.3 per cent for capital. There was actually a vast development of railroads in the area west of the Mississippi River in the decades following completion of the Union Pacific. The indirect consequences of the Union Pacific extended beyond the borders of the United States to Canada, as will be discussed in Chapter 8.

EVALUATION OF THE CONTRIBUTION OF CANALS—We turn from the

evaluation of individual projects to the problems of more general evaluation of the canals and, in the next section, of the railroads. There is no controversy as to the importance for the development of the country of the introduction of economical transportation that penetrated the interior of the continent. An attempt to quantify the impact has been made by Harvey H. Segal.[13] He states that by the criterion of financial success of the project over two-thirds of the 188 million dollars invested in ante-bellum canals was a social waste. Like most writers, he rejects this criterion as too narrow. He has assembled statistics on the cost to shippers of the freight actually moved from 1837–1846 on ten heavily used canals. One calculation, which he proposes tentatively, is a comparison of hypothetical cost per ton-mile for those shipments by wagon with actual costs by canal. The difference is a measure of the saving to shippers if volume is assumed constant. The wagon rates were about 25 cents per ton-mile, he believes, and costs by canal about 2 cents, implying a saving of 23 cents. On an average annual volume of 288 million ton-miles, the saving to shippers in the years 1837–1846 would have been 66 million dollars a year on the ten canals.

Yet, Segal argues, this estimate is too high. Most of the freight did not move at the wagon rates prior to the existence of the canals. The consumers' surplus to most of the shippers, therefore, must have been less than 23 cents per ton-mile. Much of the freight would no doubt have moved at, say, 2.36 cents. Suppose, on the average, the surplus was in fact 3.6 mills per ton-mile. That amount is of interest because a consumers' surplus of 3.6 mills per ton-mile on the 288 million ton-miles carried by his ten canals would have been enough to equal the annual deficit on the national canal system as a whole during the period. The social gain would have offset the loss to the canals. Part of the cost of the system was met from tolls, of course. The addition of only another 1 million dollars would have matched the loss. If a consumers' surplus to shippers of 66 million dollars is too high, 1 million dollars is too low.[14] The canal system as a whole undoubtedly produced a net gain to society.

RAILROADS AS A LEADING SECTOR—One of the most widely read

13. Harvey H. Segal, "Canals and Economic Devlopment," in Goodrich, *Canals and American Economic Development.*

14. Consider the shape of the demand curve implied by Segal's estimates. A small amount of freight did move by wagon. It is not too far wrong, then, to say the demand curve intersects the vertical axis above but near the value of 25 cents per ton-mile. We also know the point on the demand curve observed at the time, at a price of 2 cents a volume of 288 million ton-miles. Any reasonable demand curve passing through those points would be such that at prices of 3 or 4 cents considerable volumes would have moved.

analyses of the economic development of the United States in the last century is that of W. W. Rostow.[15] Rostow's main thesis is that there are five stages of economic growth, and that at any given time any society may be classified in one of these stages: the traditional society; the precondition for take-off; the take-off; the drive to maturity; and the age of high mass-consumption. Of these, the crucial stage is the take-off, in which growth becomes the normal condition for the society. As far as the United States is concerned, Rostow places the take-off in the brief span from 1843 to 1860, and he assigns to the railroads a crucial role as the leading sector, the most powerful single initiator of the take-off. This view of the economic development of the United States implies that the indirect social benefits from investment in railroads in the period of take-off were very large indeed.

The position taken by Rostow and scholars who agree with him has been challenged by other economic historians, notably by Fogel.[16] Fogel presents a much less enthusiastic estimate of the contributions made by the railroads in the nineteenth century as a whole and the years 1843–1860 in particular.

Rostow's argument is that in the United States and in many other countries railroads have had three major kinds of impact.[17] First, by lowering the cost of transportation railroads brought new areas and new products into the market. They broadened the market and thus facilitated the division of labor. Second, railroads have been a prerequisite to the development of a major new export sector. Third, the development of railroads has led to the development of industries to supply the factors of production required by the railroads, namely, coal, iron, and engineering industries. Specifically, in the United States in the 1840s railway and manufacturing development occurred in the East, while in the 1850s there was the railway push into the Middle West.

Fogel attempts to estimate the effect on the national income if the economy had relied on water transportation plus highways with no railroads whatsoever. He devotes most of his attention to the movement of major agricultural commodities, which he divides into two parts. One part is interregional distribution, defined as movement from the primary markets in the major cities of the Midwest to the secondary markets in the large cities of the East and South. The second part, in-

15. W. W. Rostow, *The Stages of Economic Growth,* Cambridge University Press, 1960.

16. Robert William Fogel, *Railroads and American Economic Growth: Essays in Econometric History,* The Johns Hopkins Press, 1964.

17. Rostow, *op. cit.,* p. 55.

traregional distribution, is movement from farms to the primary markets and from the secondary markets to nearby points of consumption. For the movement between primary markets the principal advantages of the railroads were speed and ability to operate twelve months in the year. As we have noted, average charges per ton-mile were higher by rail than by water. For example, Fogel reports the rate for wheat in 1890 from Chicago to New York was 0.52 cents per ton-mile by rail, three times the charge by water. The central problem in evaluating the gain by rail on such a route is one of evaluating the advantage to shippers of the speed and reliability of rail. Fogel approaches the problem primarily by estimating costs of carrying inventories. It is possible to estimate the cost per month of carrying inventory, which is composed of storage charges plus interest on the capital employed. The difficulty is how much inventory to consider and for how long. Fogel's estimate is that exclusive reliance on water would have involved a maximum of one month longer in transit for interregional shipments. He also allows for an extra five months' stock of produce in inventory, to cover the full period when the waterways are frozen. Both estimates seem generous. Indeed, stocks must be held somewhere through the year to allow for the fact that the harvest is seasonal while consumption is at a constant rate. It is hard to see how reliance on water transportation could have increased the total period for which stocks were needed by an average of six months. Fogel's main conclusion is that even with his generous estimate of the savings in costs of carrying stocks the reduction in cost of interregional movement by the shift from water to rail must have been small, less than 1 per cent of national income. If anything, he seems to have overstated the saving.[18]

The gains in intraregional distribution from the development of railroads were larger. The developing rail network reduced the necessary wagon haul from farm to terminal, and transportation by railroad was certainly much cheaper than by wagon. By 1890, according to one set of estimates, costs by wagon averaged 17 cents and by rail under 1 cent per ton-mile. This set of estimates seems to overstate the saving

18. Indeed, Fogel leaves one searching for a fuller explanation of why shippers of grain switched to rail. One possibility is that transit rates had the effect of "holding to the rails" traffic that could economically have moved by water. (See Chapter 19 for a more extensive discussion of transit rates.) In effect the railroads may have succeeded in using special through rates to exploit their advantage in the intraregional movement of traffic in such a manner as to dominate the interregional movement of agricultural products even though the social cost of interregional movement by rail was about the same as the social cost of movement by water. If this conjecture should prove correct, the effect, of course, would be to strengthen Fogel's main contention as far as grain movements are concerned: that they could have been handled tolerably well by water.

by using rail. If the average cost for all railroad transportation was 1 cent, the cost of that part of rail service involved in assembling full freight trains from local stations must have been higher than 1 cent. Nevertheless, the costs of the collection function and the distribution function of the transportation system were undoubtedly lower by rail than by wagon.

Fogel's central thesis is that these savings were not large enough so that railroads were indispensable to economic growth in the United States. The country could have been opened to settlement relying on water and road transport. As far as agriculture is concerned, Fogel demonstrates at least that such a possibility existed. The West could have shipped all of its grain to market by water.

Fogel also reviews in detail the role of the railroads as customers for the iron, coal, and engineering industries. Fogel's most important estimate is that railroads accounted for about 25 per cent of pig iron production during some of Rostow's crucial eighteen years, but only for 10 per cent during the five years ending in 1849, averaging 17 per cent over the two decades. It seems reasonable to conclude that direct use of iron by the railroads was not essential to the development of the iron industry.

The crucial contribution of the railroads may well have been in the effects of the provision of fast, reliable, year-round service in facilitating the movement of semifinished and finished goods. It has been argued by Nathan Rosenberg, for example, that specialized machinery producers began appearing at the time of the development of the railroad network. Until 1840 machinery production was unspecialized and for a local market because of the high cost of transporting machinery. After 1840 there were large numbers of producers who typically specialized by types of machinery.[19]

One wonders, also, what the arrangements for communication and for business travel would have been without the railroads. Would Andrew Carnegie have set out from Pittsburgh for New York by stage coach in, say, the winter of 1890?

As is common in intellectual controversies, the final verdict may well be that there is truth both in the view that railroads were important and in the view that their importance was limited. Further historical research and analysis, we hope, will contribute to fuller understanding of their economic impact.

19. Nathan Rosenberg, "Technological Changes in the Machine Tool Industry, 1840–1910," *Journal of Economic History,* December 1963.

Concluding Comments

The main strategy adopted by the public authorities in the United States in the nineteenth century, to bring about the development of the country, reflected the geography of the country and the shifting border of the settled parts of the country. Transportation was of central importance and the development of transportation facilities was a central feature of public policy. That policy was essentially: Do what is necessary to build the transportation facilities and leave the rest to private initiative.

With regard to the development of transportation facilities the choice of instruments was flexible. Sometimes public agencies were relied upon, sometimes private, and sometimes mixed, with the reliance on unaided private business tending to increase as time went on. Where precise calculations of costs and benefits were not possible, in assessing proposed transportation facilities there was frequently a willingness to take an optimistic view and push hopefully ahead.

Broadly speaking this strategy was a success if the rate of growth of gross national product may be taken as the criterion. While the record of individual projects in transportation is mixed, the country did develop —rapidly. Both canals and railroads made major contributions to the development. Progress was achieved, however, only at the cost of some waste, and some individual projects were mistakes.

8

Transportation in the Economic Development of Canada to 1923

THE PART PLAYED by transportation in the economic development of Canada is of interest because of the sheer magnitude of the transportation problems relative to the population and resources of the country. The inevitable consequence was that public policy toward transportation became political to a greater extent than it did in the United States. The history of Canadian transportation illustrates how political and economic considerations jointly can influence the development of transportation policy.

Difficulties of Canadian Geography

The geography of Canada, while it presented some major advantages, presented extraordinary difficulties. The Saint Lawrence-Great Lakes Waterway provided a route to the interior of the continent without the difficulties confronting the early settlers in the United States in the form of the Appalachian barrier. This waterway, however, has disadvantages: it freezes in the winter, and there are major natural obstacles to navigation in the rapids and falls in the St. Lawrence and Niagara Rivers.

A geographic barrier unique to Canada is the Canadian Shield. This geological formation covers nearly half of Canada. It is at its widest in the north and narrows to the south, but it is still so wide that it reaches the United States at Lake Superior and at the Thousand Islands in the St. Lawrence River. The area is made up of ancient rocks that have been much glaciated, and as a result, the soil is sparse. It is not suitable to agriculture. The region is characterized by rocky hills and innumerable lakes. In fact, in some parts of the Shield, which have been carefully studied, the lakes cover 40 per cent of the surface. The area contains important mineral deposits. One indication of the difficulty of the terrain is that until about 1960 it was impossible to cross the Shield by automobile from the Great Plains to the fertile and populous areas of the St. Lawrence Valley and southeastern Ontario. Canadian motorists could cross the continent only through the United States.

To the west of the Canadian Shield, the plains region is about 800 miles wide at the American border, and somewhat narrower to the north. Further west is the Cordillera, a second formidable barrier. The Canadian Rockies have an average width of about 400 miles, and an elevation of 10,000 feet above sea level for much of their area.

Finally, to the north the climate of the arctic and subarctic regions presents major difficulties for transportation, and provides serious limitations to the usefulness of the access to the sea by way of the Hudson Bay.

These geographic difficulties had consequences for the development of the country. Very heavy investments in transportation facilities had to be made and these investments have been closely tied to the economic history of Canada.

From the point of view of transportation policy, the history of the development of Canada may be divided into three phases. The earliest phase is that of the fur trade. This trade involved the transportation of small volumes of commodities, which were high in value in relation to their bulk, over natural waterways in canoes—and later in open boats and sailing ships on the lakes. This period is not of special interest here. The second period was that of the opening up of the country to agriculture, and the establishment of transportation lines from the Atlantic to the Pacific, with the early development in the form of canals and later emphasis on the railways. This period extended to approximately the time of World War I. It is the major focus of attention here. The third period is characterized by increasing importance of industry relative to agriculture and, from a transportation point of view, by increasing development of major transportation lines running north and south within the country.

Development of Transportation Lines from East to West

The development of transportation from east to west in Canada falls into two periods: an earlier period in which reliance was exclusively on water transportation, and a later period in which railroads were of central importance. Within the railway period two developments are of special interest: the construction of the Intercolonial as an example of a major road whose purpose was primarily political, and the construction of the transcontinental roads that are excellent examples of railroads designed to develop new country. Political considerations were also involved, however, in the decision to build the first transcontinental line.

WATERWAYS—Until 1850 the major efforts to improve the transportation system were the improvements to the natural waterways and the canals. In 1850 only sixty-six miles of railroad were in operation. The development of Canadian waterways must be understood in the light of events south as well as north of the American border. The impact of the success of the Erie Canal was felt in Canada just as it was felt up and down the Atlantic seaboard. Until the completion of the Erie Canal, much of the commerce of the western part of the United States had gone through Montreal. Easterbrook and Aitken put it dramatically: the effect of the Erie was to cut Montreal's economic hinterland in half.[1] The development of Canadian canals was in part intended to recover that lost position, and the economic success of the canals depended upon success in this respect. It was not until 1848, however, that Canada had a water route reasonably competitive with the Erie, and by that time the American railroads were being developed as formidable competitors for all the waterways.

A canal was constructed at the Lachine Rapids in the St. Lawrence River and completed as early as 1825, the same year as the Erie Canal, but to a depth of only four feet. The Rideau Canal, completed in 1832, provided a circuitous route from Montreal to Lake Ontario by way of Ottawa and Kingston, but with a depth of only five feet. It was built to provide a military route remote from American attack and never was of much commercial importance.

A major effort in this period was the construction of the Welland Canal from Lake Ontario to Lake Erie surmounting the Niagara escarpment. It was built to a depth of eight feet, with completion in 1829

1. W. T. Easterbrook and Hugh G. J. Aitken, *Canadian Economic History*, The Macmillan Company of Canada, Limited, 1958, p. 255.

and the first traffic in 1830. This Canal is a classic example of a facility constructed before its time. Completion had been possible only after repeated appeals for public funds to supplement the original private capital. As a result of the scarcity of funds, the Canal was cheaply built, and shortly incurred high expenses for maintenance. Meanwhile the traffic that had been anticipated from new settlers in the area to the west of the canal failed to materialize. Something of the tenor of the contemporary comment may be inferred from newspaper articles by W. L. Mackenzie in the *Colonial Advocate*. He wrote: "Economy and the Welland Canal are as far apart as earth and heaven." And again: "The Welland Canal has been a hoax from first to last."[2]

In retrospect it seems clear that an eight-foot Welland Canal would make sense economically only if it was joined with a canal at Lachine of a greater depth than four feet. Mary Q. Innis has pointed out that at this period the cost of shipping a ton of merchandise from London, England to Montreal, a distance of 3,200 miles, was one pound, while to ship the same ton 130 miles up river to Prescott cost 2.5 pounds because of the necessity for trans-shipment at the rapids of the river.[3]

The loss incurred as a result of the early errors of judgment in connection with the Welland Canal was borne primarily by the government, which bought out the private interests in 1839. By 1848 the canals on the St. Lawrence had been built to match the Welland Canal, which also was improved. The improved system, however, never rivaled the Erie as an outlet for the American Middle West.

The subsequent history is one of gradual improvement of the entire Great Lakes-St. Lawrence system. The problem of balance between the capacity of the Welland Canal and the capacity of the canals along the St. Lawrence recurred as late as the period of the first operations of the St. Lawrence Seaway, with the Welland Canal the bottleneck this time.

RAILWAYS—Railway construction in Canada was delayed until the second half of the nineteenth century. Until 1850, as previously noted, there were only sixty-six miles in operation in the country. Some idea of the magnitude of the problem of raising the money for railroads may be inferred from the fact that by 1867 a total of 2,459 miles had been built at a cost estimated to be about 155 million dollars. This amount may be compared with an estimate of the gross national product

2. Quoted by G. P. de T. Glazebrook, *A History of Transportation in Canada*, The Ryerson Press, 1938, p. 87.

3. Mary Quayle Innis, *An Economic History of Canada*, Riverson Press, Revised edition, 1954.

of the country in current dollars in 1867 of 419 million dollars.[4] Thus the investment in railroads was roughly equal to one-third of the GNP for one year. At the present time a comparable investment in the United States over a period of eighteen years would be 200 billion dollars, or roughly four times the total cost of the Interstate System of highways.

The money for the early Canadian railroads was partly English capital lent either to the government or directly to the railroads. There was also private lending from the United States in addition to the Canadian funds employed. As the early Canadian roads were constructed, they tended to run into financial difficulties. Glazebrook observes that "all the railways cost more than the estimates, whether those estimates were made by English, American, or Canadian engineers." On the other hand the estimates of traffic were invariably optimistic guesses: the traffic failed to materialize. Two of the railways developed in Canada in the second half of the century deserve detailed discussion as examples, one of a railroad developed primarily for political purposes, and one of a railroad developed for mixed political and economic purposes.

THE INTERCOLONIAL RAILROAD—When it was proposed to combine the Maritime Provinces of the Atlantic seaboard in political union with the rest of Canada it was clearly recognized by contemporaries that union would be possible only if a railway existed. The direct route from Montreal to Nova Scotia and New Brunswick passes through the State of Maine. But could the unity of Canada be achieved by a route across Maine? The decision was taken to develop the road on a route on Canadian soil close to the St. Lawrence River and as far as possible from the American frontier.

The Intercolonial Railroad, completed in 1876, was publicly constructed and publicly owned. The cost estimate of the line had been 20 million dollars, but the actual construction cost was over 34 million dollars. The line never paid for the capital investment, but it seems to have been justified both in the minds of contemporaries and in the minds of modern Canadian historians as a contribution to the political development of the country. The road no doubt would have been more successful financially if later the Canadian Pacific had not taken advantage of reduced fears of war with the United States to construct across Maine a short line to St. John with lower operating costs than the Intercolonial.

THE CANADIAN PACIFIC—The railway to the Pacific was a political necessity as well as an economic one. The political pressures came in

4. O. J. Firestone, *Canada's Economic Development, 1867–1953*, Bowes and Bowes, 1958.

part from the decision to combine British Columbia with the Dominion of Canada. The negotiations for the admission of British Columbia to the Dominion included discussions of the development of transcontinental transportation. In 1870 the Dominion Government agreed with the representatives of British Columbia that it would begin a railroad within two years and complete it within ten years. Note that the date of the agreement is the year after the completion of the Union Pacific. The spirit of this agreement was kept, but the date had to be renegotiated, and actual completion of the railway to the Pacific did not come until 1885.

A second form of political pressure arose because the vast uninhabited stretches of the Canadian plains were more easily accessible from the United States than they were from Canada. The small settlements in the Red River Valley, which had developed as a result of the fur trade, were close to rapidly developing portions of the United States. As early as 1858 freight could reach St. Paul overland from the Red River by cart and then proceed down river to New Orleans and to Liverpool more cheaply than it could be shipped to York Factory on the Hudson Bay and thence across the Atlantic. By 1859 there were steamboats on the Red River, and in 1871 the Northern Pacific Railway reached the Red River making the carts obsolete and providing mechanized transportation from Winnipeg to the outside world via the Mississippi Valley.

The political danger of this situation was emphasized by an actual rebellion in 1869–1870 under a halfbreed named Louis Riel. Only a very few men were involved, but the rebellion was put down slowly and with difficulty because of the lack of communications with the Red River area from eastern Canada. It did not take much imagination to foresee a situation with settlers moving into the empty Canadian plains from the United States with efficient transportation to the United States and out of the effective reach of the Canadian Government. The Canadian Pacific, thus, was a response to the Union Pacific just as the early work on the Great Lakes–St. Lawrence waterway was a response to the Erie Canal. These events illustrate how competitive pressure can play a major part in investment decisions by forcing reevaluation of the situation as it would exist without a proposed investment.

The Canadian Government made the decision to proceed with a railway and chose the method of subsidizing a private company. Events did not proceed smoothly. A major political scandal developed, "the Pacific scandal," involving contributions to campaign funds of the Ministers in the Government and the question of who should receive the contract to build the railway. This scandal caused the resignation of the Government. The new Government, while accepting the necessity for the railroad, took the position that the wisest course would be to proceed slowly and make use of the connection through the United States for a few years. The work, however, proceeded, and this period was used for careful surveys. With return to power of the Government of Sir John A. MacDonald, work proceeded more rapidly and the road was eventually pushed through in 1885.

These political events emphasize the importance of the railway in the political situation at the time and afford some indication of the economic strain that was involved in the project. What was required was a railway to cross approximately 2,000 miles of virtually uninhabited country crossing both the Canadian Shield and the Rocky Mountains. With regard to the Shield country, Sanford Fleming, the Engineer in Chief of the Canadian Pacific Railway, wrote: "No civilized man, as far as known, had ever passed from the valley of the Upper Ottawa through the intervening wilderness to Lake Superior. The country east and west of Lake Nipigon was all but a *terra incognita*."[5] The cost of the project far exceeded the estimates, and repeated government loans were necessary, notably a loan from the British House of Commons in 1883 of 22,500,000 dollars. The Government gave assistance in several forms to the project, including a subsidy of 25 million dollars in cash, extensive land grants, and turning over without charge 710 miles of line built at government expense at a cost of 38 million dollars.[6]

Once completed, however, the railway was a grand success both from a financial and from a developmental point of view. One incident of its construction had been the discovery of the major source of nickel and copper in the vicinity of Sudbury, north of Lake Huron. The whole of the plains area was opened to agricultural settlement. In 1871 the population of the entire western part of Canada, including the settlements in British Columbia, had been about 100,000. After the Canadian Pacific was completed in 1885 the population increased, and, by 1901, the population of the area was 600,000. The great growth in population came from 1901 to 1911, however. In that period the population of Manitoba, Saskatchewan, Alberta, British Columbia, and Yukon went from 600,000 to 1,700,000.[7] Note that this period is sixteen to twenty-six years after the initial completion of the railroad.

5. Quoted by Glazebrook, *op. cit.*, pp. 257–258.
6. See Easterbrook and Aitken, *op. cit.*, Ch. XVIII.
7. Glazebrook, *op. cit.*, p. 316.

The very success of the railway created political repercussions. Protests had become increasingly vociferous by the end of the century. The people in the newly settled regions felt that they were at the mercy of a railway monopoly that charged exorbitant freight rates and appropriated to its own benefit the fruits of their labor. Hearings were held and statistics cited to show, for example, that the through rates on wheat from Winnipeg to Toronto, over the Shield, a distance of 1,287 miles, were 50 cents per 100 pounds; whereas similar rates on the Grand Trunk from Ingersoll to Halifax, an almost identical distance, 1,283 miles, were only 31.5 cents per 100 pounds. The defenders of the company, of course, argued in terms of the high cost of operation over the "bridge" across the Shield.[8]

Private monopoly, however, proved politically intolerable. The result was that not one but two new railroads were constructed! One of these, the Grand Trunk Pacific, required government support for construction. Plans were crystallized in 1903 and the road was put through by September 1914. The Canadian Northern, meanwhile, was stitched together out of a group of prairie lines. It was built in a patchwork way, with much cheaper original construction than had characterized the Grand Trunk Pacific. Public assistance was not on a large scale, though it was involved because of contracts that existed with the constituent railways. This through line to the Pacific was completed in 1915. Although the Canadian Pacific had made money as soon as it was running, the Grand Trunk Pacific and the Canadian Northern were in financial difficulties. The two lines were built to compete with each other, and in some areas went side by side along the same route. Through the major pass in the Rockies, Yellowhead Pass, for example, the two lines went side by side!

Later economic commentators have looked back at this development without enthusiasm. Easterbrook and Aitken observe that there were alternative policies not adequately considered. Private monopoly can be curbed by government regulation. If competition is a necessity, might not one competitor be enough? They note that government approval of the additional roads was given in an "atmosphere of optimism and nationalistic self-confidence."[9] Caves and Holton observe wryly that the second and third transcontinental roads can be excluded from any list of investments necessary to develop wheat production. They trace the successful development to the original railroad and branch lines, the

8. Glazebrook, *op. cit.*, p. 306.
9. Easterbrook and Aitken, *op. cit.*, Ch. XIV.

long rise in grain prices on the world market up to 1920, and such factors as the development of strains of wheat with a shorter growing season more suitable for a northern climate.[10] It is hard to escape the conclusion that overoptimism led to overinvestment in the Canadian railroad system in the period 1900–1915.

It became painfully apparent that the country could not afford three transcontinental systems and soon the government nationalized and consolidated the two new lines. This reorganization was completed in 1923: the combined railroads becoming the Canadian National Railways with total assets of over 2 billion dollars. An idea of the continuing importance of the railways in Canada may be gleaned from the fact that the gross national product of Canada in current dollars in 1920 was about 5.5 billion. The continuing burden on the economy may be indicated by the fact that in the 1930s the deficit on the Canadian National Railways accounted for up to 11 per cent of the federal budget.

The solution to the problem of the organization of transportation, which was adopted in 1923 and has stood the test of time, was to have two major transportation companies. Of the two companies one continues to be privately owned and managed, the second is a nationalized undertaking. The policy of the Canadian Government has been to permit each of these two corporations to develop as a general transportation company with investments in other kinds of transportation in addition to railways. This form of organization of the transportation industry is distinctively Canadian. It is in sharp contrast to American policy of the separation of the ownership of different modes of transportation.[11]

By World War I industry accounted for approximately the same proportion of the national product of Canada as agriculture. Since that time, and especially since World War II, there has been a tremendous industrial development in Canada that has been closely linked to the United States and has involved such industries as petroleum, wood pulp and paper, and iron ore. From a transportation point of view this development has been associated with the development of railways, especially the development of trunk lines in a north-south direction, which represented the last major phase in the development of the Canadian railway network. Since 1920 there has been little expansion in the total number of miles of railway in operation in Canada.

10. Richard E. Caves and Richard H. Holton, *The Canadian Economy: Prospect and Retrospect,* Harvard University Press, 1959, pp. 198–199.

11. See the discussion of "Diversification of railroads into other forms of transportation," Chapter 13.

CONCLUDING COMMENTS—In the development of Canada, public policy with respect to transportation was essentially similar to that in the United States and in contrast to that, for example, in Great Britain. Transportation networks had to be constructed. Both the political integration of the country and its future economic development required transportation. The sums involved were too large and the risk of financial failure too great for reliance on private enterprise. In the United States the role of public initiative and support gradually diminished especially after the completion of the early transcontinental railroads. By the end of the nineteenth century it was possible in the United States for the government to leave the further development and operation of the railroads in private hands subject only to regulation by the government. In Canada, however, the national government was forced to take over the railways that became the Canadian National, essentially because of the smaller population of the country and the slower rate of economic development. The necessity for subsidies still continues in some parts of the country. For example, in the maritime provinces, southeastern Quebec, and Newfoundland, the shipment of freight is subsidized, the government paying from 20 to 30 per cent of the normal charge and the shipper paying the rest—according to arrangements concluded in 1957.

Canada has been described as "an experiment in transportation." The successful economic development of the country has been the result of the success of that experiment. As a country characterized by difficult terrain and long distances, Canada has benefited in the past and stands to benefit in the future from any improvements in technology that reduce the cost of transportation.

9

Transportation in the Economic Development of the Soviet Union

THIS CHAPTER will focus attention on the broad choices of policy made in the period between the accession to power of the Communists and World War II, by which time the Soviet Union had become an industrial power. There was already in existence a reasonably complete railroad network at the beginning of this period. This discussion, therefore, is concerned with a later stage in the development of the country than that discussed in the preceding chapters. For example, the parallel to the development of the Canadian Pacific would be the construction of the railway across Siberia, which will not be considered. In Tsarist Russia, railroads were regarded by the government as the foundation of industrialization and were pushed forward ahead of demand. The Soviets, as will be discussed below, reversed this policy.[1]

In any consideration of the relation between transportation and economic growth the more recent experience in the Union of Soviet Socialist Republics is of interest because of the size and importance of the Soviet Union. The difference in political and economic organization

1. See the account in J. N. Westwood, *A History of Russian Railways,* George Allen and Unwin, Ltd., 1964.

between the Soviet Union and the free world presents leads to interesting differences in transportation policy, yet there are also similarities.

There are special difficulties for the Western or American economist in the study of Soviet transportation. When the language barrier has been surmounted, there is still the difference in intellectual approach. The Soviet discussions of economic problems have a political, almost a theological, tone often foreign to the Western academic economist. Finally, much statistical information is not completely available outside the Soviet Union. Much information is available, however, and a small group of specialists on the subject have been able to piece together and make available to economists generally a reasonably complete and intelligible picture of the main course of events with regard to transportation. The emphasis in the following discussion is on four topics: the choice of means of transportation; the policy of utilization of railroads to the maximum of their capacity; location policy; and rate policy. It may be noted at the outset that any one of these four topics could be discussed in the context of a capitalist economy. It is the choice of *organization* of the industry that is restricted in the Soviet Union, public ownership is the only politically acceptable arrangement.

Choice of Means of Transportation

In any modern economy there is a choice among several systems of transportation. Emphasis can be placed on railroads, highways, pipelines, inland waterways, air transportation, or on a wide variety of combinations of these methods. By some means or other this choice must be made in a communist economy as well as in a capitalist economy. There is no doubt of the choice made by the Soviet planners. The whole emphasis has been on transportation by railway. In 1963 the railroads handled 88 per cent of the freight, in terms of ton-miles of traffic.[2, 3] Furthermore, the percentage of freight traffic carried by the railroads has shown a tendency to rise slowly since the period of the First Five-Year Plan, 1928–1932. While the future may bring some change in this picture, any change is likely to be gradual, and it can

2. *Annual Economic Indicators for the U.S.S.R.*, prepared for the Joint Economic Committee, Congress of the United States, United States Government Printing Office, 1964. (In 1963 the railroads handled 1,745 of a total of 1,984 billion ton-kilometers of freight traffic exclusive of freight moved by sea. See p. 218.)

3. James H. Blackman, "Transport Development and Locomotive Technology in the Soviet Union," University of South Carolina, Bureau of Business and Economic Research, *Essays in Economics*, No. 3, February 1957.

be expected that for years to come the main emphasis in freight transportation in the Soviet Union will be on the railroads. Certainly, the
railroads moved the bulk freight throughout the period of industrialization discussed here.

ECONOMIC GEOGRAPHY AS A REASON FOR THE EMPHASIS ON RAIL-
ROADS—In part the explanation of this emphasis on railroads is to be
found in the economic geography of the Soviet Union. Distances are
long, there are few mountains, and most of the country is remarkably
flat. As a result, more than half of the main line trackage has gradients
below one-half of 1 per cent. Less than 5 per cent of the total first main
track operated has a ruling gradient in excess of 1 per cent.[4]

The rivers of Russia, historically, had been famous transportation
systems. The ancient route between the Byzantine Empire and Scan-
dinavia on the Dnepr River and the traffic on the Volga River are well
known. But from a modern point of view these rivers suffer from several
disadvantages. Roughly speaking the rivers flow north and south both
in European Russia and in Siberia. The main flow of freight traffic,
however, is now east and west, especially in Siberia and in the region
beyond the Urals. The Siberian rivers suffer from the additional disadvantage that they freeze in the winter throughout their length and
then melt in the spring, but the southern part of the river melts first.
The ice in the northern stretches dams up the waters and produces formidable floods. The Volga and the Dnepr do not suffer from this type
of flood, but they are frozen for several months. Rivers in flat country
tend to flow in serpentine channels so that distances by river are typically much longer than by rail in the Soviet plains.

The possibilities of development of coastal shipping in the Soviet
Union also are seriously limited by geography. Shipping on the Caspian
and the Black Seas is basically limited by the extent of the seas themselves. The northern oceans along the Arctic frontier of the Soviet
Union, of course, are frequently icebound.

Although these geographical conditions limit the possibilities and
make railroads particularly attractive in the Soviet Union a range of
choice still remains. It is official Soviet policy to develop a unified deep
water transportation system within the Soviet Union although actual
development has been slow.[5] From 1913 to 1957 waterborne commerce

4. See for a detailed distribution of miles of roadway by class of ruling gradient in
1933, Holland Hunter, *Soviet Transportation Policy,* Harvard University Press, 1957,
pp. 18–19.

5. Andrei Lebed and Boris Yakovlev, *Soviet Waterways, the Development of the
Inland Navigation System in the U.S.S.R.,* Institute for the Study of the U.S.S.R.,
December 1956.

grew by less than three times while rail traffic grew eighteen times.[6] In 1963 rivers carried only 6 per cent of all ton-kilometers of freight in inland transport.[7]

PIPELINES—From a technical point of view it would have been possible for the Soviets to develop a network of pipelines to move petroleum products over long distances much more rapidly than they have chosen to proceed. Until the last few years no pipelines over twelve inches in diameter existed in the Soviet Union, whereas twenty-four to thirty inch lines have been common in the United States since World War II. As late as 1959, Williams reported no lines over twelve inches whatsoever in the Soviet Union, but more recently there has been a development of large diameter pipelines. By 1963 pipelines accounted for 5 per cent of ton-kilometers of freight movement, the number of ton-kilometers moved by pipeline having more than doubled from 1959 to 1963.

HIGHWAYS—The development of highway transportation is technically an additional possibility. There were about three million trucks in the Soviet Union in 1959 compared to nearly twelve million in the United States at that date. Williams reports that the average length of haul by truck in 1956 was only 11.5 km., implying use of trucks for local service to the exclusion of line-haul movements. In 1963 only 2 per cent of freight ton-kilometers were by truck.[8] Here, also, further expansion at an earlier date would have been possible. Westwood suggests one reason for the lack of development of highway transport. It is usually the responsibility of the users of the transportation system to pay the cost of loading and unloading vehicles. Soviet transport planners tend to ignore costs paid by others.[9] Advantages of trucks in low terminal costs may have been underestimated. Further, in the United States a highway system was developed largely in response to public desire for travel in private automobiles. Trucks could take advantage of this system, paying only part of the cost. No comparable development of passenger cars has taken place in the Soviet Union. Development of trucking implied development of a highway system for the use of the trucks.

Were the economic planners in the Soviet Union justified in the decision to rely primarily on one means of transportation during the

6. Ernest W. Williams, *Freight Transportation in the Soviet Union,* Occasional Paper 65, National Bureau of Economic Research, 1959.
7. *Annual Economic Indicators for the U.S.S.R.,* p. 218.
8. Williams, *op. cit.* See also *Annual Economic Indicators for the U.S.S.R.,* p. 218.
9. Westwood, *op. cit.,* p. 291.

early period of industrialization? This question can be answered only by an expert in Soviet economics. In the United States use of more than one method of transportation is necessary to achieve the lowest possible cost of production and distribution of goods including the cost of transportation. One may speculate that concentration on a single mode made more sense for the Soviet Union as a temporary strategy for rapid industrialization, under the conditions inherited by the Soviets, than as a long run strategy for obtaining efficiency in the use of resources.

Policy of Maximum Utilization of Railroads

A second choice to be made by any government which assumes responsibility for developing its transportation system is where to aim between the extremes of building well ahead of the demand or investing in its transportation system only as it is forced to invest to meet present needs. Again, there is no doubt as to the choice made by the Soviets: it was to invest no more than absolutely necessary. The counterpart of the policy of concentrating freight movement on the railroads was a policy of minimizing investment in railroads. This strategy is shown most clearly by the history of the First Five-Year Plan.

TRANSPORTATION IN THE FIRST FIVE-YEAR PLAN—The forced industrialization of the Soviet Union began with the First Five-Year Plan in 1928. The Soviets had inherited a railway system that in 1916 carried about 91 billions of metric ton-kilometers. The history of the years from 1916 to 1928 is one of disorganization and subsequent reconstruction, and it was not until 1928 that the volume of freight traffic reached the 1916 level.[10]

The position adopted by the planners, especially from 1928 on, was that the task of all the transport media, especially the railroads, was to provide the necessary accommodation for economic growth, but not to precede growth or to induce it. As already noted, this position is the exact opposite of the strategy followed in the early economic development under the Tsars, as well as in the United States and Canada where transportation came first.

How successful the planners were in increasing the output of transportation in the First Five-Year Plan while concentrating investment in heavy industry rather than transportation may be indicated by the following index numbers. In each case the 1928 figure is set as 100.

10. Hunter, *op. cit.*, p. 331.

On this basis the number of freight locomotives had increased by 1933 to 125.5, the number of freight cars to 143.6, but the volume of freight traffic had increased to 181.5.[11] How was the increase in output per unit of capital achieved?

In the early years of the First Five-Year Plan the policy of holding down investment in the railways while forcing up their output can only be regarded as a success. The excess capacity that seems to have existed in the system in 1928 could be utilized. But by the end of the period the policy had been pushed too far. The result was a bottleneck so serious that it enlisted Stalin's personal direct attention. The usual symptom of an overburdened transportation system is a backlog of unshipped freight. By the end of 1932 there was in the Soviet Union a huge backlog of unshipped freight that has been estimated at about twenty million tons. This situation did not develop without some preliminary warning. Apparently the difficulty in completing all shipments required of grain and iron ore in 1929 and 1930 was not of a magnitude to create a general economic crisis. But by 1934, Stalin was saying to the Seventeenth Party Congress: "Transportation is a bottleneck that can check, and is already beginning to check, our whole economic policy, and first of all our distribution of commodities." He went on to say: ". . . in addition to helping the transportation system by providing workers and equipment, our task is to root out the bureaucratic-routine attitude prevalent in transportation administration and make it more efficient." In case any of the audience had missed the point, in a subsequent address Voroshilov stated: "Now that Comrade Stalin is really turning his attention to transportation, comrades, you may be sure that all joking is going to be laid aside."[12]

The transportation bottleneck was in fact broken in a period of approximately two years. Additional equipment was provided at a more rapid rate, but output rose even faster than the number of cars and locomotives added to the system. There was success in increasing the weight and speed of trains, as measured, for example, by gross freight ton-kilometers per freight train hour. There was also success in increasing the number of kilometers per locomotive day and in reducing the turnaround time for freight cars. The turnaround time fell from 10.6 days in 1928 to 8.8 days in 1934 and 7 days in 1937.[13] By 1936–1937 the average time for freight cars was sixteen hours at each end of the trip. In other words, the freight car would be emptied, reloaded, and

11. Hunter, *op. cit.*, p. 316.
12. Quoted by Hunter, *op. cit.*, pp. 55–56.
13. Westwood, *op. cit.*, p. 232.

sent on its way again in an average period of sixteen hours.[14] This speed is greater than anything attained in the United States. It must have been attained not only by exertions on the part of the railroad workers, but at the cost of trouble and expense to the shippers and receivers of commodities. The speed of freight trains increased from 14 kms. per hour in 1928, and also in 1934, to 19 kms. per hour in 1937, and later to 38 kms. per hour in 1956.[15] The doubling of traffic from 1928 to 1934, with total length of line little changed, meant that the density of traffic also doubled, from 1.2 million ton-kilometers per kilometer to 2.5 million. The total effect was to push hard against the limits of capacity. The Soviets, one might say, were exploring the shape of the short run cost curve as far to the right as they possibly could.

The government employed two techniques to shake up the routine of railroad operation: the carrot and the stick. The carrot was in the form of special rewards to Stakhanovites who achieved record performance. The successful individuals and their techniques were given wide publicity. A variant was socialist competition between work groups engaged in parallel tasks. The stick was the use of purges. The two groups who suffered most in the purges were army officers and railway managers.[16] Comrade Stalin was indeed a man to be taken seriously. Whether the results were achieved because of these measures or in spite of them, it is, of course, impossible to know.

The strategy with regard to investment in transportation, however, is clear. Both the problem of forecasting the probable use of the transportation system and the problem of estimating the amount of investment in transportation required for the movement of freight were solved by the heroic strategy of pushing vigorously ahead in other parts of the economy and adding to the investment in transportation only when the system obviously could not carry the load placed upon it.

COMPARISON WITH THE UNITED STATES IN INTENSIVENESS OF CAPITAL PLANT USE—Williams has assembled statistics that summarize the difference between the United States and the Soviet Union with respect to the utilization of capital in railroads. They highlight the Soviet policy of intensive utilization of plant. At the time he wrote (1959) the railroads in the Soviet Union moved more ton-miles of freight than the railroads in the United States. They did so with less than half the mileage of line, thus achieving more than double the number of ton-

14. Hunter, *op. cit.*, p. 82.
15. Westwood, *op. cit.*, p. 233.
16. See the account in Westwood, *op. cit.*, Chapter VII.

miles moved per mile of line. The freight car stock was about half that of the United States, and it was primarily in two axle units rather than the four axle units common in the United States. Thus the freight car stock was used twice as intensively or more than twice. This achievement was possible because of a difference in average freight car turn-around time, then less than seven days in the Soviet Union but fifteen or more in the United States. The aggregate tractive power of the stock of locomotives, similarly, was just over half as great in the Soviet Union as in the United States.

For the policy of intensive utilization the same type of questions arise as for the policy of concentration on the railroads. Are the economic planners of the Soviet Union justified in pushing so far in their efforts to maximize output per unit investment? From the point of view of the economic theorist, a policy of minimizing the use of capital in one industry at all costs in terms of other inputs cannot be defended as a general policy. The efficient entrepreneur is thought of as adjusting the proportions of inputs that he employs for a given purpose taking into account the relative prices of the inputs and their relative contributions to output. In the simple case of two factors of production he will arrive ideally at a solution where:

$$\frac{\text{price of a unit of factor } a}{\text{price of a unit of factor } b} = \frac{\text{marginal output of a unit of } a}{\text{marginal output of a unit of } b}$$

In the Soviet Union, however, the planners may proceed as if unskilled labor were in excess supply, a free factor of production. If such labor is factor a, it would be efficient to add labor wherever it can be used to generate any marginal output. For example, it would be efficient to have laborers at a shipping point ready to unload or reload freight cars immediately whenever the cars were received even if the laborers had to wait for the cars or work at inconvenient hours. The Soviets have a policy of loading and unloading transportation equipment on a seven day week basis.

There may be a case for proceeding as if unskilled labor were free in a developing economy. It seems doubtful that it is ever efficient to ignore all costs incurred by the plants served by the transportation facilities because of the limited availability of transportation. For example, what inventory policy do plant managers adopt in order to protect themselves against difficulties in obtaining transportation at times of peak loads on the railroads? What costs are involved when shortages of key materials or machines disrupt production? Such questions are not easily answered in any country, and for the Soviet Union may be unanswerable altogether.

Location Policy and Transport Policy

There is a necessary relationship in long run economic planning between decisions as to the location of industrial activity and decisions as to transportation. The objectives of location policy in the Soviet Union, however, were complex and changed over the period 1928–1941. Broadly speaking it was the objective of the economic planners in the Soviet Union to increase regional self-sufficiency. This objective was established in part for the purpose of cutting down on freight shipments. Similarly, a more even development of the country has been an objective. In the years prior to World War II, it was the economic strategy of the Soviet planners to shift industrial development outward from the older centers, especially eastward—away from the frontier.

GIANT PLANTS AND SUPER TRUNK LINES—This broad objective, however, had to be reconciled with another basic goal of the planners that was maximum speed in economic development. If one wishes to develop an economy rapidly, in general it is easier to do so in existing centers of production. Another basic characteristic of the Five-Year Plans, especially in the early years of industrialization, was emphasis on obtaining maximum economies of scale and centralizing production in giant plants. The policy of giant plants inevitably led to a policy of developing intensively the rail lines that served those plants. Thus, the policy of centralization of production was matched with a policy of centralization of railroad activities on a limited number of trunk lines, or super trunk lines, that were utilized to a maximum of capacity. The result of all these forces was a pattern in which a limited number of new plants appeared, which were widely scattered, but formed definite clusters in about five districts. By the end of the 1930s, however, there was a shift in this policy away from emphasis on the giant plants and toward the completion of smaller facilities. It was found that the smaller factories could be brought into production more rapidly than some of the giant installations.[17]

SHIFT TO THE "EAST"—The part played by the "East" in the success of the Russians in withstanding the attack of the Germans in World War II is an interesting topic in itself, but is beyond the scope

17. See Hunter, *op. cit.*, p. 24ff., for a general discussion of locational policy and its relation to transportation.

of this chapter. A discussion of the shift in the location of industrial output may be found in Hunter. He comes to the conclusion that the shift in economic activity to the eastward was important but less important than the impression that has been given in some of the accounts. The importance of the East seems to have been exaggerated and its growth over-emphasized by the simple device of shifting the dividing line between the West and the East, so that more of what was formerly the West was included with the East.

The choice of location of economic activity is a topic inherently complex, and the best solutions to problems of location are not easily arrived at. It is not clear, however, that the planners of the Soviet Union have been sophisticated in their approach to the problem. Some of their discussions in print, in fact, give the impression that the achievement of gains in the reduction of transportation costs should be equated with the achievement of net gains for the economy. Such a view rules out a priori the possibility of substituting transportation for other inputs in the productive process. The practical policies may have been better than the theory. The early policy of giant plants, for example, may have been an efficient means of utilizing a limited supply of skilled engineering personnel. We may note that this policy has been followed much less persistently than the policy of relying on the railroads for freight movement.

Policy in Rate Making

USE OF FREIGHT RATES TO REGULATE THE ECONOMY—In view of the extraordinary amount of attention that has been paid to railroad freight rates in Western economics, it is a matter of interest to examine how freight rates are determined in the Soviet Union and what their relation is to the overall objectives of Soviet economic policy. Immediately after the Revolution much traffic was moved free. The rate structure that was established with the New Economic Policy was extremely simple. In 1920 all commodities were classified into seven categories. These categories reflected basic policy objectives. Special low carload rates were provided for four of the seven that were believed to be of the greatest national importance. The remaining three categories were classified by size of shipment. From this early date, therefore, freight rates were used by the government as an instrument of economic policy. The favored commodities were the bulk commodities essential to the economy.

The rate structure developed gradually through the 1920s with a steadily increasing margin between the most favored and least favored categories of freight. By 1929, Westwood reports, the ratio of lowest to highest rates had reached 1 to 28. Use of railroad rates was made to curb the private sector of the economy when the transition was being made from the New Economic Policy to the First Five-Year Plan. A 50 to 100 per cent surcharge was added to the charges for the movement of private freight beginning in 1926.[18] A formal review of freight rates was undertaken which led to introduction of a new rate system in 1931. The principles proposed at that time were that individual freight rates should be "brought close to" the cost of shipping for each commodity. Commodities selected for special treatment should be charged 65 per cent of their shipping costs, and all others should be charged enough to make up the implied deficit. The policy of using railroad rates to regulate the economy, however, was continued. The structure was designed in such a way as to afford a subsidy to heavy industry. Thus, the freight rate structure was used as one device in the government's policy of stimulating overall economic development through the development of heavy industry at the expense of the development of the rest of the economy. The policy of extra charges for any goods not belonging to the socialist sector was continued. In contrast to recent American experience, profits on passenger service have helped to subsidize freight service since about 1930.

USE OF FREIGHT RATES TO PROMOTE REGIONAL SELF-SUFFICIENCY —An additional feature of the freight rate policy was the shape of the relation of rates to length of haul. During the 1930s the rates on long hauls were kept low relative to short hauls—probably lower than would have been justified by the relative cost of shipment over different distances. Near the end of the 1930s, however, official attention was directed increasingly to problems of excessive shipments and waste of transportation facilities through long hauls. The rate structure was changed and the rates for the very long hauls sharply increased. The objective was to further the objective of increased regional self-sufficiency.

USE OF FREIGHT RATES TO MAXIMIZE UTILIZATION OF EQUIPMENT —An additional feature of Soviet rate policy has been the use of demurrage charges to expedite car movements. Westwood reports that as of 1955 receivers of shipments had one clear day to unload a car, with fines at 3 roubles per car hour for the first six hours rising to 15 roubles per car hour after eighteen hours.[19]

18. Westwood, *op. cit.*, p. 218.
19. Westwood, *op. cit.*, p. 263.

This very brief review of Soviet policy with regard to freight rates is intended to emphasize two aspects of that policy: first, the government used freight rates, even as early as 1920, to control the development of the economy and stimulate certain parts of the economy while holding back the development of other parts. Second, policy with regard to freight rates was closely tied to policy with regard to the location of industry. Freight rates were used as tools in achieving broad objectives with regard to the location of economic activity.

An alternative policy would have been to base freight rates strictly on the relative cost of freight shipments. As indicated, cost considerations did play an important part in the development of the freight rate structure, but costs were subordinated to other economic considerations. This tendency to emphasize other considerations is consistent with the overall policy of the planners of the Soviet economy, who always have been less interested in the efficient allocation of resources than in the rapid industrialization of the country.

CONCLUDING COMMENTS—The whole emphasis in Soviet transport policy has been on extracting as much service as possible from a minimal capital investment in a single transportation system, the railroads. It is apparent from the record that this policy has been a success in that large volumes of freight have been moved and bottlenecks in transportation have not ordinarily limited economic development. Whether the policy of minimizing transport inputs has been pushed too far and has led to excessive use of other inputs is a possibility, but the evidence to date seems inconclusive.

10

Transportation in India

IN A DISCUSSION of the role of transportation in economic development, attention should be paid to countries that have failed to indus-
trialize as well as to those that have in this respect succeeded.

India is one of the largest underdeveloped countries of the world.
It is easier for Western economists to obtain access to the materials
necessary to study Indian than Chinese transportation policy, because
of the political situation and because the Indians write in the English
language. The population of India is of the magnitude of 450 millions,
of whom about one-fifth live in cities and four-fifths in villages. Average
per capita income is currently estimated to be in the neighborhood of
65 to 70 dollars a year. Such statistics cannot convey the difference in
the way of life between India and the United States, but do help to convey the correct impression that most people in India are poor. Many
live at the margin of existence, and others at standards that are in
varying degrees higher but still represent poverty by American standards.

Two periods are of interest in connection with economic policy
toward transportation in India. Before independence the questions of
interest are related to the introduction of mechanized transportation in
the country in the second half of the nineteenth century and its consequences. In the period since its independence, the questions of inter-

est in India concern the role of transportation in the national effort to develop the resources of the country and raise the standard of living.

Introduction of Mechanized Transportation

In the history of Indian transportation before independence two facts stand out: (1) railways were built, and (2) the country failed to develop economically. While the development of a mechanized system of transportation is a necessary condition for the development of a country, the Indian experience demonstrates that it is not a sufficient condition. A general discussion of the other prerequisites of the development of an industrial society is beyond the scope of this analysis. No doubt it is possible to point to various crucial factors that were missing in India. Here the question is raised: did some characteristics of policy toward transportation reduce the contribution to economic development made by the railways? In this context it is relevant to ask what the objectives of the British government were in the construction of the system and especially how those objectives related to economic development.

OBJECTIVES OF THE BRITISH IN DEVELOPING RAILROADS—The objectives of the British government in developing railways in India were explicitly stated in 1853 by the then Governor-General of India, Lord Dalhousie.[1] These objectives included increased facility in the administration of the country and the greater mobility that railways gave to military forces. The events of the Indian Mutiny a few years later in which a revolt led by Indians in the British army seriously challenged British rule must have strengthened this consideration in the minds of the authorities.

Lord Dalhousie also visualized a prospect of "Indian cotton for English textile mills and of a vast market for British manufacturers." This objective is economic, but it is hardly equivalent to the objective of the development of Indian manufactures. No doubt the Viceroy had in mind terms of trade that would not be too unfavorable to the English manufacturers. The possibility of losses on the operation of the railroads was envisaged, but these losses were believed to be justified by the political advantages of the railroads. They were to be borne by the Indian taxpayers.

A further objective of the development of railroads in India, the prevention of famines, was especially emphasized in the latter part of

1. Lord Dalhousie's "Minute on Railways," 4 July 1850 and 20 April 1853. In Amba Prasad, *Indian Railways*, Asia Publishing House, 1960.

the nineteenth century, subsequent to the first years of construction. On investigating a serious famine the official *Famine Commissioners* found in 1880 that the mortality due to famine was greatest in those areas where the transportation facilities were the worst. Their recommendations played a part in the subsequent period of railroad development.[2] On humanitarian grounds one can only applaud the construction of railroads to prevent famines, but the economist must note that the resulting increase in population in a poor, agricultural country must contribute to the pressure of the population on the means of subsistence.

One must conclude that the Imperial Government in the construction of railways in India in the nineteenth century did not seek primarily the economic development of the country. Of course, it does not follow that the roads would not be used for economic development, but in the details of the planning and operation of the system other considerations were paramount.

FINANCIAL STRAIN IN THE EARLY PERIOD—Construction was actually begun in 1853 by private companies who found the capital for the enterprises and carried out the construction of the railroads. They operated under a policy by which the government guaranteed a return of 5 per cent interest on their money to the investors. The contracts provided for surplus profits over 10 per cent to be divided between the companies and the government. The government also had the right to purchase the guaranteed roads after a period of twenty-five to fifty years. It was originally expected that the roads would soon make more than the 5 per cent per annum. These expectations were not justified and for years the government found itself in the position of paying a substantial sum because of the guarantees.[3]

This system of finance led to waste, in the building of the railroads, that was widely criticised at the time. For example, Sir John Lawrence, Viceroy of India, was quoted in a dispatch from his successor, Lord Mayo, on March 11, 1869, as follows:

The history of the actual operations of railway companies in India gives illustration of management as bad and extravagant as anything that the strongest opponent of government agency could suggest as likely to result from that system.

The Finance Minister of India under both these Viceroys, William N. Massey, commented:

2. D. R. Gadgil, *The Industrial Revolution of India in Recent Times,* Oxford University Press, Fourth Edition, 1942.
3. *Ibid.,* Chapter IX.

All the money came from the English capitalist, and so long as he was guaranteed five per cent on the revenues of India, it was immaterial to him whether the funds that he lent were thrown into the Hooghly or converted into brick and mortar.[4]

As a result of such criticism the government policy was changed and for a decade, beginning in 1869, construction was carried forward under state auspices. Subsequent to 1882 there was a policy of private construction without guarantees but with financial assistance from the government. In almost every case during this period, land was given free to the private company.[5] The later strategy of the government seems to have been to proceed cautiously, taking each case on its merits as it came along, without attempting to develop a clearcut national policy such as existed earlier. During this period there was some construction by the government itself. With regard to the roads that had been privately constructed, the general policy was to take up the options for government purchase as they came due, with the result that gradually the system came under government ownership and operation. Government ownership is now complete. We must conclude that the problem of finding the necessary large sums of capital for the India railroads was solved only after some costly initial errors. It would be unfair to be too harshly critical of the authorities, however, in view of the errors made elsewhere at about this time, for example by the American Congress in regard to the financing of the Union Pacific.

THE GAUGE PROBLEM AS THE HERITAGE OF EARLY DIFFICULTIES— During this period there was one major technical miscalculation the consequences of which are still felt. Some of the early roads were constructed with a broad gauge of 5 feet 6 inches. The use of a broad gauge reduces operating costs, but it requires more capital outlay per mile of line. The early financial results, as noted above, were disappointing. As a consequence the system was not completed with the broad gauge. Large sections of line were built to a gauge of one meter and some use was made of a narrow gauge of 2 feet 6 inches. The number of route kilometers for each type currently are:

Broad gauge	27,359
Meter gauge	25,063
Narrow gauge	4,320
Total	56,742

4. Quoted by Romesh Dutt, *The Economic History of India in the Victorian Age*, K. Paul, Tench, Trubner & Co. Second Edition, 1906, p. 356. Dutt is critical of British policy in India. He quotes favorably statements by Sir Arthur Cotton, the leading advocate of canals as opposed to railroads.

5. Gadgil, *op. cit.*, p. 132.

The broad gauge lines are more heavily used and account for about 83 per cent of the traffic.[6]

Viewed as a whole, the record of the development of the railroads is not impressive. The social cost was higher than it need have been and the gauge problem was not well handled. The Indian railway grid has also been criticized as providing better connections to the ports than among inland centers. From the point of view of the British, the need was for roads to the ports, but internal development would have been better served by a different arrangement.

In spite of the difficulties, however, railways were built. By 1880 the combined expenditure by the Guaranteed Companies and the State came to 125 million pounds sterling.[7] By that year there were two rail routes from the capital, Delhi, in the center of the country to Bombay on the west coast.[8] The Indian railway grid has always remained a coarse network in comparison to more developed countries. At the present time the 35,000 miles of railroad route in India contrast to about 230,000 in the United States.

RATE POLICY—The economic consequences of any railroad system reflect its rate structure. Rates can be powerful economic forces in determining what traffic will move. The main outlines of the government policy with regard to the regulation of rates were established in 1887. The policy was announced of establishing maxima and minima for railroad rates but leaving a margin within which the companies were free to set rates as they chose. For the most part the companies seem to have used a value of service principle in pricing not dissimilar to that found in other parts of the world, that is, with substantial departures from cost but with cost still a conspicuous factor.

PORT RATES—A special feature of rate policy in India was the establishment of low rates to ports. This policy favored the import of foreign goods and the export of raw materials and, in the view of the Indian commercial interests, discouraged the industrial development of the country. The policy was not officially stated as such and publicly defended, but was brought out in the proceedings before a series of investigation commissions. Thus, an *Industrial Commission* in 1916–1918 chaired by Sir Thomas Holland recommended that:

6. *Report by the Railway Board on Indian Railways for 1962–63,* Ministry of Railways, 1964, Table I and p. 92.
7. Dutt, *op. cit.,* p. 362.
8. *Report of the Railway Freight Structure Enquiry Committee,* Government of India, Ministry of Railways, 1955–1957, Vol. 1, Part 1.

Internal traffic should be rated as nearly as possible on an equality with traffic of the same class and over similar distances to and from the ports [and particularly so] in the case of raw materials to and from an Indian manufacturing center.[9]

Yet, the *Wedgwood Committee* (1937) still was "impressed with the feeling of grievance that appeared to exist in regard to these [port] rates."[10] The rate for cotton from the sources of production to the principal Indian ports was higher than the rate to interior towns. For example, the rate from Navsari to Calcutta, a distance of 1,168 miles, was less than the rate from the same production center to the interior town of Kanpur, a distance of only 831 miles. Similarly, rates were less from the cotton producing center of Barwal to Calcutta than to Kanpur, even though the difference in mileage was even more extreme, 1,191 to Calcutta against 761 miles to Kanpur.

ECONOMIC CONSEQUENCES OF THE RAILWAYS—Given the nature of the railroad route structure and the system of low port rates, it followed that the inland centers of production were at a disadvantage. First, the indigenous handicraft industries were put at an economic disadvantage since they had to compete with the ports and with foreign production. Authors differ in the emphasis placed on the destructive consequences to Indian industry. There is no question of the destruction to the Indian handicraft industries. In particular, the machine made British textiles pre-empted the important market for cloth. Daniel Thorner, however, unlike some earlier writers, dates the destruction of Indian handicrafts prior to the railroads.[11] No doubt the railroads played a part in the process, however. Thus they contributed to technological unemployment among such groups as the weavers. This process was essentially the same as that which destroyed the same handicrafts in Europe. The result in both cases was increasing reliance on the economies of scale of factory production. The difference was that the factories were in England, and not in India, at least in the early days.

The development of railroads also tended to stimulate the growth of the principal ports, especially Bombay and Calcutta, which were unimportant before the British period. The stimulation to the ports came partly from the increased flow of exports and imports through their facilities. It also came from the development of industry in the ports,

---

9. In the *Railway Freight Structure Enquiry Committee,* 1955–1957.

10. This discussion follows Prasad, *op. cit.,* pp. 236–237.

11. Daniel Thorner, *Investment in Empire, British Railway and Steam Shipping Enterprise in India 1825–1849,* University of Pennsylvania Press, 1950.

since the local entrepreneurs as well as foreign traders were benefited by the low rates from interior centers to the ports. Low rates on cotton and wool to Bombay contributed to the development of the manufacture of textiles in Bombay. Low rates on wheat, oilseeds, and jute to Calcutta stimulated exports but also led to flour, oil, and jute mills.

Thus, the development of the railroads tended to stimulate the growth of these industries. It also stimulated the coal mining industry. A basic problem of the coal mining industry everywhere is transferring the coal from pit head to the ultimate consumer. Without railroads, or another system of bulk transportation, coal mining is economically impossible.

Finally there was a leveling of prices throughout India, especially the prices on food grains. This leveling of prices, and especially the improvement of the distribution of supplies, undoubtedly helped to prevent local shortages and famines as the *Famine Commissioners* had desired.

The economic effects of the railways were not entirely beneficial to the Indian economy. The handicrafts were destroyed and replaced, partly by factories located primarily in the port cities of India, and partly by factories in Europe. Coal mining was stimulated and with it industries based on the use of coal, but heavy industry developed only to a very limited extent. There were inefficiencies in the development of the railways. (Some inefficiency can be found in the development of railways elsewhere, as illustrated in previous chapters.) While a railroad system developed in a different manner with a different rate structure would have been more beneficial to the development of Indian industry, the principal reasons for the slow rate of growth of the country prior to independence are not to be found in the lack of mechanized transportation or in the operation of the railroads.

Policy Since Independence

India since independence has been engaged in an ambitious program of stimulating economic growth. Investment policy, therefore, tends to occupy the center of attention. As in other countries there are two basic questions of investment policy: the level of investment in transportation as opposed to other sectors of the economy; and the allocation of transportation investment among the modes of transportation. Should the economic planners follow the pattern of the Soviet Union and concentrate on a single system of transportation for the movement of heavy freight? Should they develop transportation only to the extent absolutely necessary to permit the development of heavy industry? Or should the strategy be similar to that followed in the United States: active encouragement of investment in transportation ahead of demand; and reliance on more than one system of transportation? As we shall see, the policy has been different with regard to the different modes of transportation.

INLAND WATER TRANSPORT—In India, as in the other countries discussed, there was a period prior to the construction of the first railroads when water transportation was developed. Boats powered by steam appeared as early as 1832 in the vicinity of Calcutta and in 1842 service was extended for a long distance inland on the Ganga River system to Agra. This development was not as revolutionary as the first English and American canals since country boats had long operated on the Ganga, the principal river of India. New motive power was applied in new vehicles but on an existing route.

While this service was important prior to the railroads, inland water transportation in India has deteriorated. Traffic over government maintained channels has been estimated at approximately 1 per cent of the tonnage of goods moved by the railways.[12] On the Ganga on January 1, 1958 the steamers that had plied that river for many years closed down their operation. They claimed that they lost money because of competition from roads and railroads, difficulties of navigation, aging of their vessels, and the difficulty of replacing them with new equipment.

The river was thus left to the country boats, which work today as they have for centuries. It has been estimated that there are about 2,000 such boats employing four or five men each and costing about 5,000 rupees (approximately 1,000 dollars). These boats are towed upstream by ropes pulled by men. No mechanical power is employed.

Would an investment of public money be justified to expand river transport on the Ganga system? There are basic difficulties in operating boats on this river and its tributaries owing to the nature of the river. The flow varies widely during the year from the monsoon to the dry season. During the flood season the discharge from the river is about nine times as great as it is during the rest of the year. This extreme fluctuation in flow creates problems not the least of which is the tendency for changes to occur in the course of the river where it flows through flat country. These changes are so drastic as to make it difficult to locate shore facilities in such a way that they can be relied on for perma-

12. S. C. Bose, *Modern Economic Geography*, Fifth Edition, 1958.

nent use. These characteristics have made bridging it a difficult problem, with consequences for the development of railroads and highways, which will be discussed below. They would make expensive the construction of channels, docks, and harbor facilities. The failure of the authorities to act to preserve the river steamers implies a policy of avoiding massive investment in river transportation. The technical difficulties certainly make this policy understandable.

ROAD TRANSPORT—Transport by road is of basic importance in India because of the limitations of the rail grid. The rural areas that are not in close touch with a railroad must depend upon roads and highways for economic communication with the rest of the country.

A brief description of the existing system is necessary to an understanding of the question of policy. The basic form of transportation in rural India, as it has been for centuries, is the bullock cart. One estimate is that there are about nine million bullock carts in India.[13] There were in 1962 about 321,000 passenger cars and 275,000 commercial vehicles.[14]

CHARACTERISTICS OF THE ROAD NETWORK—These vehicles operate on a rudimentary system of roads. The defects in the Indian road network are somewhat characteristic of the road systems of underdeveloped countries. Bose in 1958 listed the following: a) Large gaps in the network especially in hilly regions where circuitous routes often must be used. b) The roads often are narrow, and bridges very narrow. In this connection it may be noted that the objective of the *Nagpur Plan,* described below, has been to provide on all arterial routes, road services improved at least to *one* lane in width. On the main roads in the vicinity of large towns it is planned to widen the roads to two lanes. c) Many rivers are unbridged. Ferries are provided at some points but arrangements for crossing are not available at all points. Long lines of cars and trucks may often have to wait hours for ferries. d) Surfaces are not always well kept. e) Especially in eastern India there are disjoined links from one point to another and few trunk roads. The large rivers typically are not bridged.

Nevertheless the total mileage of surfaced rural roads had been increased under the Second Five-Year Plan to about 144,000 miles in 1960–1961. Hence, roughly speaking there was one quarter of a mile of surfaced rural road per motor vehicle. The number of motor vehicles per mile of road is sensitive to what definition of road is used. *Basic Road Statistics of India* published an estimate of 1.3 motor vehicles per

13. *Ibid.,* p. 608.
14. *United Nations Statistical Yearbook,* 1963.

mile of road in India in 1956 as against 21.4 in the United States. Whatever the exact calculation, traffic densities on rural roads in India are very low by American standards. It also follows that expenditure on highway per motor vehicle in India is high. Wilfred Owen cites an estimate of 342.0 dollars per vehicle in India in 1960 compared to 151.3 dollars in the United States.[15]

INVESTMENT PLANNING FOR ROADS—Plans for major programs of investment in Indian roads have been proposed. In 1943, a detailed plan for the development of the road network was developed known as the *Nagpur Plan*. This scheme called for a division of roads into four classes based on the governmental agency that maintained and developed that part of the road network: national highways, state highways, district roads, and village roads. This classification has been retained. The *Nagpur Plan* called for trebling the road mileage in ten years; this ambitious program was drastically curtailed. The amount proposed in 1946 of 145 crores of rupees may be compared to Rs. 27 crores actually spent under the First Five-Year Plan. Nevertheless, in the ten years of the first two Five-Year Plans, the mileage of surfaced roads other than municipal roads was increased from about 98,000 in 1950–1951 to about 144,000 in 1960–1961. In the Third Five-Year Plan it was proposed to add about 20,000 more miles of surfaced roads, a less rapid rate of expansion than in the first two plans. Some additional mileage was to be constructed in the local programs.[16]

By 1960 a new twenty-year plan had been developed by highway officials for the period ending in 1980–1981. The following statistics indicate the nature of the plan:[17]

	Nagpur Plan Mileage	Mileage Expected in 1960–61	Target Proposed by 1980–81
National Highways	20,000	13,800	32,000
State Highways	53,000	35,000	70,000
Major District Roads	50,000	95,200	150,000
Other District Roads	70,000	78,300	180,000
Village Roads	138,000	156,700	225,000
Total	331,000	379,000	657,000

Study of these statistics shows how the mileage of national and state highways in 1960–1961 was much less than the *Nagpur Plan* objectives, while the local roads met the *Nagpur Plan* targets in terms of mileage.

15. Wilfred Owen, *Strategy for Mobility*, Brookings Institution, p. 209.
16. *Third Five-Year Plan: A Draft Outline*, Planning Commission, Government of India, 1960, pp. 247–248.
17. *Indian Roads Congress*, Silver Jubilee Souvenir, January 1960, p. 69.

The meaning of the 1980–1981 target may be understood in terms of the stated objectives:

The broad objective of the Plan is to bring every Village:
(i) in a developed and agricultural area within 4 miles of a metalled road and 1.5 miles of any road;
(ii) in a semideveloped area within 8 miles of a metalled road and 3 miles of any road; and
(iii) in an underdeveloped and uncultivable area within 12 miles of a metalled road and 5 miles of any road.[18]

Note that in order to reach this goal, total mileage must increase by about 73 per cent over 1961. The required annual expenditure on road development is estimated at 80 crores of rupees in 1961–1962, rising annually to a level of 440 crores of rupees in 1981–1982.

In terms of the amount of money to be invested under the Third Five-Year Plan the amount projected for roads may be contrasted with that for railways. The original allocation for the Railway Development Program was 890 crores of rupees (i.e., 8,900 million of rupees) plus 330 crores of rupees from the Railway Depreciation Reserve Fund or a total of 1,220 crores of rupees. The allotment for roads was 272 crores of rupees, or 54 crores of rupees a year average. Thus, the major emphasis has continued to be on the railroads. The roads have received some attention in the development program, but nowhere near what some have proposed. Revised estimates for 1961–1966 made in the middle of the Third Five-Year Plan increased the allocation of 890 crores of rupees to 1,196 for the railways, and the allocation for roads from 272 to 416.[19]

VEHICLES—The second half of a system of highway transportation, of course, is the vehicles. Road transport services for people in India have been largely nationalized and are operated either by the national or by the state governments. The transport of goods by road has been left primarily in the hands of private operators. The Third Five-Year Plan provision for road transport was modest, 25 crores of rupees originally planned, and 23 crores of rupees according to the revised estimates for 1961–1966.

Note that the objectives of the highway program are stated in terms of making roads available. It is not a question of meeting known needs, but of building ahead of the traffic. Such a policy can succeed only if the other preconditions for development of traffic are met.

18. *Ibid.*, p. 69.
19. *The Third Plan, Mid-Term Appraisal,* Government of India, Planning Commission, November 1963, p. 139.

RESTRICTIONS ON ROAD TRANSPORT—In the early years after independence, regulation of road transport was left very largely up to the state governments. They adopted a policy that only can be described as restrictive! For interstate movement vehicles were required to have permits recommended by the state of registration for counter-signature by the other state in which the operator wished to do business. The number of permits, routes, and conditions of operation were subject to interstate agreements. These measures were operated in such a way as to restrict the development of the industry. Black markets in permits actually developed.

Limits have been placed on the length of truck haul. At one time the limit was 50 miles, and later 75 miles. In practice, since lifting of these restrictions, operating permits are administered to prohibit truck operation over 300 miles.

An additional difficulty confronting private operators in the industry has been the difficulty of obtaining a supply of new vehicles. Such difficulties have persisted into the Third Five-Year Plan.[20] Most of the trucks in India seem to be operated by small operators who start out by buying a single vehicle on hire purchase, that is, on the installment plan. Credit costs 12 per cent or more per annum. Nevertheless, the number of commercial vehicles in India has risen at a rapid rate. During the period 1948–1962, the number of commercial vehicles of all kinds increased from 86,000 to 274,000.[21]

Public policy toward the trucking industry seems to have taken a more favorable turn in recent years with some relaxation of licensing policies, the revision of the railroad rate structure to discourage the use of rail for hauls of 25 miles or less, and the appointment of a committee on transport policy and coordination to examine policy toward the development of road transport and other means of transportation. The tone of the comments on road transport in the *Planning Commission's Mid-Term Appraisal* of the Third Five-Year Plan was favorable, with references to measures to facilitate interstate traffic and financial assistance to road transport operators. In this more favorable environment it will be interesting to observe the rate of development of road transport in India in the late 1960s and 1970s. There seems to be recognition of the inconsistency between a policy of investing scarce capital in the development of a road network and a policy of restricting the development of the trucking industry.

20. *Ibid.*, p. 144.
21. *United Nations Statistical Yearbook,* 1963.

Whether the policy of investing in highways ahead of demand has been a success does not seem to be definitely known although it could be investigated. What would be required would be study of the economic impact of better roads. The difference in economic level of villages before and after roads are built could be measured, for example. Present knowledge on the subject seems inadequate to estimate the social benefits.

RAIL TRANSPORT—From the preceding discussion it will be apparent that apart from local service the main reliance for the movement both of people and freight in India has been on the railroads. Of the total freight traffic roughly 88 per cent moves by rail. Investment policy toward the railroads since independence in 1948 has been closely tied to industrial development.

At the beginning of the period the railroads were in poor shape. The generally worn out condition of the rolling stock and the poor condition of the roadway were the heritage of World War II and the transitional years immediately following the War. Investment policy during the first years of independence necessarily was directed to the remedy of these deficiencies.

INDIAN STANDARDS OF RAILROAD EQUIPMENT—It should not be inferred that Indian railways have been brought up to American standards with regard to equipment. The policy for the replacement of capital equipment on the railways in the form of rolling stock indicates clearly that the objective is to get the most out of existing facilities. The assumption made in drawing up the requirements for rolling stock for the Third Five-Year Plan was that *all* locomotives and wagons (freight cars) up to the age of forty-five years would be retained. In contrast, of the locomotives in service on Class I Railroads in the United States only about 4 per cent are twenty years old or more.[22] Note that the Third Five-Year Plan provides for the retention of all locomotives age forty-five years or less but does *not* necessarily provide for the replacement of all locomotives of that age or more. For the coaches, thirty-six years is the minimum age of retirement on broad gauge, forty years on meter gauge, and forty-five years on narrow gauge. The emphasis in retirement policy is clearly on condition, based on actual physical wearing out, rather than on any criterion of obsolescence.

INVESTMENT PLANNING FOR RAILROADS—Currently, investment in railways is part of the Five-Year Plans, the outlay for transportation

22. At the beginning of the Third Five-Year Plan, December 31, 1959, in the United States there were 29,465 locomotives of which 1,180 were built prior to December 31, 1939. I.C.C., *Transport Statistics in the United States.*

amounting to about a quarter of the total outlay in the public sector under the Plans. The procedure in developing the investment plan is to make estimates of the volume of production that will be obtained in various industries by the end of the Plan. Thus, it is stated in *Third Five-Year Plan, A Draft Outline:*[23]

The estimates of traffic for the last year of the third plan are based on the following estimates of production: Steel ingot 8.7 million tons, pig iron 1.5 million tons, coal 95 million tons, cement 13 million tons. The estimate for steel is exclusive of the production envisaged from the new steel plant at Bakaro. The provision for railway facilities required in connection with the Bakaro steel plant forms part of the overall allocation for the steel plant. . . . As regards miscellaneous traffic, the estimate has been worked out with regard to the targets of production of important industries like cotton textiles, sugar, jute manufactures, paper, tea, fertilizers, vegetable oils, etc. The estimate also takes into account the traffic relating to mineral oils and mineral ores. On the whole, on basis of the above targets, the increase during the third plan in miscellaneous traffic is estimated to be of the order of 5 per cent per annum which is the minimum to be expected in keeping with the trend shown by this type of traffic on the railways in the last few years.

As this statement makes clear, there has been in India a systematic attempt by the *Planning Commission* to work out the transportation requirements implied by estimated production elsewhere in the economy. At the middle of the Third Five-Year Plan period, investment in railways was reconsidered in the light of experience. In particular the original estimate that coal traffic would increase from about 50 million tons in 1960–61 to 95 million in 1965–1966 was revised downward to about 88 million tons in 1965–1966.

Broad generalizations are hazardous, but perhaps it would be close to correct to say that Indian railroad policy reflects the same general approach as Soviet policy. Transport will be provided as necessary. Shortages will be permitted to develop on occasion. If an error is to be made, it is generally preferable to permit these shortages rather than to build too far in advance of the need for transportation. It is a symptom of difficulties in India that pressure on the capacity of the railroads has been reduced in the Third Five-Year Plan. In 1965–1966 line capacity for 260 million tons is expected to be provided against a traffic forecast of 241.

OVERCROWDING OF PASSENGER TRAINS—With regard to facilities for passenger travel, in both the Second and Third Five-Year Plans, provi-

23. Page 243.

sion was made for expansion of rail facilities at a rate expected to match the annual growth in traffic. Overcrowding on trains existed at the beginning of the period and was expected to continue. Policy, in other words, has been to use the capital equipment to capacity, or beyond. The crowding is most serious in the third-class passenger facilities, which account for the bulk of the traffic. According to one official body which examined the question: "It would, therefore, not be an exaggeration to say that chronic overcrowding is more or less a normal feature of all trains."[24] Two other choices of policy exist: it would be possible to raise the fares and discourage third-class passenger travel, which might be undesirable because of the incidence of the tax on the lower income groups; or it would be possible to expand capacity, which would require allocation of a share of the limited available resources of capital. Both these choices have been rejected implicitly in favor of the policy of permitting crowding to continue. The growth in rail passenger traffic has been substantial, from 62.8 million passenger kilometer in 1955–1956 to 84.5 million in 1962–1963. Average revenue per passenger kilometer has remained low, 2.02 n.P. (naya paisa) in 1962–1963, or about 0.4 cents![25]

AIR TRANSPORT—At first thought it may seem remarkable that an underdeveloped country like India should devote any of its scarce resources to the development of air transport. But air transport has unusual advantages in India, in addition to those found in all parts of the world, which arise from the size of the country and the slowness of the competing means of transportation. India has an area of about a million and a quarter square miles, which means the distances from one end of the country to the other are long. The railroads, as indicated, tend to rely, to a considerable extent, on obsolescent capital equipment. Furthermore, the rail lines are much better developed in certain directions than in others. The rail service between Assam in the far northeast and the rest of India has not been very satisfactory since the partition of India from Pakistan. Rail service from northern to southern India is not as well developed as the service between the capital, Delhi, and the largest ports, Bombay and Calcutta. On the other hand, the Indian airlines can make use of modern capital equipment. As of 1964 Indian Airlines Corporation, the domestic airline organization, was operating with a fleet including Boeing jet aircraft as well as Douglas D-C 3's, and Vickers Viscounts. The service offered by a modern aircraft is, of

24. Estimates Committee, 25th Report, 1955–56, p. 23. In Amba Prasad, *op. cit.*, p. 206.
25. *Report by the Railway Board on Indian Railways for 1962–63*, Table I. (There are 100 naya paisa to one rupee.)

course, the same in India as it is in other parts of the world. Freight trains on broad gauge average about 15.4 km. p.h., or about 10 m.p.h. The relative advantage in speed of air freight is far greater than in the United States.

There are three main classes of passengers on the airlines in India, government officials, private business men, and foreign tourists. Travel by Indian citizens for other than business reasons seems to be unimportant.[26] From the point of view of public policy it may be argued that all three of these principal classes of travelers are important, the government officials and businessmen because of the nature of their activities, and the tourists because of their contributions to the foreign exchange position of the country. From a political point of view the advantages of tying the country together by the rapid movement of persons are particularly important to a nation in which there are many divisive forces.

CONCLUDING COMMENTS—The basic modern transport network in India is the railroad system. In developing it, the policy of the government has been to provide only for the amount of freight that has to be moved in order to permit completion of the Five-Year Plans. This strategy is reminiscent of that used in the early stages of forced industrialization in the Soviet Union. It is difficult to make more than a gross judgment of the success of this policy. We may note, however, that the index of Indian industrial produced moved from 100 in 1950–1951 to 195 in 1960–1961 and an estimated 222 in 1962–1963. Transport does not appear to have been a bottleneck.

Allowing for the fact that room for private enterprise has been left in the Indian economy, the government may have been unduly restrictive in its attitude toward that part of the transport system that has been left to the private sector, especially transport of freight by highway.

It is difficult to evaluate the investment made to date in rural roads. The level of agricultural production has been disappointing.[27] Data are not available to permit an evaluation of the actual and the potential contribution of transport to agricultural production. It is easier to assess success than relative failure. When several factors of production are

26. The impression that these three main classes are the important ones is derived from: *Report on Indian Airlines Corporations Fares and Freight Rates* (May 1957), Government of India, Air Transport Council, 1957.

27. The index of agricultural production rose over the period of the Second Five-Year Plan from 116.8 to 139.6 in 1960–1961. In 1961–1962 the index reached 141.8, but fell to 136.8 in 1962–1963. These numbers must be interpreted in the light of the increase in population.

needed to achieve a result and the result is achieved, as in Indian industrial development, it is clear that each factor must have been present in at least the minimum required quantity. When the result is not achieved, as in Indian agriculture, it takes detailed analysis to know which were the critical deficiencies.

11

Transportation Policy in Underdeveloped Countries

$\mathbf{T}$HE PRINCIPLES of economic theory do not differ from developed to underdeveloped countries or from one century to the next, in spite of the variation in situation from country to country illustrated in the previous chapters. Although in this sense the theoretical discussion in Part I is general, it is the basic purpose of Part II to indicate how much variation there is in the important problems of policy and what courses of action are appropriate. A brief discussion of current problems of transportation policy in underdeveloped countries, therefore, cannot present a set of solutions to fit all possible circumstances. It is the purpose of this chapter to indicate the nature of the main choices, to suggest something of the range of possible strategies in making these choices, and also to point out something of the range of possible errors. The problem falls into two groups, those related to investment, and those related to the operation of transportation systems. Of the two, the investment choices are the more important for the process of development and will receive more extended discussion.

151

Investment Policy

The choices to be made concerning investment in transportation may be divided into three categories that concern, first, the total amount to be invested in transportation (as opposed to investment in other sectors of the economy); second, the basic choice as to the division of investment among the different modes of transportation (rail, highway, water, pipeline, and air); and third, the remaining choices of investment policy subsequent to these basic decisions.

Although it is convenient to use these three categories in discussing the subject, it should be understood that the actual sequence of decision making will not proceed in this order. One of the problems to be faced is how to fit together the decisions concerning transportation and decisions concerning other parts of the economy. Yet, whatever the sequence of steps, the total investment in transportation is of interest.

TOTAL INVESTMENT IN TRANSPORTATION—One simple way to approach the question of how much investment should be made in transportation is by rule of thumb. The rule of thumb approach is to think in terms of the average percentage of total gross capital formation allocated to different purposes in different countries. About one-third of all loans by the International Bank for Reconstruction and Development and about one-fifth of American aid for development projects is for transport. About 20 to 25 per cent of all public and private investment in transportation is typical. With such averages in mind, one can say that 41 per cent of all investment in transport and 3 per cent in education seems questionable. These percentages at one time (1939) applied to government investment in Colombia.[1]

Yet, it is hardly safe to conclude that an average percentage will always be optimal. A starting point for analysis is the exhortation to plan investment in transportation in a developing country in a manner that is integrated with general economic policy in that country since general economic development is the goal. At a theoretical level this integration has received considerable attention. The basic characteristics of underdeveloped countries are a scarcity of capital and a desire to proceed rapidly toward a higher level of output per capita. Consideration of the problems of economic policy under such conditions has led economic theorists to the development of growth models. These theoretical models are concerned with the conditions under which the economy will grow at the maximum attainable rate. Discussion of growth models

1. Wilfred Owen, *Strategy for Mobility,* The Brookings Institution, 1964, Ch. II.

is beyond the scope of this volume except to point out that they require consideration of investment in transportation in the context of a complete model of the growth process.[2]

Fromm has proposed a method of bringing comprehensive planning into line with a sophisticated model. His sequence of steps can be used without a complete mathematical statement at each step if resources do not permit. He proposes that long term economic goals should be specified at five year intervals for thirty to forty years. A long range dynamic development plan should then be specified. Near-term plans should be developed in this context. The detailed analysis of prospective individual investments then should be undertaken within the framework thus prepared. Finally, the entire process should be reviewed, considerations not previously taken into account should be introduced, and the stages made consistent. Successive iterations of the procedure may be needed to achieve this result.[3]

Such dynamic programing, of course, is ambitious. It would be beyond the intellectual and statistical resources of many countries to carry out Fromm's proposals in full, as he is well aware. The approach would take into account, however, the interconnections between different parts of the economy and would solve the problem of evaluating transportation investments in their proper context. It would meet the requirement of considering investments in transportation in relation to the rest of the economy as the economy is expected to develop in the long run.

A simpler, practical procedure for taking into account the major interconnections between transportation and the rest of the economy is reported by Robert Sadove of the staff of the World Bank. Three steps are involved; first, a general review of the economy of a country and its investment program; second, a judgment as to whether the transportation sector of the economy is a "priority" sector in which investment should be made to stimulate development of the economy; and third, a study of whether the particular project is the most beneficial that might be undertaken.[4] This method is essentially a method for evaluating a particular project in the context of the economy of the country in question.

WHETHER TO BUILD AHEAD OF KNOWN DEMAND—Whatever the intellectual context in which decisions are taken, a strategic choice must be made as to whether to minimize total investment in transportation

2. See Gary Fromm, editor, *Transport Investment and Economic Development,* The Brookings Institution, 1965, Ch. VI.

3. *Ibid.,* Ch. I.

4. *Ibid.,* Ch. XI.

or to build ahead of demand. As already indicated, the policy of building the minimum transportation system absolutely necessary to achieve a given increase in the level of economic activity was followed by the Soviet Union in its First Five-Year Plan. It is being followed by India in its policy toward railroads. The opposite strategy, to build ahead of demand in the expectation that the development of demand will ensue, was followed by America and Canada in the last century and by India in its highway policy. The possible strategies fall on a continuum; how far ahead of known demand one builds is a question of degree. It should be understood that the choice arises fundamentally out of the difficulty of making accurate forecasts of demand. If precise forecasts of demand could be relied on, there would be much less difference of opinion about the correct level of investment in transportation in a given situation.

The "tight" strategy assumes that economic development will be pushed forward in sectors other than transportation by some economic force, such as investments under the control of the central planners in a controlled economy. The obvious risk inherent in the strategy is that the development of the transportation system will be too slow and will act as a brake on production in other sectors. A subtle but basic risk is that transportation will be minimized when it should be substituted for other inputs in production.

The "loose" strategy assumes that either the other necessary preconditions for development exist or that they will come into existence as a result of the development of transportation so the transportation system will be used. It is consistent with reliance on private enterprise and initiative. In the American West, for example, when the railroads reached into new territory, they could become profitable only if, first, the area rendered accessible was suitable for farming (or some other use), second, people were ready to move into the territory to develop it, and third, a market existed for the products. The obvious risk inherent in this strategy is that the transportation system will be built too soon or even permanently overbuilt. A more subtle risk is inconsistent policies, that is, the policy of the public and private agencies involved may be such as to discourage the development needed to stimulate demand to make use of the investment in transportation. It is also possible to substitute transportation in excessive amounts for other inputs.

AN EXAMPLE OF THE IMPLICATIONS FOR TRANSPORT OF A SPECIFIC PROJECT—Some of the possible connections between investment in a transportation facility and general economic planning may be indicated by a specific example. A report on transportation in Nigeria in 1961 spelled out some of the implications of the construction of a proposed dam, the Kainji Dam on the Niger River. It was noted that this project would require 500,000 tons of construction provisions and other freight to be moved over four years, an amount equal to the total annual northbound movement of freight for one year on the Nigerian railroad at the time. Once completed, furthermore, the project would provide electricity in large quantities at a cost low enough to raise the question of whether the railroad should be electrified.[5] Note that both demand for the services of the railroad and the supply of factors of production available to the railroad are involved. Note the importance of a single large project in a developing country. And note that the implied demand for transportation is not a general demand but a specific requirement for movement of certain commodities to a particular site.

CHOICE OF MODE—The allocation of investment funds among the several modes of transportation is the second problem of investment strategy for economic development. The primary criterion is cost minimization. The costs to be minimized, however, must not be defined too narrowly. Both costs of vehicles and roads must be considered in highway transportation for example. Costs of shippers other than their outlays on transportation must also be taken into account when these costs vary depending on the transportation service provided. Thus, allowances may be necessary for difference in the service offered by different modes, especially differences in speed and reliability. Analysis requires consideration both of the available technology and the geography of the area as well as the existing transport system.

CHOICE OF MODE IN PERU—To indicate the kind of analysis that can be made of choice of mode in an underdeveloped country, two examples will be discussed in detail: proposed investments in Peru and Chile. The government of Peru in 1960 engaged economic consultants to consider, among other problems, the method of transportation to be used for opening an area for development on the inland side of the Andes, known as Peru-via. At the time of the study the region was partially unexplored and transportation in the area was extremely limited, with air taxi the most widespread type of service. Development of the area clearly required either road or rail service. Forecasts of traffic in such a situation could hardly be reliable, but analysis of the choice-of-mode problem required some assumption as to the volume of traffic. The method used was to make assumptions that covered a wide range

5. Hamlin Robinson, Stanton R. Smith, Kenneth G. Clare, *The Economic Coordination of Transport Development in Nigeria,* (Joint Planning Committee, National Economic Council, Federation of Nigeria, February 1961.)

of possibilities. Three possible assumptions were made as to the extent
of the geographic area to be covered. For each of the three areas, small,
medium, and large, a low and a high volume of traffic was assumed.
Thus, six possibilities in all were envisaged. The range of the assumptions may be seen from the fact that the two levels of traffic assumed
for the smallest area were 40 million ton-kilometers per year and 150
million. The higher volume chosen was close to that actually handled
by the most comparable existing railroad.

The next steps in the analysis were to assemble relevant information
on the cost of constructing and operating railroads and the cost of
building highways and operating trucks. The method was to obtain data
from the most comparable transport systems in Peru and nearby areas.
Further assumptions had to be made as to such matters as the probable
mix of trucks of different carrying capacity, the standards to which
highways might be constructed, and the weight of rail and type of
locomotives to be used. A single estimate was made on each of these
points.

The results of the calculations may be summarized in terms of money
cost per ton-kilometer:

AREA AND TRAFFIC ASSUMPTIONS	TOTAL COST OF FREIGHT MOVEMENT IN SOLES PER TON-KILOMETER	
Area A	Railway	Highway
Low traffic	3.53	0.80
High traffic	1.32	0.80
Area B		
Low traffic	3.13	1.37
High traffic	1.22	0.80
Area C		
Low traffic	3.10	1.41
High Traffic	1.18	0.80

The results show total cost of highway transport far lower than rail
transport in all six situations. The conclusion in favor of highway transport, of course, is no more reliable than the cost information that went
into the estimates. But the margin of superiority is large enough so that
the cost estimates could be considerably in error and the choice of
method of transportation would be the same. A closer decision would
require a more refined estimating procedure.[6]

6. *A Program for the Industrial and Regional Development of Peru,* A Report to the
Government of Peru, by Arthur D. Little, Inc., 1960, pp. 98–111. (Nelson Sharfman of
Wyer, Dick and Company served as transportation consultant on the project.)

CHOICE OF MODE IN CHILE—The investment decision made by the government of Chile in 1959 was of a different character. There was already in existence a national railroad system owned by the government, as are nearly all railroad systems outside the United States. The question was whether to make the substantial investment necessary to renovate and modernize the system. The choice actually made was to invest over 200 million dollars for a complete modernization of the system.

This choice has been criticized by Robert T. Brown.[7] The fundamental objection Brown makes is that the decision was taken without careful consideration of the possibility of substituting highway for rail transportation. He shows that the possibility of such a substitution could be considered by estimating the cost of transporting by highway the entire volume of railway traffic moved in one year, 1961, by a part of the railroad system, the Southern System. His estimate is that the total cost to society of movement of all of the traffic by highway would have been in the range of 64 to 76 million escudos. The cost of moving the traffic by rail as published by the State Railways was 95 million escudos. Brown believes that 97 million escudos would be a more accurate estimate of social costs. Taking the higher estimates for both systems, his estimate is that the highways could have handled all the rail traffic for 21 million escudos less. The discrepancy in favor of the highway does not mean that all traffic should in fact move by highway. It is entirely possible that certain classes of traffic on certain routes could be handled more economically by the railroad. The point of the criticism is that the whole subject should have been investigated before the decision to invest heavily in the railroad was made. The analysis actually made was in terms of the cost saving of the railroad from the improvements at projected levels of traffic movement. The cost savings envisaged were substantial, and, on the basis of rather optimistic estimates of traffic, it appeared the program could convert a substantial and continuing deficit for the Railways into a surplus within six years. It is easy to understand the appeal to the responsible government officials of the prospect of ending the deficits, but from the point of view of the economy their perspective was too narrow.

FURTHER COMMENTS ON THE CHOICE BETWEEN HIGHWAYS AND RAILWAYS—In both of these situations economic analysis pointed in the direction of reliance on highway transport rather than rail. Do the results always come out that way? Not necessarily.

Owen cites an example of a new railroad in Venezuelan Guiana only

7. Fromm, *op. cit.*, Ch. XII.

146 km. long carrying five or six trains of ore per day, each with
10,000 tons of ore.[8] In this instance it seems to be the heavy volume
between individual points rather than length of haul that justifies the
railroad. (An example of a situation in Nigeria will be discussed below
in which the social cost of truck transport exceeded the cost of using
an existing railroad.)

Truck transport is generally believed to be the most economical
choice for short hauls on the ground that terminal costs are low for
trucks. The argument is that line-haul costs for trucks may be high
compared to railroads, but terminal costs are low. For considerable
distances, total cost may be less by truck, but beyond some critical
distance total cost by truck will be greater than by rail.

There is considerable truth in this view, but also a degree of over-
simplification. The subject of cost estimates for trucks will be discussed
in Chapter 13 and for railroads in Chapter 14. It should be understood
immediately, however, that short hauls are not invariably cheaper by
truck. Terminal costs, defined to include all costs incurred before the
main line rail movement can begin or the loaded truck can depart, will
vary both according to volume, and according to the type of equipment.
On a railroad, terminal costs for boxcars are much higher than for
containers shipped on flatcars, for example. Costs also depend on whether
use of a local train or a switching engine is required for assembly of a
full train for main line movement. Shipment in trainload volume from
a single point to a single destination is by no means the same as handling an equal tonnage of less-than-carload lots. For line-haul costs per
ton-mile there is also diversity. This diversity makes impossible precise
and simple statements about the general relation between truck and rail
terminal costs.

LACK OF COORDINATION—A related error in allocation of investment
across modes is failure to exploit the potential advantage of coordination
of different modes. This error is most easily made when there is an
atmosphere of hostility between modes, say, between rail and trucks, or
rail and water transport agencies. It is possible to use trucks to handle
pickup and delivery service for rail. The use of containers and transfer-
able trailer bodies can reduce costs. By the use of a crane or a ramp
the container or trailer can be loaded on a flatcar. A recent study of
the Department of Economic Affairs of the Pan American Union notes
these possibilities. It also comments on the use of containers as a means
of reducing the expense of a break in gauge. But the report notes that

8. Owen, *op. cit.*, pp. 32–33.

the practices are not frequently used in Latin America though recommended in specific situations in Brazil and Colombia.[9] Lack of coordination, unfortunately, is a worldwide problem.

OTHER CHOICES OF INVESTMENT POLICY—Even given a choice among the modes of transportation, and given an estimate of the load to be carried, there is a further choice as to how much capital to invest in the system. This choice arises because of the possibilities of substitution between initial capital outlay and operating costs. Systems can be overdesigned. They can be built to an unnecessarily high standard of performance and durability. Systems can be underdesigned. They can be built to low standards without adequate consideration of operating costs and requirements for maintenance. Roads can be built without regard to the increased operating costs and wear and tear on vehicles resulting from deterioration of the surface.

INADEQUATE VS. EXCESSIVE MAINTENANCE—Maintenance, in the same way, can be inadequate and can be excessive. Failure to maintain a transportation system can amount to negative investment, that is, withdrawal of investment from the system. *General Problems of Transportation in Latin America* cites deplorable lack of maintenance on many systems in Latin America. Its comments on the condition of the Bolivian railroads at the time they were observed include:

The condition of the roadbeds is deplorable. There is almost no ballast; the sleepers have not been replaced when needed; and the rails are badly worn. Only the small volume of freight carried has made it possible to continue service at all.[10]

Comparable problems have occurred elsewhere. One of the reasons was that some railroads were operated on a concession system. As the date approached for the railroad to revert to public ownership the standard of maintenance declined. A policy of disinvestment was advantageous to the operators of the concession, if not to the developing economy.

Excessive maintenance also can occur. Facilities can be maintained when substitute facilities ought to be built. The same report notes that there are cases of roads laid out in colonial or even precolonial times in Latin America. The geometric design and location of these roads is obsolete and cannot be improved by expenditures to improve their sur-

9. *General Problems of Transportation in Latin America,* Pan American Union, 1963, p. 14. On one Brazilian railroad the cost of transferring goods because of a break in gauge reached 70 per cent of operating expenses.

10. *Ibid.,* p. 8.

face.[11] Some transport facilities ought to be worn out and discarded rather than maintained in perpetuity.

IMBALANCE IN CAPACITY—Another area in which there are possible difficulties is in achieving a balance of capacity across the elements of a transportation system. While imbalance among the capacity of vehicles, power plant, and way may occur, lack of terminal capacity provides some of the most dramatic examples of difficulties. In Latin America, for example, port facilities have been bottlenecks. Long lines of trucks waiting in streets leading to wharves, or rolling stock on sidings are said to be common. An estimate was made in the port of Callao of an annual cost of congestion of 16 million dollars, the largest components of the cost of congestion being theft and illegal removal, and damage to the freight. In this instance considerable success in relieving congestion resulted from a warehouse fee charged on goods in the port.[12] (It is doubtful, however, that congestion in Latin America ever reached the monumental proportions achieved on the east coast of the United States during World War I.)

DISCONTINUITIES—An extreme form of disorganization of a system results from sections that do not connect, roads to nowhere, like the West Virginia Turnpike. The Colombian Parliament, for example, was criticized in 1961 for this defect, "fragmenting the Highway Budget over many dispersed areas."[13]

Discontinuities in railroad systems may take the form of breaks in gauge, which are particularly likely at international frontiers. There is such a division, for example, where the Uruguayan broad gauge meets the Brazilian narrow gauge. The same problem exists in Africa where the meter gauge of Dahomey lies between the 3 foot 6 inch gauge of Nigeria on the one frontier and Ghana on the other. The consequence is that the total investment is less useful than it might have been had policy been coordinated and international trade encouraged.

Operation of Transport Systems

The problems in the operation of transport systems in underdeveloped countries are not fundamentally different from those elsewhere. A complete discussion of the operation of transport systems is beyond the scope of this book, but four topics deserve brief mention here: the

11. *Ibid.,* p. 11.
12. *Ibid.,* p. 15.
13. *Ibid.,* p. 40.

excessive use of one factor of production relative to others; the effect of rate policies on use of different modes of transportation; excessive regulation and formalities; and failure to assemble adequate statistical information.

DISPROPORTIONATE USE OF ONE FACTOR OF PRODUCTION—There may be a tendency in underdeveloped countries, especially under conditions of excess labor supply, to use labor in unreasonable quantities. An example of this kind is Lloyd Aereo Boliviano, which at the time of one report had a total staff of 1,511 persons—and only eighteen planes. There were eighty-four employees per plane in service![14]

A less conspicuous waste may occur in the employment of scarce resources of skilled managerial personnel. It is urged by advocates of highway transportation that small operators who own and drive their own trucks are being trained as entrepreneurs while large-scale bureaucracies needed for railroads absorb scarce executives.[15] It may be wasteful to use scarce trained personnel to manage railroads when trucks could supply the transport.

EFFECT OF RATES—The type of misallocation of resources that can result from inappropriate rate structures may be illustrated by an episode reported in the study of transport in Nigeria, to which reference has been made.[16] A principal export from Nigeria is groundnuts (peanuts). The groundnuts are grown 700 to 1,000 miles from sea. There are three technically possible methods of shipment, by rail, by truck, and by a mixture of land and water shipments down the Niger and Benue Rivers. Of these methods, truck shipment is the most expensive to society especially in a period such as 1959–1960 when the railroad had excess capacity. Average cost per ton-mile for rail was 2.2 pence, but rail direct operating cost for distances over 650 miles for groundnuts was only 1.55 pence, compared to about 6 pence for the truck operators. Yet about 22,000 tons of groundnuts moved to the sea by truck. The amount involved is only a fraction of the total exports, which were about 480,000 tons, but waste was involved in all such shipments.

The explanation seems to have been in part the railroad rate structure. Groundnuts paid high freight rates. They accounted for one-third of total revenue but only one-fourth of revenue tons shipped. The diversion to road transport led to a reduction in railroad rates for groundnuts in 1960. There also is a question whether the charges paid by truck

14. *Ibid.*, p. 30.
15. This point was stressed by E. K. Hawkins, *Road Transport in Nigeria,* Oxford University Press, 1958.
16. Robinson, Smith, Clare, *op. cit.,* pp. 43–45, 78, 84.

operators for the use of highways reflected an appropriate share of the true economic cost of the highways, but the amounts involved are not a large fraction of the total costs of the truck operators. An idea of the magnitude may be obtained from the fact that a proposed increase in fuel taxes of one-fifth would increase total costs of road transport by about 3 per cent.

Note the contrast between the situation in Nigeria and the investment decision in Peru mentioned above. In Nigeria, long haul shipment of a basic commodity in bulk by a railroad with excess capacity was involved. In Peru, the involvement was a decision to construct an entirely new transportation system to handle the full range of shipments in and out of a completely undeveloped region.

RED TAPE—The proliferation of administrative requirements, documents, entry and clearance permits, and the like can impede the effective use of a transportation system. Difficulties of this type on Indian highways have been mentioned. Similar problems exist elsewhere, especially at international frontiers. A particularly unfortunate situation exists on the River Plate, and has had a serious effect on the development of the river fleets of Argentina, Paraguay, and Uruguay. The Pan American Union study referred to this situation as involving "lack of coordination—which could even be called antagonism." Consequences include both partial idleness of river vessels and congestion in the ports.[17] It is only fair to add that there have been efforts to reduce trade barriers among developing countries by common markets in East Africa and, since 1960, by the Latin American Free Trade Association. For trade among Latin American countries, maritime transport is of predominant importance but progress to date toward more economical and efficient maritime transportation has been disappointing.

LACK OF STATISTICAL INFORMATION—A final problem in the operation of transport systems in underdeveloped countries, which aggravates other difficulties, is the lack of adequate statistical information. The difficulty may not be so much a question of the *quantity* of statistics as of the *quality*. There may not be a shortage of numbers so much as a lack of reliable statistics relevant to the analysis of the important problems of operating the industry. Serious statistical deficiencies, however, are found even in the United States, as the next chapter will make clear.

CONCLUSION—In the operation of a transportation system, as with any economic enterprise, the possibilities of waste and inefficiency are

17. *Ibid.,* p. 16.

legion. Examples have been cited in underdeveloped countries of the following: excessive use of labor, excessive use of scarce managerial talent, rate structures that encourage inefficient choice of means of transport, and lack of coordination at international frontiers.

III

Modern Transportation
in the United States

12

Introduction to Statistical Analysis of Transportation in the United States

CHAPTERS 12 THROUGH 20 are devoted to the modern transportation industry in the United States. The subject has an obvious special interest for Americans and perhaps an international interest owing to the leading economic position of the nation. Chapter 12 is devoted to a general consideration of the available statistical information that may serve to convey something of the relative position of the different methods of transportation in the total American market. Chapters 13 through 18 consider the individual methods of transportation.

The sequence of these six chapters deserves a word of explanation. Railroads are discussed first, essentially for chronological reasons. Highway transportation is considered next, partly because it closely competes with rail and partly because of the need for coordination of the two. Urban highways are a part of the same highway system as rural highways; however they must be treated separately. The connection between urban transport and air transport is less intimate, but surface transport in urban areas is an important part of journeys by air. Marine transport in its international aspects presents problems analogous to those of international air transport. Finally, the inland waterways and pipelines are grouped together as bulk carriers operating within the country. The pipelines are highly specialized and are treated briefly here. An argument could be developed that long distance transmission of electricity might also have been included. Transmission of electricity, however, seems more a substitute for transportation than a form of transportation.

Each of these chapters considers the major issues of public policy concerning the industry in question. The organization of the industry is considered, including the nature and extent of competition and the functions of the relevant public agencies. The topics emphasized vary from chapter to chapter. Problems of investment policy are central with regard to highways and urban transportation but not railroads. Rate policy, on the other hand, and the regulation of rates by the I.C.C. (Interstate Commerce Commission), are important to the railroad industry.

The two final chapters again cut across the methods of transportation. Chapter 19 considers two areas of competition among methods of transportation, competition for the movement of grain, and competition for passenger business. The final chapter is a general summary of current issues of public policy in the field and of positions taken in this volume with regard to some of these issues.

In order to analyze the modern transportation industry in the United States an economist must rely on statistical information. In this chapter, we shall begin by considering at an introductory level the nature of the information that would be useful to an economic analyst with some examples of the available statistics. Later chapters will consider the several methods of transportation separately and will describe the institutional arrangements.

From the earlier theoretical discussion it is possible to infer in general what types of statistics an economist would like to have. Measures of output are a basic requirement. Without measures of output it is impossible, for example, to construct cost curves. Data on price are equally fundamental. Measures of total revenue are closely related to price and output. To understand the forces that determine price and revenue it is essential to obtain measures of the structure of costs on one side of the market and of the structure of market demand on the other. In addition, the behavior of firms in an industry must be understood in the light of information about the extent of competition or, more comprehensively, the market structure of the industry. Finally, informed evaluation of an industry requires statistics of market performance. The discussion, therefore, is organized under the following subheads: statistics of output; statistics of price and revenue; statistics of cost and capacity; statistics of the structure of market demand; statistics of competition and market structure; and statistics of performance. Each section contains a brief statement of the purpose of the statistics considered and the nature and limitations of the available data.

It should be recognized that the needs for data of interested parties differ according to the problems with which they are concerned and the approaches they take to those problems. For example, much of the available information about cost has been compiled by the I.C.C. for use in rate regulation. The economic analyst interested in transportation in underdeveloped countries must adapt it as best he can.

Statistics of Output

Statistics of output are useful both directly in themselves and in combination with other measures. They may be prepared for different geographic areas, different markets for transportation, different business enterprises, and so forth, in great variety. Used by themselves they reveal that a particular branch of the industry is growing or declining and the rates of growth or decline. They are also required for many problems for use in connection with other measures. Measures of efficiency, for example, since they indicate output per unit input, require measures of output in the numerator of the fraction. Empirical cost curves and demand curves require measures of output.

The most elementary statistics of output are measures of the total number of tons of freight moved, or the total number of passengers carried. There is a fundamental difficulty in the preparation of this type of summary statistic that is well illustrated by consideration of two types of things to be moved, people and freight. How can a measure of total output be constructed for an enterprise, say, a railroad, which transports both? Should one simply add together so many pounds of people and so many pounds of coal? One might calculate that 16 people at 125 pounds each make one ton, and the weight of people can be added to the weight of coal accordingly.

What might make this procedure unreasonable? It is that the accommodations for people on a train are not the same as those for coal, and are much more expensive to provide. One choice for the analyst is to opt for keeping statistics about people and coal entirely separate. But once he accepts this division, other questions arise. If people must be kept separate in the statistics, how about pigs? They require different facilities from those appropriate for coal—they need food, water, and air. Even when inanimate freight is considered, some is perishable and must be kept refrigerated, some requires protection from the elements, some is fragile, and some is compact. Cargo space may be full of light freight when a vehicle could carry much more weight, or only partly full of heavy freight when the weight limit is reached. Yet, some aggregation must take place.

One system of aggregation that may be used is to combine tons, weighting them in proportion to a measure of cost. An index of output may be constructed. Weights may be set up on the basis, for example, of the marginal cost per ton of moving each type of traffic. This type of measure has much to recommend it for comparisons among technically similar modes of transport—say, for comparing output of two railroads that haul different mixes of freight. It is less useful for comparison between modes when the marginal costs of different classes of traffic are not the same on one mode as another. On an aircraft when a plane is to be loaded to a certain weight, a ton of people may very well be a close substitute for a ton of packages that otherwise could be loaded onto the same vehicle—but not on a railroad. Another possibility is to use weights based on revenue, for example, revenue per passenger-mile and revenue per ton-mile. There is no general solution to this problem of the heterogeneity of tons, but there is a general warning to beware of inferences based on measures not appropriate to a particular inquiry.[1]

Output of transportation is not only a question of how *many* tons are moved. It also involves how *far* they are moved. Output of the transportation industry, therefore, is ordinarily measured in ton-miles or passenger-miles. These measures represent a major advance over statistics that show only the total number of tons moved without indicating the length of the average movement. They are used for comparisons among transportation systems, from one area to another for the same mode of transport, and from one means of transport to another.

The introduction of distance into the calculation, however, introduces another set of measurement problems. Consider, for example, the effects on the statistics of output of expenditures to straighten a railroad. After

1. See for discussions of measurement of output, Harold Barger, *The Transportation Industries, 1889–1946* National Bureau of Economic Research, 1951; and George W. Wilson, *Essays on Some Unsettled Questions in the Economics of Transportation* Indiana University, 1962.

the road has been straightened, if exactly the same commodities move
as before, the output of the railroad measured in ton-miles will *fall*. Yet
the railroad will be performing exactly the same economic function as
before, and, if anything, performing it better than before since there
is likely to be some improvement in the speed of the service associated
with the shortening of the route. The service provided is essentially
movement of goods between two points.

An alternative measure of output would measure the distance between these points by the shortest theoretically possible route between
the two points regardless of distance traveled, that is, by a straight line
or, more exactly, by the great circle route between the two points. This
measure would have the advantage that it would not vary according to
the method of transportation selected. Thus, movement of a given shipment between two points would represent the same number of ton-miles
whether the movement was by air, rail, pipeline, highway, or water. As
a rule of thumb, distances by air average about 15 per cent less than
by highway. If people leave the highways and take to the airways, one
would prefer that the shift not show up in the statistics as a decline
in total passenger miles. Water routes for inland transport tend to be
in varying degree circuitous; hence, miles by air and by water may be
very different.

There is one additional complication associated with ton-mile statistics. For most modes of transportation cost per ton-mile is not independent of length of haul. One reason for the association between cost
per mile and number of miles, to which reference was made in Chapter
11, is that some costs will be incurred at the terminal before any
movement takes place. In effect, the longer the haul, the more miles of
movement over which to spread the terminal costs. Average cost per
ton-mile, and also average revenue per ton-mile, falls with distance. For
comparisons of output over time or from one situation to another, therefore, it may be important also to be able to compare length of haul.[2]

Examples of the type of statistics of output frequently cited appear
in Tables 12.1 and 12.2, which show trends in intercity freight traffic
and passenger-miles by kind of transport agency. These estimates are
subject to the errors and difficulties just discussed. Table 12.1 excludes
deep-sea domestic waterborne traffic which amounted to about 312.5

2. It should be understood that traffic does not necessarily move over the shortest route.
If there are two or more rail routes, not all traffic will proceed by the short-line route. The
I.C.C.'s Bureau of Accounts has used estimates of average circuity of 13 per cent. (State-
ment 4–64, May 1964, *Rail Carload Unit Costs by Territories for the Year 1962.*, p. 9.)

billion ton-miles in 1963. Of that total by far the largest part is 271.7 billion ton-miles accounted for by tankers.[3]

Table 12.1—Intercity Freight Traffic, Public and Private, in Ton-Miles, by Kinds of Transport Agency, 1939–1963 (percentage distribution)

Year	Railway	Motor Vehicle	Inland Waterway1	Oil Pipelines	Airways	Total	Total (billions)
1939	62.34	9.72	17.71	10.23	.002	100.00	543
1949	58.38	13.83	15.22	12.55	.026	100.00	916
1959	45.55	21.52	15.26	17.61	.052	100.00	1278
1964	42.9	23.8	15.9	17.2	.1	100.00	1555

1. Includes Great Lakes. Data for inland waterways are not strictly comparable over the period owing to increases in waterways covered introduced in 1947–1953.
Source: I.C.C., *Transport Economics*, February 1965. (See I.C.C., *Annual Report* for earlier years.)

Table 12.2—Intercity Passenger-Miles, by Kinds of Transport Agency, 1950–1964

Agency	1950	PERCENT 1960	1964
Railways	46.3	27.6	19.7
Buses	37.7	25.5	24.3
Inland waterways, including Great Lakes	1.7	3.4	3.0
Airways	14.3	43.5	53.0
Total	100.0	100.0	100.0
Billions of passenger miles	70.2	78.1	93.4

Source: *Transport Economics*, February 1965; *Moody's Transportation Manual*, 1964, p. a30. From *Yearbook of Railroad Information*. (See I.C.C. *Annual Report*.)

As will be discussed below, since the type of freight moved and the type of service provided vary from one mode to another, the value of the ton-miles varies. In an important sense, therefore, Table 12.1 understates the economic importance of the movement of freight by air and motor vehicle and overstates the importance of the railways, pipelines, and inland waterways. The airlines, and in some degree the trucking companies, are producing and selling a premium service.

In addition to estimates of passenger-miles by common carrier we have estimates of the division of intercity passenger travel among the several modes including auto. Since these estimates can be broken down into subdivisions of the market, they are presented below in the discussion of competition and market structure.

3. I.C.C., *Transport Economics*, July 1965. Deep-sea domestic waterborne commerce consists primarily of coastwise movement by ocean-going vessels. It also includes intercoastal movement and traffic with non-contiguous areas such as Alaska and Hawaii.

While this brief discussion does not exhaust the difficulties in the measurement of output, it may at least warn of the heterogeneity of ton-miles and passenger-miles. It must be emphasized that output is a fundamental variable, and these difficulties permeate discussions of the statistics of transportation.

Statistics of Price and Revenue

The basic difficulty that confronts the economist interested in the price of transportation is the enormous variety of prices offered. This difficulty is greater for some branches of the industry than for others. It is less for the transport of people than for goods. There is also the possibility of separate prices for each pair of points. There is the possibility of elaborate systems of classification of the goods or persons to be moved. The possible number of prices is the product of the number of pairs of points and the number of types of commodity or service. To trace movements in such a large number of prices presents a series of formidable, if not impossible, statistical problems. What is required is a set of price indices, but, in general, indices of transportation prices unfortunately are not available.

The simplest approach to price movements is to use measures of average revenue. For example, it is possible to divide total output in ton-miles or passenger-miles into the total gross receipts. The resulting average, however, is far from ideal as a measure of price. Consider the situation when several prices are quoted for different types of commodity. If the highest of these prices is raised to the point where no shipments at all take place, the average price paid will fall. If a railroad raised its price on one type of freight to the point where that type of freight no longer moved by rail, shall we infer that the railroad cut its price? Should we note that the road then lost business and conclude, therefore, that the demand was not price elastic?

There is something to be learned, however, from measures of average revenue about gross differences among transport agencies. The average revenue received by railroads per passenger per mile was approximately 3.2 cents in 1963. This price compares to an average revenue of approximately 6.1 cents per passenger-mile received by the air transport carriers. The revenue per passenger-mile received by the bus companies engaged in the intercity movement of passengers was 2.8 cents. As this comparison makes clear, the average price of air travel is substantially higher than the price of travel by bus or by rail. Such comparisons conceal variations in fares from first-class to second-class fares and from the fares for single adults to family plan fares for children or complete families traveling together.

The diversity of prices concealed by an average rate is even greater when attention is turned to freight movements. Nevertheless, it is worth noting that average revenue per ton-mile of different types of carriers was estimated recently by the I.C.C. as follows:[4]

	Cents per Ton-Mile
Class I intercity motor carriers:	
Common carriers	6.5
Contract carriers	7.4
Class I railroads	1.3
Pipe lines (oil)	0.3

Air freight, of course, is much more expensive. In 1963 the average revenue of the domestic trunklines from freight carried on their scheduled operations was about 22 cents.

Statistics of total revenue exhibit the same deficiencies as statistics of average revenue. Information is available compiled by the I.C.C., however, showing total revenue by mode of transportation:[5]

Transport Agency	Revenue (millions of dollars)
Railroads	$10,229
Motor carriers of property	9,282
Motor carriers of passengers	809
Domestic scheduled air carrier operations	3,169
Pipe lines under I.C.C. jurisdiction	870

Note especially that the revenue of motor carriers is approximately equal in total to that of the railroads.

Statistics of Cost and Capacity

The uses of statistics of cost are numerous and important. Investment planning requires cost estimates. For a choice between two methods of transport, comparative costs are needed. Rate policy requires knowledge of costs. If a rate is to be set at long run marginal

4. I.C.C., *Transport Economics*, July 1964. Class I motor carriers are those with annual revenue over one million dollars.

5. I.C.C., *Transport Economics*, April 1965 (data are for 1964 and refer to regulated carriers only.)

cost for a certain type of shipment, it is necessary to estimate what that cost may be. If a rate is to be set at short run marginal cost under conditions of excess capacity, it is necessary to estimate that magnitude. It is also necessary to know what capacity may be in order to state that there is a certain amount of excess capacity.

Very extensive statistics of cost are available for the transportation industry. Regulatory bodies require complete information about the industries under their jurisdiction, and they insist upon at least approximately comparable systems of accounts from one enterprise to the next. The most thoroughly regulated industries, therefore, provide the most comprehensive statistics. The statistical information about the cost of American railroads under the jurisdiction of the Interstate Commerce Commission is particularly extensive. Yet it remains extremely difficult to answer crucial questions about the cost of transportation.

There are two main classes of sources of information about the costs of transportation. The most familiar consists of the accounting data and operating data collected by the enterprises engaged in the transportation of goods and people in the course of their operations. Accounting data on costs will be introduced in later chapters in the course of the discussion on individual industries. This information is essential to financial analysis and forms the raw material for statistical studies of cost. A second source of information about costs consists of engineering cost studies. These studies consist of estimates of the costs of different methods of providing a given service prepared for purpose of analysis.

STATISTICAL STUDIES OF AVERAGE COSTS AND MARGINAL COSTS— What the economist wants to know is the shape of the long run, intermediate run, and short run cost curves of firms in the several parts of the transportation industry. What the regulatory agencies collect are statistics of historical cost. As a first approximation, statistical analysts may try to estimate long run relationships by comparing firms of different sizes at the same point of time. They observe "plants" of different scales and hope to remove influences on costs other than the differences in scale.[6]

Analysts may try to estimate short run cost curves by observing changes in cost over time for a given firm during periods short enough so that the plant remained roughly constant but output varied. The object is to estimate the effect of changes in rate of operation, other factors held constant. These studies involve complex and difficult statistical problems that will not be discussed in detail here. One central problem

6. See Meyer, Peck, Stenason, and Zwick for such a study, *The Economics of Competition in the Transportation Industries,* Harvard University Press, 1959.

that may be mentioned is the difference in time between the movement of traffic and the expense for maintenance incurred as a consequence of that movement. The management of a railroad has considerable discretion as to the timing of maintenance work, to the analyst's discomfort.

ENGINEERING STUDIES OF ECONOMIES OF SCALE—Engineering studies of economies of scale in the transportation industry to supplement the statistical studies are less plentiful than might be desired. In some industries, however, such measures are available. The oil pipeline industry is one characterized by important economies of scale. One measure of these economies may be stated as follows: one ton of steel on a 30-inch pipeline will accommodate two and a half to three times as much petroleum as the same ton of steel on 8-inch line. In addition, less than half as many pumping stations are required on a 30-inch line as on a 8-inch line. This type of information, which comes from engineering sources as well as from the experience of the industry, is convincing evidence of the importance of economies of scale in oil pipelines.[7]

On the basis of all sources of information, it is safe to say that it is usually true that economies of scale exist in the use of larger vehicles. These economies are important, for example, in over-the-road motor trucks, as is discussed in Chapter 14. Recently the railroads have been actively exploring the economies both of large size freight cars and of handling freight in train load lots, say, trains of coal from mine to power plant. Another type of transportation in which there is much interest currently in economies of large "vehicles" is in tankers for the movement of petroleum on the high seas.

MEASURES OF CAPACITY—Measures of the capacity of a transportation industry may be employed to give an indication of the adequacy of existing facilities. The relation to investment policy is obvious. Measures of capacity may be used in conjunction with measures of output to indicate the percentage utilization of the facilities. Such measures may also be employed to predict and to avoid the development of bottlenecks in the system.

Analytically one may mean by the capacity of an industry the physical maximum output that could be produced by the industry with its present capital stock. It is impossible, for example, to move more than a certain number of vehicles per hour down a particular stretch of highway, and the attempt to do so by adding more vehicles will eventually create such a traffic jam that movement will stop.

Capacity may also be defined as that output at which average cost per unit output begins to rise. For example, it may be possible to in-

7. See Leslie Cookenboo, *Crude Oil Pipelines and Competition in the Oil Industry,* Harvard University Press, 1955.

crease the number of serviceable locomotives on a railroad by putting on extra men and working overtime in the repair shops. Train crews can be worked longer hours, but at overtime rates. Capacity is that level of output at which such expedients cause average cost per unit output to increase.

Overall measures of capacity divide into measures of the capacity of the system network and measures of the capacity of available vehicles and power plants. The two need not be the same. Recently the American railroads have had trouble finding the rolling stock to move the fall harvest of grain, but they seem to have excess capacity in the way.

The simplest measure of the capacity of the way is the number of route-miles available, whether of highway, railroad, airline routes, pipelines, or inland waterways. Measures of number of miles are incomplete without an indication of the capacity per mile. Obviously, railroads may vary in terms of number of tracks, highways in terms of number of lanes, pipelines in diameter, waterways in depth. Even this added dimension tends to give only a very imperfect idea of capacity. For example, the capacity of a single-track railroad will vary according to the number, length, and positions of the sidings provided and the signaling system employed. The capacity of a highway will depend upon the degree to which access to the highway is controlled and upon the number of intersections without grade separations.

In spite of these limitations statistics of total route mileage are useful. The totals change only slowly. The United States Air Transport carriers operated about 67,000 route miles in domestic trunkline operations as of 1963. This figure has grown slowly at the rate of about 12,000 route miles for the trunklines over a ten year period. In 1962, the pipelines engaged in interstate operations operated about 48,000 miles of gathering lines and about 107,000 miles of trunklines, or a total of 155,000 miles of line. The total mileage operated by these organizations also was increasing at a moderate rate, as shown by the increase from 1952 to 1962 of approximately 22,000 route miles. The increase was entirely in trunklines. The railroads (including all railroads in the United States) operated about 250,000 miles of road from 1916 to 1931, but by 1962 were down to 228,000 miles, or a decline of about 1000 miles a year on the average over a 30 year period.

Since either the way or the number of vehicles may be the limiting factor, studies of capacity in the transportation industry must take into account the vehicles available. The simplest measures are counts of numbers of vehicles, e.g., of railroad cars or airplanes. More sophisticated measures take into account the carrying capacity of the vehicles.

An example of a problem in the measurement of capacity of rolling

stock by counts of units is the change in the number of railroad locomotives owned by Class I railroads, which fell by about 6,600 locomotives from 1953 to 1963, the total count being 28,416 in the latter year.
The locomotives of 1963 were not identical with those of 1953, however.
The rise of the diesel, and the decline of the coal-burning steam locomotive, were major changes. The steam locomotives had ceased to haul any
appreciable volume of freight by 1961. Statistics on the capacity of
freight cars present similar problems of interpretation. The aggregate
capacity of freight cars in terms of millions of tons of carrying capacity
was approximately 92 million in 1949 and 94 million in 1958, a small
percentage of increase, but there seems to have been an improvement
both in reliability and in quality of ride—freedom from damage to the
contents. The average capacity of a single freight car is about 56 tons
as of 1962. (The average *load* has been rising and reached 38 tons by
1964.) Over the years the number of passenger cars has fallen with the
decline in service, from 38,000 in 1949 to 23,000 by 1963. The number
of motor trucks registered in the United States has been increasing
rapidly. The total number of trucks was 1.0 million in 1920, 4.6 millions
in 1940, and 11.9 millions in 1960 and 13.4 millions in 1963.

PEAK LOAD PROBLEMS—Since it is a basic characteristic of the transportation industry that transportation services cannot be stored, the
capacity of the industry must be considered in the context of the time
dimension of demand. Customers seek transportation at specific hours of
the day, days of the week, and weeks of the year. In this respect the
transportation industry is similar to the electric power industry and the
telephone industry. Telephone calls also cannot be stored; they must be
completed at the time the customer places his call if they are to be completed at all.

The characteristics of the load curves confronting the various
branches of the transportation industry are of the greatest importance
to the industry. Anything that tends to increase the business of a transport agency during an off-peak period will have a favorable effect on its
costs, while anything that makes the peak more jagged will tend to
increase average cost. The loss of off-peak business in recent years has
been a cause of distress in the urban transit industry. The peaks in
demand, therefore, have been attracting increasing attention by transportation economists.[8] Among the most complete statistics on the subject are those for urban transportation discussed in Chapter 15.

8. See the work of Tillo Kuhn presented to the National Bureau Conference on Transportation in 1963.

Statistics of the Structure of Market Demand

Study of the determinants of the market demand for transportation is essential to accurate prediction of events in the industry and to the intelligent formulation of economic policy. Forecasts of future demand are obviously necessary for investment policy, for price policy, and for product policy. The economist would like to know not only the price elasticity of demand but the elasticity of curves showing the relation of demand to every other major variable relevant to demand. In the market for passenger transportation the income elasticity of demand is fundamental. The effects of changes in all those attitudes and preferences that economists customarily group as "tastes" are also relevant. These subjects have been studied increasingly in recent years using the technology of the sample survey, but much remains as yet unknown.[9]

Analysis of the demand for the movement of freight should begin with the study of the location of economic activity, which has been discussed briefly above. Once a firm has selected the location of a plant, to a large extent it has made the basic decisions about the transportation requirements of the plant. The choice of means of transportation among the several modes may still remain to be made, or may be modified, and adjustments made in the modal split as opportunities arise for cost reductions.

On the passenger side of the market there are analagous problems: the investigation of the determinants of the total volume of passenger transportation and the determinants of mode choice. These problems arise both in the study of urban and intercity passenger travel. Mode choice in intercity travel is discussed in Chapter 19.

Statistics of Competition and Market Structure

For purposes of the analysis of the extent of competition and the nature of the relationship among sellers in an industry, as discussed in Chapter 5, it is of basic importance to know how many sellers there are in the market. Is there a single seller who has a monopoly in the market? Are there two sellers, three sellers, four sellers, or a large number of sellers in this market? What are their relative sizes? On the

9. See United States Department of Commerce, Bureau of the Census, *1963 Census of Passenger Transportation;* the National Travel Market Surveys of the Survey Research Center; the studies of demand for urban transportation referred to in Chapter 15.

other side of the market, is there a single buyer, a monopsonist, or are there two, three, four buyers? What is the number of purchasers of the service being offered for sale?

The type of information readily available is very different: there are about 100 Class I line-haul operating railroads in the United States, Class I roads being those with operating revenues of 3,000,000 dollars or more. There are roughly 1000 Class I motor carriers of property with operating revenue over 1 million dollars engaged in intercity service that report statistical information to the I.C.C.[10] There are about thirty-seven scheduled air carriers on domestic routes including both passenger and cargo carriers.

Statistics of this sort are open to several major objections as measures of the number of sellers in a market. They fail to take into account the possibility of competition by other unregulated or private carriers. Regulated motor carriers cannot ignore the possibility that a shipper may buy his own trucks. Second, statistics of the type shown fail to take into account competition between different transport agencies. An airline that is the sole concern offering transportation by air on a particular segment may be in active competition with a railroad, a bus company, or with the services offered by individuals driving their own cars on the public highways. Third, in order to measure statistically the number of buyers and sellers in a market, it is first necessary to define the market. As discussed earlier, there are many markets for transportation, not one single market covering the nation. These complexities are sufficiently troublesome so that no effort to summarize the extent of concentration in the transportation industry in the United States has ever been made. The best available statistics are for the airlines, and they will be discussed in Chapter 16. The number of airlines serving each pair of cities is known, and can be summarized. Even here, however, no measures of intermode competition exist.

Statistical analysis of the number and size distribution of *buyers* in particular markets for transportation is even less satisfactory. When a single buyer of transportation services is large enough, he may be in a very powerful bargaining position. One thinks, for example, of the actions of Andrew Carnegie and the steel company under his control in the controversy with the Pennsylvania Railroad in the nineteenth century when Carnegie actually began construction on a competing railroad line (the tunnels eventually became the route of the Pennsylvania Turnpike). The outcome in such circumstances will depend on

10. I.C.C., *Transport Statistics in the United States* (published annually).

bargaining between the buyer and the seller of the transportation services. Very little statistical information is available, however, on the frequency of such situations.

There is available some information relating to the problem of how the total transportation market is divided among the competing modes. For passenger transportation, the I.C.C. has published estimates of average length of passenger journey by mode, which are as follows:[11]

Mode of Transport	Average Length of Passenger Journey (Miles)
Class I rail	
Coach (excluding commutation)	116
Parlor and sleeping car	448
Class I motor carriers, intercity schedules	85
Scheduled domestic air carriers	601

If attention is restricted to trips to places 100 miles away or more, it is also possible to assemble estimates of the distribution of total passenger trips by distance and mode of transport used. (See Table 12.3 below.) The table emphasizes the dominance of the auto in the market

Table 12.3—Estimated Distribution of All Trips by Mode and Distance, 1963
(Percentage distribution of all trips of 100 miles or more)

Mode	All (100 miles or more)	DISTANCE (MILES) 100–199	200–499	500 +
Air	10.6	1.1	4.3	5.2
Rail	4.3	1.4	1.6	1.3
Bus	5.1	2.6	1.8	0.7
Auto	80.0	50.0	23.3	6.7
Total	100.0	55.1	31.0	13.9

Sources: The distribution of trips by mode and distance was calculated from the 1963 Census of Transportation, Passenger Transportation Survey, National Travel, 1963 Summary, TC 63 (A)-P4, November 1964. See Table 7 especially.

as a whole. Note that the share of the market taken by each of the modes varies with distance, however, with air important for the long distances but not for trips under 200 miles.

The competitive parts of the market are those where the shares of the modes are nearly equal. For example, the market for long haul travel is now divided between air and auto. A comparable table for 1950 would show a very different situation with regard to the relative position

11. I.C.C., *Transport Economics*, January 1964.

of air and other modes of travel, but the data needed for its construction do not exist.

A breakdown of total freight traffic by type of commodity must be based on a standard classification of commodities. Since 1964 a standard *Commodity Classification for Transportation Statistics* sponsored by the Bureau of the Budget has come into increasing use. This system of classification is based on the *Standard Industrial Classification*. With its application there is reason to hope for more nearly adequate statistics of freight transportation that will permit comparison across modes of transport.

A recent major addition to statistical knowledge of freight transportation has been made by the 1963 Census of Transportation. The Commodity Transportation Survey, which is a part of the 1963 Census, measured the volume and characteristics of shipments to markets outside of the local area of the plant for a sample of all plants in manufacturing. The resulting information was tabulated for 23 groups of industries within manufacturing. In the Census the estimates of distance are estimates of straight-line distance calculated by a computer program to which the inputs include the origin and destination shown on the shipping paper.

The nature of the results may be indicated by the findings for meat and dairy products (group 1). A total of 43 million tons were shipped, generating 13 billion ton-miles. Of the ton-miles nearly half, 49 per cent, were by rail, 34 per cent by motor carrier, and 15 per cent by private truck, the three principal means of transporting meat and dairy products.

A major contribution to knowledge is made by the breakdown of these totals. The most important division is by size of shipment, that is, by the number of pounds shipped as shown on the individual bill of lading, sales invoice, or other shipping paper. The breakdown of shipments by weight is as follows:[12]

Means of Transport	All Weights	WEIGHT OF SHIPMENT (POUNDS)				
		Under 1,000	1,000– 9,999	10,000– 29,999	30,000– 59,999	60,000 +
Rail	31	1	6	20	37	54
Motor carrier	28	13	24	42	41	12
Private truck	40	86	69	38	22	33
Other; unknown	1	—	1	—	—	1
Total	100	100	100	100	100	100

12. See *1963 Census of Transportation, Commodity Transportation Survey, Shipper Series, Meat and Dairy Products,* Preliminary Report TC63 (P)C1–1. United States Department of Commerce, Bureau of the Census, 1965.

These figures show that although rail accounts for more than half (54 per cent) of the largest shipments of 60,000 pounds or more, virtually none of the shipments under 1,000 pounds are made by rail. The bulk of these shipments (86 per cent) are made by private trucks. The motor carriers compete most effectively for the broad middle range of shipments, shipments of from 1,000 to 59,999 pounds.

Statistics of Performance

The student of any industry who wishes to form a judgment as to the economic performance of that industry will wish to have statistical measures of that performance. Without them he is likely to be reduced to the most subjective judgments.

DIMENSIONS OF OUTPUT—A variety of measures of technical performance have been developed for transportation. One class of measures concerns those dimensions of output that everyone will agree are desirable. It is desirable, other things being equal, for service to operate on time, for people to arrive safely, for vehicles to move at a high rate of speed rather than a low rate of speed, etc.

For example, the average rate of train speed has changed as follows:[13]

AVERAGE TRAIN SPEED

Year	Freight	Passenger
1941	16.5	36.1
1950	16.8	37.4
1959	19.5	40.3
1961	19.9	40.9
1963	20.1	40.9

The speed of aircraft has increased rapidly in recent years as the following series shows:[14]

AVERAGE SPEED, DOMESTIC FLIGHTS

Year	m.p.h.
1950	180
1960	235
1961	252
1963	287

13. I.C.C. *Transport Statistics in the United States.* The series shown is average train-miles per train-hour.
14. As reported in the *Statistical Abstract of the United States,* 1963, p. 586.

These figures represent what is known as block speed, that is the quotient arrived at by dividing the distance between two points by the time from the moment of leaving the first to the arrival at the destination. In order to achieve a given block speed an aircraft must travel at substantially more than that speed during part of its trip in order to make up for time lost in taxiing along runways, waiting for traffic clearance, and the like.

Data on comparative accident rates are usually cited in fatalities per 100,000,000 passenger miles. The rate for deaths of air passengers shows a tendency to fluctuate from year to year since many deaths may be caused by a single crash. The rate was as low as 0.1 per 100 million passenger miles in 1963. More typical rates are probably those for 1961 and 1962, which were about 0.4 for domestic scheduled airlines. Rates for rail and bus are lower, on the order of 0.1 to 0.2. For private passenger cars the death rates are much higher, in the vicinity of 5.6 per 100 million passenger miles in 1964.[15]

QUANTITY OF INPUTS—Another class of measures refers to quantity of inputs or inputs per unit output. To an economist such measures of performance are partial measures. It is not enough to know about a single input; it is necessary to know about all inputs for a complete picture. Such simple measures, however, can be useful.

One type of measure concerns the quantity of some variable input used. One example is the total number of hours worked by employees of Class I railroads, which recently has declined as follows:[16]

Year	Millions of man-hours
1922	4,311
1930	3,760
1940	2,616
1950	2,877
1959	1,924
1963	1,641

This measure of an input can be related to measures of output. Ton-miles of revenue freight were 589 billion in 1950 and 575 billion in 1959. Revenue passenger miles fell from 32 billion to 22 billion from 1950 to 1959.

Other measures concern utilization of some part of the plant or the quality of the plant. The number of miles per locomotive day in freight

15. See *Traffic Safety,* published by the National Safety Council, for motor vehicle death rates. Figures for the common carriers are compiled by the I.C.C. and F.A.A. (See F.A.A., *Statistical Handbook of Aviation.*)

16. Source: I.C.C., reprinted in *Moody's Transportation Manual.*

service for serviceable locomotives, a measure of the utilization of equipment, rose as follows:[17]

Year	Miles per locomotive day
1939	93
1950	119
1959	145
1963	150

Another example of a series that shows a measure of utilization is the revenue passenger load factor for United States air carriers. It measures the proportion of seat miles flown that were actually sold to paying passengers. In 1964, the revenue passenger load factor for the domestic trunklines was 55 per cent. For United States international air carriers, the rate was 53 per cent in 1963.

Such a series is not always available; for example, it is not shown in the *Transit Fact Book*, published by the American Transit Association. It cannot even be approximated without a measure of passenger miles sold, which is lacking. In 1963 the urban transit industry operated 2,022 million vehicle miles and carried 8,400 million revenue passengers, primarily in motor buses. How far those passengers moved, however, is unknown. Even such a relatively simple measure as load factor cannot be computed without a series that measures the output of the industry.

There are a variety of other measures of performance in use, especially for the railroads. For the most part these series involve ratios, usually of some measure of output to an input, such as ton-miles per locomotive day. These measures can be enlightening for particular problems. More sophisticated study of performance may lead, and conceptually it should lead, to attempts to consider simultaneously all inputs and outputs of a given transportation agency in an econometric production function. Some studies of this nature have been made, but we shall not consider them in this chapter.

CONCLUDING COMMENT—Perhaps the major conclusion of this brief review of the statistics of the American transportation industry is that in spite of the large mass of statistics available many major gaps in statistical knowledge remain for the economic analyst. The state of statistical knowledge is unven. We are relatively well informed on some subjects for some industries and poorly informed about others. We know least about the unregulated types of transportation and about those topics that require sophisticated analysis or specially collected data.

17. Source: *Ibid.*

13

Railroads

The "Railroad Problem"

MOST PEOPLE turning their attention to a discussion of the railroads do so with the feeling that there is a "railroad problem." "Things are not good" with the railroad industry. Often such views, upon examination, are based on statistics of output. There are a number of different series used to measure the total output of the railroads. None of them in recent years have shown trends that can be described as indicating rapid growth for the industry as a whole. One series shows the tons of revenue freight carried by all Class I Railways, i.e., those roads with operating revenues in excess of 3,000,000 dollars.

Billions of Tons of Revenue Freight Carried by Class I Railroads

1955	2.62
1958	2.20
1960	2.29
1964	2.50

This series shows an absolute decline in the volume of freight moved from 1955 to 1958 in spite of the general growth of the economy but then shows a modest upward trend from 1958 to 1964.

Another basic series concerns revenue ton-miles of freight movement:

Billions of Revenue Ton-Miles of Freight by Class I Railways

1920	410
1930	383
1940	373
1950	589
1955	624
1960	572
1963	622
1964	659

This series shows the same absolute decline followed by recovery.

Statistics showing estimates of the per cent of total intercity freight traffic which moves by rail are also relevant:

Per Cent of Ton-Miles by Rail of Total Intercity Freight Traffic

1940	61
1950	56
1955	49
1959	45
1963	43

As these statistics make clear, the proportion of ton-miles of freight moved by rail has been falling and continues to fall (at the time of writing). The recovery in the absolute volume of railroad freight movement has been made possible by the expansion of the economy and associated increase in total freight movement. The railroads have been receiving a decreasing share of the pie, but the pie is getting larger.

Estimates of the per cent of total *revenue* received by the railroads cannot be exact since much of the movement by truck is not regulated and the statistics for the unregulated part of the transportation industry are inadequate. There is no doubt, however, that the railroads share of total revenue from freight shipments is lower than their share of ton-miles. A few years ago the I.C.C. estimated about a quarter of the total intercity freight transportation dollar goes to railroads.[1]

Turning to the passenger business, the number of revenue passenger miles sold by the railroads has been declining since 1920:

1. I.C.C., *Seventy-first Annual Report*, p. 3. (A basic source for statistics of railroad output and other statistical information about carriers regulated by the I.C.C. is *Transport Statistics in the United States*, published annually. A convenient compilation appears in *Moody's Transportation Manual*, also annual. For more current statistics see *Transport Economics* published monthly by the I.C.C.)

Billions of Revenue Passenger-Miles Class I Railroads

1920	47.4
1930	26.9
1940	23.8
1950	31.8
1960	21.3
1964	18.3

Unlike freight movement the absolute volume of railroad passenger business has continued to decline in recent years.

Whatever statistical measure is chosen, it is clear that the per cent of all traffic carried by the rails has been falling for some time and the total absolute volume of some parts but not all of their business appears also to have entered a decline that may prove to be permanent.

Associated with the trends in output has been a tendency toward narrow profit margins for the railroads. The operating ratio shows the percentage of total railway operating income required to meet railway operating expenses. This ratio has been about 79 per cent in recent years, e.g., 78.51 per cent in 1962. (The remaining 21 per cent covers taxes and return on capital.) The operating ratio in 1950 was 74.4 per cent; but in the early years, say, 1900, it was about 65 per cent. The American railroad system as a whole does earn a profit, according to the Association of American Railroads in 1964 699 million dollars on revenues of 9.9 billion dollars for Class I roads, but the margin is narrow for such a capital-intensive industry.

The decline of an industry should not be in itself a matter of public concern. Even the extinction of some industries has been necessary. Who will argue that the development of railroads should not have been permitted to destroy the stagecoach industry? In the case of the railroads nothing so drastic is possible in the foreseeable future. Some industries *should* decline. There may be problems associated with their decline in terms of efficient withdrawal of resources without undue loss or unfair burdens on individuals. In general, however, the decline of an industry is an economic misfortune only if it occurs for noneconomic reasons or at a noneconomic rate.

Is there, then, a railroad problem? There is a reasonable consensus of opinion that there is, indeed, a railroad problem—or a series of railroad problems. The problems essentially are problems of adjustment to an environment in which the railroads must meet competition from other modes of transport. The economic environment of the railroads has changed fundamentally. Some types of service must be given to the competition and others must be performed with increasing efficiency. Adjustments to this end have been required and continue to be required in the policy of the government, of railroad management, and of the other interests concerned with the railroads. The following discussion is centrally concerned with the problem of the adjustment of the railroads to a competitive environment although some attention is paid to other topics. There is no special difficulty in outlining the economically desirable policy that should be followed by an industry faced with competition from new technology. Such a policy would include the abandonment of activities or types of service that no longer can meet the market test, search for and adoption of innovations that can reduce costs or increase demand for types of service that can be continued or expanded, and adjustment of pricing policy to take into account the new competition.

The modern problems of the railroads must be dealt with by institutions that have developed over a long period of time. Present policy should be understood in historical context. It must also be understood in the context of railroad costs. Only following a discussion of these two topics, then, will we turn to recent developments in railroad mergers and the organization of the industry and to a discussion of railroad rates and rate policy.

The Development of Public Policy Toward the Railroads

Public policy toward railroads in the United States has passed through three distinct periods that may be distinguished according to the shifts in the dominant objectives of public policy from one period to the next. The first period was one wherein the main objective was the stimulation of development of the railroads, as discussed in Chapter 7. Both the national government and the state and local governments were principally concerned with the problem of getting the railroads built in order to stimulate the economic growth of the country. Land grants and grants of money were made in order to assist in the raising of capital for the railroads in a period when capital scarcity was chronic in the United States and profitability had to await the growth of traffic. Extensive use was made of European capital.

The second period may be dated roughly from the passage of the *Act to Regulate Commerce* in 1887. During this period the dominant objective of public policy was to protect shippers and the public from the monopoly power of the railroads and to prevent inequity in the use of that power. There was much public concern over the railroads. Profits were believed to be unfairly high. Unjust discrimination among shippers and among communities and regions was a cause of complaint. The principal feature of the early part of the period was a struggle for power between the regulatory authorities and the railroads that eventually resulted in the effective domination of the industry by the regulatory commission. The history of this period and of the Interstate Commerce Commission will be discussed in more detail below.

The third period, which continues to the present time, is the period of adjustment to competing modes of transportation whose central problem already has been mentioned. In this period public policy has had multiple purposes. The existence of an efficient railroad industry has again become a matter of public concern although there has been continued emphasis on the control of monopoly power. The technological changes in highway transportation that presented to the railroads the problem of adjustment were well begun by about 1920. A change in public attitudes was brought about by the experience of World War I. During that war "the railroad problem" consisted in the technical problems railroads faced in meeting the demands for traffic that arose out of the war period. The federal government found it necessary to take over the railroads and operate them for a period during the war. At the conclusion of the episode of government operation, the Commission was given new responsibilities relating to the development of the railroads as an integrated and effective transportation system through consolidations and cooperation in car interchanges, and the like. The emphasis was on the national need for a transportation system adequate to meet the demands placed on it by the economy either in peace or in war. As time passed, the relation of the railroads to other forms of transportation has become increasingly important. The National Transportation Policy incorporated in the *Transportation Act* of 1940 is an explicit but not particularly successful attempt to set guidelines of policy concerning the relations among different modes of transportation.

It is not accidental that the period in which comparatively little attention was paid to the contribution of transportation to the development of the country was the shortest of the three and appears in retrospect as a comparatively brief episode in the long history of public policy toward transportation. It is always the most fundamental requirement of public policy that there should be an adequate transportation system that can play an appropriate part in the economic life of the country. The development of such a system may under some circumstances place undue power in the hands of a limited number of organizations or individuals, and it may become necessary to take special measures to control this power. But a prior requirement is that an adequate transportation system should be provided. The development of regulatory power, however, was a critical part of the evolution of transportation policy and regulatory objectives continue to be important.

GRANGER MOVEMENT—The business depression of 1873, like other major depressions, created a climate that was favorable for the development of popular movements for reform. Sentiment became strong among farmers in the West for regulation of the railroads. The people in the newly settled agrarian states felt themselves at the mercy of the railroads, without which they would be cut off equally from supplies and from markets. They were well aware of the public assistance given to the railroads and of contributions of capital by private citizens who lived in the areas served. Something of the state of public opinion at the time may be conveyed by a quotation from an address of the Grand Master of the Grange in 1874, in which he made the following observations about the railroads: "When we plant a crop we can only guess what it will cost to send it to market, for we are the slaves of those whom we erected [the railroads] . . . in our inmost soul we feel deeply wronged at the return made for the kind and liberal spirit we have shown them."[2] The grievances of the western farmers against the railroads were threefold: (1) the rate levels were believed too high; (2) unfair price discrimination was believed to exist; and (3) investors who lost money in railroad stock believed that promoters had cheated them. Hadley wrote in 1885 that the farmers in the early 1870s were "dangerously near the point where revolutions begin."[3]

A series of laws known as the Granger Laws were passed in 1871–1874. In part they were ill-considered, and most of them were shortly repealed. Their constitutionality was tested in the courts, however, and it is a matter of major importance in the legal history of economic regulation that the right to regulate was upheld. The leading case is *Munn vs. Illinois.*[4] *The Illinois Act* of 1870 required the licensing of public warehouses and set maximum rates for the storage of grain. The power of the government, in this instance the state, to pass a law providing for economic regulation of a private business was upheld by the Supreme Court. Railroads, because of economic similarity to warehouses, were deemed to be covered by this interpretation.

2. This famous quotation comes originally from the *Proceedings, National Grange of Patrons of Husbandry,* 1874.
3. A. T. Hadley, *Railroad Transportation,* New York, 1885, p. 134. (This quotation has been cited by Locklin.)
4. 94 U.S. 113 (1876).

The second major constitutional issue had to do with which branch of government should have the power of regulation of interstate commerce. In *Wabash, St. Louis and Pacific Railway vs. Illinois,*[5] the Supreme Court held that the interstate commerce clause gave to the Congress the *exclusive* right to regulate interstate commerce. Since most railroad traffic is interstate in character, including the movement of western grain to market, this decision made federal regulation essential.

RATE MAKING BEFORE THE ACT—One type of practice objected to by the public was subsequently described by the I.C.C. in its First Annual Report:[6]

The system of making special arrangements with shippers was in many parts of the country not confined to large manufacturers and dealers, but was extended from person to person under the pressure of alleged business necessity, or because of personal importunity or favoritism, and even in some cases from a desire to relieve individuals from the consequences of previous unfair concessions to rivals in business. The result was that shipments of importance were commonly made under special bargains entered into for the occasion, or to stand until revoked, of which the shipper and the representative of the road were the only parties having knowledge. These arrangements took the form of special rates, rebates, and drawbacks, underbilling, reduced classification, or whatever might be best adapted to keep the transaction from the public; but the public well understood that private arrangements were to be had if the proper motives were presented. The memorandum-book carried in the pocket of the general freight agent often contained the only record of the rates made to the different patrons of the road, and it was in his power to place a man or a community under an immense obligation by conceding a special rate on one day, and to nullify the effect of it on the next day by doing even better by a competitor.

THE ACT TO REGULATE COMMERCE—The law as passed in 1887 applied to all common carriers by rail engaged in interstate or foreign commerce. The central provisions with respect to rates were contained in four sections:

Section 1 required all rates to be "just and reasonable," employing a phrase from the common law. Thus, extortionate charges were prohibited.

Section 2 was directed at personal discrimination such as the above. It provided "that if any common carrier subject to the provisions of this act shall . . . by any special rate, rebate, . . . or other device, charge . . . any person a greater or less compensation for any service rendered,

5. 118 U.S. 557 (1886).
6. See I.C.C., *First Annual Report,* pp. 5–6.

in the transportation of persons or property . . . than it charges . . . any other person . . . for doing . . . a like and contemporaneous service in the transportation of a like kind of traffic under substantially similar circumstances . . . such common carrier shall be deemed guilty of unjust discrimination." In effect, this section thus defines "unjust discrimination" among persons and prohibits it. ("Persons," of course, includes legal "persons" such as corporations as well as natural persons.)

Section 3 deals with "undue preference and prejudice." It prohibits "undue preference or advantage to any particular person . . . corporation, or locality . . . or to any particular description of traffic." Note that geographical discrimination is specifically mentioned. Note also, it is "undue" preference that is forbidden.

Section 4, known as the long- and short-haul clause, deals with a specific form of geographic discrimination. It provides that except in "special cases" it shall be "unlawful to charge greater compensation for the transportation of passengers or of like kind of property under substantially similar circumstances and conditions for a shorter than for a longer distance over the same line in the same direction, the shorter being included within the longer distance." Section 4 can be most easily understood with the aid of a simplified diagram of a rail line joining three cities:

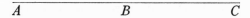

A B C

It prohibits charging a larger total amount for a shipment from A to B than for a shipment from A to C.

The law also prohibited pooling. It provided that rates were to be public knowledge. Tariffs were to be printed and copies filed with the Commission.

From the point of view of a modern economist with the theory of price discrimination in mind, was this law an attempt to prohibit price discrimination by the railroads subject to the jurisdiction of the Commission? Most emphatically the law was not an attempt to prohibit price discrimination in general. It was an attempt to prevent discrimination that was believed to be unjust. What was unreasonable, unjust, or undue was largely left to the Commission and the courts to determine. From time to time Congress also has intervened in the process by the passage of new legislation. As will be discussed in more detail below, the long history of interpretation and amendment of the act has left obscure the meaning of the law in some situations.

The early court decisions were surprisingly unfavorable to the Com-

mission. Within a period of a little more than ten years, judicial interpretation left the Commission with little important regulatory power.[7]
The courts refused to expedite injunctions to enforce I.C.C. orders.
Without injunctions the orders were unenforceable. Further, the courts
reviewed the facts of the cases and took new testimony in addition to
reviewing the law. The power of the I.C.C. to control the rate level was
interpreted not to include power to set rates that would be just and
reasonable. All the I.C.C. could do was to declare that a particular exact
rate was illegal. The phrase in Section 4 with regard to "substantially
similar circumstances and conditions" was interpreted to require that the
competitive conditions must be similar. This interpretation made the
clause meaningless. A rational railroad manager would charge more for
a long than short haul only if the demand curves in the two markets
differed in elasticity. It was precisely because competition from other
railroads or from water transportation made the demand curve elastic in
the long haul market that there was reason to charge more for the short
haul. If the law meant anything it was that the railroad manager was
forbidden to take advantage of the difference in elasticity arising from
the difference in competition beyond the point of charging the same
amount for the short and the long hauls.

ELKINS ACT OF 1903—It is noteworthy that the first important
amendment to strengthen the law, the *Elkins Act* of 1903, was put
through in large part by the railroads themselves. This legislation was
aimed at the regulation of price competition by providing effective control of departures from published rates. Its purpose, which was largely
achieved, was to make Section 2 effective and stop unjust personal discrimination of the type described above in the quotation from the
I.C.C.'s *First Annual Report*. The railroads themselves as well as their
officers and agents were made subject to fines for violations. Shippers
also were subjected to penalties. The railroads had discovered that
while a requirement of published charges to which all sellers adhere may
have advantages from the point of view of fairness among purchasers
of railroad services it also has advantages to the sellers because it makes
it much easier to maintain a monopoly price level in the industry. High
price levels in oligopolistic industries are much easier to maintain if all
price shading is publicized. Few modern economists would advocate the
passage of such legislation in the absence of effective regulatory control.
But such control came shortly thereafter.

HEPBURN ACT—The *Hepburn Act* of 1906 marked the beginning of

7. *I.C.C., Activities 1887–1937*, p. 35. The legislative history of the Commission in the
earlier period is well summarized in this report.

effective railway regulation by the Interstate Commerce Commission. The outstanding provision of this *Act* was the authority given the Commission to prescribe maximum rates. The law provided that orders specifying such rates were to be effective as determined by the Commission with the burden on the carriers of testing the validity of the orders before the courts. Thus the procedural need of enforcing injunctions was removed.

MANN-ELKINS ACT—The next step in the strengthening of the power of the Commission came with the *Mann-Elkins Act* of 1910. The authority of the Commission to prescribe maximum rates under the *Hepburn Act* could be used only on complaint concerning rates which were already in effect. The Commission had not enjoyed the power to determine the reasonableness of a proposed rate before the rate was put into effect. The procedure had been that complaints were made before the Commission and the Commission might then find a rate to be unreasonable. But now the *Mann-Elkins Act* provided that the Commission could suspend new schedules before they went into effect, make its investigation, and prescribe maximum rates if it considered that such rates were appropriate.

PANAMA CANAL ACT—The *Panama Canal Act* of 1912 was intended to foster competition between rail transport across the continent and water transport through the Canal, but its provisions were drafted in general language. It forbade railways to own or operate water lines when competition would thereby be lessened. This legislation was subsequently applied to the ownership of freighters on the Great Lakes by the railroads, and the railroads were forced out of the freight business on the Lakes.

TRANSPORTATION ACT OF 1920—The railroads had very serious difficulty in coping with the increased traffic during World War I. Under wartime conditions the collapse of the system could not be permitted. On January 1, 1918 the railroads were taken over by the federal government as a wartime measure, and they continued under federal operation until March 1, 1920. The *Transportation Act* of 1920 returned the roads to private ownership.

It was a critical stage in the history of the American railroads. In a different political climate nationalization might have become permanent. The question had to be faced of how the industry should be organized.

The general philosophy of the *Transportation Act* of 1920 was that although the railroads should be returned to private ownership the government should take the responsibility to see that adequate transportation was supplied. The Commission was directed to propose a plan for regrouping the railways into a limited number of systems. Competition, however, was required to be preserved under the plan. This provision of the law proved in the end a failure and was repealed; the regrouping envisioned has yet to be carried out. The present status of the merger question will be discussed below.

The *Act* also strengthened the powers of the Commission in several areas. The Commission was given authority over railway security issues and over abandonments of railway lines. Pooling, which earlier had been prohibited absolutely, might be permitted by the Commission. The Commission was given power to set minimum as well as maximum rates. This provision was introduced to prevent rate wars among railroads. In the coming struggle for business between the railroads and the trucks, this power of the Commission over minimum rates was to be of central importance in the regulation of intermodal competition. The I.C.C. was also given control over the division of rates, which is necessary when one shipment uses several roads, enabling it to protect weak roads.

HOCH-SMITH RESOLUTION—The *Hoch-Smith Resolution* of 1925 was pushed through by the farm bloc. Its language is vague: it directs the Commission to adjust freight rates "to the end that commodities may freely move." The Commission is to give due regard to such factors as the market value of commodities. The Commission is directed to set the lowest possible lawful rates for the products of agriculture. As finally interpreted by the Supreme Court the *Resolution* did not add to the powers of the Commission.

Yet, the *Resolution* helped the members of the farm bloc in Congress make clear to the I.C.C. that they wanted low rates on farm products to relieve the economic problems of the farmers. If rates less than the full cost of service were charged for such service, correspondingly higher rates would have to be charged for other products, such as manufactured products. A rate structure involving low rates on agricultural products and high rates on such items as manufactured goods is inherently vulnerable to competition from motor carriers.

The depression of the 1930s produced financial distress among the railroads but little basic change in railroad regulation. The emergency provisions of the *Emergency Transportation Act* of 1933 were largely unsuccessful, and little was done of a permanent character. Other legislation enacted in the 1930s included an amendment to the *Bankruptcy Act* of March 3, 1933, which changed the legal arrangements for the reorganization of insolvent railroads and imposed duties on the Interstate Commerce Commission in that connection. Legislation concerning motor carriers will be discussed in Chapter 14.

TRANSPORTATION ACT OF 1940—Congress made an attempt at a basic reformulation of transportation policy in 1940. Perhaps the most noteworthy feature of the *Transportation Act* of 1940 was the statement in the preamble of a National Transportation Policy. This Policy represents an attempt to deal with the problem of competing modes of transportation. It reads as follows:

It is hereby declared to be the national transportation policy of the Congress to provide for fair and impartial regulation of all modes of transportation subject to the provisions of this Act, so administered as to recognize and preserve the inherent advantages of each; to promote safe, adequate, economical, and efficient service and foster sound economic conditions in transportation and among the several carriers; to encourage the establishment and maintenance of reasonable charges for transportation services, without unjust or destructive competitive practices; to cooperate with the several States and the duly authorized officials thereof; and to encourage fair wages and equitable working conditions; all to the end of developing, coordinating, and preserving a national transportation system by water, highway, and rail, as well as other means, adequate to meet the needs of the commerce of the United States, of the Postal Service, and of the national defense. All of the provisions of this Act shall be administered and enforced with a view to carrying out the above declaration of policy.[8]

From this statement it is clear the Congress is in favor of preserving "the inherent advantages" of each mode of transportation, but it is obscure what these advantages may be. Does a mode have "inherent advantages" for a given type of traffic even if its costs are higher than those of alternative modes of transport? Should it, therefore, be regarded as having some right to a "fair share" of the traffic? What costs are relevant to such a determination? On such questions the policy is unclear.

Beyond this statement, the *Transportation Act* of 1940 made a contribution to the literature in the field by the creation of a Board of Investigation and Research, which was responsible for a series of reports in its two years of existence. This law also brought interstate common carriers by water under the jurisdiction of the I.C.C. Carriers by water of commodities in bulk, however, were exempted, provided that not more than three commodities at a time were transported. Otherwise, basic policy was unchanged.

REED-BULWINKLE ACT—The *Reed-Bulwinkle Act* of 1948 provided specific exemption from the antitrust laws for rate bureaus subject to

8. 54 Stat. 899.

the Interstate Commerce Act, as amended, confirming a long-existing situation. Rate bureaus are associations of railroads for the purpose of setting rates. Their activities will be discussed below in connection with the discussion of railroad rates.

TRANSPORTATION ACT OF 1958—The *Transportation Act* of 1958 was largely motivated by a desire to assist the railroads. It authorizes the Commission to guarantee loans made to the railroads. This provision was intended to assist the railroads in obtaining capital. It has been little used. The loans may be for capital improvements or for maintenance only. No dividends can be paid while a loan for maintenance is outstanding.

The *Act* gives to the Commission the authority to permit the reduction or abandonment of service by railroads even when the trains involved operate within a state and the state authority had denied a petition to discontinue service. This provision has been effective in circumventing state regulatory bodies that had sometimes been reluctant to permit railroads to withdraw unprofitable service.

Finally, the *Transportation Act* of 1958 directs the I.C.C. in setting rates to consider the costs of the carrier to which the rate is applicable and *not* to set rates at a level to protect traffic of other modes, *but* to give due consideration to the National Transportation Policy, which lays emphasis on preserving the inherent advantages of each mode. As a result the law with regard to rate making when competition between modes is involved, as it usually is involved, can only be described as obscure.

CONCLUDING COMMENT—The history of the legislation having to do with the regulation of railroads by the Interstate Commerce Commission shows a remarkable degree of continuity of development over a period that now exceeds three quarters of a century. The provisions of the law as initially passed are still important at the present. The sense of steady progress with which one reads the history of the development of the powers of the Commission up to the *Transportation Act* of 1920, however, is difficult to sustain in the later years. By 1920 the Commission was fully empowered to deal with the problems of railroad monopoly. It was less well equipped to deal with the emerging problems of competition among modes.

There are two main areas of regulatory policy toward railroads that have importance for competition among modes. Both involve controversy. The first to be discussed is the policy toward mergers and the organization of the industry; the second, rates and rate policy. Both areas, however, can be better understood in the light of a discussion of railroad costs.

Introduction to Railroad Costs

The following discussion of railroad costs begins with a general examination of the subject based on data assembled by the I.C.C. for the industry as a whole. The sense in which the railroad industry is capital intensive is discussed, together with the consequences of the capital intensive character of the industry for economic policy. Subsequent sections concern the problems of estimating costs for particular shipments or types of shipments, and describe briefly the methods that have been used to develop estimates of costs on a disaggregated basis.

RAILROADS AS CAPITAL INTENSIVE—The most important special characteristic of railroads from the point of view of cost is that they are extremely capital intensive. The total investment in road and equipment of Class I and II railroads is estimated by the I.C.C. at about 34.4 billion dollars.[9] Deducting from the book value of 34.4 billion dollars depreciation reserves of 9.0 billion dollars, net investment is about 25.4 billion dollars. Operating revenues of 9.5 billion dollars imply a capital-output ratio of about 2.8. By comparison, consider that the 65 Class A carriers by inland and coastal waterways (those with annual operating revenue of over 500,000 dollars) had an investment net of depreciation of 195 million dollars and operating revenue of 244 million dollars. The capital-output ratio would 0.8. (This estimate refers only to carriers under the jurisdiction of the I.C.C.) The 1004 motor carriers in intercity service reporting to the I.C.C. in 1961 had carrier operating property revenue of 5,428 million dollars, for a ratio of only 0.2. The railroads are more capital intensive than other modes of transportation mainly because they provide their own way. Highways, waterways, and airways are provided by the government. To the extent that they are paid for by the carriers the charges are mostly in the form of user charges like taxes on fuel, which to the carriers are variable costs.

It is true that there is a range of choice as to how capital intensive a railroad is to be. For example, there is a choice as to whether to electrify a length of line. Electrification is expensive, but yields fuel economy; in the use of coal the economy is on the order of 4 to 1 over steam locomotives. Such a choice, however, is a matter of degree. There is no choice as to whether a railroad is to be capital intensive.

Important consequences follow. In the first place, since railroads are

9. I.C.C., *Transport Statistics in the United States, 1962, Part I: Railroads*, p. 104. Data are for 1962. Class I roads have operating revenue of 3,000,000 dollars annually or more; Class II, less than that amount. Switching and terminal companies are excluded from these statistics. These companies account for about 2 percent of all railway operating revenues.

capital intensive they require large initial investments. The history of the early roads is largely the history of efforts to raise enough capital. In the second place, after a railroad has been built, that is, after the necessary heavy investment has been made in right-of-way, track, yards, terminals, rolling stock, and all necessary facilities, the profitability of the investment will depend heavily on how intensively it is used. A third consequence is the difficulty of allocating costs to particular traffic. When a given fixed plant consisting of all kinds of capital goods (way, rolling stock, terminals) is used to move a wide variety of commodities and passengers, as is true on the railroads, it is not easy to say how the costs should be allocated among the several kinds of traffic. In economics, there is no unique solution to the problem of the allocation of common costs. The more important these costs are, the more important the arbitrary elements in cost allocation.

It is possible as a practical matter to estimate the total costs of a railroad and to divide those costs over the traffic, but it is *not* possible to arrive at a uniquely correct division of the costs. More than one method of allocating costs being possible, the search for *the* full cost of a given shipment is a will-o'-the-wisp. Much, however, can be done and is being done to increase knowledge of the behavior of rail costs and to reduce the areas of uncertainty.

Information about railroad costs is published by the I.C.C., which requires reports based on a prescribed system of accounts. A summary of these costs is shown by the following tabulations for all Class I Line-Haul Railroads. The total annual average railway operating expense may be broken down as follows:[10]

Type of Expense	Per Cent of Operating Revenue
Compensation to employees	49
Fuel	4
Depreciation	6
Loss and damage; injuries to persons	2
Insurance; stationery and printing; advertising	1
Pensions	1
All other (being materials other than fuel and miscellaneous)	17
All operating expenses	79 per cent

The first impression one receives is that the compensation of employees dominates the cost structure to a surprising extent for a capital intensive industry. The compensation of employees is important partly because

10. *Ibid.*, p. 62. Percentages shown are averages for the five years 1957–1961. Detail in the tabulation will not add to the total owing to rounding.

what is sold is a service. Expense for materials to be processed is, therefore, less important than in manufacturing. The compensation of employees is important, also, because of the importance of employees engaged in maintenance.

Maintenance bulks large in railroad costs, as is shown by a breakdown of operating expenses by group of accounts, which follows:[11]

Group of Accounts	Per Cent
Maintenance of way and structures	16
Maintenance of equipment	23
Traffic	3
Transportation-rail line	51
Miscellaneous operations	1
General	6
Total	100

Maintenance, thus, amounts to 39 per cent of operating expenses. The importance of maintenance may be expressed, also, by the percentage of maintenance charges to operating revenues, about 21 per cent.[12]

Maintenance policy, therefore, is an important aspect of railroad operating policy. Maintenance costs can be deferred in the short run. They can be deferred by a road in financial straits to meet interest payments, or for other purposes, even including making a killing for the owners or operators of the road. (All that is required is invention of a system for diversion into their pockets of the funds that should be going into maintenance.) There will be an interval before the equipment reaches a state of physical collapse and in periods of low traffic much equipment is not used. Failure to maintain is economically justified in some circumstances, especially when the railroad should be abandoned. The most economic usefulness should be obtained from the capital equipment before the line is abandoned.

A fundamental reason for the importance of maintenance charges in railroad costs is that railroad managements depreciate their equipment slowly, making expenditures as needed to keep it in operation. Railroad managements have been criticized for failure to replace equipment when its economic life is over—as opposed to its physical life, which may be longer. Within the industry there appears to be a difference of opinion on the question of depreciation policy. Railroads differ in depreciation rates for similar equipment. Statistics on the diversity of practice with regard to depreciation rates among different railroads are published by the I.C.C. For freight-train cars, for example, the figures were as follows in 1962:[13]

11. *Ibid.*, p. 57. Data for Class I Line-Haul railroads.
12. *Ibid.*, p. 63.
13. *Ibid.*, p. 60, Table 96.

Depreciation Percentage Rate	Number of Class I Companies
Under 2.00	1
2.00–2.49	12
2.50–2.99	21
3.00–3.49	42
3.50–3.99	13
4.00–4.49	4
Over 4.50	5
Average rate (per cent credits to depreciation reserve of base)	3.14

Such dispersion implies a diversity of judgment from one railroad to another. Some economists believe that the railroads with low rates would be well advised to depreciate their equipment and replace it faster in order to compete more effectively.[14] (Fast write-offs do not necessarily imply early replacement, or any replacement. If early replacement is planned, however, fast write-offs would be appropriate.)

The cost of capital to the railroads also takes the form of the necessary net return to investors, which may be paid out in interest and dividends or retained. For all railroads regarded as one system the I.C.C. summarizes financial results as follows (in millions of dollars):[15]

Operating revenues	$9,792
Operating expenses	7,692
Taxes and net equipment and joint facility rents	1,340
Net railway operating income	760
Other income	294
Total income	1,054
Rent for leased roads and equipment	6
Interest on funded debt	386
Other deductions	91
Net income	571
Dividends	362
Balance	209

Note that interest on funded debt of 386 million dollars plus dividends of 362 million dollars total 748 million dollars paid for long term capital, or about 8 per cent of operating revenue. That payments for long term capital are relatively high as a per cent of revenue is a consequence of the capital intensive nature of the industry. By way of contrast, the motor-carrier statistics for Class I common carriers show interest of 28 million dollars and dividends of 18 million dollars, 46 million dollars

14. Meyer, Peck, Stenason, Zwick, *The Economics of Competition in the Transportation Industries,* Harvard University Press, 1959, pp. 56–61.
15. I.C.C., *Transport Statistics, op. cit.,* p. 65.

total on operating revenues of 3,785 million dollars, or about 1 per cent.[16] The railroads, thus, do make substantial payments to investors, but there has been no complaint in recent years that returns on railroad investments have been excessive. The I.C.C. estimates the long run average return realized by carriers on their investment in road and equipment at 4 per cent.[17]

DISAGGREGATION OF COSTS—For the study of competition among modes, however, it is not the total costs of railroad operation that are of interest, it is costs per unit of service provided. Furthermore, an analyst would like to know the responsiveness of costs to changes in the situation. For studies of competition it is important to know marginal costs. For studies of mergers it is important to know how costs will respond in the long run to changes in plant and equipment, for example, to such changes as re-routing over a single line of traffic which formerly used two parallel lines.

If we are prepared to assume, as a rough approximation, that the rate of return to railroad investors is on the average at a normal rate, as a starting point the economic cost of railroad freight service including normal return on capital may be regarded as approximately equal to average revenue per ton-mile, or about 1.4 cents. Such an average, however, covers such a wide variety of types of service rendered under such varying conditions as to be of limited usefulness.

One simple method of disaggregation is to examine the same statistic, total freight revenue per ton-mile, for different regions of the country. Revenue per ton-mile does vary by district as follows:[18]

District	Freight Revenue Per Ton-Mile (mills)
New England region	22
Great Lakes region	15
Central Eastern region	15
Eastern district	15
Pocahontas region	11
South region	13
Northwestern region	13
Central western region	13
Southwestern region	13
Western district	13
All districts	14

16. *Ibid.*, Part 7, p. 10–12. Statistics shown are for Class I common carriers of general freight in intercity service for 1962.

17. I.C.C., Bureau of Accounts, Statement 4–64, May 1964, *Rail Carload Unit Costs by Territories for the Year 1962*, p. 5.

18. I.C.C., *Transport Statistics, 1962, Part I*, p. 134, Table 162.

Variation among districts, however, itself requires explanation, and variation within districts remains unexplained. More refined statistical procedures and further breakdowns of costs are a necessity. What is required is detailed knowledge of the determinants of railroad costs. We may indicate the problem by posing a question. Why should the railroads, with costs and revenue averaging in the range 11 to 22 mills, have lost a large fraction of their business to trucks, with average revenue per ton-mile several times as high? Another way of putting the question is to ask, under what circumstances is truck service less expensive than railroad freight?

The work that has been done on railroad costs may be divided for convenience of discussion into the cost studies done by the staff of the I.C.C., and the cost studies done by others, primarily academic economists. Each will be discussed briefly.

Cost Studies by the I.C.C.—An extensive body of data on American railroad costs has been collected by the I.C.C. and a large number of studies of railroad costs have been made by its staff. These studies may appear as Statements of the Bureau of Accounts, Section of Cost Finding.

This body of work has been built up using a set of definitions and procedures that must be understood in order to understand the meaning of the results. Two types of costs are of basic importance in this work, *out-of-pocket costs* and *fully distributed costs*. Both are essentially long run costs. Out-of-pocket costs ". . . reflect costs which over the long-run period, and at the average density of traffic, have been found to be variable with traffic changes." They include, for freight service, 80 per cent of freight operating expenses, rents and taxes, plus a return of 4 per cent after Federal income taxes on that part of the plant that is believed to be variable with traffic volume, which is 50 per cent of the road property and 100 per cent of the equipment used in freight service.[19] "Fully distributed costs" include in addition the remaining 20 per cent of freight operating expenses, rents, and taxes plus added revenue as needed to provide a return of 4 per cent after Federal income taxes on the property as a whole after meeting operating deficits on passenger-train and less-than-carload service.

It should be clearly understood that out-of-pocket costs as defined include more than short run variable costs. Rents, for example, are fixed costs in the short run, but are included in part in out-of-pocket

19. I.C.C., Bureau of Accounts, *op. cit.*, pp. 4–5.

costs. Out-of-pocket costs are conceptually much closer to long run marginal costs, leaving aside the question of how closely out-of-pocket costs as measured approximate the long run cost curves of economic theory.

How did the Cost Finding Section come to the 80–20 division of freight operating expense? Two methods were used, both of which are statistically simple. Method I was to observe over a period of time the effect of traffic changes on the expenses of a given carrier or group of carriers. A study was made of changes from before World War II to the postwar period, i.e., 1939 or 1940 to 1944 to 1946, during which there were large changes in the volume of traffic. During this period two things happened, the railroads moved from a condition of excess capacity to a high level of operations, and they made changes in their plant and equipment. The movement of costs involved both movement along short run cost curves and movement to new short run cost curves along long run cost curves. Method I, therefore, produces results not easy to interpret.

Method II was to observe differences from road to road at the same time. The objective was to detect changes in costs associated with long run changes in traffic volume. The method assumes that the differences in costs among roads reflect primarily differences in volume of traffic, and that the roads have had time to adjust their plant and equipment to the volume of traffic. It is upon the results of Method II that principal reliance is placed.

The procedure may be illustrated with reference to Chart 2 of the I.C.C.'s report.[20] This chart was prepared for the Eastern District in 1946 for those roads with average haul of 100 miles and over. The unit of observation is the road. The scatter diagram plots a measure of output as independent variable: thousands of gross ton-miles per mile of road. This variable measures the total ton-miles of trains *and* their contents generated by a railroad divided by the number of miles of road. It is, thus, a measure of density of traffic. The dependent variable is a category of expense, in this example, freight service operating expenses, rents, and taxes, also expressed in dollars per mile of road. The Cost Finding Unit pays special attention to the value of costs corresponding to the observed average density of traffic. The essentials of the results are illustrated in Figure 13.1.

20. I.C.C., *Explanation of Rail Cost Finding Procedures and Principles Relating to the Use of Costs*, Statement No. 7–63, November 1963. This publication is similar in many respects to an earlier publication of November 1954.

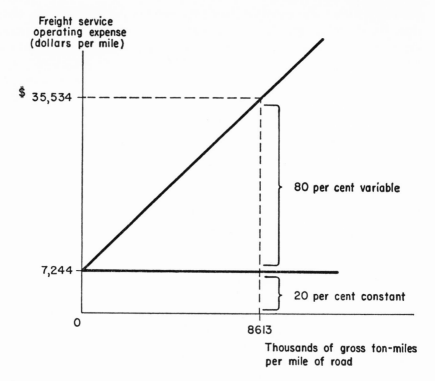

Figure 13.1—Freight Service Operating Expenses, Rents, and Taxes per Mile of Road (Eastern District—1946)

The equation of the line of relation may be inferred to be:

$$Expense = \$7,244 + \frac{(\$35,534 - 7,244)}{8,613} \cdot (\text{Gross ton-miles})$$

$$E = \$7,244 + \frac{\$28,290}{8,613} \cdot G$$

$$E = \$7,244 + \$3.28\ G$$

In this district in 1946, the average variable freight operating expense of moving 1,000 gross ton-miles was, thus, $3.28, which converts to $.00328 per gross ton-mile. Total freight service operating expenses for any individual road may be estimated as $7,244 per mile of road plus $.00328 per gross ton-mile.

Figure 13.1 is a simplified version of a graph published by the Cost

Finding Section. The equation, however, was not published by the Section. Its attention was directed to the division between constant and variable cost at a particular level of traffic, that level corresponding to the average number of gross ton-miles per mile of road which obtained in this district in 1946, or 8,613. What the Section calculated and published is an estimate of the "percent variable" at average density. Thus, in Figure 13.1, the total freight operating expense at 8,613 ton-miles is 20 per cent constant and "80 per cent variable."

The estimate of "80 per cent variable" strictly speaking is justified only at a density of traffic of 8,613 gross ton-miles per mile of road. As one departs from average density of 8,613 it ceases to be true that 80 per cent of freight service operating expenses are variable. (At zero level of traffic costs would be 0 per cent variable by this method of calculation.) The Section, of course, is aware of this fact, but nevertheless feels that the use of an 80–20 division of freight expenses for purposes of estimating out-of-pocket costs is justifiable as an approximate procedure.

The implications of this type of calculation may be indicated by converting from the total cost curve shown above to the corresponding average cost curve. The calculations would be as follows:

Level of Output (Thousands of Gross Ton-Miles per Mile of Road)	Constant Cost	Variable Cost ($3.28 × G)	Total Cost	Average Cost per 1000 Gross Ton-Miles
1,000	$7,244	$3,280	$10,524	$10.52
3,000	7,244	9,840	17,084	5.69
5,000	7,244	16,400	23,644	4.73
8,000	7,244	26,240	33,484	4.18
10,000	7,244	32,800	40,044	4.00

Since average freight service operating expenses fall with output, the implication is that there are decreasing costs or increasing returns to scale. Note once more, the long run character of these estimates. These costs are assumed to reflect the adjustment of plant and equipment to operation at different levels of output. Average cost falls with output because of the economies of scale associated with increased density of traffic.

The Cost Finding Section has prepared some interesting estimates of variations in out-of-pocket costs under different conditions. The division between terminal costs and line-haul costs is particularly crucial for intermodal competition. Trucks are generally supposed to have lower terminal costs but higher line-haul costs than railroads. The Section has published estimates for 1962 operations of out-of-pocket expenses for three types of train showing separately line-haul and terminal expenses. The estimates were made for 13 types of equipment, from general service box cars to tank cars, and for different regions.[21]

For box cars in general service in Region II (Eastern District excluding New England) the estimates were as follows for through trains:

Type of Out-of-Pocket Expense	Cost in Cents per Hundredweight
Line-haul	
Per car-mile	19.84
Per hundredweight mile	.0109
Terminal	
Per carload	7335.
Per hundredweight	1.019

Thus, the line-haul cost for one box-car in general service was 19.8 cents per mile plus about .01 cents per mile per hundredweight of contents. The terminal costs were $73.35 per carload plus about one cent per hundredweight.

The average weight load for this type of car in this district was 29.0 tons. The costs above, then, may be converted to costs per ton and per ton-mile for an average load.

Type of Out-of-Pocket Expense	Cost in Cents per Hundredweight	Costs per Ton or Ton-Mile for an Average Load of 29 Tons
Line-haul		
A) Per car-mile	19.84	0.68¢ per ton-mile
B) Per hundredweight mile	.01093	0.22¢ per ton-mile
Total		0.90¢ per ton-mile
Terminal		
C) Per carload	7335.	$2.52 per ton
D) Per hundredweight	1.0193	0.20 per ton
Total		$2.72 per ton

The total cost of the shipment becomes, under these assumptions, $2.72 per ton plus 0.90 cents per ton-mile. One way of stating this result is that terminal costs would be equal to line-haul costs at a distance of about 300 miles. For shorter hauls the line-haul cost would come to less than $2.72 per ton, the amount of the terminal costs. For longer hauls the line-haul costs would be the larger.

There is considerable variation in these costs. The component of terminal costs which increases in proportion to weight (line D) is much smaller for types of equipment such as gondola cars, hopper cars, tank

21. I.C.C., Bureau of Accounts, *op. cit.*

cars, and TOFC flat cars than it is for boxcars. (In Region II the cost for boxcars is 1.019 cents; for TOFC flat cars only .029 cents.) Line-haul costs are substantially different for way trains and through trains. In Region II the cost for through trains is .01093 cents (line B); for way trains it is .01726 cents, i.e., 58 per cent higher. Costs also vary by Region. Line-haul costs per car-mile, which are 19.84 cents (line A) in Region II for through trains, are 29.15 cents in Region I (New England).

It is this type of specific, detailed information that is needed by the I.C.C., by the railroads in fixing rates, and by anyone concerned with competition among modes. If anything, even more specific data are necessary for particular movements of particular commodities.

COST STUDIES BY OTHERS—Cost studies carried out by academic economists in the railroad field in general show much more statistical sophistication than the work of the Cost Finding Section. The academic studies tend, however, as one might expect, to be carried out on a more aggregated basis and without benefit of special efforts to collect new data required for the purposes at hand.

One of the best known studies is that by Meyer, Peck, Stenason, and Zwick.[22] These investigators applied multiple regression techniques to the problem of estimating long run marginal costs. They used a cross-section of railroads, and combined the years 1952 to 1955. In any study that relates railroad costs to output a basic problem is, that although outlay for maintenance depends in large part upon output, the money may be spent in a different time period from that in which the output is produced. By combining years they hoped to reduce the problem created by the lack of association of maintenance costs and output in any one year. The details of their statistical approach to the data are beyond the scope of this discussion, but their conclusions are of interest. They estimated total long run marginal operating costs at 2.8 mills per gross ton-mile of freight traffic (in 1952–1955 mills) and the variable portion of capital costs at 0.4 mills, with total long-run marginal operating and capital costs at about 3.27 mills per gross ton-mile. Converting to revenue ton-miles and assuming a 20 per cent cost increase from 1952–1955 to 1958, they estimate an average cost of 9–10 mills per revenue ton-mile of freight traffic. (For passenger traffic they estimate 1.3 cents to 1.4 cents per seat mile.) As a comparison, note that in 1958 average revenue per ton-mile for all Class I roads was 1.46 cents.

Another study of railroad cost functions was published in 1960 by

22. Meyer, Peck, Stenason, Zwick, *op. cit.*, Appendix A (for a critique of the I.C.C.'s statistical costing methods).

George H. Borts.[23] Borts includes a summary of sources of error in statistical cost functions. He finds it useful in estimating long run costs to stratify his observations both by region and by size of firm. (The I.C.C. study discussed above uses a regional breakdown but not a breakdown by size of firm.) Borts finds regional differences in his results, with long run costs apparently increasing as output increases in the East and decreasing or constant in the West. Note that his results raise a question about the Cost Finding Section's decreasing costs shown above.

Detailed consideration of this research and similar studies requires a knowledge of statistics that is beyond the limits of this discussion. For present purposes, perhaps the most important conclusion to which these studies lead is that results reached by methods such as those used by the I.C.C.'s Cost Finding Section must be regarded as approximations subject to considerable margins of error. Knowledge of long run marginal costs is directly relevant both in consideration of potential economies from mergers and in rate-making.

Railroad Mergers and the Organization of the Industry

One of the possible responses of the railroad industry to increased pressure from other methods of transportation is by basic reorganization of the industry. There has been some interest in the possibility that the railroads might take a step toward becoming general transportation companies by expanding into highway transportation. Even more attention has been devoted to railroad mergers, and it is to railroad mergers we first turn our attention. For half a century the subject has been extensively debated, discussed, and investigated; repeatedly, legislation has been passed by Congress dealing with it; and gradually, mergers have taken place.

For purposes of discussion by economists, a merger of two railroads means effective consolidation of the two from an operating point of view. It is possible for one railroad to own a controlling interest in another, or for a third party to obtain control of two railroads, without combination of the properties into a single operating unit. Such combinations are not discussed here.

In evaluating the merits of any merger of business enterprises in any industry, from the point of view of the public, two broad sets of considerations apply. First, are there cost reductions that can be achieved by the proposed merger which could not otherwise be realized? If there are important economies of scale in the industry, it may be that the

23. "The Estimation of Rail Cost Functions," *Econometrica*, January 1960, pp. 108–131.

combination of two or more small, inefficient firms may make possible
the creation of one large efficient firm. On the other hand, the combination of competing firms must reduce the number of firms in an
industry. An increase in the degree of monopoly in an industry may
lead to any of the possible evils familiar from discussion of the case
against monopoly: high prices, excessive profits, reduced output, and a
lazy toleration of inefficiency and high costs of production. How do
these general considerations apply to the railroads? The case for and
against mergers of railroads will be outlined briefly.[24]

THE CASE FOR MERGERS—The advocates of railroad mergers rest
their case primarily on the savings in cost they expect will result. Why
should there be economies from mergers that could not be realized apart
from the mergers? To this question, the answer in specific situations may
be a matter of geography. When there are parallel lines between two
points one may have the advantage of superior geographic location with
lower ruling gradient, fewer curves, or shorter mileage. When two railroads maintain terminal facilities in an area, one may be better located
than the other. Whether such a situation exists is a specific question that
must be analyzed in detail for any proposed merger.

Apart from geography, economies of consolidation, as already suggested, may result from economies of scale. In principle there may be
economies of scale in each of the elements of a railroad system. There
may be economies of scale in terminal operations, in line haul, in repair
shops and maintenance facilities, and in management. As noted in the
previous section, the I.C.C.'s Cost Finding Section finds evidence of
economies of scale. A related possibility is excess capacity in one or
more of the component parts of a railroad system resulting from a decline in utilization or from technical innovations that make possible
increased output from a given installation.

A detailed review of available evidence will not be attempted here.
As a first approximation, as far as line hauls are concerned, there is
not much evidence of major gains from longer total mileage. As already
discussed, even though the evidence is not entirely satisfactory there
do seem to be gains from increased density of traffic. Certainly there are
minimum densities below which rail service is uneconomic.

Another category of facilities of importance for competition are terminals and the associated yards and facilities. Two lines that enter a
metropolitan area and compete for traffic between that area and other
points will both be anxious to maintain direct contact with shippers

---

24. For a review of the problem see the "Doyle report," *National Transportation Policy*,
printed for the Committee on Interstate and Foreign Commerce, 87th Congress, 1st Session,
January 1961, ch. 4, pp. 224–272.

whose goods move on the route in question. Both will have an interest in maintaining terminal facilities as a means of preserving their competitive identity. Combination of the roads with elimination of the competition between them may open up opportunities for consolidation of terminals with resulting economies.

Estimates of the total saving that might be made from complete consolidation of all roads range from 200 million to 2 billion dollars. Gilbert Burck, in an influential article in *Fortune*,[25] estimated a potential total of 1 billion dollars. Burck envisioned savings in each of the main elements of the transportation system distributed as follows:

Category	Potential Saving (millions of dollars)
Terminal operations	400
Reduced maintenance and operation of abandoned trackage	100
Improved routing and utilization of equipment	300
Purchasing, repair shops, reorganization of less than carload traffic	75 or more

Total railway operating expenses at the date of these estimates were on the order of 8 billion dollars a year (7.6 billion dollars in 1958) so that a saving of 1 billion dollars would be one-eighth. Such economies, it should be understood, could be realized only after some time for carrying through reorganization and after investment in such facilities as connecting line.

As an example of what may be involved in a merger in the way of cost reduction, consider a summary of estimates reported by the same author (in a more recent article)[26] concerning a proposed merger of the Atlantic Coast Line and Seaboard Air Line. That merger, it was estimated, would save 38 million dollars a year before taxes, the following being the major economies:

19 million dollars: rearrangement of physical facilities, especially elimination and abandonment of 1,100 miles of duplicate track
10 million dollars: office consolidation
6 million dollars: rerouting traffic

25. "A Plan to Save the Railroads," *Fortune*, August 1958.
26. "Mating Time for the Railroads," *Fortune*, January 1961.

These savings, however, were to be realized only after a new capital investment of 66 million dollars, including 20 million dollars in new yards, 6 million dollars in signalling, and 14.5 million dollars in payments to employees to be dropped.

Such estimates must rest upon detailed study of the operations of the two roads and the accuracy of the estimates must rest essentially upon the quality of the study. It is not remarkable that estimates of the potential cost savings from mergers differ widely.

There are other advantages of mergers that are sometimes urged. Many of the day by day problems of the Commission would be simplified or completely solved by consolidation. Examples are regulations concerning access to terminal areas, routing of traffic, and the division of rates where service is provided by two or more carriers.

There is another, less tangible consideration that is mentioned in connection with discussions of railroad mergers. It is frequently observed by persons close to the railroad industry that the management of railroads is on the average less progressive than management of other modern industries. Various uncomplimentary adjectives have been used to describe railroad managements. The accuracy of the adjectives no doubt depends on which management is being characterized, in what manner, and at what time.[27] (Railroad managers are likely to respond

27. The authors of the "Doyle report" observed in 1961 (*op. cit.*, pp. 292–293): "(1) There is a great resistance to change, particularly in operating procedures. Such a resistance is observable in many managements but even bankers and stockbrokers have accomplished more important changes in methods than have the railroads.

"(2) The railroads remain strongly production oriented in an age where most managements, even in other transportation media, are primarily distribution oriented, sales oriented, or customer oriented, depending on just the flavor each management wishes to impart.

"(3) There has been, until the past 5 years, an almost complete lack of the basic economic and market research which many other industries initiated back in the 1930s. Present research in the railroad industry is making very deliberate headway in an uphill battle. This relates to the basic lack of sales orientation.

"(4) With a very few notable exceptions railroad financial management seems to be one of the aspects least changed since the end of monopoly. The accountants have allowed themselves to be captured by the I.C.C. accounting and reporting requirements primarily geared to ascertaining financial soundness and the current value of the property for earnings regulation. This system is in no way adequate for the provision of the unit-cost data, and cost-control information, that are universally accepted in modern business. The I.C.C., of course, must bear much of the responsibility for this condition. The Commission is now prevented by its own lapse from acting on the basis of sound data at a time when costs are of great importance in the fixing of individual rates. A related aspect of rail fiscal management is the lack of profit centering in divisions or product departments and an inability to clearly focus responsibility for the profit of any segment of the traffic on a single responsible executive.

"(5) Most important of all, perhaps, the railroads are doing little to seek out, or encourage, able and educated young men for careers in the industry. A 1954 study of this matter* revealed that only 17 out of the 115 class I railroads regularly contacted college campuses

with comments which reflect a certain lack of enthusiasm for the policies of Congress and the regulatory agencies.) The main thrust of these
comments, however, is that *any* drastic revision of the arrangements in
the industry has advantages because it will force a reconsideration of
traditional practices. It is at least possible, however, that necessary
changes could be made with no mergers. The case for mergers rests
primarily on the possibilities of cost reduction. Although the amounts
which can be saved are known only approximately, there is evidence
that considerable savings are possible.

THE CASE AGAINST MERGERS—The case against mergers arises out
of the implied reduction in competition. Even in a regulated industry in
which direct price competition does not exist, competition among a
limited number of sellers may serve a useful purpose in keeping the
rivals under pressure to innovate either by reducing costs or by improving the product. There are two types of mergers that reduce competition, but in different ways. The simplest to understand is the merger
of parallel lines. When two lines running side by side are combined, there
is an obvious reduction in the number of sellers in the markets for
traffic between the pairs of points served by the two. Railroads may
also combine by end-to-end mergers. Consider a situation such as the
following, with two lines from city A to city B and one line from B to C:

$$\text{City } A \overset{\text{I}}{\underset{\text{II}}{=\!=\!=}} \text{City } B \overset{\text{III}}{=\!=\!=} \text{City } C$$

A merger of lines I and III would not reduce the number of lines from
A to B, nor would it reduce the number from B to C. Such a merger,
however, would be a source of consternation to the management of railroad II. The management of the combined road would be in a position
to influence the routing of traffic from C to A since all such traffic must
pass over its line at least from C to B and would be booked by its agents
who would be in direct contact with shippers in C. Nothing would be
easier and more natural than to arrange matters so that all such traffic
moved over lines III and I. The loss of business to line II could mean
the difference between profitable operation and bankruptcy.

The same fundamental issue of control over the routing of traffic can

where specialized engineering and transportation training was given. A key problem in the
railroad personnel scene is the extension of labor union control up into the ranks of middle
management and a strong adhesion to rigid seniority. It has also been observed that in
terms of quality and expertness most railroads have too few staff personnel. The top
executives are relatively uninformed simply because there are not enough of the right kind
of people in middle management."

*Robert L. Banks, "The College Graduate and the Railroad Industry" (for the Feder-
ation for Railway Progress), 1954.

arise in a variety of situations. If there were two railroads, III and IV, from city *B* to *C,* for example, a merger of I and IV would tend to drive II and III into a defensive alliance, while a combination of any three of the roads would leave the fourth in a weak position. Competition among railroads, thus, is partly a question of the number of sellers in any one market, and partly a question of the strategy of the relations among different, related markets.

Weak railroads are particularly vulnerable to competition. The problem of weak and strong roads is a classic problem of railroad regulation. It came up in 1890. The I.C.C. found, side by side, from Chicago to Kansas City, two railroads with comparable facilities. One was capitalized at 46,000 dollars per mile and the other at 92,000 dollars. For the same services the two would have to charge the same rates. How could I.C.C. set a rate that would permit a fair return for the weak road and would not provide an excessive return for the strong road?[28] Such problems could be avoided—if not solved—by merger of the two lines. But the risk is a series of mergers might take place that would greatly exacerbate the problem of weak roads. Lines left out of the mergers that were not already weak might well become so. The I.C.C. and other public agencies would be left with an assortment of roads for which the choice would be subsidy or liquidation.

These difficulties could be avoided by a strong hand of the regulators in the arrangement of the mergers. Compulsory mergers could have solved this problem. Nationalization could have solved the problem. These drastic solutions, however, have been set aside in favor of voluntary, private mergers under public control, with some degree of competition preserved.

HISTORY OF POLICY TOWARD MERGERS—The idea of merging railroads is an old one, and public policy in the area has a long history. Up to 1904, when the *Sherman Act* was applied to railroads, there was no legal barrier to consolidation and the process went forward rapidly. The early roads were typically short. The New York Central, for example, was created by end-to-end mergers. In the latter part of the nineteenth century, there were also many mergers that involved consolidation of a trunk line and the associated feeder lines. This period was culminated in 1899–1900 when in a period of 16 months one-sixth of the total mileage was absorbed by other lines.[29]

In 1904, in the Northern Securities case the Supreme Court applied the *Sherman Act* to the railroads, preventing a combination of the Great

28. See I. L. Sharfman, *The I.C.C.,* Vol. III-B.
29. "Doyle report," *op. cit.,* p. 231.

Northern and Northern Pacific. A period of legal discouragement of railroad mergers is customarily dated from 1904 to 1920. The *Clayton Act* in 1914 explicitly applied the antitrust principle to railroads by giving to the I.C.C. jurisdiction of the enforcement of *Section 7* insofar as it might affect a common carrier under the Commission's jurisdiction. The language of *Section 7* forbids purchase of the stock of one corporation by another when the effect would be to substantially lessen competition or tend to create a monopoly.

Since the *Transportation Act* of 1920, the stated objective of public policy has been to encourage mergers. While this *Act* proposed consolidation, the railroads were to be arranged in systems so competition could be preserved as fully as possible. The I.C.C. was to prepare a master plan. The actual consolidations were to be according to this plan, but to be entered into voluntarily by the railroads. The purpose envisioned was primarily the solution of the strong road–weak road problem.

The basic policy of voluntary mergers under I.C.C. supervision was set in 1920. The I.C.C. retained William Z. Ripley to prepare a plan. He carried out the assignment. The Commission itself released, as early as 1921, a plan showing tentative groupings into twenty-one systems, but never allocated Class II and III carriers, involving 39,000 miles of line, to those systems. By 1925, the I.C.C. asked to be relieved of the legislative requirement of preparing a full plan but it did approve a nineteen-system plan in 1929.

Various efforts in the 1930s led to no legislation. In 1938 President Roosevelt appointed a committee of three of the Commissioners. They recommended that authority be given to the I.C.C. to compel mergers when sought by at least one carrier. A committee of six, three railroad executives and three representatives of railway labor, opposed compulsion of any kind.

The *Transportation Act* of 1940, which is now in force, left the power to initiate a plan in the hands of the private carriers, not the I.C.C. The I.C.C. is directed by the *Act* to determine whether a plan is in the public interest. The I.C.C. is to take into account the following: (1) the effect of the proposed transaction upon adequate transportation service to the public; (2) the effect upon the public interest of the inclusion or failure to include other railroads in the territory involved in a proposed merger; (3) the total fixed charges resulting from the proposed action; and (4) the interests of the employees of the carriers. The I.C.C. is given authority to attach conditions to approval of a plan designed to safeguard the rights of the employees. It is directed to include a provision that during a four-year period, from the effective date of the plan, no employee of four years standing shall suffer loss of job or shall be made worse off otherwise.[30] For employees of less than four years standing the protected period is equal to their length of service. Some mergers have taken place under this law, and more are in prospect, but the process of consolidation proceeds slowly.

In the northeastern part of the country, after years of proposals and negotiations, three consolidated systems are taking shape. They involve the combination of the Chesapeake and Ohio with the Baltimore and Ohio (1963); the Norfolk and Western with the Nickelplate, the Wabash, and the Pittsburgh and West Virginia (1964); and the Pennsylvania with the New York Central.[31] Recently the further combination of the first two of these consolidated systems has been proposed.

Has the policy toward mergers, which has evolved gradually, been the correct policy? The savings in operating costs, the existence of which is agreed upon though the magnitude of which is not known, seem to justify the price of a reduction in the number of sellers. Under modern conditions the need for competition among railroads is clearly less than in the days when railroads were the only means of mass transportation available in the country. The potential spur to innovation remains as long as at least two railroads compete in the major markets. Mergers of railroads do not seem to involve too great a risk of monopoly. The principal complaint, which seems justified, is that the mergers are being brought about so very slowly.

DIVERSIFICATION OF RAILROADS INTO OTHER FORMS OF TRANSPORTATION—Consolidation of railroads through mergers into more efficient operating units is not the only possible organizational response to pressure from competing modes of transportation. A second basic possibility is for the railroads themselves to own other carriers. The most debated question is whether railroads should own motor carriers.

Present public policy is to restrict rail ownership of motor carriers. The I.C.C. under the *Motor Carrier Act* of 1935 permits railroads to operate motor carriers only if the operations are "auxiliary or supplementary" to train service.[32] Service is confined to points which are sta-

30. *Ibid.*, p. 242.

31. This last merger is expected to lead to annual savings after the first few years of 80,000,000 to 100,000,000 dollars according to press accounts. *Wall Street Journal*, March 5, 1965, p. 22.

32. For a brief review of the relevant law and the issues of policy see Roger C. Cramton, "Diversification of Ownership in the Regulated Industries—the Folklore of Regulation," *Public Utility Law*, 1961, pp. 24–31. (Reprinted from *Public Utilities Fortnightly*, September 14 and October 26, 1961.)

tions on the railroad and must not include long hauls even parallel to the rail line.

The truckers insist that such restrictions are necessary. They argue that the railroads are large corporations with substantial capital, and might engage in aggressive competitive practices designed to drive out of business any motor carriers with whom they were in direct competition. This argument would be more convincing if it were not for low economic barriers that make entry into the trucking business easy. To enter the trucking business requires a relatively small amount of capital; and there are no major barriers such as patents, secret processes, etc. Even if some firms were driven out of the industry others would enter it. Re-entry of truckers would be possible at any time assuming no legal barriers to entry into trucking. When the trucking industry was in its infancy, there may have been some dangers that attempts would be made by rail-owned trucking companies to inhibit growth of other truckers by predatory practices. Any such danger would now seem to be small. The same argument would apply to bus service.

The railroads argue that integration of railroads and trucking companies would provide economies of joint operation. Coordination of the two methods of transportation could be achieved. This argument implies that coordination cannot be achieved without joint ownership. Yet, where there is a profit to be made by cooperation of firms in different industries, one would expect the cooperation to take place. There is evidence, furthermore, of the actual development of coordination across modes in the growth of "piggyback" (trailer-on-flatcar) service. Thus, both the potential risks to competition and the potential gains in improved coordination from unrestricted ownership of motor carriers may be exaggerated.

Rates and Rate Policy

At the center of the problem of competition between railroads and other forms of transportation is the subject of railroad rates. Shippers make choices among the alternatives open to them on the basis of the prices they must pay for the services they require. Price, of course, is not the sole consideration. Shippers may also take into account differences in the speed, reliability, or other aspects of the service. Price, however, is a central consideration.

The subject of railroad rates is one of the most complex and difficult, as well as most important, topics in the field of transportation. It will be approached here in the following order: a description of the actual rate structure; a discussion of the role of the I.C.C. in rate determination; a discussion of the costs of railroads in relation to their rates; and a brief discussion of the differences in cost between railroads and other modes.

ACTUAL RATE STRUCTURES—Railroad rates exist in principle for all of the thousands of articles known to commerce between any pair of freight stations in the country. Consider only one thousand stations and one thousand commodities. A matrix of stations of origin and stations of destination would have 1,000 columns and 1,000 rows. Rates in opposite directions may be and often are unequal and shipments within a city cannot be excluded. Hence, each cell in the table specifies a possible route. For each of the 1,000,000 routes, one freight rate per commodity would bring the total to an unmanageable 1,000,000,000 rates! And the commodities and stations both greatly exceed 1,000!

Faced with the problem of simplifying such a structure, one might reasonably propose to begin by classifying the commodities. If the thousands of commodities could be grouped together into a small number of categories, the problem would be greatly simplified. This idea occurred to railroad men many years ago, but there was originally no single intelligence with the responsibility of organizing a system of freight classes for the nation as a whole. Independently, different systems of classification developed in different parts of the country. As of the outbreak of World War I there were three major systems of freight classification, and one of the consequences of the period of government operation was that these three were coordinated to the point where they at least were printed in parallel in one publication. Eventually, in the 1950s a Uniform Freight Classification was adopted. The Classification is complete in that it covers every commodity moved by the railroads. More precisely, it covers every description of traffic, since a commodity may be shipped in various forms. There are a total of 30 classes ranging from Class 400 down to Class 13. Taking Class 100 as base, the rate for a commodity placed in Class 400 is four times the base, while the rate for Class 13 is 13 per cent of the base; Class 40 is 40 per cent; and so forth.[33]

The second essential element in the structure of class rates is a distance scale. As previously discussed, it is expensive for a railroad to assemble the freight into loaded freight cars and assemble the cars into trains ready to move. Actual distance scales, therefore, incorporate

33. See Fair and Williams, *Economics of Transportation*, Harper & Brothers, revised 1959, p. 371.

a terminal charge. As the freight moves, costs will rise with distance but less than proportionately. There are economies in costs per mile as distance increases arising, for example, out of better vehicle utilization (i.e., more car-miles per day). Distance scales, for these reasons, are ordinarily graduated, or tapered. The freight rate thus increases with distance at a decreasing rate.

The rail class rate scale now in force was prescribed by the I.C.C. in 1952. A simplified algebraic representation of this distance scale has been prepared by Herbert O. Whitten.[34] The distance scale may be decomposed into two parts, a fixed sum that does not vary with distance, and a cost per mile, which, of course, tends to increase total cost with distance. The fixed sum may be thought of as equivalent to the cost of a certain number of miles. Whitten speaks of that fixed amount as the "Terminal Mileage Revenue Equivalent." He also notes that the number of miles must be discounted to allow for the usual taper.

In effect, the rate for Class 100 as prescribed in 1952 was as follows:

Rate = Terminal Mileage Revenue Equivalent + Miles (Mileage Discount)

If: R = Rate in cents per ton
     d = distance in miles

$$R = 6.33¢ \left[270 + d \left(1 - \frac{1.56d}{10,000} \right) \right]$$

That is, the rate is 6.33 cents times the discounted distance in miles plus a fixed amount which is equal to 6.33 cents per mile for 270 miles. The discount factor is equivalent to 1.56 per cent per 100 miles traveled. Note that the structure of the rate with respect to distance does not depend on the use of a rate of 6.33 cents. In the years 1952 to 1963 there were five general rate increases, which in effect increased this factor for Class 100 to 8.65 cents; no doubt further increases may occur. The effect of considering freight of a different class is merely to apply a factor of proportionality to this amount. Thus, for Class 50, divide 8.65 cents by 2.

This distance structure has been criticized by Whitten. He believes that it fails to take into account truck competition. It contains too high a terminal mileage revenue equivalent—he believes 150 to 200 would make competition with trucks feasible—and too large a mileage discount

34. Whitten, Herbert O., "Maximum Pricing at the Demand Rate Level for Rail Service," *Papers, Fourth Annual Meeting, Transportation Research Forum*, December 1963, pp. 198–218.

factor. Thus, he would like to reduce railroad rates for short hauls and increase the rate at which railroad rates rise with distance, thereby competing more effectively with trucks for the moderate length hauls.

It should be understood that most freight does not move at the class rates. Whitten's estimate is that only 4 per cent moves at these rates. A. P. Bukovsky of the General Services Administration of the federal government recently estimated that in the East only about one per cent of all railroad carload tonnage moves on class rates.[35] These rates are maximum rates; most freight moves either under exception ratings or under commodity rates. Exception ratings rely on the class rate structure, but the items covered in the exception sheet are recategorized into a classification with a lower rating. Most traffic, however, moves under commodity rates, which are specific rates for the movement of specific commodities between named points of origin and destination. The low commodity rates supersede the class rates and are commonly used for those goods that are the most important items of railroad freight.

Although the distance scale prescribed for the class rate system is not important insofar as it applies to class rates since these rates are little used, it is important because of its effect on the rate scales used in commodity rates. Whitten investigated a sample of 103 rate scales (out of 500 he found) and estimated for each the terminal mileage revenue equivalent. He found one-third of the scales had terminal equivalents of over 300 miles, and 90 per cent over 200 miles, the maximum he believes consistent with effective competition with motor carriers.

Distance scales are by no means the only type of rate structure in use. *Modified distance scales* are sometimes used in which rates are constant over broad zones and rise in steps at the zone boundaries. It then becomes a matter of concern exactly where the zone boundaries fall. The amount of geographical price discrimination increases as the width of the zone increases.

Route equalization structures are designed to make the rates on competing routes equal or to introduce a fixed differential between routes. The classic example is the rate structure involving the Missouri River Crossings. The rates from the Mississippi River to the Missouri River on different roads are the same even though the distance varies from 212 to 414 miles. In the same manner the rates from the several

35. A. P. Bukovsky, "Rate Structures and National Transportation Policy," speech delivered before the National Transportation Policy Symposium, November 19, 1964 (mimeographed).

crossings of the Mississippi west of Chicago to that city are the same in spite of variations in distance. It is obviously demand rather than cost considerations that lead to this forced equality. The demand considerations involve water-borne competition on the rivers as well as pressure for equality from the cities whose shippers otherwise would be at a disadvantage in shipment to Chicago.

The North Atlantic port differentials illustrate the creation of *fixed differentials* among competing points. For export and import traffic between the ports and territory west of Buffalo and Pittsburgh there are fixed differentials in class rates. Portland and Boston were given the New York rates; Philadelphia rates 2 cents below New York; and Baltimore, rates 3 cents below New York.[36] Such a pattern, of course, reflects efforts to rationalize relationships among competing ports.

Group rate systems are essentially commodity rate systems that apply the same rate to a large area with many points of origin, or to an area with many points of destination, or both. This type of grouping simplifies the rate structure by reducing the fineness of the distinction made among geographic areas. An example is the rate structure for oranges shipped east from California. Until 1945 one rate was charged from California to all points east of the Rockies and north of the Ohio River! In 1945 four blanket rates were introduced. The rates for canned goods from San Francisco rise sharply at first as one moves east. Four hundred miles from San Francisco the rate is half the rate across the continent to New York![37]

These group rate systems obviously are not based on costs. They are based primarily on differences in the elasticity of demand arising out of competition, either competition from competing modes of transportation such as water transportation, or competition from competing sources of supply of the commodity in question, perhaps served by different railroads. Thus, rates from San Francisco east on canned goods can rise sharply because of the absence of water competition in the desert and mountain states. But there is downward pressure on rates to New York from water transportation to that city. The effects of that competition extend inland since canned goods can be moved from California to New York by ship and then inland by rail. A rate that would be higher from San Francisco to, say, Buffalo than from San Francisco to New York would be the best system of meeting such competition— were it not for two factors: the Fourth Section of the *Interstate Commerce Act* and the pressure of competition from canners in the area

36. Fair and Williams, *op. cit.,* p. 394. This pattern is historical, not current.
37. See Fair and Williams, *op. cit.,* p. 396.

south of the Great Lakes. A high rate to Buffalo might in effect abandon that city to the competition of middle western canners. The group rate adopted thus represents a response to a whole set of market forces.

The railroad rate structure, in brief, is a highly complex system of prices based both on costs and on considerations of demand. The pattern of rates is determined by the efforts of the railroads to maximize their profits as modified by the influence of the Interstate Commerce Commission. The rate structure as it developed historically has been criticized as poorly adapted to the needs of the railroads in their competitive struggle with the trucks because the rate relationships best suited to attracting traffic are changed greatly.

Even apart from intermodal competition, there is concern with the complexity of the rate structure. Complexity leads to aberrations, rates that have no rational basis, and to much effort expended just to find out what the rate is for a shipment.[38] A recent improvement in the classification of freight is, in its initial stages, a statistical innovation rather than a change in the Uniform Freight Classification. The Bureau of the Budget has adopted a Commodity Classification for Transportation Statistics based on the widely used system of defining industries, the Standard Industrial Classification. All carriers reporting to the I.C.C. since 1964 are using a code with 410 groups of commodities based on the new classification, and the classification is coming into use elsewhere in the government. The improvement in statistics of freight movements is likely to be dramatic. The effect on railroad rates may be even more important. The simplification resulting from the improved classification may lead to the use of computers for rate quotation. The problem is one of storing the rates in a computer's memory and obtaining access to the memory as required. It seems reasonable to hope for improvement in the rate structure based on computerized rates in the next few years.

ROLE OF THE I.C.C. IN RATE DETERMINATION—In his monumental study of the Commission, I. L. Sharfman wrote:

. . . the Commission, despite its continuous striving to achieve rationalization of rate relationships, has been guided in large measure by pragmatic considerations and has found a presumptive starting point for the solution of the vast majority of controversial issues in the existing arrangement.[39]

38. Bukovsky, *op. cit.*, writes: "Huge traffic departments of shippers and carriers are still at work trying to determine the lowest applicable rates in a veritable maze of tariffs. I am not a rate man myself. I do know, however, that rate people do not always come up with the same figure if you ask them to look up a rate the second time."

39. Sharfman, *op. cit.*, Vol. III-B, p. 5.

In the years since Sharfman wrote this generalization has continued to be appropriate.

In discussing the role of the I.C.C. in rate determination at the present it may be helpful to review the present provisions of the law relative to rates before discussing the procedure of the Commission. Section 15a of the Interstate Commerce Act, the "rule of rate making," was enacted in 1920 and revised most recently in 1958. It reads as follows:

Sec. 15a (1) When used in this section the term "rates" means rates, fares, and charges, and all classifications, regulations, and practices relating thereto.

(2) In the exercise of its power to prescribe just and reasonable rates the Commission shall give due consideration, among other factors, to the effect of rates on the movement of traffic by the carrier or carriers for which the rates are prescribed; to the need, in the public interest, of adequate and efficient railway transportation service at the lowest cost consistent with the furnishing of such service, and to the need of revenues sufficient to enable the carriers, under honest, economical, and efficient management to provide such service.

(3) In a proceeding involving competition between carriers of different modes of transportation subject to this Act, the Commission, in determining whether a rate is lower than a reasonable minimum rate, shall consider the facts and circumstances attending the movement of the traffic by the carrier or carriers to which the rate is applicable. Rates of a carrier shall not be held up to a particular level to protect the traffic of any other mode of transportation, giving due consideration to the objectives of the national transportation policy declared in this Act.

The National Transportation Policy specifically referred to here has been quoted earlier in this chapter.

Basic provisions of the original law remain relevant. They are supplemented, not supplanted, by the "rule of rate making." Section 1 requires that charges be "just and reasonable." Sec. 2 forbids "unjust discrimination" between persons. Section 3 prohibits "undue or unreasonable preference or advantage." Section 4 governs the relation of long and short hauls. The *Hoch-Smith Resolution* of 1925 directs the Commission to adjust freight rates "to the end that commodities may freely move." It also "in view of the existing depression in agriculture" directs the Commission to promote the freedom of movement of the products of agriculture "at the lowest possible rates compatible with the maintenance of adequate transportation service."[40]

Rates are ordinarily made in the first instance by the carriers themselves acting individually or through their rate bureaus. In an unregu-

40. 49 U.S. Code 55.

lated industry the activities of the rate bureaus would be condemned
under the antitrust laws as conspiracies to fix prices, but specific exemption from the antitrust laws for the activities of rate bureaus in the
railroad industry is provided by the *Reed-Bulwinkle Act,* as noted
earlier. The I.C.C. has the power to act on its own initiative in rate
matters but does not ordinarily do so.

Rate matters may come to the Board informally. During 1960 about
11,000 letters of complaint were received. These complaints may concern misapplications of rates as in overcharges, misrouting, etc., but
many of them involve the legality of rates under one of the relevant
sections. The staff of the I.C.C. may handle these informal complaints
by such action as assisting a shipper in obtaining an adjustment, interpreting tariffs, and the like.

Formal rate proceedings, in contrast, result in binding orders of the
Commission. There are four types: (1) complaint cases; (2) investigation and suspension cases; (3) fourth section applications; and (4) general investigations initiated by the Commission on its own volition.[41]

In formal complaint cases the shipper or another railroad charges a
violation of the law. For example, a charge is made of unreasonableness,
undue preference, violation of the Fourth Section, or deviation from a
published tariff. The burden of proof is on the complainant, who seeks
reparation or an order fixing rates. Such proceedings are now far less
important than previously. In 1930 there were 1412 formal complaints
but in 1960 only 164, of which 142 were against railroads and 22 against
motor carriers.

Investigation and suspension cases deal with newly filed rates. Any
interested person may protest a newly filed rate. Thirty days notice is
required before the rate goes into effect; protest may be filed up to
twelve days before the expiration of the thirty-day period. Suspension
for up to seven months may be requested. The Suspension Board has
ten days to take action on the request to suspend, an extremely short
time to take what may be an important action. The rate is not in effect
while its lawfulness is determined, and the burden of proof is on the

41. See the discussion in the following sources:
Administrative Conference of the United States. Committee on Rulemaking. *The Conduct
of Rate Proceedings in the Interstate Commerce Commission.* Report of a Study Conducted
by the Staff Director, Roger C. Cramton, University of Michigan Law School, December
1, 1961.
Administrative Conference of the United States. Committee on Rulemaking. *Improvement
in the Conduct of Federal Rate Proceedings.* October 2, 1962. Reprinted in Selected Reports
of the Administrative Conference of the United States, Senate Committee on the Judiciary,
Subcommittee on Administrative Practice and Procedure, Sen. Doc. No. 24, 88th Congress,
1st Session 69–114 (1963).

carrier filing the rate. These cases are of increasing importance. In 1930, 153 "I & S" cases were instituted; in 1960 there were 1,137. The cases concern primarily motor carrier rates; in one period studied 83 per cent concerned such rates. It does not require much imagination to see the possibilities of this type of proceeding as a defense against competition. Delay of up to seven months may in itself be a matter of importance regardless of final determination of the case.

Fourth Section applications are requests to the I.C.C. to exercise its power to grant relief from the restriction on rates in the long and short haul clause in the Fourth Section. A special Fourth Section Board considers these applications. In 1960 it entered 960 orders of which 808 granted continuing relief.

A wide variety of general investigations have been conducted, 45 of them in one recent year, October 1960–September 1961. Commonly what is involved is an effort by railroads to raise a wide range of rates. Procedures followed resemble those in a court of law.

From the point of view of intermodal competition, minimum rate cases are of primary importance. In essence the I.C.C. asks two questions in such rate cases: is the rate compensatory? If so, is the rate unlawful though compensatory? It is not entirely clear what is meant by "compensatory." It seems to be true that, to be compensatory in the eyes of the I.C.C., a rate must at least cover "out-of-pocket costs." What is meant by "out-of-pocket costs" and how these costs are to be determined is, therefore, a matter of importance. The Commission, as previously described, *also* considers full costs. It holds that full costs are ultimately controlling as to which is the most economical carrier.

Should the I.C.C. allow a carrier, which is not the most economical carrier by this standard, to compete for traffic by charging rates more than out-of-pocket costs but less than full costs? The law is not clear on this point. The practice of "umbrella" rate-making, i.e., maintaining arbitrary fixed differentials between rates so that each mode may share in the traffic, was apparently condemned by the clause in Section 15a (3) enacted in 1958: "Rates of a carrier shall not be held up to a particular level to protect the traffic of any other mode of transportation. . . ." Clear enough! The remainder of the sentence, however, reads as follows: ". . . giving due consideration to the objectives of the national transportation policy declared by this Act." That policy directs the I.C.C. to "preserve the inherent advantages" of each mode of transportation. It is not surprising, therefore, that the Commission does not have a single standard of what is a compensatory rate. A clarification of policy would be in the public interest.

Even if a rate is compensatory, the Commission may still hold the rate to be unlawful as being "unreasonable" or a "destructive competitive practice." The Commission tends to find objectionable undue disruption of existing traffic patterns and existing rate structures. As Cramton puts it, in plain language, a more efficient carrier can "nibble away" at the status quo but may not swallow a large chunk at one time.

Some regulatory agencies have adopted a policy of framing general rules to be followed by individualized staff applications. The I.C.C. has not followed this policy in rate cases. Its practice has been one of case-by-case adjudication. Critics have objected to this strategy as leading to uncertainty and unpredictability of actions of the I.C.C. The fundamental difficulty, however, with regard to minimum rates, is the lack of clarity of the law itself.

STATISTICAL SUMMARY OF THE EFFECTS OF THE RATE STRUCTURE— The I.C.C. has published estimates of the ratio of revenues to out-of-pocket costs by commodity group and of total dollar contributions to revenue in excess of out-of-pocket costs by commodities. These studies serve to summarize the results of the railroad rate structure viewed as a source of revenue. If the rate system is regarded as an example of a system of economic price discrimination, as it is in this discussion, these statistics indicate approximately the nature of that system.

The following tabulation shows ratios to out-of-pocket costs:[42]

Ratio of the United States Carload Revenues to Out-of-Pocket Costs

Commodity Group	1961	1952
Products of Agriculture	118	137
Animals and Products	111	121
Products of Mines	106	125
Products of Forests	117	132
Manufactures and Misc.	148	185
Forwarder	111	156
Ratio for all commodity groups	127	152

Note the shifts away from high ratios to out-of-pocket costs from 1952–1961, presumably reflecting competitive pressures. For the "manufactures and miscellaneous" group the fall from a ratio of 185 to 148 is especially noteworthy.

42. I.C.C., Bureau of Accounts, Statement No. 6–64, June 1964, *Distribution of the Rail Revenue Contribution by Commodity Groups, 1961.*

Further information as to what commodities now are crucial to the railroads is provided in the following tabulation:

Ten Leading Commodities in Producing Aggregate Dollars of Contribution to Revenue in Excess of Out-of-Pocket Costs as Estimated by I.C.C.

Commodity	CONTRIBUTION (MILLIONS OF DOLLARS)	
	1961	1959
Wheat	121	117
Manufactured iron and steel	105	132
Vehicle parts, N.O.S.	91	124
Lumber, shingles, lath	74	101
Bituminous coal	69	126
Chemicals, N.O.S.	52	62
Paperboard, fibreboard	48	46
Automobiles, passenger	45	21
Food products, N.O.S.	44	41
Fertilizers, N.O.S.	41	45

Note that the ranking of the top ten commodities is not constant but fluctuated even over a two year period, 1959 to 1961. Wheat, coal, and lumber are basic components of railroad traffic. Manufactured iron and steel and vehicle parts are also very important contributors to revenues.

Concluding Comments: Directions of Public Policy

In considering public policy toward the competitive struggle between the railroads and other modes of transportation, there are two levels of public policy toward the railroad industry that are distinguished here. They are public policy toward the basic organization of the industry and public policy designed to influence the market practices of the industry, especially practices in the determination of rates. The most important problems of organizational policy concern mergers. The railroad merger question is centrally a question of railroad efficiency. It has been reviewed above, and the conclusion reached that the social gains from mergers outweigh the social losses.

Discussion of the problems of railroad rate policy in competition with other modes of transportation cannot be concluded without discussion of the economic characteristics of the competing modes, especially highway transportation. Some observations on the problem can be made at this point, however.

A case might be developed for a railroad rate structure based exclusively on the full cost of service. Railroads discriminate in price, however, because it is profitable to do so. They will abandon price discrimination only if forced to do so. It seems improbable that such an effort will be made by the public. In a situation in which a basic difficulty is that many roads are not profitable, a policy of prices based on costs only, abandonment of discrimination, and, hence, lower profits, seems unreasonable. It is also difficult to envisage a system of rates based on costs prescribed by public authority in the present state of knowledge of costs. Furthermore, efficient use of existing capacity may require price less than full cost of service.

What are the possibilities of reduced regulation in connection with rates? Regulation certainly could be reduced by making it simpler. Congress could clarify the law with regard to rates, for example, by repealing the reference to the National Transportation Policy in the rule on rate making. The Commission could clarify its position as to what cost estimates it will accept. A more drastic proposal would be to eliminate entirely control by the I.C.C. over minimum rates. The wisdom of this policy can only be evaluated in the light of a discussion of highway transportation and the trucking industry.

14

Highway Transportation

A BASIC CHARACTERISTIC of highway transportation is that while the roadway is publicly owned and maintained the vehicles for the most part are privately owned. The private owners, furthermore, are numerous and diverse, ranging from households who own one or two cars to business enterprises that own cars and trucks for their own use and firms engaged in the transport of people or goods for hire. This diversity of interests complicates the problems of public policy toward highways.

The questions of public policy toward highways are, first, questions having to do with the provision of highways, questions of investment policy. How much money should be spent on highways? Who should pay the bill for the highway program and in what form should the charges be levied? Another set of questions concerns economic regulation of the trucking industry. The first two sections of this chapter are devoted to investment decisions and finance, respectively, and the third section to a brief discussion of the economic regulation of the trucking industry.

As has been noted earlier, trucking companies are often in the same industry as railroads in the sense that they compete directly. There is, therefore, a close connection between the problems of railroad regula-

230

tion and the regulation of trucking. Much of highway transportation, of course, is not subject to economic regulation. Private passenger cars are unregulated except for regulations concerned with safety or the control of pollution of the atmosphere by exhaust fumes. These problems are beyond the scope of this discussion, as are problems of the economic losses resulting from motor vehicle accidents except as these losses enter into discussions of investment policy.[1]

Investment Decisions

HISTORY OF INVESTMENT IN HIGHWAYS—In the early years of the nineteenth century in the United States there was an active period of road construction financed in substantial part by the levying of tolls. With the successful development of railroads and the demonstration of the superiority of the iron horse, interest in highways was much reduced. Rural roads existed primarily to serve local purposes.

With the development of the automobile a system of highways had to be created. The method of construction originally adopted was to surface the existing network. This was the period of getting the motorist "out of the mud." Changes might be made in the curvature; grades and bridges might be constructed; but the main reliance was on the existing right of way and on modernizing the existing structure of the highway. A national network of surfaced roads evolved from the original primitive system.

The growth of the network may be summarized by statistics of the existing surfaced mileage of rural roads and municipal streets at selected dates:

	Existing Surfaced Mileage (thousands of miles)
1904	154
1910	204
1920	369
1930	694
1940	1,367
1950	1,939
1962	2,647

(*Historical Statistics of the United States,* Bureau of the Census with the cooperation of the Social Science Research Council, 1960, p. 458. 1962 data from *Highway Statistics, 1962,* March 1964, Bureau of Public Roads, p. 137.)

1. For a more general discussion of accidents see S. Valavanis, "Traffic Safety from an Economist's Point of View," *Quarterly Journal of Economics,* November 1958, pp. 477–484.

The gradual improvement of the existing network has continued, but in the late 1930s it became apparent that improvement was not enough. This method became increasingly unsatisfactory as the automobile evolved. The more important changes were in speeds.[2] In 1925 only expensive automobiles could travel 60 miles an hour, and in the low price cars 40 miles per hour was fast. By the late 1930s, however, even the lower priced cars were capable of sustained speeds on the order of 60 m.p.h. It was becoming clear by the late 1930s that completely new highways with new rights of way, designed according to new principles, were far better adapted to the characteristics of motor vehicles than the existing road networks. In 1937, for example, an article appeared evaluating the results of the operation of motor vehicles on the new highways that had been built in Germany essentially for military reasons. A comparison was made between an expressway and a parallel existing pre-expressway highway. The mileage between two points on the expressway was 92 miles, on the older road 101 miles. On the parallel road the highest possible speed was 44 miles per hour, and for purposes of comparison speed on the expressway was held down to the same 44 miles per hour. In a test run there were 444 speed changes on the parallel road compared to one speed change on the expressway. The number of manipulations of the steering wheel involving a movement of 2.3 inches or more differed by a ratio of 570 to 1. Fuel consumption on the parallel road was 14.2 miles per gallon compared to 22.3 miles per gallon on the expressway.

It was also discovered that there was a measurable difference in accident rate between a limited access expressway and a conventional highway. One of the early results was that on the Merritt Parkway in Connecticut the fatality rate per vehicle mile was one-third the rate on the parallel Boston Post Road. This improvement was achieved by limiting access, eliminating foot traffic, dividing the two streams of traffic in opposite directions by a median (which reduced head-on accidents by three-fourths), and by provision of grade separations at intersections. As information of this kind continued to accumulate it began to appear by the end of the 1930s that construction of a new network of main rural highways would be necessary.

Neither the costs nor the benefits from such a system, however, were known with any precision. In particular, reliable forecasts of future use presented difficulties. Such forecasts are, of course, essential to rational

2. See the discussion in Wilfred Owen, *Automotive Transportation: Trends and Problems,* Brookings Institution, 1949.

planning of investment in a manner consistent with the theoretical model outlined in Chapter 3.

It is relevant to examine in somewhat more detail this aspect of the history of the new highways. In 1939, the United States Bureau of Public Roads issued a report, *Toll Roads and Free Roads,* which was essentially a statement of opposition to the principle of toll highways. It was directed primarily against a proposal for three superhighways east and west across the United States and three north and south, for a total of 14,336 miles, which had been suggested as a toll network. The bureau doubted that at a toll of 1 cent per mile for passenger cars the proposed network would pay more than 45 per cent of its cost. It did find some mileage feasible, especially in the northeast in the area between Washington D.C. and Boston.

As events developed, a series of toll roads were built and the traffic on these roads can be compared with the estimates. The comparison illustrates the difficulty of making intelligent forecasts of the economic impact of a completely new facility such as a new national system of superhighways. The Pennsylvania Turnpike was not opened until 1940. The Bureau estimated that traffic on the Pennsylvania Turnpike would be about 715 vehicles per day. By 1947 the actual traffic count was 10,000 vehicles per day. Between Portland, Maine and the New Hampshire border the report estimated the traffic at 1,348 per day. Traffic in 1949, the first year of operation of the Maine Turnpike, was 4,000 and more vehicles per day, with traffic of 5,000 vehicles per day by 1950.[3]

Two turnpikes constructed subsequent to the Maine Turnpike may be mentioned as further examples of the difficulties of forecasting demand. Reference has been made earlier to the success of the New Jersey Turnpike. In November of 1951, the first section was opened; by December of 1951, 90 miles of highway had been opened. In September of 1952, the authority reported to the bond-holders that traffic through August 15, 1952 had been twice what was expected; to be exact, it was 111.6 per cent above the estimates! The West Virginia Turnpike, the "turnpike to nowhere," and its financial difficulties were reported in Chapter 3.

The early turnpikes came into existence for a variety of reasons. The first of the major turnpikes, the Pennsylvania Turnpike, actually was built in part as an antidepression measure and in part as a result of an historical accident. The Pennsylvania Turnpike Commission was estab-

3. See Wilfred Owen and Charles L. Dearing, *Toll Roads and the Problem of Highway Modernization,* Brookings Institution, 1951.

lished in 1937 and the original section of the turnpike, 160 miles long, was opened in 1940. There was in existence a right of way that had been partially developed with the intention of constructing a railroad from the vicinity of Pittsburgh to the vicinity of Harrisburg. About half of the tunnel boring required had been completed and the tunnels were in good order. This partially developed right of way was purchased by the Pennsylvania Turnpike Authority at the bargain price of 2 million dollars. The project also received substantial federal assistance from the Public Works Administration that gave a grant equal to 45 per cent of the cost estimate. A loan equal to 55 per cent of the funds was received from the Reconstruction Finance Corporation, which later transferred this obligation to private interests. Federal assistance to the project was, thus, part of the program of an agency whose principal mission was to combat the great depression. Once built, the Pennsylvania Turnpike was a success, as the German experience had foreshadowed.

Another of the early turnpikes, the Maine Turnpike, was undertaken essentially to solve a problem of highway finance, as will be discussed in the next section. Once built, however, and proven to be financially successful, the Maine Turnpike also led to increased interest in investment in other turnpikes. Something of a boom followed.

The postwar boom in the construction of toll roads was brought to an end in 1956 by the passage of the legislation providing for the construction of the Interstate System under the auspices of the federal government. This legislation will be discussed below in the comparison of different methods of highway finance. The extent of the toll roads constructed by the states from 1940 to 1959 was as follows:[4]

Total mileage	3,257 miles
Total cost	5,052,611,000 dollars
Total number of states with toll roads	19
Average cost per mile	1,550,000 dollars

Thus, the period left as its tangible contribution to the transportation of the nation about 5 billion dollars worth of highways, and as its intangible contribution a demonstration of the value of modern main rural highways.

INVESTMENT CRITERIA FOR HIGHWAYS—Implicit in the toll road development was a definite financial criterion for highways. Only roads that would pay their cost through tolls should be built. The greater

4. These statistics refer to the situation as of October 1, 1959, by which date only 5.7 miles of toll roads remained under construction. See *Highway Statistics, 1958*, Bureau of Public Roads, 1960, pp. 59–60.

separation of investment decisions and financing decisions in the more recent policy leaves the investment decisions still to be faced. What is required is analysis of the costs and the gains of each proposed project even though there is no authority set up to collect tolls and pay the costs of each length of road.

Typical procedure in highway investment, according to a report prepared for a recent transportation study of the United States Department of Commerce by John E. Clayton,[5] is as follows:

(1) an estimate of the total future travel is made;
(2) design standards for the various systems and routes are established by considering average daily traffic on the various highways in conjunction with such other factors as safety, comfort, types of vehicle, weight of vehicles, etc.;
(3) the present condition of the highways is determined by use of some type of rating process;
(4) the total investment needed to raise the efficiency of the highway plant to the desired level is computed. . . .

Each of these steps requires some explanation.

(1) The estimates of total future travel usually make use of such variables as population, vehicle registrations, income, and motor fuel consumption. For example, total population may be projected over a period of thirty years. A second projection will be made of the number of persons per vehicle. These two series will then yield an estimate of vehicle registrations by a process of division. The next stage will be to prepare a series of miles traveled per vehicle, which also must be projected for thirty years. Multiplication of the number of vehicles and miles per vehicle will yield projected vehicle miles traveled in each year.

(2) The establishment of design standards involves two types of standards, geometric and structural. The geometry of a highway involves the number and width of lanes, the width of the shoulders, curvature, sight distance, design of intersections, width of bridges, and grades. The structural standards refer to the composition and thickness of the pavement and the character and load-carrying capacity of the subgrade.

Design standards depend in large part on traffic density, the character of the traffic, and the assumed design speed. The procedure with regard to traffic density is to estimate hourly traffic for some future year, called the design year, which may be fifteen years in the future,

---

5. John E. Clayton, *Highway Investment Theories and Practices*, Staff paper prepared for the Federal Transportation Study, October 1959 (mimeographed).

and then establish standards to handle the thirtieth highest hour out of all the hours in that year at the assumed design speed. That volume of traffic is the "design hour volume." The character of the traffic represents the mix of passenger cars and trucks of different weights. The design speed is that at which the user will wish to travel. It is the "maximum approximately uniform speed which will be adopted by the faster group of drivers."

(3) The evaluation of the present condition of the highways may use a concept of "tolerable standards" that are not so high as would be applied to new roads. The considerations are not entirely clear which underlie these standards; such phrases are used as "reasonable safety and without serious inconvenience to traffic." An inventory of roads will be made, with an evaluation of each section of each road.

(4) The final stage involves the more or less elaborate and careful preparation of a set of cost estimates to bring the system up to standard.

Procedures of this sort are certainly improvements over unsystematic methods of tackling the problems. This approach, however, is deficient in one major respect: there is no explicit treatment of the benefits from the investment. The problem of estimating benefits is avoided by the adoption of design standards. The underlying issues remain: What are to be accepted as standards? How is one to know whether standards are too high or too low? Uncertainty about standards implies uncertainty about whether particular projects should be built.

There is a tradition of thought, however, that treats benefits explicitly. The benefits ordinarily considered are the benefits to the users of the proposed facility. They fall into two broad groups, reductions in operating costs of motor vehicles resulting from the proposed investment in a new or improved road, and other gains to users, from improved service, especially in time saved, reduced risk of accident, and comfort and convenience. As will be developed below, gains to others than the users of the road in question should also be taken into account.

The development of this line of reasoning over several decades has led to detailed studies of the costs of operating motor vehicles and to attempts to relate these costs to the characteristics of the highways involved. Such studies have been made by the Highway Research Board and the American Association of State Highway Officials (AASHO). They are summarized in textbooks on highway engineering.[6]

Fuel costs are a function of the speed attempted by the driver rather

6. See, for example, Lawrence I. Hewes and Clarkson H. Oglesby, *Highway Engineering*, Wiley, 1954.

than the actual speed. The two may be the same under ideal conditions. When a driver must slow down to less than the desired speed and then accelerate to the desired speed, the extra fuel required in acceleration tends to wipe out the savings in fuel from travel for a period at a slower rate. Fuel consumption also depends on grades. Curves do not matter *provided* there is proper superelevation to keep the vehicle in its curved path.

Fuel consumption is related to the nature of the surface, especially at moderate to high speeds. One study showed, for example, that at 15 m.p.h. for passenger cars fuel consumption is about 7 per cent less on a concrete road than a gravel road. At 45 m.p.h. the difference in fuel consumption is 20 per cent.[7]

Oil consumption is related to speed and to the surface of the highway, being higher on gravel than on paved roads. Tire wear depends on the surface as well as on speed, grades, curvature and traffic conditions. Repair and maintenance costs also vary with the surface. The principle is clear and estimates have been made by engineers of the effects of the character of the road on each of these types of cost. For example, at 40 m.p.h. tire life is about three times as many miles on pavements in good condition as on unsurfaced roads.[8]

Depreciation is partly a function of time and partly of use. The conventional division is to assume a total cost, total years of life, and total mileage (e.g., 2,000 dollars total cost, ten years life, 10,000 miles a year) and divide depreciation evenly between time and use. To the extent that depreciation is a function of use, that is, of distance traveled, shorter roads save money. If the previous figures are used, the saving is 1 cent per vehicle mile of distance saved.

Stopping a car costs some extra amount. Hence, such structures as grade separations that eliminate stops save money for motorists. The cost is in fuel and in wear on tires and brakes, and varies with the speed before (and after) the stop. The standard estimate at 30 m.p.h. is 0.74 cents and at 60 m.p.h., 2.94 cents. The length of the standing delay will also influence costs.

Up to this point the questions are essentially problems in engineering estimates of cost reductions. From this stage onwards questions of valuation must be introduced. Prices must somehow be placed on the time of the driver (and others in the vehicle), their comfort and convenience, and accidents if these items are to enter into the calculations.

7. Paul J. Claffey, "Time and Fuel Consumption for Highway User Benefit Studies," Highway Research Board, *Bulletin 276, Motor Vehicle Time and Fuel Consumption.*
8. Hewes and Oglesby, *op. cit.,* p. 48.

In total estimates of highway benefits this trilogy of time, comfort, and safety is likely to bulk large.

Time is clearly a cost to the owner of a bus or truck who must pay the wages of a driver while he operates their vehicle. For private cars an arbitrary rate of $1.55 per vehicle hour has been adopted by the American Association of State Highway Officials. Allowing 1.8 people/vehicle, the implied rate is 86 cents per person per hour. Economists tend to criticize such rates as too low. As an approximation, people's time may be valued at the price at which they sell it to their employers. Even minimum hourly wage rates are higher, and average hourly earnings are much higher than 86 cents.

Driver comfort and convenience have been valued by the same organization at 1 cent per mile. This figure, also, is obviously arbitrary. Conservative practice is to carry it separately through the calculations.[9]

Accidents certainly represent a cost. Attempts can be made to estimate the dollar value of the savings of modern highways in reduced accident rates. The National Safety Council uses the rule of thumb of multiplying the number of deaths by a round number to take into account the fact that for every death there will be personal injury accidents and property damage accidents. In 1952 the figure was 95,000 dollars and the estimate was, for every death there were thirty-five personal injury accidents, and 225 property damage accidents. An alternative approach is to calculate the expense of accidents in terms of average estimated cost of each type of accident, for example, 21,800 dollars per death, 950 dollars per injury, and 180 dollars per property damage accident have been used. There is a need for more thorough study of accident costs. (One study will be discussed briefly in Chapter 15.) An estimate made by the American Insurance Association, and reported in *Insurance Facts,* 1965, by the Insurance Information Institute, is that the economic loss from traffic accidents reached 10 billion dollars in 1964 including property damage; legal and medical costs; loss of income from absence from work; and the administrative costs of insurance. There were in that year 47,700 deaths caused by motor vehicle accidents. By the National Safety Council rule of thumb the economic loss was 210,000 dollars per fatality.

When the gains from all these sources have been estimated they can be discounted back to the present, as in Chapter 3, or annual averages may be entered in a formula showing the benefit-cost ratio, that is, the ratio of annual benefits to annual costs. Presentation of the results of the analysis may be in the form of an estimate of the rate of return

9. American Association of State Highway Officials. *Road User Benefit Analyses for Highway Improvements,* 1960.

the proposed investment would earn. Such a presentation is desirable because of the possibility of comparison with rates of return on other projects.

This approach brings into one calculation the elements of the total cost to society of producing a given volume of transportation services including both the cost to the operator of the vehicle and the cost to the public of providing the highway. It is certainly appropriate to minimize the sum of these two types of cost rather than to minimize one to the neglect of the other. Criticisms of the method concern (1) problems of estimation of the components included, and (2) the question of what components to include. There are obvious problems of estimation in the use of this approach in treating the components included in the calculation. Further research can be expected to lead to refinements and improvements. Comparisons of projects also may be possible that do not rely on the exact value placed on components that are inherently hard to estimate in dollars and cents, such as the gains in comfort and convenience. For example, if two competing projects look the same in this respect the choice between them may be based on the components that can better be quantified.

The general method has been criticized by Mohring and Harwitz on the grounds that calculations are incomplete. They take what may be regarded as the extreme position in favor of conceptual completeness.[10] They make a sharp distinction between benefits to existing traffic and benefits to new traffic, and argue that the cost-benefit calculations usually carried out understate the benefits, especially those arising from new traffic. Even on existing traffic, they argue, the benefits are understated.

There are benefits, first, not only to *users* of the proposed new highway itself but also to *users of substitute facilities.* Congestion on the substitute facilities may be reduced by diversion to the new road. The drivers who continue to use the old road will gain from the reduced congestion. For example, drivers who continued to use Route U.S. 1 after the opening of the Maine Turnpike found the driving both faster and pleasanter. In principle it would be possible to make quantitative estimates of the value of these gains and include them in the calculation of the benefits of the Maine Turnpike.

Time saved by users of the proposed road is commonly taken into account. (Mohring and Harwitz argue that it is underestimated, as suggested above.) But the time of goods in transit is not explicitly considered. There is a direct gain in reduced cost of inventory because of

10. Herbert Mohring and Mitchell Harwitz, *Highway Benefits, An Analytical Framework,* Northwestern University Press, 1962.

the reduced time that goods spend in transit. Fewer goods in transit means a lower total inventory of goods needed in production. There is an additional indirect gain in that reduced congestion tends to reduce the uncertainty about time in transit. It is no longer necessary to hold reserve stocks lest shipments be delayed.

The benefits arising from *increased traffic* on the improved road are more complex. They are benefits from substitution, and may be classified according to the type of substitution involved.

There will be substitution, first, by shippers who now will be more likely to use highway transportation in preference to other modes. The shippers will gain by the amount of the reduction in their costs owing to the better service now available to them. For example, a firm operating both in Portland and Boston may have switched from rail to highway after completion of the Maine Turnpike and found its total shipping costs lower.

Consumers of goods and services involving transportation will be able to substitute transportation-intensive goods and services for other goods and services. A family may, for example, take a vacation involving an automobile trip instead of staying at home after completion of a section of the Interstate System. The family is better off because the choice of goods and services within its means of time and money was made wider by the completion of the road. The gain to the family is derived from the difference in satisfaction between the bundle of goods and services it consumed, given the highway, and the bundle it would have consumed, *sans* highway.

Finally, there may be substitution by producers of transport intensive means of production for other means of production. The classic example of this type of benefit is the gain that resulted from the increased use of coal to produce power for industrial production in the nineteenth century. Methods of production using coal were more transportation intensive than those relying on the muscles of men or animals. Reductions in total cost of production arising from such changes are difficult to quantify, but, nevertheless, they exist.

There is no question that this analysis is correct in the sense that all these gains do exist. It has yet to be demonstrated, however, that they can be quantified in such a manner as to be usefully taken into account in making comparisons among competing projects. The best practical approach may be to go as far as possible in basing comparisons among projects on considerations that can be quantified, leaving some scope for judgments based on any existing differences that cannot be reduced to dollars.

An opposite error is also possible. It would be an error to include in the estimate of benefits the full area under the demand curve, that is, the entire consumers' surplus. Such elements are not reflected in the prices of products that are rivals for the same resources.

Financing Highways

The problems of highway finance are the problems of allocating the burden of highway costs. The question is, who is going to pay? Should nonusers contribute, and, if so, in what amounts? The remaining burden must then be allocated among the many users of highways. It must be allocated among types of vehicles, and it must also be allocated geographically, which implies allocation among political units. The allocation of the financial burden is accomplished through the use of some selection among four principal sources of revenue: general taxation, taxes on land and real property specially benefited, tolls, and taxes on motor vehicles and the operation thereof.

The subject of highway finance is complex and controversial, and only the outlines of the problems can be indicated here. The discussion will proceed in the following order: a brief treatment of principles of highway finance, a description of the main features of the administrative framework of the highway system, the mix of methods of finance, and problems of cross-subsidization. Discussion of congestion on urban highways and the cost of peak load service versus off-peak service will be postponed until the next chapter.

PRINCIPLES OF HIGHWAY FINANCE—The basic considerations involved are in part questions of equity. It is consistent with principles of equity to propose that there should be no subsidization of one group of highway users by another or by nonusers unless cause for subsidy can be shown. Ordinarily, those who use services should pay for them. The burden of proof is on those who propose the subsidy. That this burden of proof can be successfully carried may be illustrated by the decision of Congress and the President to use federal money to construct an improved system of roads in Appalachia. Criteria for subsidies are discussed below.

Another basic consideration is economic efficiency. This consideration is one of the foundations of the user charge principle, the principle that users of transportation facilities provided by the government should pay the cost of those facilities. The level of user charges to trucks, it has been urged, is important for competition between trucks and railroads.

Purchasers of transportation services, it is argued, will make the correct choice between the two if the price of each includes the cost of the resources used to provide the service.

The view has been urged by many economists that public subsidy in the form of contributions from general funds should be paid only in those markets in which the market otherwise would fail to produce enough of goods or services which yield benefits to nonusers.[11] As far as highways are concerned, the implication is that charges to nonusers are necessary only to the extent that user charges would fail to cover the cost of providing needed roads and streets. A method of distinguishing when a subsidy from nonusers is appropriate from when it is not appropriate has been presented by Kafoglis. This approach can be most easily understood with the aid of a diagram. Assume for simplicity that marginal cost is constant, and that there is only one class of vehicle. Individual *a*, a user, may be thought of as having a demand for highway services represented by a demand curve, *Da*. If the price is set equal

Figure 14.1—Subsidy of Highways by Nonusers

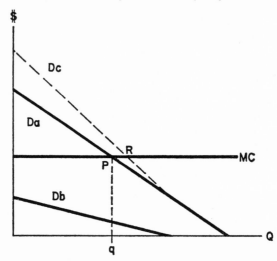

to marginal cost by a user charge (or system of charges), individual *a* will consume (and pay for) an amount of highway services indicated by *q* determined by the intersection of *Da* and *MC* at *P*. Suppose, now, that individual *b*, a nonuser, receives some benefits from the use of the highway by individual *a*. Then *b* may be thought of as having a demand

11. This position is summarized in Milton Z. Kafoglis, "Highway Policy and External Economies," *National Tax Journal,* March 1963, pp. 68–80.

curve for use of the highway by *a*, which is shown by *Db*. Assume *b* actually stands ready to pay for use of the highway by *a* as his demand curve indicates. Total demand for use of the highway by *a* then may be found by adding together demand by *a* and *b*, as in the dotted line, *Dc*. Total output will then be determined by the intersection of *Dc* and *MC*, at point *R*, which is to the right of the point *P*.

Note that a subsidy will be offered by *b* only if his demand for the use of the highway by *a* has a value greater than zero at the point of equilibrium that would be reached without subsidy. There may be benefits to *b* that are intramarginal, which will not result in any offer of subsidy, as in the situation in Figure 14.2. In this situation *Dc* differs from *Da* only to the left of *P*, that is, in the area where the shape of *Dc*

Figure 14.2—Benefits to Nonusers of Highways without Subsidies Paid by Nonusers

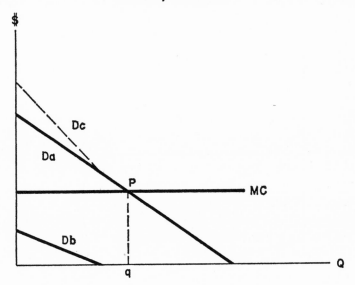

makes no difference to the value of the equilibrium output. The nonuser gets a windfall—like many other windfalls that accrue both to firms and households in the economy.

According to this approach the first reliance should be on user charges, and subsidies by nonusers should be used in situations as shown in Figure 14.1 but should not be used in situations as shown in Figure 14.2. That is, there should be subsidies only when exclusive reliance on user charges would lead to inadequate highways. The focus of attention is on the situation at the margin. The question is not whether nonusers derive some benefits from highways. The question is whether they desire more or better highways than would otherwise be provided and are willing to pay for them. Their concern may not be narrowly selfish. For example, they may believe it to be in the national interest that roads be improved in impoverished areas such as Appalachia as a means of assisting the long-run economic development of those areas in order to reduce the disparity in economic well-being between rich and poor geographic areas. Note, however, that this approach would lead to restriction of the use of general funds for highways to special cases such as the construction of roads in depressed or underdeveloped areas.

A variety of methods have been proposed for allocating charges between motor vehicle operators and property owners.[12] One of the simpler methods, known as the predominant use method, would assign to property owners the full cost of access roads; to road users the full cost of trunk routes; and to the community to be paid from general funds the cost of the remaining local roads. This method is inconsistent with the principles just proposed to the extent that it involves a subsidy to roads from general funds.

The earnings credit method involves an averaging between two opposite approaches. The first starts from the idea that motorists should pay the full cost of the primary system (i.e., main rural roads). Rates should be set for taxes on fuel, registration fees, and other charges to cover full cost per vehicle mile for travel on the primary system. These rates applied to travel on lightly used local roads will pay for part of the cost of those roads. According to the first approach after deduction of this credit the balance of these costs should be paid by local taxpayers and property holders. The second approach starts from the idea that local roads should be paid for entirely by local taxpayers. Charges not thus met remain to be allocated to motor vehicle operators. This approach will lead to a different allocation from the first, and the two results may then be averaged. The reasoning would seem more straightforward if the first approach only were used.

The second stage in the problem of allocating highway costs is the division among different classes of vehicles of that part of the cost of highways allocated to tolls and taxes on motor vehicles and the operation thereof. The need for differentiated charges arises from differences in the cost of providing the highway services used by different classes of vehicles. The customary approach to the problem is through consider-

12. For a summary and references to recent literature see A. D. Le Baron, "The Theory of Highway Finance: Roots, Aims and Accomplishments," *National Tax Journal,* September 1963, pp. 307–319.

ation of the weight of the (loaded) vehicle and the number of miles it travels. Ton-miles are sometimes considered.

However, there are objections to the ton-mile as a measure of highway movement. Highway construction involves structural design and geometric design. Structural design includes, especially, specification of pavement characteristics. Costs incurred for the provision of pavement are a function of wheel load, not of gross vehicle weight. The same gross vehicle weight may be distributed over different numbers of wheels, of course, by varying the design of the truck. This point has been urged by Grubbs, who has worked out some of the anomalies that may result from vehicles of similar gross weight but different numbers of axles.[13] Grubbs further discusses the relation between trucks and the geometric design of highways. Again the use of the ton-mile as a measure is unfortunate. The engineering approach is to use what is called the truck factor, that is, a conversion factor by which to estimate the number of passenger cars to which a truck is equivalent in its use of highway capacity. The truck factor does not depend on the weight of the truck. It depends primarily on its speed. A case might be made that it also depends on the ability of the truck to change speed, or to maintain constant speed in hilly terrain. What is required, it would seem, is a method of taxing trucks which requires low-powered trucks to pay the social cost of the amount of highway they consume and thus provides an incentive to the use of more powerful engines in trucks. Such charges could be combined with charges based on wheel loads, not gross vehicle weight, to reflect the cost of heavier construction or greater maintenance.

Such a system of allocation would be based primarily on costs rather than on benefits. As has been repeatedly pointed out, the use of charges based on costs is advantageous because of the contribution to economic efficiency. The case for charges based on demand considerations is strongest where such charges are necessary to meet the full cost of the service. In highway transportation, however, experience shows that demand for highway services is price inelastic. Taxes based on cost-of-service can meet the full cost of providing highways.

CLASSIFICATION OF HIGHWAYS—The decisions as to the allocation of funds for highway purposes are made within a system of classification of highways, which has been developed by law. The federal primary system of main roads was set up in 1921. Since 1944 a federal-aid secondary system of important feeder roads also has been established. The Interstate System is legally part of the federal-aid primary system.

13. Clifton M. Grubbs, "Problems of Highway Cost Allocation," *National Tax Journal*, December 1963, pp. 416–425.

Intraurban segments of main highways, which previous to 1944 had been denied federal aid, since then have been part of the federal-aid system.

The Interstate System is financed 90 per cent from federal funds and 10 per cent from state funds. The other federal-aid systems are financed on a fifty-fifty basis by the federal government and the states. The allocation of funds among the states is based on a formula which takes into account the population of the states, the area of the states, the mileage for the three types of roads, and the estimated cost of completing the Interstate System in each state. Roads within national parks are entirely paid for by the federal government.

The laws of states vary, and therefore, the situation at the state level cannot be described adequately in a few words. The main facts include the following. The states collect substantial sums of money from highway-user taxes, especially taxes on gasoline. Most segregate these revenues in a general highway fund or funds dedicated to particular highway purposes, but a few do not keep the money separate from the general revenue. The states, in addition to their own expenditures on highways, allocate a substantial share of their receipts from highway users to local governments for the provision of local roads and streets. The relation of the states to the localities, thus, is similar to the relation of the federal government to the states in matters of highway finance.

The counties and other rural units rely on state transfers for more than half of their support, property taxes being their other main source of income. For local urban units state transfers are also important, but aggregate less than half of their revenue for roads.

While the varied methods by which the funds are allocated will not be further analyzed here, it is within this framework that the decisions are taken as to where roads will be built and where they will not be built and who will pay for them. The decision in 1944 to allocate federal funds to roads within urban areas, for example, has had far-reaching effects. It obviously changed the allocation of funds as between rural and urban uses.

THE MIX OF METHODS OF FINANCE—As noted above, there are four basic sources of funds for highways: tolls, general taxation, taxes on land and real property especially benefited, and taxes on motor vehicles and their operation. Each has been used to some extent in recent years. Each has characteristics as a method of distributing the cost of highways. How they have been used will be briefly discussed.

Tolls made possible the rapid construction of modern road systems in those rural areas where they most needed in the period after World War II. The usefulness of tolls has been limited by several considerations. Users of toll roads make a double contribution to the cost of highways. They pay tolls plus the same user taxes (gasoline taxes, etc.) as users of other roads, thus paying for roads they are not using as well as the toll road. Another limitation, especially in urban areas, has been the mechanical problem of toll collection. It is some trouble and expense to stop to pay a toll, in addition to the direct cost of building and operating the collection facility.

Not all intercity roads have enough traffic volume to support themselves through tolls when most roads are toll-free. There were about 3,257 miles of toll roads in operation by October 1, 1959 with only an additional 5.7 miles under construction. These roads had been built or were under construction by the end of 1956, for the most part; that year is taken as marking the end of the postwar boom in toll road construction. They were, in general, the roads most likely to pay for themselves. Viewed financially, added mileage would become increasingly risky. No doubt many more miles of road would have paid, but not all roads. Which roads would pay would depend in considerable part on the development of the network as a whole, which was not easy for a state agency to control. Only about 5 per cent of the total receipts of all units of government from current imposts for highways are from tolls.[14]

The use for highway purposes of the general revenue is also relatively small but it is a more important source of funds than tolls, amounting to about 10 per cent of receipts from current imposts. There is also some diversion of highway revenue by states to nonhighway purposes equal in the aggregate to about half the amount of general funds used for highways. Taxes on land and real property are the third type of taxation. Particular property may be directly benefited by highways. Of receipts for highways from current imposts, about 9 per cent now come from the taxation of real estate.

The principal sources of funds for highway purposes, however, remain taxes on motor vehicles. There is general agreement on the principle that these charges should be the principal source of funds. About 76 per cent of current imposts used for highway purposes are of this type.

Relatively little use is made of bonds for highway finance. In 1961, for example, only about 11 per cent of total receipts for highways came from the sale of bonds.[15] Bond proceeds equaled only about 19 per cent of the total capital outlay.

14. *Highway Statistics, 1962, op. cit.*, p. 115.
15. *Highway Statistics, 1962, op. cit.*, p. 115.

Within the total of user charges, there are a variety of taxes used for allocation of the burden among users. There are two main classes of user fees, those that do not vary with miles driven, such as registration fees and excise taxes on motor vehicles, and those that do vary with miles driven, such as taxes on fuel and tires.

License fees have the advantage that they can be adjusted to the weight and other characteristics of vehicles. They are invariant with respect to mileage of use, and, therefore, offer the possibility of including an element in the tax structure to cover those costs incurred in the provision of the highway network that also are invariant with respect to the number of vehicle miles.

Fuel taxes have two basic advantages. The amount of fuel consumed increases with use of the highways. The fuel taxes provide, thus, a method of charging more of those who make greater use of the roads. Also, they are economical to collect.

These are important advantages. A limitation is that there are economies of scale in fuel consumption as the size of the vehicle increases. For passenger cars the result is roughly satisfactory. High fuel taxes provide an incentive to consumers to operate smaller cars. Smaller cars use less highway, both in the sense of occupying less space, and in the sense of causing less wear and tear. It is not a matter of major concern that the larger autos use less fuel per ton-mile.

The effect of high fuel taxes on the economies of trucks is less satisfactory. As the size of the truck increases the cost of fuel per ton-mile decreases. The quantity of gasoline consumed per mile increases much less than proportionally to the vehicle weight. The following figures indicate the relationship:[16]

Average Gross Vehicle Weight (pounds)	GASOLINE CONSUMPTION	
	Gallons per Mile	Gallons per Ton per Mile
20,000	.161	.016
30,000	.191	.013
40,000	.221	.011
50,000	.251	.010
60,000	.281	.009
70,000	.311	.009

These economies of scale are substantial. Note, for example, that as the average gross vehicle weight of a gasoline powered line-haul truck is multiplied by three (20,000 to 60,000), the fuel consumed per ton per mile falls from .016 to .009 gallons. Truckers have strong incentives to

16. Malcolm F. Kent, "Fuel and Time Consumption Rates for Trucks in Freight Service," in *Highway Research Board Bulletin 276, Motor Vehicle Time and Fuel Consumption*, pp. 1–19. See p. 11.

operate large vehicles. The effect of high fuel taxes is to increase the economies of scale in operating large trucks—from the point of view of the trucker. From the point of view of the highway department, many small vehicles would produce less wear and tear on the roads. High fuel taxes tend to encourage use of large, underpowered trucks.[17]

There has been some interest among those concerned with highway finance in "third structure" taxes. Third structure taxes are charges based on gross vehicle weight. The purpose is a finer adjustment of charges to use than is possible with the combination of fixed fees such as license fees plus taxes on fuel. The limitations of this approach have been discussed above. The refinement should relate to axle load or wheel load.

THE FEDERAL TAX STRUCTURE AS AN ILLUSTRATION OF HOW TAXES MAY BE COMBINED—The provisions of the Federal legislation of 1956 may be regarded as an attempt to develop a tax structure by a judicious combination of taxes. The taxes were intended to provide the financial base for a greatly expanded long range construction program whose most prominent feature is the Interstate System. The legislation provided for the creation of a special trust fund, the United States Highway Trust Fund, set up in the Treasury, to which new taxes plus certain existing taxes were to be diverted and from which highways were to be financed. The main reliance continued to be taxes on fuel. The federal tax on gasoline was raised from 2 to 3 cents a gallon in 1956, and further increased to 4 cents in 1959. The tax on tires was increased to 10 cents after 1961, and a new tax on camelback (tread rubber) was introduced, 5 cents per pound after 1961. These taxes, like those on fuel, are paid by highway users in amounts that vary with their use of the roads. The structure also includes since 1956 a federal registration fee for large trucks. The amounts set since 1961 are $3.00 per 1000 pounds on the gross weight of the vehicle if its gross weight exceeds 26,000 pounds when loaded. Prior to 1961 this rate was $1.50. Adjustment of this rate offers the possibility of changing the share of highway costs borne by large trucks as opposed to smaller vehicles. There is also an excise tax on trucks, buses, and trailers of 10 per cent of the manufacturer's whole-

17. The bitter opposition to fuel taxes on the part of some oil companies has been criticized by some economists as shortsighted from the oil companies' point of view. See, for example, John F. Due, "The Rise and Fall of the Toll Principle in Highway Finance— 1940–1957," *National Tax Journal,* June 1957. Better roads lead to the generation of new traffic and, hence, increased total fuel consumption. The stimulating effect on travel by highway of better roads very probably exceeds the depressing effect of the tax on fuel. If it were not for the rule that only public agencies may build roads, it would very likely pay the oil companies to raise their prices and spend the money on providing free highways for people to induce them to consume petroleum.

sale price and the proceeds accrue to the Highway Trust Fund. (Excises on passenger cars currently do not go to the Fund.) Further adjustments of rates seem probable. By suitable manipulation of these rates it is clearly possible to shift the burden as between passenger cars and trucks. It is not possible to go as far as would be desirable in basing charges to trucks on the cost of providing highways to different types of truck.

PROBLEMS OF CROSS-SUBSIDIZATION—A complex system of financing such as that used in highway finance offers possibilities of cross-subsidization of one category of highway users by another. Two possible types of cross-subsidy have attracted particular attention, geographic apportionment that provides roads for people living in one area at the expense of people living elsewhere, and subsidy of trucks by passenger vehicles. The nature of possible cross-subsidization may be indicated by a case history of a problem in highway finance in Maine.

At the conclusion of World War II the State of Maine was faced with the problem of providing highways to meet a seasonal need.[18] In the summer there is a heavy flow of vehicles from the Boston metropolitan area north along the coastline into southern Maine. The existing highway in that part of the state, Route 1, had been improved in a patchwork manner, most of the improvements consisting in widening of the road. There were no grade separations even though there were seventy-six important intersections between Kittery and Portland. At the same time, according to a study made in 1947, the highway network of the state as a whole was seriously deficient.

Furthermore, state law provided for "equitable" distribution of highway funds among counties on the basis of population and mileage of roads eligible for federal aid. The formula in use gave *no* weight to traffic. Thus, the formula did not take into account the existence of the seasonal flow of traffic in the southern part of the state. The tendency as a result of the formula was for the state to spend what funds were available in building disconnected stretches of highway here and there through the state. Meanwhile, the affected towns were opposed to bypassing by construction of a new highway. They were not interested in pressing the state government for a revision of the allocation formula, which would result in the construction of a new highway that they feared would remove the summer visitors from their streets.

Ordinarily the recourse of a state government that needs revenue for highways is to increase the gasoline tax. Already, however, the state gas

18. See Owen, *op. cit.*, for a detailed account of the situation in Maine.

tax in Maine was 6 cents per gallon compared to 3 cents per gallon in Massachusetts. There was a natural tendency for the summer visitors, and especially the weekend vacationers, to fill up their gas tanks in Massachusetts in preference to purchasing gasoline in Maine. As a result there was considerable public feeling in Maine that the out-of-state traffic was not paying its fair share of highway expenses.

Another common recourse for funds for highway construction is to a bond issue by the state. In Maine, however, constitutional provisions made such borrowing impossible during this period.

The solution adopted, as previously noted, was the construction of a toll road. The toll system solved the problem of geographic allocation of the burden, of course, since the users paid the tolls even if they were not residents of Maine. It is difficult to see that any alternative system of financing existed by which the State of Maine could have paid for a modern highway from the border to Portland. There was only one conceivable political solution of the problem of financing a modern highway in southern Maine without the use of tolls, and that was the construction of a national system of such highways by the federal government. Such a program was eventually inaugurated, but the legislation was not passed until 1956. Maine would have had to wait at least a decade for its highway.

A general geographic question concerns the allocation of expenditures between urban and rural areas. Are urban road users being subsidized by rural road users? Statistical study of this question has established that in fact the urban road users as a group are more than paying their own way. A study made using data for 1960 by Bielak and McCarthy estimated for forty-six Standard Metropolitan Statistical Areas the road-user revenues to the government from motor vehicle travel. They also estimated highway expenditures. The ratio of earnings to expenditures was 1.11:1. Overall, drivers in metropolitan areas are more than paying their own way. Whether there is cross-subsidization within metropolitan areas is another question which will be considered in Chapter 15.[19]

The problem in this example was geographic. The second type of possible cross-subsidization that has attracted attention has been among classes of vehicles, especially large trucks as against other vehicles. The most extensive study yet made of the problem was the Highway Cost

19. Stanley F. Bielak and James F. McCarthy, "Highway Income, Expenditures, and Highway-User Earnings in 46 Standard Metropolitan Statistical Areas," *Public Roads,* August 1965, p. 185.

Allocation Study of the Bureau of Public Roads. The *Final Report* of that study in 1961 (which was not really final, see below) came to the conclusion that contributions by large trucks to the Highway Trust Fund would be too small at the rates then obtaining and should be increased. Increases were made by the Congress in that year to the levels mentioned above.

To the economic analyst interested in intermodal competition, it is important to have at least some impression of the importance of taxes in the competition between trucks and other methods of transportation. *The Supplementary Report of the Highway Cost Allocation Study,* which finally appeared in 1965, does contain the final results of the very extensive investigation that was made. The most interesting of the methods of allocation used is the incremental method. Cost of facilities adequate for the lightest vehicles (cars and light trucks) was divided evenly among all vehicles. Successive increments of cost were assigned to successive vehicle groups of increasing size and weight. Each successive group excluded the vehicles of such size and weight as not to require the additional increment of cost. Taxes paid were estimated for each vehicle for comparison with the allocated cost responsibility for support of Federal-aid highways. In general, the two were quite close. An average automobile was allocated a cost responsibility of 31 dollars as against estimated 1964 payment of taxes to the highway trust fund of 30 dollars. A three-axle tractor-semitrailer combination with registered gross weight of 45,000 pounds was allocated a cost responsibility of 462 dollars as against estimated payment of 466 dollars. This vehicle is assumed to be gasoline-powered. Major discrepancies appeared for the larger diesel trucks, which enjoy an advantage in miles per gallon over comparable gasoline-powered vehicles. For a five-axle 66,000 pound diesel-powered semitrailer, the estimates were cost responsibility, 1,369 dollars, and payments, 923 dollars.

Even if new legislation shortly corrects this discrepancy, it is clear that for some time the large diesel trucks have enjoyed favorable tax treatment.

Economic Regulation of Trucking

Interstate motor carriers for hire are under the economic regulation of the Interstate Commerce Commission. The following discussion commences with a brief description of the history and content of that regulation. The basic question of whether continuing economic regulation of the industry is necessary is postponed so that it can be evaluated in the light of an analysis of the economic characteristics of the industry. Economic regulation of trucking by states will not be discussed explicitly, but it presents economic questions similar to regulation of interstate commerce.

REGULATION OF TRUCKING—Regulation of intrastate carriers by the states developed by the 1920s. Regulation of motor carriers by the I.C.C. dates from the *Motor Carrier Act* of 1935, which was incorporated in the *Interstate Commerce Act* of 1940 as Part II of that *Act*. The *Transportation Act* of 1958 amended the earlier legislation. As mentioned above, under the law rates charged by interstate motor carriers for hire are regulated. The language of the sections of the law concerning rates parallel those for railroads. The Commission requires records and accounts to be kept and reports to be made that are necessary for regulation and also form a major source of information about the operations of the interstate trucking industry. The Commission also has power over the issuance of securities by the industry if the amount is more than a certain minimum. Consolidations and mergers require the approval of the Commission. Perhaps the most important provision gives the I.C.C. control over the entry of new firms into the industry, and the expansion of existing firms into new territory. Operators of trucks may be classified into four categories according to their activities:

(1) *Local cartage*. Truckers engaged in local cartage transport commodities within a radius, say, of 20 miles.
(2) *Intercity common carriage*. These carriers offer their services to the general public.
(3) *Intercity contract carriage*. These carriers limit their offers of service to particular shippers.
(4) *Private trucking*. Private truckers are engaged in the carriage of goods that are owned by the same individuals or business enterprises that own the trucks in contrast both to common and to contract carriers, who transport the property of others.

The I.C.C. does not regulate categories (1) and (4). It does regulate those intercity carriers for hire who operate across state lines. Carriers of agricultural commodities across state lines have been specially exempted from regulation by the Congress. This exemption, however, does not extend to products manufactured from agricultural commodities.

The Automobile Manufacturers Association has estimated on the basis of I.C.C. data that the total volume of intercity truck ton-miles, 348 billion, is distributed as follows:[19]

	Per Cent
Holders of I.C.C. operating authorities	33
Common carriers	31
Contract carriers	2
Other intercity carriers	67
Total	100

Motor carriers were brought under the regulation of the Commission in the depths of the depression. The industry was in economic difficulties like most of the rest of the economy. The spirit of the legislation was one of relieving economic distress by restricting competition. This philosophy influenced interpretation of the law, especially the provisions concerning entry.

The legislation required the Commission to grant certificates of public convenience and necessity to existing carriers under a "grand-father clause." The spirit in which the Commission has approached its responsibilities regarding entry under the legislation may be indicated by the following quotation: "Curtailment of entries for the purpose of limiting competition often is warranted as a means of developing a financially responsible and reliable transportation industry."[20] In the administration of this part of the legislation the I.C.C. had to decide what should be covered by the certificate granted to a carrier. To this end it had to interpret phrases like "bonafide operation" and "over the route or routes or within the territory." The proceedings often went to hearings, the burden of proof was placed on the carriers, challenges were filed by the railroads and by the large motor carriers. The issuance of these certificates took over a decade. More than 40,000 protests were filed with the Commission. The Commission put the burden of proof on the applicant. It required operation *continuously* since the grandfather date. As time passed and routes changed, the effect was that some carriers lost routes. There were approximately 90,000 of the "grandfather" applications, and a large majority of them were not settled for six years or more. The Commission also required proof not only that there had been a shipment but, at least in some cases, it required proof of shipment in substantial amounts and with a sufficient degree of regularity.

19. Source: Automobile Manufacturers Association, *Motor Truck Facts*, 1964, p. 38.

20. Quoted by James C. Nelson, *Controls of Entry into Domestic Surface Transportation under the Interstate Commerce Act*, p. 323. The discussion of entry relies extensively on Nelson's paper which is a Staff Paper prepared for the Federal Transportation Study, October 1959 (mimeographed).

In a particular certificate restrictions might be entered with regard both to commodities and to routes. New roads, which might have developed in the interval, were not necessarily included. New application had to be made to the Commission to use new routes.

Another type of restriction has appeared in the regulations called a "gateway" restriction. The Commission might approve the purchase by one carrier of a connecting carrier and the consolidation of the intersecting routes. These routes might be end to end, or they might be approximately at right angles to each other. The Commission might require that service between the old and the newly acquired territories operate through points common to the operating authority of both the new and the acquiring carriers. In other words, the new company would be required to make shipments down two legs of the triangle instead of following the short route.

Another aspect of the regulation of entry has concerned restrictions on return hauls. Here a basic question has been whether the Commission would permit private carriers that had a load in one direction to operate as common or contract carriers and haul a load back. Without regulation, of course, the private carriers would yield to the economic pressure to find a back load if they could. It is wasteful to drive trucks empty if suitable back loads are available. For example, trucks hauling citrus products north from Florida to New York as private carriers might seek a load from New York south. It has been Commission policy to refuse to permit private carriers to engage in this business in order to protect the common carriers. Another type of return haul restriction might arise from commodity restrictions in the certificate of public convenience and necessity. The commodities a carrier might be authorized to move over a certain route might all tend to flow in one direction. Other commodities that flowed over the route might move in the opposite direction, but the carrier might be barred from obtaining a load of those commodities because its certificate did not permit it to engage in that part of the business.

The importance of the agricultural exemption must be understood in this context. Any carrier is free to move the exempt commodities. Hence, a carrier searching for a legal return load will tend to look for a load of grain, fruit, fresh vegetables, or the like. For example, a private carrier that hauls its own goods outbound may fill a truck with grain for the trip back.

A basic difficulty with detailed regulation of entry is its sheer complexity. It was brought out in congressional hearings in 1958 that the following was true:

Many motor carriers have accumulated certificates, as many as 200, piece by piece, some of which cover varying commodities and run into over-lapping territories. In such instances local terminal managers themselves find difficulty in interpreting and complying with certificated authority. Loose compliance results. The Commission and its staff spends a disproportionate amount of time struggling with details of this situation.

The Commission, of course, is aware of this difficulty. It was emphasized, for example, in a speech by Commissioner Kenneth H. Tuggle made in April of 1959 in which he described the situation of one large carrier holding more than 244 grants of operating authority:

These authorities are covered in 30 certificates and are set forth on 124 legal size pages. The grants spelled out in this 124 page volume range, on the broad side, from the right to transport general commodities with no exceptions, thus including the right to transport any and every type of freight, and to provide any and every type of service, to, on the narrow side, the right to handle only "such merchandise as is dealt in by wholesale, retail and chain grocery and food business houses." And on the extremely narrow side, one certificate granted the right to transport only "piano plates."

The Commissioner went on to say:

When this spectrum of commodity grants is viewed in conjunction with duplicating or at least partially overlapping territorial grants, it is obvious that the precise scope of the services authorized is difficult of comprehension, particularly when combinations of separate grants are involved. . . . We receive, in Washington, and in the field, upwards of 30,000 requests each year as to whether or not a particular carrier holds the right to transport a particular shipment. Moreover, many of these queries later come to the Commission in a formal proceeding at the cost of much time and expense to the parties and to the Commission.[21]

These pressures seem to have led the Commission to consider some relaxation of its regulations, and an attempt is being made to make regulation more efficient by the use of electronic machinery. The plan is to provide a means for electronic identification of the motor carriers in relation to the routes they are authorized to serve and the commodities they may carry.[22]

The Commission also has found itself involved in complications that concern the boundary between bona fide private carriage and for-hire

21. Quoted by Nelson, *op. cit.*, p. 145.
22. I.C.C., *Annual Report, 1960,* p. 59.

service. The marginal cases fall in what is called the "gray area" of operation. The types of arrangement include, first, buy-and-sell operations in which the owner of the truck nominally buys the goods at the point of origin and sells them at destination but actually takes title to the property only as a matter of form. Second, the shipper may lease the vehicle and its driver. As before, the purpose may be to evade regulation by creating the appearance of private carriage to conceal the reality of for-hire carriage. The Commission attempts to prevent such evasions.

The Commission does not in any way restrict the volume of business a motor carrier provides if it has the necessary authorization. Its control is over entry, and over rates, but not over output. As previously noted, the volume of shipments by truck has continued to expand since the 1935 legislation.

ECONOMIC CHARACTERISTICS OF THE TRUCKING INDUSTRY—Evaluation of the question of whether this cumbersome apparatus of regulation is necessary requires a discussion of the economic characteristics of the industry that may form the basis of a judgment as to what would happen without regulation. Economic analysts of industrial organization are concerned with what is sometimes called the market structure of an industry, the market conduct of the industry, and its economic performance. They seek to find in market structure predictors of conduct and performance.[23]

The starting point of a discussion of market structure is an estimate of the number of sellers in the market. The exact number of firms in the trucking industry is not known, but it is certainly very large. There are about 3,500 motor carriers of property under the jurisdiction of the I.C.C. of which about 1,100 are Class I. (Firms in Class I have a gross operating revenue of 1 million dollars a year or more.) These carriers can be classified according to the type of load they carry and as to whether they are common or contract carriers. About half of these Class I carriers are common carriers of general freight.[24] The number of motor carriers, thus, is much larger than the number of railroads. The number of *private* motor carriers in the United States is still larger. In 1961 the I.C.C. estimated that there were 55,000 active private motor carriers. These firms are to some degree in competition with the for-hire carriers. Competition for back-hauls has been mentioned already. And a firm with goods to ship may at any time compare its costs between its

23. For a discussion of this general approach see Richard Caves, *American Industry: Structure, Conduct, Performance,* Prentice-Hall, 1964.

24. I.C.C., *Transport Statistics in the United States,* 1962, *Part 7.*

own trucks and for-hire operators' rates. The national market for trucking services is geographically divided, of course. Even on a regional or local basis, however, the number of truck operators is large.

The conditions of entry into an industry are important because of potential changes in the number of sellers. If entry is easy, monopoly profits cannot long continue in an industry because new firms will enter to share in the high profits and output will rise until prices fall. Apart from the barriers to entry imposed by economic regulation, entry into trucking must be rated as easy. The total investment required is not large compared to the investment required to enter, say, the business of transporting people by air between large cities as a common carrier.

The required investment is small since there are only very limited economies of scale in trucking. It is true that there are substantial economies in the operation of large trucks over the road. The economies of fuel consumption have been indicated above. The operation of trucks of large capacity also permits the spreading of the driver's wages over more ton-miles of freight movement.[25]

Economies also exist in operating several trucks, but these economies are more difficult to measure and seem to be limited. There are advantages on the selling side in operating enough trucks to be able to offer to shippers a frequent and dependable service. There also may be economies of scale in the operation of truck terminals for types of service where terminals are needed. Terminals may be required, for example, for the consolidation of small shipments picked up by small trucks in a large city into a load for a large over-the-road hauler. The trend has been toward larger terminals. It is not essential, however, for one trucker to operate a terminal; union terminals also exist.

In sum, the economies of scale in trucking are not such as to give to larger firms a decisive cost advantage over smaller firms. New entrants are not confronted with the choice between beginning operations at a very large scale or suffering a decisive disadvantage in cost. Apart from the legal barriers to entry, the conditions are such as to make entry easy.

An unusual technical characteristic of the trucking industry of economic importance is the rapid wearing out of vehicles. There are considerable differences in the intensity of utilization of vehicles depending on the nature of the vehicle and of the firm (as well as on the geographic location of the business). The large regulated motor carriers

25. It was estimated in 1965 that a new truck tractor-semitrailer combination suitable for hauling perishable agricultural commodities would cost about 30,000 dollars. *Private Motor Carriers of Exempt Agricultural Commodities,* Marketing Research Report No. 696, United States Department of Agriculture, Marketing Economics Division, Economic Research Service, p. 11.

use their equipment intensively and wear it out quickly. For all trucks of all types average mileage is only about 10,000 per year, but for the large Class I common carriers of general freight in intercity service average mileage per vehicle per annum is 68,000 while private carriers studied by the Department of Agriculture averaged 31,000.[26] Useful life of a tractor-semitrailer combination in private carriage may be 4 to 6 years. For all trucks in the country useful lives would be longer. Even so, the scrapping of trucks is about 500,000 to 600,000 per year. New registrations in the United States are on the order of a million a year.

One economic consequence is that technological changes tend to be diffused rather quickly. There are no substantial numbers of obsolete trucks two decades old among the vehicles employed by truckers. A further consequence of the high rate of scrapping is that excess capacity in the industry is not likely to exist for long periods of time. A contraction in the number of trucks can be obtained by the simple expedient of not replacing trucks as they wear out and are scrapped. Excess capacity can exist, but chronic excess capacity in the trucking industry as a whole is not a danger, and especially not for the common carriers.

Market practices in the trucking industry deserve detailed economic analysis but in this brief discussion attention will be focused on rates to the exclusion of such matters as the economic role of truck brokers and freight forwarders. The establishment of rates involves the use of rate bureaus, which are legally sanctioned price fixing organizations. Without regulation, which has led to explicit legislative sanction, the activities of the rate bureaus would be illegal under the antitrust acts.

Regulation of rates of motor carriers is similar to regulation of rates of railroads. Interstate motor carriers for hire must publish their rates and file copies of the schedules with the Interstate Commerce Commission and adhere to rates filed. Changes in rates can be made only on thirty days notice. (For a description of the procedure of the I.C.C., see the discussion of railroad rates p. 223.) Formal interagency agreements are not allowed, e.g., agreements between motor truck operators and railroads. But obviously where competition between modes exists the staffs of the rival rate bureaus must pay close attention to the rates filed with the Commission by the competing mode.

In evaluating the operation of this system a crucial problem is the effectiveness of the bureaus in preventing reductions in price by their members. There is some evidence, which has been cited by Roberts, that "maverick rates" are a cause for concern to the motor carriers rate

26. *Ibid.*, pp. 17–18. Data for Class I carriers from *Transport Statistics in the United States, op. cit.*, p. 38.

bureaus.[27] More evidence on this point would be welcome, but there seem to be indications that the structural characteristics of the industry —many sellers, no major economies of scale—do produce pressure toward price competition, as one would expect they would.

There has been historically price leadership in the transportation of freight. The railroads tend to act as the price leaders. The origin of this practice goes back to the early days of the industry. Even in the 1920s it was the practice of the motor carriers to adopt the railroad classifications and rates already in existence. This practice appears to have been followed through most of the industry in 1935 when the motor carriers came under the I.C.C. The strategy was for the motor carriers to match the rates charged by the railroads for the traffic in which they were interested, which in general was the high rated traffic, and then compete with the railroads by offering better service. The truckers could offer greater speed door-to-door. Trucks have been particularly effective within the range in which they can offer overnight delivery. A second continuing advantage has been that they offer more flexible and more complete service. The possibilities of shipment by truck with only one loading operation at the origin and one unloading operation at the destination have been attractive. Associated with this advantage has been the fact that truckers have been able, for many commodities, to offer much less stringent packing requirements than the railroads were forced to insist upon.

It is hard to imagine a better strategy for invading an industry with an elaborate system of price discrimination than the strategy originally followed by the truckers. To cut rates would have been to invite counter moves. Yet a seller with inferior service can survive only if he offers lower prices. The truckers went after those shipments for which railroad rates would cover better service by truck. Only in the postwar years did the railroads generally attempt a more aggressive pricing policy.

The pattern of price leadership by the railroads has tended to continue. In the postwar rate increases the railroads tended to lead, and the motor carriers tended to follow their lead. They have not always increased to the full extent of the railroad rate increases.[28] The motor carriers have also tended to follow price cuts whenever the railroads have cut prices on those categories of traffic that are competitive. Water carriers have attempted to maintain a price differential below railroads,

27. M. J. Roberts, *Evaluation of Rate Regulation,* Staff paper prepared in 1959 for the Federal Transportation Study (mimeographed).

28. I.C.C., *Annual Report,* 1949, p. 15.

also tending to accept the railroads as price leaders. An example of inter-modal competition is presented in Chapter 19 after the discussion of inland waterways in Chapter 18.

How should the economic performance of the trucking industry be evaluated? One criterion is economic success, which may be approached either by study of the success of the industry in competition with the railroads and other means of transport or by consideration of the returns earned on investments in trucking.

The record of the successes of the trucking industry in competitive struggles with the other types of transport has not been completely com-piled. Considerable information, however, is available. For the position of all trucking in the total transportation market, see Table 12.1, p. 172. Trucks have been especially successful in competing for business on short hauls. The average length of haul for trucks is shorter than for railroads, 267 miles for Class I intercity motor carriers compared to 464 miles for the line-haul railroads.[29] The results of the 1963 Census of Transportation, Commodity Transportation Survey, indicate the share of all shipments made by specified classes of manufacturers which were handled by each means of transport. Only shipments beyond the local area of the plants are considered. The following tabulation shows the distribution of shipments by means of transport for selected types of manufacturing establishment arranged in order of the percentage shipped by truck:[30]

Type of Manufacturing Establishment	Millions of Tons Shipped (1963)	PER CENT SHIPPED BY TRUCK		
		Total by Truck	Motor Carrier	Private Truck
Candy, beverages, and tobacco products	51	79	33	46
Apparel and related products	4	73	62	11
Meat and dairy products	43	72	30	42
Canned and frozen foods and other food products	128	40	23	17
Primary iron and steel products	121	40	36	4

The motor carriers have been most successful in the market for shipping products of establishments in the apparel and related products industry, of which they carried 62 per cent in 1963. They move a substantial part of the output of the establishments in heavy industry, including 36 per

29. I.C.C., *Transport Economics*, December 1964, p. 7. Data are for 1963.
30. Source: Bureau of the Census, *1963 Census of Transportation, Commodity Trans-portation Survey*, Preliminary Reports, 1965.

cent of the tons shipped by establishments engaged in the manufacture of primary iron and steel products. Of the shipments made by that industry those least likely to move by motor carrier are the shipments for the longer distances, especially over 400 miles. Viewed as a whole the evidence certainly indicates that the motor carriers have acquired substantial shares of many of the markets for freight transportation.

The second measure of the performance of the trucking industry proposed above is the return on capital invested in the industry. Data are available for the regulated part of the industry. The net income of 3,314 Class I and II carriers of property in 1962 after federal income taxes was 146 million dollars on capital stock and unappropriated surplus of 1,251 million dollars, which is almost 12 per cent. Not every year has been so successful. In 1958, a recession year, the rate of return similarly estimated was 8 per cent. These financial results indicate reasonable economic success.

DIRECTIONS OF PUBLIC POLICY—It was proposed in Chapter 5 that economic regulation of part of transportation may become appropriate when it is not possible to rely on the normal working of competitive markets to bring about adequate social performances of the industry. This situation may develop, as in the railroad industry, when the technology of the industry is such that the number of sellers in a market must be very small, often only a single enterprise.

It is not possible to develop a strong case for regulation of trucking on any such basis. The economies of scale, as discussed above, are strictly limited. Apart from legal restrictions, entry into the business is easy. To propose economic regulation of trucking to control a natural monopoly does not make sense.

The history of the regulation of the industry indicates that it was not fear of monopoly that led to regulation, but fear of competition. Economists are in general reluctant to discard the forces of competition as instruments of social control, preferring them to the other choices. Yet competition can be a factor in economic distress in an industry. The underlying problem is ordinarily not the competition, but something else. The problem may be one of chronic excess capacity in an industry with competition driving prices below average cost and, for some reason, no response through reduction in capacity. This model hardly fits trucking, which is a growing industry with short-lived capital equipment, as pointed out above.

There may be excess competition in an industry if some sellers deliberately cut prices below cost with the intent to force rivals out of business and then to raise prices to enjoy monopoly profits. This strategy is, of course, illegal under the antitrust laws. It is also unlikely to work in an industry like trucking where entry is easy so that when monopoly profits appear new firms can crowd in.

There is a special argument for regulation of trucking that does not apply to most industries. It is that the trucking companies sell their services in the same markets as the railroads, and the railroad industry is a highly regulated industry. The I.C.C. would be in the awkward position of regulating some but not all of the sellers in a market if interstate trucking were no longer regulated. A related argument is pressed by those who are concerned with the public need to assure the existence and reasonable prosperity of common carrier service by rail. Unregulated trucking, they fear, might undermine the rate structure needed to maintain common carrier service.

Thus, there are, broadly speaking, two directions public policy can take toward the trucking industry. One possible direction of public policy would be to retain and perhaps to tighten regulation of the industry, meanwhile seeking to improve the efficiency of the regulatory process. The alternative policy is to rely more on competitive forces, remove or reduce the legal restrictions on entry, and reduce regulation by the Commission.

The second direction of policy is advocated by economists who are not impressed with the dangers of high, monopoly prices in industries with easy entry. According to their view the excess capacity in the industry in 1934–1935 and the general distress existing at that time were symptoms of the general disintegration of the economy in the Great Depression. That Depression is past and the need for these controls, if it then existed, also is past.

A policy of removing the legal barriers to entry into the trucking industry would be the logical counterpart of a policy of removing legal barriers to the reduction of railroad rates. The combined effect of free entry into trucking and no legal minimum rate regulation would be to leave the division of the market to the forces of competition to a greater degree than at present. Rail competition might force some truckers out of business, but, given free entry into trucking, it is difficult to see how monopoly prices for the movement of commodities could long survive.

Would such a policy have any serious disadvantages? There is the danger just mentioned that the result would be the reduction or even on some routes the elimination of common carrier service. The risk is that small shippers would be disadvantaged by such a reduction. It is in the public interest, therefore, to provide the common carriers with a protected market position in order to reward them for assuming the obligation of a common carrier to serve all comers. Advocates of a policy of reduced regulation argue that the market would supply the needed services without this stimulus.

15

Urban Transportation

Some of the most difficult problems of transportation policy are those concerned with urban transportation, the most conspicuous being problems of passenger movement. From the point of view of the private citizen, highway traffic jams and unsatisfactory public transportation often make getting around in urban areas frustrating or expensive or both. From the point of view of the public official it may be difficult to select an intelligent course of action and even more difficult to carry it through given the assortment of political jurisdictions concerned with urban transportation. From an intellectual point of view there are difficulties in developing the theoretical apparatus needed to handle the problems of urban transportation, in obtaining the necessary information, and in carrying through the application of the analysis to the problems.

This chapter begins with the painful difficulties of the transit industry. The subsequent sections are organized at three levels of discussion. The first concerns the short run and considers proposals for pricing existing transportation facilities. The second level is concerned with investment in transportation facilities. The third level is concerned with the economic functions of urban areas and the relation of transportation to the location of activities within urban areas. Separate sections related to the third level of discussion consider the movement of freight and choice of residential location within urban areas.

The Dilemma of Mass Transportation

The problems of transportation within urban areas may be approached from the starting point of a study of the transit industry, which as defined by the American Transit Association includes motor buses, electric street railways, elevated and subway rail lines, and trolley coaches (but not suburban railroads). Public policy toward the transit industry faces a dilemma. The transit industry, it can be forcefully argued, is in an impossible position, and must be regarded as a "sick" industry. The transit industry, it can also be argued with force, is indispensable. The result is a set of difficult choices for public officials as well as problems for the management of transit companies.

EVIDENCE OF THE DIFFICULTIES OF THE TRANSIT INDUSTRY—The long run trend in the number of passengers carried by the transit industry is down. The large increase in traffic during World War II was followed by a steady decline in the count of passengers carried, as shown in the following tabulation:[1]

Year	Total Passengers (billions)
1935	12.2
1940	13.1
1945	23.3
1950	17.2
1955	11.5
1960	9.4
1963	8.4

This series shows an even stronger downward trend when it is converted into a measure of rides per capita for the urban population. The urban population has been rising while the number of rides has been falling. From 1950 to 1960 the number of rides per capita of urban population fell from 195 to 95.

The operating revenue of the transit industry has been maintained at a level that has held fairly stable in spite of the decline in patronage, but costs have risen, as follows:[2]

1. American Transit Association, *Transit Fact Book*. Published annually.
2. *Ibid*.

Year	Transit Operating Revenue (millions of dollars)	Operating Expenses (millions of dollars)
1935	681	535
1940	737	598
1945	1380	1067
1950	1452	1297
1955	1426	1277
1960	1407	1290
1963	1390	1315

In 1963 after taxes the industry showed a deficit.

Stability of operating revenue in the face of a declining number of rides is possible only if the price per ride increases. Between 1950 and 1960 when the number of rides was nearly cut in half the average price paid per ride must nearly have doubled. To some extent higher prices per ride may reflect longer average rides—there are no data on this point—but it seems probable that most of the increase reflects higher prices. A high price policy may be successful in the short run since many transit users may have little choice. Over a period of several years, however, they may be able to reduce their use of transit, for example, by changing where they reside or by buying cars. Such long run adjustments to a high price are not easy to trace, but there is a risk that they may be important.

Have there been technological changes in the industry that offer the prospect of future reductions in cost and improvements in service? Past changes are not encouraging. The relative importance of the several methods of transportation used by the industry has shifted in favor of the motor bus. The percentage of passenger revenue accounted for by surface railways meanwhile has been declining as the following distributions show:[3]

	PER CENT OF OPERATING REVENUE	
	1950	1962
Surface railway	25	5
Subway and elevated	15	21
Trolley coach	8	5
Motor bus	52	69
Total	100	100

This shift seems to represent an adaptation to the spread of the population into the suburbs fully as much as any improvement in technology. While the performance of the industry has not been subjected to systematic analysis comparable to what has been done with some other

3. *Ibid.*

branches of the transportation industry, it is at least possible to estimate output per employee:[4]

Year	Average Number of Employees	Total Passengers (millions)	Passengers per Employee
1935	209,000	12,226	58,000
1940	203,000	13,098	65,000
1945	242,000	23,254	96,000
1950	240,000	17,246	72,000
1955	198,000	11,529	58,000
1959	159,000	9,557	60,000
1963	147,200	8,400	57,000

With the exception of the period of World War II there has been approximate stability in the number of passengers carried per employees since 1935. Gains from changes in technology appear to have been strictly limited or to have been offset by losses resulting from changes in the demand for transit rides.

The reasons for the decline of the industry in the postwar period are primarily shifts in the demand for transit. As will be discussed in the last section of this chapter, the population of urban areas is becoming less densely concentrated at the center and more diffused over the surrounding area. This trend has been accompanied, of course, by increasing reliance on private automobiles.

It is difficult to provide a thinly spread population with mass transit service. There are important economies of scale in the size of the vehicle in the transit industry just as in all branches of transportation. The larger the bus, the more passengers who can be served by a single driver, and the easier it is to pay his salary. The economic pressure toward larger vehicles is reflected in the trends toward larger carrying capacity in the buses purchased by the industry. In 1950, 40 per cent of the new buses delivered had less than forty seats, but by 1962 only 4 per cent had less than forty seats.[5] The larger the vehicle, however, the more difficult it is to obtain enough passengers to operate service at frequent intervals with a reasonable level of occupancy. The economies of scale have been pressing in one direction and the diffusion of the population in the other, to the distress of the industry, caught between the two.

A basic difficulty in the urban transportation of people has always been the concentration of the demand for transportation at peak hours.

4. See *Ibid.*, for Columns 1 and 2, from which Column 3 has been calculated.
5. *Ibid.*, 1963 edition.

In New York City the peak hour volume at the maximum load point reaches 672,000 passengers. Typically over a rapid transit system one peak hour out of twenty-four accounts for 15 per cent or more of the daily traffic while almost half of the day's total traffic moves in four peak hours. Peak hours require about four times as much equipment as can be used at other times.[6] Hence, average cost per ride tends to be much higher than if demand were evenly distributed over time.

Unfortunately for the industry, the problem of peaks in demand on transit systems has been becoming more acute. The reason for this trend is a shift toward transportation by auto in the off-peak periods when the roads and streets are not congested. That transit handles a larger share of the total volume of traffic during peak periods than during off-peak periods is well documented. In Philadelphia in 1955, for example, transit on a typical weekday accounted for 72 per cent of all peak-hour person trips leaving the central business district but for only 46 per cent in the remaining twenty-three hours.[7] In 1960 of the total volume of trans-Hudson movement in the New York area automobile travel accounted for 73 per cent on Saturdays, Sundays, and holidays but for only 11 per cent during rush hours.[8]

Are there circumstances under which consumers might change their minds and reverse the trend to the private automobile? The answer to this question must emerge from studies of consumer preferences and of the price elasticity of the demand for transit. Studies of consumer choice of mode will be considered below. As previously suggested, the available evidence indicates that the demand for transit is inelastic with respect to changes in price. In New York City in 1948 fares were increased from 5 cents to 10 cents. In the succeeding year the number of passengers declined 13.1 per cent. In 1953 a further increase from 10 cents to 15 cents led to an 11 per cent decline in passengers.[9] It is, of course, uncertain exactly what would have happened to sales if the price had remained unchanged. Some decline would probably have taken place even with no fare increase, so that the decline to be attributed to the change in price should be even smaller than would at first appear. There is no doubt that the demand was inelastic. Fitch reports that the rule

6. Wilbur Smith and Associates, *Future Highways and Urban Growth,* 1961, p. 125.
7. Cited by Wilbur Smith, *op. cit.,* p. 122.
8. *Metropolitan Transportation, 1980,* Comprehensive Planning Office, The Port of New York Authority, 1963, p. 278.
9. Cited by Wilfred Owen, *The Metropolitan Transportation Problem,* Brookings Institution, 1956, p. 92.

of thumb in the transit industry is that an increase in fares of a given percentage will reduce traffic by one-third of that percentage.[10]

There would seem to be little prospect, therefore, of reversing the downward trend in the total revenue of transit companies by reducing fares. Consideration of the income elasticity of demand, which will be discussed below, leads to the equally gloomy conclusion that, as peoples' incomes rise, they are less likely to use transit. It seems reasonable to project a downward spiral of declining total patronage and sharper peaks in demand, with consequences of losses of revenue and higher costs per ride. Such a sequence, unrelieved by advances in technique of production, can lead only to increased fares and hence, to still further declines in patronage. The logical culmination would seem to be the gradual withdrawal of service and its final abandonment.

Nobody actually expects the industry to disappear. Important examples of periods of stability can be cited such as the stability in the number of revenue passengers of the New York City Transit Authority from 1955 to 1961 (1,378 million and 1,363 respectively). Some series even show an increase, such as the number of miles of route operated by bus lines, though not by other types of service:[11]

	TOTAL MILES OF RAILWAY TRACK		Trolley Coach—Miles of Negative Overhead Wire	Motor Bus—Miles of Route Round Trip
	Surface	Subway and El		
1945	16,480	1,222	2,313	90,400
1950	9,590	1,223	3,513	98,000
1955	4,976	1,221	3,428	99,800
1960	1,900	1,243	2,196	108,700
1962	1,312	1,245	1,849	114,300

Wholesale abandonments of line have occurred only for the street railways as they lost ground to the buses. Approximate stability in number of route miles, however, is a doubtful indicator of health in an industry where output is falling. Stability of route miles under these circumstances is rather an indication of decreased density of traffic per mile of line. At best, the picture is one of an industry holding on in an increasingly difficult situation.

THE CASE FOR THE INDISPENSABILITY OF THE TRANSIT INDUSTRY— The case for the indispensability of the transit industry rests, first, upon the difficulties of providing adequate capacity to serve urban areas with transport by auto. Consider, as a starting point, the problem of pro-

10. Lyle C. Fitch and Associates, *Urban Transportation and Public Policy,* Chandler Publishing Company, 1964, p. 122.
11. *Transit Fact Book, ibid.,* 1962.

viding parking spaces to serve as terminal facilities for private automobiles. The basic fact is the number of square feet needed per vehicle. There is room for some variation depending on such matters as the dimensions of the vehicles and the generosity of the allowances for spaces between cars, but the estimates in common use are on the order of 250 to 300 square feet per car. A comparable estimate is that an office worker requires about 100 square feet of floor space. If he drives himself to work, his car will need two and a half to three times as much space as he will. Similarly, suburban shopping centers allow two and a half to three times the area in parking space that they plan for floor area.

Starting from such statistics it is possible to show what would happen if everyone entering the central business district of a large city came by car. The classic estimate was made by J. Bower and P. Costello. Taking an estimate that 3.5 million people enter Manhattan south of 52nd Street on a weekday, they calculated that if all 3.5 million came by auto, parking the cars would require five levels of storage over *all* of the usable space for buildings from 52 Street to the Battery! There would be no room for anything else![12]

The type of calculation involved is straightforward. There are about 27.9 million square feet in a square mile. Allowing for 22 per cent of land area in streets leaves about 21.7 million square feet.[13] At 300 square feet to the car about 72,000 cars could be parked on the surface. Using a figure for work trips of 1.2 people per car (from experience in Chicago) 86,000 workers would be provided for in a square mile devoted to streets plus parking. From that point it is a question of how many levels of parking structure to assume and how much land to set aside for uses other than parking. For example, on a one-story basis, with parking on the surface only, a square mile would provide for about 62,000 office workers and their cars. Three and a half million workers would require about fifty-six square miles.

The second point in the case for the indispensability of the transit industry is the superiority in capacity of transit systems for line-haul movement. A figure commonly cited is 40,000 people per track per hour

12. Owen, *op. cit.*, p. 140.

13. Whether 22 per cent is appropriate is open to debate. It has been reported by Karl Moskowitz, of the California Division of Highways, Sacramento, that the percentage of land in streets and sidewalks in Sacramento as laid out in 1850 was 38 per cent, while parts built in 1900–1930 average 21 per cent, and parts built since World War II, 15 per cent. The overall average in the city limits does equal 22 per cent. (*Dynamics of Urban Transportation,* a symposium sponsored and published by the Automobile Manufacturers Association, 1962).

for the capacity of rail rapid transit systems. Such volumes have been realized in New York City, but actual peak loads elsewhere have been in the range from 10,000 to 30,000. The 40,000 estimate assumes a ninety second headway, forty trains per track per hour each carrying 1,000 people.[14] Whether it is possible to handle that many trains depends, necessarily, on the total capacity of the system for moving the traffic and not simply on the existence of a pair of rails passing a single point. Hence, the capacity feasible per line per hour is not everywhere the same.

For highways the basic estimate of capacity is the number of passenger cars that can pass a point in one hour. Usually estimates are made per lane of highway. This number is a function of speed, the number of lanes in the highway, whether it is day or night, and weather conditions. A usual estimate of capacity under ideal conditions is 2,000 vehicles per lane per hour on multilane roads.[15] The number of *passengers* would be larger since some cars carry people other than the driver. At 1.2 people per car, 2,400 or 2,500 people would be moved per lane per hour. At a hypothetical five persons per car, one lane could carry 10,000 persons per hour. The type of comparison often made is that at, say, 20,000 people per track, one track could handle as many people as eight lanes in a given direction at 2,500 people per lane.

For buses the estimates of capacity per lane are intermediate between those for cars and trains. The maximum attainable has been estimated by the Port of New York Authority to be in excess of 600 buses or 30,000 passengers an hour. Over 20,000 passengers an hour have been observed under ideal conditions.[16] The crucial questions, however, for buses as for trains, have to do with the circumstances under which high volumes can be attained rather than theoretical maxima for individual lanes.

The complexity of the determinants of the exact, practical capacity of transportation systems should not obscure the correctness of the point that where space is scarce in a congested area it is important to economize on the width of the strip of land to be taken for a transportation system. The number of lanes, and, hence, the width of the way, undoubtedly must be greater for private automobiles than for rail transit systems or for lanes reserved for buses.

The third point in the case for the indispensability of transit is of a different character. There are groups in the population for whom

14. Wilbur Smith, *op. cit.,* p. 126.
15. Hewes and Oglesby, *op. cit.*
16. *Metropolitan Transportation, 1980, op. cit.,* p. 299.

transportation by private automobile is not available at all, or who should be encouraged to avoid the use of cars as a matter of social policy. For some, the difficulty is physical. They include handicapped persons and old people who are no longer able to drive, especially not on high speed multilane urban expressways. For example, there are in the United States millions of women over 65 who are not now married, primarily widows. The number of aged people in the population is steadily increasing. Should their needs for urban transportation be ignored?

A second group is those for whom the barrier to automobile ownership is primarily financial. Millions of urban dwellers in the lower income groups own no cars. To suggest that these people should rely on taxicabs is reminiscent of the celebrated suggestion that the French peasants who lacked bread should eat cake.

There are at the other end of the age distribution school children who rely on transit facilities. For them the alternative to transit service frequently is school bus service at public expense.

Finally, there are objections to masses of automobiles on other grounds. The evidence seems conclusive that automobiles produce fumes which pollute the air and, under unfavorable geographic conditions, contribute to the development of smog. Unless and until this difficulty can be removed, there will be an argument in favor of electrically driven means of transportation in congested urban areas.

These are forceful arguments in favor of the continuation of the transit industry. Yet as indicated earlier, transit is a sick industry.

SOLUTION BY SUBSIDY—When a transportation service seems to be indispensable but it cannot be financed out of charges for its services, the question arises, should the service be subsidized? In the field of urban transportation the argument for subsidy from the general revenue is strongest for the provision of service for the groups in the population for whom transportation by automobile is not appropriate. For the most part they are in the lower income groups, and it may be argued that in the interests of equity the community should provide some form of public transportation. Such service may be at infrequent intervals and need not have the peak load characteristics associated with the journey to work. Most of the people involved—the aged, the handicapped, children too young to drive, those in very low income groups—are not in the labor force. The type of service needed is service to make it possible for these groups to reach different parts of a community for shopping, to reach medical facilities, for social purposes, and the like.

Provision of such service is not to be confused with the larger problem of providing transportation to get people to and from work. There is no reason on grounds of equity of distribution to propose a subsidy from general revenues to pay for the journey to work. Indeed, commuters are likely to be among the more prosperous members of the community. They or conceivably their employers may reasonably be expected to pay for their journeys to work.

FEDERAL AID TO URBAN MASS TRANSPORTATION—Recently, after years of leaving cities to their own devices, the federal government has entered the field of providing mass transportation in urban areas. The *Urban Mass Transportation Act* of 1964 provides for expenditure of federal funds by the Housing and Home Finance Administrator. Whether the law marks the beginning of general, permanent subsidy to urban mass transport systems remains to be discovered. The legislation as drawn authorizes grants up to 375 million dollars for fiscal years 1965 through 1967. It emphasizes the need for developing transit facilities as part of programs for unified urban transportation systems that are part of comprehensive plans for the development of the urban areas in question. It also contains provision for research, development, and demonstration projects. The spirit of the legislation thus appears to be one of searching for new and improved urban transportation systems rather than merely meeting deficits for existing systems. The program has been described as roughly parallel to the federal aid to the urban portions of the Interstate System. As it stands the program of federal aid to urban mass transportation appears to be in a formative period: it may be expected to develop more definite character if it is continued and expanded.

TYPES OF POSSIBLE SOLUTIONS TO PROBLEMS OF MASS TRANSPORTATION—As indicated above, there are three levels at which solutions to the problems of passenger transportation in urban areas can be analyzed. These levels differ essentially in the length of time considered. Remedies have been proposed, first, that would take effect in the short run. By the short run is meant a period too brief to allow either for the construction of new facilities for transportation or for the relocation of economic activity that uses transportation. The most common remedies proposed are subsidies and revised pricing policies. Pricing policies also have long run implications. Direct restrictions on the use of private cars are possible, but are not often urged except for very limited areas such as malls reserved for pedestrians. Second, over long periods of time, investment in transportation facilities may take place. Methods of analysis of proposed investments in urban transportation will be discussed below in detail. Past urban transportation studies have tended to take the demand for transportation as given. A third type of approach considers both the transportation facilities and the location of activities within urban areas as freely variable, and considers explicitly the adjustment of the location of private homes, business enterprises, and other institutions to the new transportation facilities. Very long time periods will be required for the full working out of the types of adjustment contemplated. This type of approach differs in emphasis from the second, but elements from the two may be found in a single report.

Pricing of Urban Transportation by Highway

At first glance it may appear that no charges are made for the use of most urban streets and roads. As already discussed, however, all highways are financed primarily by a system of user charges with chief reliance on the tax on gasoline. In effect, filling stations operate as toll booths. In this way highway users pay for roads as the users of mass transit and commuter railroads pay fares.

Prices, or user charges that substitute for prices, perform several related functions. The required investment in highways will be influenced by the amount of traffic to be accommodated. The amount of traffic, at least in some degree, may be influenced by the charges made for the use of the system. Further, prices may play some part in the short run in the rationing of facilities that are in short supply. How useful they may be for this purpose in urban transportation is a matter on which opinions differ. At the same time prices or user charges serve as sources of revenue and, thus, distribute the burden of paying for the facilities.

PRICE AS A MEANS OF FINANCING URBAN HIGHWAY SYSTEMS—The overall system of highway finance relies on user charges as discussed in Chapter 14. The system of charges, however, is largely based on flat rates. Highway users as a whole pay for such outlays as those on the construction of the urban portions of the Interstate System. It is not necessarily true, however, that the burden is fairly distributed among all highway users. The provision of peak load capacity for commuters who work in the central part of major metropolitan areas is particularly expensive. This particular group of people may be subsidized by others, including other highway users in metropolitan areas.

The costs involved in provision of peak load capacity may be substantial. For example, in a study made in 1959 of the needs of the Washington metropolitan area three alternative transportation systems were proposed. Two of the three proposed systems relied more heavily on transit facilities, by express bus or by rail, than the "auto-dominant" system. The comparison between systems involved a difference in capital costs for highways of 570 million dollars if one of the transit systems was selected rather than the "auto-dominant" system.[17] An additional 250,000 trips per twenty-four hour period would be carried by highways under this plan. The capital cost works out on the average to 2,280 dollars per daily trip provided for. Interest charges alone at 6 per cent on 2,280 dollars would be 137 dollars a year or roughly 50 cents a working day. A more complex calculation has been made based on the extreme assumption that the entire cost of the incremental highways should be allocated to the traffic they would carry in the four peak hours on workdays. This calculation comes to a cost of $2.10 per vehicle for a daily peak hour trip of fifteen miles.[18]

Fitch has estimated the cost of handling peak-hour traffic by various modes under more or less typical conditions.[19] His calculation of total cost per fifteen mile round trip is $1.75 per person by private auto assuming 1.5 persons per car, 84 cents by rail transit, and 56 cents by express bus. For the private auto his estimate is that the cost to the user, consisting of operating cost plus user taxes, would be about 50 cents, leaving a required subsidy of $1.25.

Other calculations may make alternative assumptions and come to different numerical results. Yet when costs of peak hour service reach anything like such levels methods should be devised to finance the construction of these expensive highways by charges borne by those who use them. The system of charging users the same rate per vehicle mile on all parts of a system at all times is reasonable when the costs do not vary too much from one situation to another. Urban expressways for peak load service, however, present a situation in which expensive service benefits a special group.

PRICING AS A MEANS OF RATIONING EXISTING HIGHWAYS—When an economic good or service is in short supply and the supply cannot be increased quickly, the usual form of market adjustment is for the

17. See *Transportation Plan*, National Capital Region, Mass Transportation Survey Report, National Capital Planning Commission and National Capital Regional Planning Council, 1959, p. 51.

18. See Fitch, *op. cit.*, pp. 134–135.

19. *Ibid.*, pp. 265–266.

price to rise. The price ordinarily will continue to rise and the use to fall until the demand is equal to the supply. This process of adjustment will not work under all circumstances, and it is not always permitted to work, but it is the normal method in a market economy. One of the basic functions of a price in such an economy is to serve to ration scarce goods and services. To economists, therefore, it is natural to ask, why should not the price mechanism be used to ration the services of urban streets or expressways? These services certainly are in short supply in many locations, especially during the morning and evening rush hours.

As pointed out previously, at the present time there is no special charge made for the use during rush hours of most of the roads in question. The method of rationing in use is indirect. It is to permit the individuals wishing to make use of the scarce facilities to crowd into them as best they can. When the traffic jams become serious, some people take action to avoid them. This system of rationing, it is argued, is inefficient. Under it nobody enjoys a high quality of service, and the total flow of traffic may even be below the physical capacity.

If a price can be put on the delay imposed by one vehicle on all others, this type of calculation can be used to estimate the social cost of adding one more vehicle to a stream of traffic.[20] There may be disagreement as to what price to place on time, as discussed in Chapter 14, but at any reasonable price congestion costs can be substantial. The individual motorist who adds his vehicle to the stream, of course, does not pay the cost of the small increment of congestion he individually creates. He pays only the cost of operating his own vehicle. The social cost of his action in this sense exceeds the private cost to him. The suggestion, therefore, has been made that the pricing system for urban streets and roads should be changed. What is proposed is a system of charges or tolls that can be more closely related to social cost.

There would be technical difficulties in some circumstances in the use of toll booths. It would not be easy, for example, to construct booths at every point of access to an arterial street. Various mechanical devices have been suggested to overcome this difficulty (notably by William Vickrey) but none is widely used. No doubt any device would entail some expense.

It certainly would be technically feasible to move in the proposed direction by taxing parking spaces in the central business district of any metropolitan area. On-street parking is now taxed by the use of park-

20. For such a calculation see Herbert Mohring and Mitchell Harwitz, *Highway Benefits, An Analytical Framework,* Northwestern University Press, 1962.

ing meters in many areas, but commonly at a rate so low that the supply of metered parking spaces is not effectively rationed. Drivers must search for vacant spaces even when the spaces are metered. Such rates could be increased and off-street parking could also be taxed. All day rates could be set, in principle, at whatever level proved necessary to induce people to leave their cars at home and use transit facilities. There is no reason why the parking rates would have to be the same at all times of the day. It is common at present for rates to differ between day and night. The same principle could be applied in favor of, say, shoppers who reach the central business district after ten in the morning and leave before three in the afternoon. The minimum proposal that has been advanced is that facilities that do collect tolls, such as the Lincoln Tunnel, should cease to give special low rates at peak periods by selling at reduced monthly rates to commuters and similar devices.

THE CASE AGAINST REVISED PRICING POLICIES—While technical difficulties in imposing a price system based on marginal social cost of providing transportation service may prevent applicability to all classes of traffic in all times and places and may limit the precision of adjustment that is attainable, technical difficulties are certainly not sufficient to prevent adoption of the principle. A more fundamental difficulty is that the available evidence suggests that choice of mode for the journey to work is not very sensitive to price. Large changes in price are likely to be necessary in order to induce people to leave their automobiles at home or change to transit at an intermediate point. People in large numbers already accept the delay imposed by congestion in order to drive. It does not appear probable that price would prove to be a very effective instrument of social control.

Public acceptance of very large changes in price of existing highways seems doubtful. The idea of rationing the service of highways by use of the price mechanism is not likely to sweep a candidate into public office however well it might fare in a poll of the American Economic Association. Voters cannot be expected to respond with instant enthusiasm to the slogan, "Let price equal marginal social cost!" Public acceptance seems more likely for increased charges to meet the cost of new, improved, and obviously expensive facilities. If such charges can be introduced, the public can be left to make its own choices between new highways and mass transportation facilities. In whatever manner pricing policies are modified, however, problems of investment in urban transportation must be faced. However efficiently they are used, existing transportation facilities in urban areas are inadequate.

Investment in Urban Transportation Facilities

The most important problems of transportation policy in urban areas are problems of investment. An elaborate methodology has been developed for planning investment in urban transportation. This approach has not received the discussion by economists it deserves. It will be described below in some detail through an account of the most elaborate study completed to date: that done in Chicago. The approach, however, has major limitations. It assumes no basic change in pricing policy such as charging highway users at times of peak load the cost of the facilities for peak load use. It assumes a constant level of use of mass transit. And it neglects the effect of the provision of highways on the location of residences and of economic activity.

It is easy to point out that progress requires the development of plans that relax some or all of these assumptions. It is difficult to carry through the development of an actual urban transportation plan that meets such specifications, and, in fact, no such plan has been completed. The approach, which will be followed below after the discussion of the Chicago study, is to consider some of the elements that must be involved in a more generalized approach to urban transportation planning. Thus, the concluding subsection of this division of the chapter concerns studies of choice of mode of travel for the journey to work. The next division considers the determinants of the location of business enterprises in the context of a discussion of the economic functions of cities. The two following divisions consider the movement of freight in urban areas, and the determinants of residential location. Eventually, it may be hoped, the urban planning process may be developed to the stage where the whole complex of relationships will be taken into account in planning investment in transportation.

The Chicago Area Transportation Study was initiated late in 1955 by governmental agencies concerned with transportation in the area. The third and final volume of the report was published nearly seven years later, in 1962. The problem for study was to develop a long range transportation plan for the metropolitan region including both highway and mass transportation facilities. The year 1980 was selected as the target year for whose requirements plans were made.

The simplest approach to transportation planning would be to measure existing volumes on each route and build facilities to match. A second level of sophistication would be to take into account the origins and destinations of trips now made and the hypothetical straight lines between them and attempt to estimate how present trips would be routed if new facilities came into existence that were planned to take the *"desire lines"* into account. The Study went a step further and attempted to forecast for 1980 what the desired volume of travel would be between all possible pairs of areas of origin and destination in greater Chicago. Facilities were then planned to match those volumes of travel. The Study accordingly proceeded in three parts: measurement of what were believed to be the essential facts about the existing situation in 1956, projections to 1980, and development of a transportation plan based on the projections.

THE SITUATION IN 1956—The program of measurement required the definition of a Study Area and the definition of location within the Area. An area of 1,236.5 square miles was defined. A grid was constructed at one-half mile intervals yielding areas of a quarter square mile. The systematic layout of existing streets facilitated this work. In much of the analysis the data for the quarter square mile grid were summarized into 582 zones in the Study Area plus 45 zones in the surrounding region. The size of the zones was graduated according to distance from the center of the city.

Data on travel in 1956 were collected, primarily, in a home interview survey. A total of 58,000 interviews were taken at a sample of dwelling places in the Study Area. The information obtained included the demographic composition of each household, the number of cars owned, and the number of licensed drivers. In addition a report was asked covering every trip by members of the family in the twenty-four hours prior to interview. For each trip data were obtained on origin and destination, land use of origin and destination, trip purpose, mode of travel, and time of departure and arrival. The "trip ends" were summarized to the grid system so that in later analysis each trip was regarded as beginning at the center of one grid and ending at the center of another. Similarly, data on number of origins and destinations were summarized from the grid to the zone. Thus, such statistics as the number of trips originated in each zone could be calculated.

Home interviews within the Study Area were supplemented by interviews taken at roadside stations along a cordon line around the area and by mail questionnaires distributed to passengers on suburban railroads. Only about 5 per cent of trips made in the Study Area were found to have origin or destination outside the Area, a result that suggests the boundary of the Area was located at about the right distance from the Loop in downtown Chicago.

The accuracy of the home interviews was checked by a special survey. A screen line was defined along the line of the Chicago Sanitary and Ship Canal and a sample of drivers crossing the line was interviewed. From this sample an estimate of total traffic across the line was made. The trips reported in the home interview study were expanded to an estimate of all trips and the number crossing the screen line was estimated for purposes of comparison. The estimate based on home interviews was 87.6 per cent of the estimate of trips by automobile drivers based on the screen line check. Trips to work were reported more accurately than trips for social or recreational purposes. These results were used to adjust the findings of the home interview study.

Special surveys were made of commercial vehicles based on samples of the vehicles registered in the Study Area obtained from the State of Illinois.

The counterpart of the massive effort to obtain data on travel was an inventory of land use. The purpose of this inventory was to measure the relationship between land use and trip generation per unit of land area in 1956 and to use the relationships thus measured to build a forecast of trip generation in 1980 based on a forecast of land use in 1980. The types of uses of land identified were as follows:[21]

Land Use Type	Percentage
Residential	32.1
Streets and alleys	25.9
Public open space	20.4
Transportation	9.0
Manufacturing	4.4
Public buildings	4.1
Commercial	3.8
Parking and miscellaneous	0.3
Total in urban use	100.0
Total in urban use	562.8 square miles
Vacant or not in urban use	673.7 square miles
Total Study Area	1236.5 square miles

In the third main effort at data collection, the inventory of existing transportation facilities, the most difficult problem was to define and measure the capacity or carrying ability of the street network. The solution arrived at was to estimate "average maximum capacity" in vehicles per hour for expressways and for arterial streets. For the arterial

21. *Chicago Area Transportation Study, Final Report, Vol. I, Survey Findings,* December 1959, p. 17. (The report includes also *Vol. II, Data Projections,* July 1960, and *Vol. III, Transportation Plan,* April 1962.)

streets the estimates vary by width and by type of area, downtown, intermediate, or rural.

Estimates were made in the Chicago Area Transportation Study of the average maximum number of vehicles that can pass a point on a roadway in one hour. These estimates are as follows for arterial streets:[22]

	ONE-HALF PAVEMENT WIDTH		
Type of Area	10 feet	20 feet	30 feet
Downtown	480	1,080	1,800
Intermediate	600	1,320	2,160
Outlying and rural	660	1,440	2,160

Note: Vehicles are automobiles; trucks reduced to estimated equivalent number of cars.
Assumes no parking; 50 per cent green time on lights at intersections; ten per cent right turns and ten per cent left turns.

Note that doubling the width of the road more than doubles the capacity. The gains from more width are greatest downtown where "side friction" is greatest from such causes as pedestrian movements and vehicles stopping to load and unload people. This volume is "rarely exceeded." It is an approximation to the absolute limit on capacity. "Design capacity" was set at 70 per cent of maximum for arterial streets and 85 per cent for expressways; it was set somewhat higher than the level of use at which increased use leads to reduced average speed, that level being estimated to be 60 per cent of "average maximum capacity" for arterial streets and 80 per cent for expressways. The definition of design capacity thus arbitrarily assumes a certain amount of congestion.

For purposes of analysis, design capacity was expressed as twenty-four hour capacity, the conversion from hourly to daily capacity being made on the basis of the observed fluctuation of demand within a day. (The effect was to assume no change in the shape of the peaks in demand.) Twenty-four hour capacity was then converted to vehicle miles of design capacity by multiplying the design capacity of a street segment by its length. On this basis it was possible to estimate for each section of the grid the vehicle miles of design capacity in existence and compare them with actual vehicle miles of travel. No deficit appeared in the central business district or in the outlying areas but one did appear in the zone three to thirteen miles from the Loop.

No effort was made to prepare sophisticated measures of the capacity of the mass transit system. The inventory made was of the seat-miles of service actually provided. This measure also was converted to a

22. *Ibid.*, Vol. I, p. 78.

square mile basis. For example, it was found that in 1956 more than 12 miles from the Loop the level of mass transportation averaged only 3,000 to 4,000 seat-miles per square mile, which is about the amount of service provided by one bus route with fifteen minute headway.

PROJECTIONS TO 1980—From measurement, the study proceeded to forecasting. The methodology used in forecasting is not easy to summarize briefly. More than one method frequently was used to forecast a given magnitude and the final estimate would then rest upon a reconciliation of the two. The main outlines, however, appear to have been as described below.

Population growth was estimated on the basis, fundamentally, of projections by the United States Bureau of the Census. The national estimate for 1980 was converted into an estimate for the metropolitan area by assuming that Chicago would continue to represent about 3.67 per cent of the total United States as it had done with minor variations from 1930 to 1956. The estimate for the whole metropolitan area was converted into an estimate for the Study Area by extrapolating a trend: that percentage was 87.4 per cent in 1930 and 85.1 per cent for 1980. This method of forecasting by sighting along a historical trend is in common use; it is successful so long as nothing drastic happens to change the situation.

The estimate of population in 1980 had to be converted into an estimate of trips by estimating trips per capita. An elaborate estimate of the economic growth of the area was prepared based on an input-output model that yielded a forecast of employment by industry. Per capita income in 1980 was estimated much more simply by extrapolating the rise in national income per capita. An estimate of a compound rate of 1.8 per cent per year was used. This rate, of course, is no more than an educated guess. The relation between income and automobile ownership was forecast to remain constant.

To forecast the detailed origin and destination of trips required a detailed forecast of land use by zone. Fortunately a land use survey had been taken in 1940. Comparison of the results of that survey with the results of the 1956 survey showed stability in land use except for the development of vacant land.

The forecast of the development of vacant land required estimates of the total requirements for each use. The problem was made manageable in part by the existence of zoning regulations. It was assumed these would be followed. The crucial assumption was made that, in general, intensity of use would follow the present relation to distance from the Loop. In particular the future density of use for residences at a given distance from the Loop was assumed constant. For example, in outer suburban areas a rate of four to five families per acre was used. (These rates are per "net residential acre" after deduction of allowances for land use for streets and other purposes in residential districts.) Similarly, the number of workers per acre of land in manufacturing use was found to decline from 400 near the Loop to 15–20 in the suburbs; the assumption was made that this relationship would govern future developments.

Given detailed estimates of land use in 1980 by zones, an estimate of total travel in that year could be made by applying 1956 trip generation rates. This calculation was made. The trip generation rates per acre were assumed constant by type of land use by distance ring, i.e., by distance from the Loop. The total thus forecast, however, was rejected as too low. For the preferred estimate of *total* future trips a method was used based on the estimates of population, and car ownership. The method was to estimate for each zone in 1980 the number of cars per 100 dwellings and the number of dwellings per acre and to assume a constant relation between these two variables and the number of trips per dwelling unit. (This method ignores any differences in average mileage between first and second cars in multiple car families.) The number of trips per dwelling unit and the number of dwellings in the zone having been forecast, in effect an estimate has been made of the travel of the 1980 inhabitants of each zone.

It remained to convert these estimates into estimates of the number of trips by pairs of origin and destination. This task was approached in two stages. The first was to estimate the number of "trip ends" by zone. For example, about 46 per cent of all person trips begin on residential land and could be distributed with population. The land use forecast was used to distribute other trip ends to manufacturing land, public open space, and other uses.

Given the estimate of total person trips, an estimate of the division of these trips by mode of travel was required. The procedure was to estimate future usage of mass transportation directly, leaving auto travel as a residual. The report itself puts the matter as follows:

It is clear that there must be a dense Central Area and that it is Chicago's policy to promote this. To continue to have such a center, it must be fed by rail transit services. . . . In view of these considerations, the working estimate for central mass transportation journeys has been held constant.[23]

23. *Ibid.*, Vol. II, p. 73.

The projection made, in spite of the tendency to make generous estimates for mass transportation, was for a roughly constant number of trips by mass transportation and an increase of 94 per cent in the number of highway vehicle trips in 1980 over 1956.

A forecast of the number of trip ends by zone by mode of travel is not an estimate of the number of trips on any route until the ends have been matched; the loose ends must be tied together! Which ones match? This problem was attacked by developing a mathematical theory of urban travel in a form that could be tested empirically by fitting equations to the 1956 data. In selecting the destination of a particular trip a traveler is assumed to select the closest possible destination that meets his individual requirements. These requirements are assumed to be specific to the traveler and to be of such a sort that a destination of a given type has a certain probability of satisfying his needs. This coefficient, which represents the probability of success at any destination, depends on the type of trip.[24]

Estimates were made on the basis of 1956 data and used to convert the data on trip ends for 1980 into desired volumes of travel between pairs of zones. The bulk of the increase in vehicle miles of travel is expected to take place in rings six and seven, which are at mean distances of sixteen and twenty-four miles respectively from the Loop.

DEVELOPMENT OF A TRANSPORTATION PLAN—The final main problem of the Study was to develop a plan to meet the needs of the community as represented by the projected volume of traffic. The choice among different possible plans was made on the assumption that the volume of traffic would be independent of the plan adopted. This assumption is of fundamental importance and it may be challenged. Once it is made, however, the choice among competing plans is greatly simplified. A plan can be chosen that minimizes the cost of transportation. The difficult questions remaining are questions having to do with how best to estimate the total cost of transportation. The cost to be minimized was taken as the sum of measurable costs to all travelers and taxpayers. The calculations made, however, did not reopen the question of the split between mass transportation and private automobiles. Plans for the two types of transportation were developed separately, with the major effort devoted to highway planning. Thus, the main effort went into the solution of a restricted but still difficult problem, developing a minimum cost solution for a given detailed forecast of highway travel.

In estimating the cost of providing the services of highways the rate

24. *Ibid.,* Vol. II, pp. 81–86 and p. 111.

of return on the capital investment is a matter of the first importance. A rate was assumed of 10 per cent. This rate was put forward as a compromise between 3 to 6 per cent earned by low risk investments and a 10 to 20 per cent rate of return on projected capital investments required by many private companies. Highways should be built, it was proposed, only if they could repay the investment made in them in 25 years plus 10 per cent interest per year on the invested capital. That is, the least profitable, marginal section of highway would be built only if it could meet this test. As discussed in Chapter 3, not all analysts would agree on the appropriateness of this rate of return, but there would be some to whom it would seem acceptable.

To minimize total costs it is necessary to estimate them. Total costs were defined to include capital costs and travel costs, and travel costs were taken to consist of three elements: the operating cost of motor vehicles, the cost of time, and the cost of accidents. Cost functions were estimated showing average total costs as a function of daily volume of traffic for each of five different major types of street designs. The cost curves thus developed are estimates of the type of the familiar average cost curves of economic theory.

Operating costs are the costs of gasoline and oil, and wear on tires and other parts of the vehicle. These costs have been studied repeatedly and are known with reasonable accuracy. They have a U-shaped relation to average speed falling from 4.8 cents per vehicle mile at five miles per hour to 2.4 cents at thirty miles per hour, and 2.3 cents at forty miles per hour, but rising to 2.8 cents at fifty miles per hour and 3.4 cents at 60 miles per hour. Since average speed is a function of street design and volume of traffic, operating costs will be influenced by the design of highways.

The value of time saved to drivers and passengers has been studied with different results by different investigators (see Chapter 14). Time must be worth something, or cars would not be driven at speeds above the most economical operating range of 30 to 40 m.p.h. (One method of estimating the value of time is to compare operating costs at the most economical speed with those at the observed speed under favorable conditions.) For this study time was valued at $1.33 per hour for an auto, which implied 85 cents per hour per person, given the observed average occupancy in Chicago of 1.56 persons.

Accident rates are known to be a function of highway design. The *CATS* reports relied on a special study in 1958 in the Study Area based on interviews with a sample of vehicle owners that found the total cost of accidents in the Area to be 1.3 cents per vehicle mile, a surprisingly high figure. Estimates were made of direct costs in dollars exclusive of any estimate of human costs in pain and suffering. The main conclusions of the special study were as follows:

Number of Accidents Per 100,000 Vehicle Miles of Travel	STREET TYPES			
	Local Streets	Arterial Streets	Expressways	Total
Fatal	.007	.003	.001	.004
Injury	1.132	.454	.091	.531
Property damage only	9.069	1.968	.418	2.940
Total	10.208	2.425	.510	3.475
Cost of Accidents Per 100,000 Vehicle Miles of Travel				
Fatal	$ 38	$ 17	$ 10	$ 19
Injury	1,319	669	145	729
Property damage only	1,737	386	153	576
Total	$3,094	$1,072	$308	$1,324

The implication of these estimates is that from a social point of view there is a major saving by getting traffic off local streets and onto expressways. The saving is represented by the difference between a cost of 3.1 cents per vehicle mile and a cost of .3 cents. Study of the economic cost of accidents and a review of the methods of such studies are areas of potential value for urban transportation analysis.

Study of the total average cost curves by type of street (including operating, time, and accident costs) led to the conclusion that intermediate facilities are inefficient. Three types of streets were efficient: local streets, arterial streets, and expressways. How should these types of streets be combined into a system? The solution proposed was to use local streets for access to property only, and to lay them out in such a manner that it would be difficult to use them for any other purpose. The result would be a series of local traffic islands, of a size suggested as one-fourth square mile in and near the central business district, and one square mile elsewhere. The optimum size in suburban areas is based on the proposition that each "island" should be large enough for one elementary school to which all children would have access without crossing an arterial street. The calculation is that 5,000 people will need 500 to 600 acres of land allowing for all neighborhood land uses. This reasoning obviously rests on the assumption that suburban densities of population will continue to be of the order of magnitude of ten people to the acre.

In planning the highway system the most difficult problem of the mix of streets was the problem of how much traffic should be handled by expressways and how much by arterial streets. This problem could be handled mathematically. The construction costs of expressways are known and the difference in travel costs between arterial streets and expressways had been estimated. Given the estimates of traffic, a least cost estimate could be made for a regular grid of expressways. That estimate was that the least cost spacing for such a grid is every three miles in rings 2–4, every four miles in ring 5, and every six miles in rings 6 and 7.

These calculations led to a preliminary plan for an expressway system. This plan, of course, had to be developed taking into account existing and committed highways and the geography of the area. The preliminary plan went through an extensive process of refinement. A central part of this process of review was the assignment of the predicted future traffic to a proposed road network. In effect, a computer was used to simulate the working of the proposed system. The input to the computer included a representation of the proposed network of arterial roads and expressways and an estimate of future vehicle trip origins at each zone. The computer then was instructed to compute the travel volume between zones; place the traffic on the network; make allowances for reduced speeds as and where congestion appeared; and make adjustments as necessary in estimated travel time and travel volume between zones. The output of the computer was a total traffic distribution on the future network, which was converted to total cost estimates by the rules outlined above. The lowest total cost in cents per vehicle mile was the recommended plan. It called for a total of 520 miles of expressway within the Study Area including 232 miles not yet committed. In contrast with the radial rail network the new expressways are proposed to take the form of a grid. Total capital cost was estimated at 2 billion dollars to be spend at about 100 million dollars a year for 20 years.

The Chicago Area Transportation Study is the most comprehensive effort at the rational planning of transportation in an urban area that has been completed. Later studies now in progress undoubtedly will remedy some of its weaknesses and improve on the techniques of analysis just as it has built on earlier studies. The next two sections of this chapter, as previously indicated, are concerned with two topics not extensively discussed in the study. Choice of mode for the journey to work is treated below. Of the assumptions made in the study the most fundamental is that the future development of the metropolitan area will be essentially independent of the transportation network which is built. The next section of this chapter after the discussion of mode choice will be concerned with the forces that shape the development of cities, among which transportation facilities will be discussed. Nevertheless, the methods used in the Study comprise an intellectual framework which, though it will be superseded, provides a point of departure for future work.

MODE CHOICE FOR THE JOURNEY TO WORK—The question of how to provide transportation for the journey to work is of basic importance in metropolitan transportation planning. Mode choice must be considered in any forecast of transportation needs. Its relevance to the success of efforts to aid mass transit systems such as that begun in 1964 under the *Urban Mass Transportation Act* hardly needs emphasis.

There have been two methods of attack on the empirical problem of analyzing choice of mode. One method is to develop "diversion curves." A study that may illustrate this approach was carried out by Donald M. Hill and Hans G. von Cube.[25] They brought together data from four surveys in three metropolitan areas. These surveys of the origin and destination of trips were based on home interviews similar to those already mentioned in Chicago. In the analysis the data were grouped by zones, and the unit of analysis was the traffic between a pair of zones. For each line of travel the transit share of work trips was measured. Variations in this share were to be explained.

Five factors were found important: (1) relative travel time by public transit and auto; (2) relative cost; (3) relative level of service; (4) level of income per worker; and (5) trip purpose.

This technique is based on aggregated data rather than on analysis of individuals' choices. From a technical statistical point of view the use of aggregate data is a risky expedient owing to the risk of introducing what is known as aggregation bias.[26]

The method consists essentially in the development of graphs showing the relation between the transit share and the ratio of travel time door-to-door by public transit to time by private auto. Other variables were handled by grouping the data into subgroups that were homogeneous with respect to these variables. For example, one graph would be for a certain economic status and a certain cost ratio. The basic results, thus, are in the form of a large number of graphs.

A second approach is to rely on formal multivariate statistical analy-

25. "Development of a Model for Forecasting Travel Mode Choice in Urban Areas," *Highway Research Record, Number 38, Travel Forecasting,* Highway Research Board Publication 1158, 1963.

26. For a discussion of the problem see Guy Orcutt, *et al, Microanalysis of Socioeconomic Systems: A Simulation Study,* Harpers, 1961.

sis of choices by individual travelers for particular trips. This method of analysis has been used by Stanley L. Warner.[27] Warner found relative times and relative costs to be consistently important, and he also found it useful to distinguish trips by purpose. Warner, however, in contrast to Hill and von Cube, found income of little importance. He also found women less likely to drive to work than men, and, for work trips, the more potential drivers per car owned by a family the less likely a person would be to drive to work.

A study also making use of multivariate analysis of data for individuals' journeys to work has been conducted by the Survey Research Center of the University of Michigan.[28] The statistical results are broadly similar to those reported by Warner. The effect of income on mode choice was found to operate through the effect of income on car ownership. Women again proved less likely to drive to work than men. For people who have a choice of how to get to work the comparative comfort of the alternative modes of travel as they perceive them was also found to be a factor in mode choice. For workers who reported they had a choice between car and common carrier to get to work, a hypothetical question was asked: "Imagine that these two ways to get to work cost the same, and took the same amount of time. Which way would [the worker] go?" Eighty-six per cent chose the car. Comfort, convenience, dislike of waiting, freedom of movement with a car, are all factors in preferences. On the other hand, a series of questions made clear that most people have only vague ideas of the cost of driving to work. Three out of four persons said they had never estimated the cost per day of driving to work. This result, of course, is consistent with the evidence reported earlier in the chapter that the use of transit is relatively inelastic with respect to changes in transit fares.

In spite of the effort that has gone into these and other studies the subject of choice of mode deserves further attention. The most difficult problems are those that have to do with the probable effects of dramatically different methods of mass transportation. There is at present under development in the San Francisco area an entirely new mass transit system for the Bay area, which is expected to cost about one billion dollars by the time it is completed in 1972. Top speeds are to reach seventy miles per hour with schedule speed including station stops

27. *Stochastic Choice of Mode in Urban Travel: A Study in Binary Choice,* Northwestern University Press, 1962.

28. John B. Lansing and Nancy Barth, *Residential Location and Urban Mobility: A Multivariate Analysis,* Institute for Social Research, Ann Arbor, 1964. See also the first report in this series, John B. Lansing and Eva Mueller, *Residential Location and Urban Mobility.*

about fifty miles per hour. Such speeds are much higher than are realized by existing services elsewhere, and forecasts of demand are correspondingly difficult.[29]

Transportation and the Location of Activities within Urban Areas

The Chicago Area Transportation Study, in spite of the elaborate
character of its methodology, was not essentially a study of the functioning of urban areas. It did not consider the possibility of any basic
reconstruction or reorganization of the city.

An urban area provides locations for economic activities and for
private residences. We may attempt to specify the economic functions
the city performs, and to raise the question whether its transportation
system contributes to performing those functions well. We may also
consider the nature of people's preferences with regard to their place of
residence and attempt to understand the implications of those preferences for the organization of residential areas.

The contrast between this long run approach and the earlier discussion may be illustrated by returning to the case for the indispensability of transit presented earlier in this chapter. That case, upon
examination, is not a general case; it is a case convincing for particular
situations. For example, it must be conceded that New York City could
not continue to exist in its present physical form without public transportation. Over a period of time long enough to permit consideration of
the reorganization of the location of economic activity in the New York
area, however, the case for the indispensability of transit is less clear.
One must compare current locational patterns with current transit to
other patterns of location that may involve more or less transit. Similarly, restrictions on space for transportation are more if no reorganization of spatial arrangements in urban areas is considered than if
decentralization is allowed. In the long run the problem of transit must
be considered in the context of the problem of the future of the central
business district and the center of metropolitan areas in general. In the
long run, then, in contrast to the short run, the problem is one of the
advantages of transit, not its indispensability.

ECONOMIC FUNCTIONS OF URBAN AREAS—Of what economic use are
cities? Why is economic activity concentrated in urban areas? There is

29. Improvements in technology unfortunately seem to be more easily achieved in line-
haul travel than in the collection and distribution of passengers, the functions in which
rapid transit systems are least satisfactory.

prima facie a case against locating any given economic enterprise in a central city. Space there is expensive. Improved land, which may cost 20,000 dollars an acre (or less) in suburban areas, costs several hundred thousand dollars an acre or more in the central city.[30] Loft space in 1956, when in Manhattan it cost on the average 98 cents per square foot per year, cost about 78 cents in Bergen, Essex, and Hudson counties in New Jersey. Taxes also are in general higher near the center. Vernon and his associates worked out an index of tax burden at 64 locations in the New York metropolitan area in 1955. His estimate was, if an average of all 64 locations is 100, then an index of 129.6 in Manhattan is appropriate, 160.1 in Jersey City, but only 92.5 in New Jersey areas outside of Newark and Jersey City. Finally, transportation costs are in general higher in the central city.

What are the advantages of a central location to offset all these disadvantages? Advantages of geographic concentration of economic activity were discussed in general in Chapter 2. Benjamin Chintiz provided an answer to the question in one specific urban situation in analyzing the reasons for the rise of the Port of New York in the nineteenth century.[31] The question he sought to answer is why New York, which was one of several ports of roughly equal importance in 1800, rose to a position of dominance over its rivals.

Internal improvements that took advantage of the Hudson-Mohawk Valley were one contributing factor. New York owed much to the Erie Canal and, later, the New York Central.

A second factor was the developing need of merchants for regular transatlantic service. Early ships sailed at the convenience of owners and captains, commonly when they were loaded. The first liner, the James Monroe, of the Black Ball Line, inaugurated scheduled service January 5, 1818. Thereafter there was scheduled service from New York. Other ports also came to offer liner service, but New York retained an advantage in frequency of sailings to a variety of destinations overseas.

New York provided a central point for domestic distribution of imported commodities. Buyers of textiles, for example, would come to New York and buy from an agent located there. It was convenient to assemble the merchants and their goods in a single port.

New York became a center for specialized middlemen in the export trade. Foreign trade merchants purchased goods on their own account

30. Raymond Vernon, *The Changing Economic Functions of the Central City,* Area Development Committee of CED, 1959.

31. Benjamin Chinitz, *Freight and the Metropolis,* Harvard University Press, 1960.

for sale abroad. They bought from many producers and developed special knowledge of which American products could be sold advantageously in foreign ports. It was convenient for a merchant engaged in this business to locate his enterprise in New York.

A variety of other specialists concerned with foreign trade developed in New York. Banks in the area did a large business in financing many merchants. They were able to spread their risk over many enterprises. They developed expert knowledge of foreign trade and the associated financial transactions. Insurance companies were able to spread the risks of marine insurance in an analogous manner. Specialists also developed in such minor arts as clearing goods through customs and packaging goods for shipment overseas.

All of these advantages (apart from the geographic circumstances of the break in the chain of the Appalachian Mountains) arise from the division of labor. As economists have understood since Adam Smith, the division of labor is limited by the extent of the market. The growing volume of trade through the Port of New York represented a broadening of the market for a variety of economic activities. Economic gains from an increasingly refined division of labor became possible. From the point of view of any one firm these gains took the form of external economies, that is, economies arising from locating in the proximity of other business enterprises.

The principles involved apply to other forms of economic activity as well as to foreign trade. An analysis of the role of the central city in one metropolitan area has been provided by Raymond Vernon.[32] Vernon suggests three reasons for the congregating of firms at the center of metropolitan areas, that is, three types of external economies arising from location in the central area.

There is, first, the need for fast communication and transportation. This requirement is important for the specialized printer of legal briefs, financial prospectuses, advertising brochures and the like. These products are ordinarily wanted quickly, and a firm with a short total production cycle has a competitive advantage. Metal working and machine shops producing custom-made parts are in a similar situation. Time may be important not only in dealing with customers but in obtaining materials that could be as specialized as the final product.

The need for personal communication is illustrated by the organization of the garment district. Apparel buyers must see the product before purchase, and they must see a great deal in a brief time. As a result

32. Raymond Vernon, *op. cit.*

90 per cent of the showrooms in the garment district are located in only four city blocks.

Personal communication must also take place between executives of large business enterprises and those with whom they transact business. The subtleties of communication must be face-to-face. There is a tendency for the headquarters of large corporations to be located in New York even though their physical plant is elsewhere.

A second reason for locating a business in a large city applies primarily to small firms. It is the need to control the costs of uncertainty. If a firm sells in markets with constantly changing products or highly variable rate of output, or both, it must seek to avoid high fixed costs. Economies of scale and vertical integration lead to fixed costs. A more appropriate strategy is to rely to the fullest extent possible on subcontractors and outside sources of supply. A small advertising agency which "lands" a large account will purchase the art work required for a series of magazine advertisements from a firm specializing in art work. To start work it is not necessary to build an art staff, and if the account is lost, there are no commercial artists expecting regular salaries. The subcontractor can survive in this situation because he relies on diversity of demand and the existence of many potential buyers for his services. The principle is essentially the same as the principle of fire insurance: the risk is spread.

Firms that purchase services from outside suppliers are themselves often relatively small. It is important that the supplier of services itself become large enough to perform its services at minimum cost. An example of a supplier of services to small firms is a freight forwarder. A freight forwarder is in the business of consolidating small lots of freight for shipment. He takes advantage, for example, of the spread between rail rates for less than carload lots and for carload lots. He may specialize in other directions; for example, he may become an air freight forwarder. It is an advantage to firms with small volumes of goods to ship to one or more destinations to locate in areas where the services of freight forwarders are readily available.

It follows that the basic economic function of transportation within urban areas is to permit business enterprises to enjoy the advantages of external economies. What is required is speed, reliability, and economy in the movement both of people and of goods. The better the internal transportation system, the better the city can do its job as a location for economic activity.

It also follows that improvements in transportation lead to the spreading out of cities. With each improvement in transportation it becomes less necessary for firms to pay the social and private costs of close physical proximity in order to have fast access to the markets in which they buy and sell.

Facilities for the Movement of Freight in Urban Areas

Although public attention is often focussed on the problems of the movement of people in urban areas, the movement of freight is of basic importance. The facilities overlap, in the obvious sense that both private autos and trucks use the streets and highways, and both people and goods are occasionally moved on suburban railroads. There are, however, extensive transportation facilities in metropolitan areas designed primarily for the movement of goods. These facilities deserve a brief description.

The rail complex in a typical large city consists, first, of main line trackage that radiates outward from the central area. Links among the main lines may be provided by one or more belt lines, which take the form of circles around the city, geography permitting. There are in addition railroad yards for the sorting of cars and the assembly and disassembly of trains. Terminals, spurs, and sidings providing direct access to shipper's plants, to warehouses, or to docks are used for the receipt and distribution of freight.

The whole network provides intricate problems of movement, interchange, and storage of equipment. Consider, as a simple example, the possibilities of delay and interruption of the flow of traffic where a main line crosses a belt line. Another source of difficulty of movement is that urban rail systems were not planned as unified wholes. They were laid out by competing systems; efficiency of interchange of freight was not the first consideration.

The initial effect of the introduction of rail service was to make the movement of goods over land much faster and more efficient than when it was necessary to rely on vehicles drawn by animals. Cities, therefore, tended to spread out.

Facilities requiring space, such as freight classification yards, were located on the edges of urban areas. It is always easier to build new facilities in areas not already congested. The typical rail-dominated pattern of development was star shaped, with cities growing out along the lines radiating from the central business district.

Trucks represented an additional improvement in the efficiency of the movement of freight over land. A further spreading out has been taking place. Trucks may proceed directly from one loading dock to another. There is an obvious efficiency in direct movement from factory or warehouse to final destination.

Intercity common carriers by truck tend to operate differently, at least in the New York area, which has been studied carefully.[33] The equipment used over the road tends to become specialized. The weight of the average shipment by truck to and from the Manhattan central business district is only 739 pounds, in contrast to 1,157 pounds for the rest of the metropolitan area.[34]

It is efficient to provide pickup and delivery service in Manhattan with a straight truck, a smaller vehicle than the trailer or semitrailer ordinarily used for line-haul. In addition to the difference in vehicles, drivers of line-haul trucks work on a different basis from local drivers. The latter may load their own truck, for example. The terminal then is the place where freight is transferred from truck to truck. In addition to the break bulk function a terminal will contain the offices of the trucking company and facilities for storage and maintenance of equipment. Terminals for intercity carriers tend to be located conveniently to main highways.

Local cartage firms within metropolitan areas have a diversity of equipment and facilities. In some instances a group of local cartage firms maintain a union truck terminal at which freight is interchanged between them and firms specializing in over the road hauling.

Truck terminals tend to be relatively small and numerous. In 1960, 299 Class I and II intercity motor common carriers maintained 373 terminals in the New York area. About half of them had more than 10 truck bays in 1960. The average size of terminals has been rising, however, since World War II, with the maximum over 100 truck bays by 1960.[35]

Terminals for air freight are a specialized type of local facility equipped to provide local pickup and delivery service. The shipments are relatively small, and there are special problems of speed of handling to prevent loss on the ground of the advantage of speed in the air.

Piggyback service and containerized service requires special yards for the interchange of trailers between railroad flatcars and tractor units. Trailers may move from these yards either to the consignee or to a truck terminal operated by a freight forwarder. The effect of the introduction of such service has been to shift outward the location of the railroads' terminal facilities. The new facilities tend to be located in outlying

33. See *Metropolitan Transportation 1980, op. cit.,* Chapter 14.
34. *Ibid.,* p. 217.
35. *Ibid.,* p. 212.

areas, and to rely on urban freeways and belt highways for distribution of vans to customers. The terminal space and trackage required is less than for conventional freight terminals. As a result, the tendency is to make possible the release by the railroads of land in the central part of the city for other uses.[36] A parallel development that tends to have similar consequences is the construction of special facilities for bulk handling of commodities such as cement. The use of integral trains running direct from coal fields to large urban consumers such as public utilities also leads to bulk unloading facilities outside congested areas.[37]

Marine terminals present yet another set of specialized facilities with problems of their own. Traditional practice in the Port of New York is for general cargo in foreign trade to move primarily through a limited number of lighterage stations maintained by the railroads. There were eleven such stations in 1960. Outbound freight was floated from these stations by lighter or carfloat to the appropriate berth. There are also some direct rail connections to docks. In recent decades much freight has been moved by truck between the railroads' lighter stations and the docks. Some freight also moves entirely by truck from shipper to dock. The increasing volume of truck service to docks amounted to about three-quarters of all freight delivered at the steamship terminals in 1959.[38] A consequence has been difficulties in handling truck movements at steamship terminals that were not originally planned with trucks in mind.

There are three types of proposals for the improvement of the local distribution of freight. The first category, just as for movement of people, involves efforts at more efficient use of existing facilities. Regulations about the use of streets fall under this head. A second category is the provision of terminal facilities either at public expense or by the use of public authority. Proposals have been made, for example, for the construction of truck terminal facilities in the garment district of New York for the purpose of relieving the acute congestion of the streets in that area.

A third and more fundamental type of remedy proposes the selective encouragement of shifts of various types of activity out of congested areas. The development of local distribution by truck has brought about a situation in which the most efficient location for economic activities oriented toward broad distribution throughout a metropolitan area is no

36. See Arthur E. Baylis (Vice-President, Marketing, New York Central System), "Changing Technology and Land Requirements in Urban Rail Freight Distribution," in *Dynamics of Urban Transportation,* a symposium sponsored and published by the Automobile Manufacturers Association, 1962.

37. *Ibid.*

38. *Metropolitan Transportation, 1980, op. cit.,* p. 160.

longer in the center of the city but just outside the area of maximum congestion. A bakery is an example of an enterprise which must be located primarily with local distribution in mind. Chinitz in 1960 cited as an example of such a shift the fact that not a single warehouse has been built in Manhattan south of 59th Street since World War II. In 1918 the five boroughs accounted for 90 per cent of the New York area's public warehouse space; in 1956, for only 56 per cent of warehouse employment.[39] Wholesale markets for fresh fruits and vegetables, similarly, are candidates for relocation. Their historic reason for location in the center of the city at the hub of the distribution system is no longer valid now that the truck has given flexibility to the local transportation of goods. In the long run there is no longer any need to pay the double cost of a central location in high rent and congestion for any activity primarily oriented toward distribution throughout a metropolitan area. Not every economic activity, however, is a candidate for relocation. Each represents a problem in analysis of locational advantages.

Residential Location within Urban Areas

The second set of location decisions concern peoples' residences. The percentage of the population of the United States living in urban areas has been increasing steadily since the first census in 1790. By 1950, 64.0 per cent of the population lived in urban places; by 1960, 69.9 per cent.[40] In absolute numbers the population of urban areas rose 28 million in that decade, while the rural population remained almost unchanged.

At the same time the density of population of the great urban centers has been decreasing for a century. In the New York region the density of population of the urbanized area was 65,000 per square mile in 1860 and under 40,000 in 1900. Between 1900 and 1940 the average density of population was roughly halved again. Thereafter, the rate of diffusion increased. Whereas between 1900 and 1940 each additional million of population had been accompanied by the urbanization of 70 square miles, between 1940 and 1954 each million was accompanied by the urbanization of 185 square miles.

Consider also the distribution of population within metropolitan areas. In 1960 half of the population of metropolitan areas was outside the central cities. The growth rate of the population in these outer areas

39. Chinitz, *op. cit.*, p. 156.
40. United States Government, *1960 Census of Population*, Vol. 1, Part A.

was 49 per cent from 1950 to 1960. The total population of central cities also increased somewhat over the decade, but the average population per square mile of land area in the central cities *fell* from 7786 to 5349. This contradiction was possible because of an increase in the area of the central cities through annexations during the period. At the same time there has been an absolute decline in population in the center of large cities. For example, four out of five of the central counties in New York lost population from 1950 to 1960.

A critical question is whether this dispersion of population into the suburbs is likely to continue, or whether people may move back into the city. A survey conducted by the Survey Research Center of the University of Michigan in 1963 indicates that people continue to prefer suburban living. The following findings of this survey, which was taken in a sample of all metropolitan areas exclusive of New York, are particularly relevant:

(1) Asked, "If you could do as you please, would you live in a single family house, or an apartment house, or what?", 84 per cent preferred a single family house. Only 67 per cent live in single family houses.
(2) People were asked, "If you could do as you please, would you like to live closer to the center of (this city) or farther from the center or just where you are?" Of the whole sample, 21 per cent said farther out, and only 7, closer in. Even of those now 15 miles or more from the center of the city, 20 per cent said farther out and only 10 per cent said, closer in.
(3) People were asked, "Suppose you had to choose between a house in the suburbs on a paved street with sidewalks and lawns, or a house in the country with woods, or a field between you and the next house—which would you choose?" The extremely rural setting was chosen over the suburban location by 45 per cent of the population.

Actual choices are constrained, and not all the people are likely to move to the country who would like to do so. People's preferences, however, are in the direction of increased dispersion of cities.[41]

Concluding Comments

The usual emphasis, in discussions of urban expansion, has been on what has been happening in the outer fringes of urban influence. Jean Gottman extended the area of scrutiny even farther out.[42] Gottman defined an area which he called "megalopolis" along the Atlantic seaboard

41. Lansing and Mueller, *op. cit.*
42. Jean Gottman, *Megalopolis, The Urbanized Northeastern Seaboard of the United States,* Twentieth Century Fund, 1961.

from Portland, Maine, to Washington, D.C. He has assembled information to show that there has been an increasing diffusion of economic activity throughout this area. The distinction between rural and urban has become blurred. Sections that look rural function as suburbs. The suburbs of one city melt into those of another, especially along the main lines of transportation. What is developing, he says, is a complex pattern of relations among a series of centers and subcenters. Agriculture survives, but only specialized, intensive agriculture with high value of output per acre. Factories are built in the suburbs. Those enterprises that require extensive areas for large scale operations tend to locate there. Activities requiring close connection with other enterprises, the activities for which external economies are important, remain closer to the central business districts. Plants producing for a broad market, perhaps a regional or even a national market, are more likely to locate in the suburbs than those oriented toward a local market.

The fundamental cause of this long process of diffusion, as has been stressed repeatedly, is the development of improved transportation. The history of the expansion of cities is the history of their means of local transportation. The dates have been assembled for Chicago.[43] To 1859, people moved on foot at a rate of three miles per hour, or by horse and buggy. 1859–1892 was the period of the horse cars for mass transportation, which were drawn at about six miles per hour. From 1892 electric street cars were introduced and during the 1890s elevated rapid transit. Recently, of course, there has been the gradual introduction of motor vehicles.

There is a tendency to think of the automobile and the truck as old inventions that have been with us for many decades since, say, the period of World War I when the Model T became popular. While the vehicle was well developed by that period, it has been substantially improved, the most important changes being in speed and reliability. The way and terminal facilities to match the improved vehicles are still in process of construction. In urban areas progress in these respects has been slower than in rural areas because of the peculiarities of the system by which highways are financed. The urban transportation *system* based on the motor vehicle, therefore, is new.

The full impact of that system on urban areas will be felt only very gradually. The reason, fundamentally, is the tremendous investment already made in urban buildings and facilities. The sunk costs are very large. And the life of buildings is long. Fifty years is not unusual. Other facilities last even longer. For example, in October 1960 of 173 general

43. *CATS, op. cit.,* Vol. 11, Chapter III.

cargo berths for ocean going vessels actually in use in New York, 44 had been constructed prior to 1909. Finally, some facilities such as docks must be located within a limited area for geographic reasons. These considerations combined with considerations having to do with external economies of central locations virtually guarantee that the process of adjustment to the new method of transportation will not be fully completed for decades to come.

16

Air Transport

AIR TRANSPORT is the newest of the major modes of transportation, but in the decades since World War II air transport has grown rapidly. As the industry matures, the central problems of public policy have been changing. Historically the emphasis has been on the broad objective of the development of aviation. Among the issues related to this goal are the following: Is there reason for public assistance to aviation? If so, in what form should subsidies be given to the industry to be most effective? To what specific ends should these subsidies be directed? What indirect means can public agencies use to stimulate the growth of the industry?

Although as the industry matures there continues to be public concern with its further development, other objectives of economic policy become increasingly important. Problems arise similar to those in the regulation of other transportation industries. Such questions as the following tend to receive increased emphasis: Is the level of profits reasonable? Are the costs of the carriers excessive or not? Is the structure of prices for different types of service optimal? Is the competition between air and other modes of transportation on a reasonable basis or is it in some sense unfair, or likely to lead to inefficient use of resources? How much competition is desirable within the industry? To what extent is it possible to rely on indirect methods of social control through competition to prevent the development of excessive monopoly power? The central problem of public policy in the 1960s, therefore, might be regarded as one of successful negotiation of a shift in emphasis to match the changing situation in the industry.

It is convenient for purposes of economic analysis to separate the discussion of air freight from the discussion of the movement of passengers, and to separate the domestic from the international movement of passengers. Viewed from the demand side of the market there is obvious reason for the separation of these markets. Domestic movement of freight is no substitute to the buyer for international movement of people! Furthermore, in the regulation of international air transport the pursuit of the objectives of national policy must take into account the policy of other nations. Most of the following account of the industry is concerned with the domestic movement of passengers but brief sections are included on air freight and on international air transportation.

The objectives of public policy toward the domestic air transport industry are partly noneconomic. From a military point of view a well-developed domestic air transport industry has advantages. It provides a pool of qualified personnel and of aircraft and equipment, which may be used in the event of a war. The airways and air terminals have uses of a military character. The same manufacturing facilities can be used for civilian as for military aircraft, and the technology of the two is closely related. While military considerations tend to support a policy of government assistance to the domestic air transport industry they have not been of overriding importance in the development of the American air transport network, as they have been, for example, in connection with American maritime policy.

Air transport also makes a contribution to the political unity of the United States. The speed of air service makes possible closer political ties with the outlying sections of the country than otherwise would be possible. It is interesting to speculate, for example, on whether Alaska and Hawaii would have attained statehood at the time they did if there had been no air transport to those parts of the country.

The approach taken in this chapter is to consider first the structure of the domestic air transport industry, including under that heading the number of sellers in the industry, and the conditions of entry. A closely related topic is the demand for air transport. The nature of costs in the industry is then discussed. With this background the public agencies concerned with the industry and their mandates are considered. There follows a discussion of regulatory policy of the Civil Aeronautics Board (C.A.B.) and its consequences. The special sections devoted to American policy toward international air transportation and to air freight are at the end of the chapter.

Structure of the Domestic Air Transport Industry

The basic organization of the industry consists of the following: provision of the airways and a variety of services such as research and analysis of accidents by the federal government; provision of airport facilities by cooperative arrangements involving different units of governments and the airlines; and provision of airline service itself by private enterprises regulated by the federal government. The public agencies will be considered in more detail below.

Consideration of the nature of the air carrier industry requires consideration of the number and relative size of the carriers both in the total national market and in local markets. Possibilities of competition from supplemental carriers and private aircraft and from entry of new sellers must be considered in addition to competition among the scheduled airlines. The nature and extent of the differentiation of service offered by the different sellers, a topic frequently considered part of market structure, will be treated below in the context of the discussion of the demand for air transport.[1] Understanding of the competitive position of the carriers will be found below to be important in understanding the policy of the regulatory agency and its consequences.

NUMBER OF REGULAR CERTIFICATED CARRIERS PER CITY AND PER PAIR—Analysis of the extent of competition in the industry must take into account the geographic distribution of the market. The most useful measure is the number of carriers by city pair. If city pairs are ranked by number of passenger miles flown and the fifty leading pairs of cities selected, the distribution of the number of sellers in those fifty markets is as follows:[2]

1. For a discussion of market structure and related concepts see J. S. Bain, *Industrial Organization,* Wiley, 1959.

2. Computed from Civil Aeronautics Board, *Competition Among Domestic Air Carriers from January 1, 1961 through December 31, 1961,* Vol. II, Part 5, see Table 3.

Number of Carriers	Number of City Pairs
12	1
11	0
10	2
9	6
8	4
7	4
6	10
5	10
4	9
3	4
2	0
1	0
Total	50

Thus, in the largest markets there are three or more carriers, but more than nine carriers appear only in three markets, with five or six carriers the typical number. Of course, the number of carriers is smaller on the lightly traveled routes. The least frequently traveled routes are served by single carriers. The important markets, however, are oligopolistic.

SUPPLEMENTAL AIR CARRIERS—There is limited competition on the fringes of the industry provided by the supplemental air carriers. These carriers, however, are restricted in important respects by the C.A.B. They may provide charter service, and they may schedule up to ten round trips a month but no more between any pair of points. These carriers have found their largest market in charter flights for the armed forces. Their total revenue is on the order of magnitude of 2 per cent of the total revenue of the scheduled airlines.

GENERAL AVIATION—An additional source of potential competition for the scheduled airlines (apart from ground transportation) is from aircraft not in the hands of air carriers. General aviation, in the terminology of the industry, includes all such civil aviation. Competition is possible from aircraft owned by business enterprises for their own use and from air-taxi operators, if not from crop dusters, patrol and survey flyers, instructors in flying, or private citizens who fly their own planes. There are large numbers of civil aircraft in the country, 137,000 as of 1965, including 42,000 business planes. (Only about 2,000 aircraft of the 137,000 are owned by the air carriers.) There are about 3,000 air taxi operators.[3]

To some extent these planes offer a service which complements that of the trunklines. It is possible to arrive at a major airport by scheduled

3. Air Transport Association, *American Aviation*, May 1965.

service and continue by air taxi to final destination. To what extent do such aircraft compete with the common carriers? There is not enough information available to provide an adequate answer. Some of the main outlines of the situation are reasonably clear as far as business planes are concerned. Company owned planes enjoy a special advantage in service to areas that are not served at all or are served only infrequently by commercial airlines. A majority of flights may be of this type.[4] Even where there is occasional commercial service—say, two flights a day offered by a local service carrier—the savings in executive time from use of company aircraft may be substantial. Flights can be scheduled at the convenience of the company officials involved. This advantage of the business aircraft is smaller on routes where there are many scheduled flights. As will be discussed below, there are economies of scale in the use of large aircraft. The scheduled airlines, therefore, which can use larger planes, tend to enjoy a cost advantage over private aircraft. This advantage should be less important on routes where a particular company has a large volume of traffic, sufficient to provide reasonable load factors for large modern aircraft. The future of the use of business-owned aircraft for the transport of company personnel is likely to be strongly influenced by the success of the manufacturers in producing small planes which can offer a high quality of service at costs not too much above those of the larger aircraft ordinarily used in scheduled service. There appears to be at least the possibility of effective competition with the common carriers from private aircraft, especially on the thinly traveled routes.

ENTRY—Only with the permission of the Civil Aeronautics Board is it possible for a new firm to enter into the business of providing common carrier service by air in interstate commerce. The Board and its policies will be discussed below, but on the question of entry into the trunk carrier market its policy has been simplicity itself. There have been no new trunk carriers since the Board was set up in 1938. (The debated question, to which we shall return, has been how many carriers to allow on any route.) The Board has permitted entry, however, into the ranks of the local service carriers, and it also has permitted and encouraged new firms to develop as "specialist carriers." These firms specialize in the provision of helicopter service, all cargo service, or all expense air tours rather than competing directly in the principal mar-

4. Claw estimated in 1956 that 70 per cent of all business flights started or ended at points not accessible by commercial airlines. Spencer Claw, "12,000 Company Airplanes," *Fortune*, January 1956.

kets for scheduled passenger service. Reference has been made already to the major restrictions imposed by the Board on the "non-skeds," as the supplemental air carriers are commonly called. There are no important legal barriers to the entry of a business enterprise into the private carriage of its own personnel in its own aircraft. There is also a limited amount of service provided by common carriers operating wholly within a single state. Entry into this type of activity is not under federal economic regulation. In brief, the picture is one of legal entry into fringe activities but tight legal control over entry into the ranks of the common carriers.

What would be the conditions of entry in the absence of economic regulations? The situation has been changing with the development of aircraft of increasing size and efficiency. It was estimated by Caves in 1962 that a new trunk carrier would need five or six long range jet aircraft to operate efficiently and compete successfully.[5] The total investment required he estimated at 46 to 47 million dollars including ground installations. If anything, he believed more than this number of aircraft would be needed rather than less, implying an initial investment of over 50 million dollars. Whatever the situation may have been in the early years, an investment of this order of magnitude is large enough to curtail the number of potential entrants, entirely apart from any legal obstacles. Studies of the historical costs of trunk carriers of different sizes also have shown that the smallest trunks are likely to have higher average costs than those selling over 2–4 per cent of the industry output of revenue passenger miles.

Entry into the parts of the industry other than trunk line operation would be less difficult in the absence of regulation. The aircraft used are smaller and less expensive. Used aircraft can be purchased. Possibilities seem to exist for avoiding large initial capital outlays by leasing equipment and by arranging for maintenance work on the planes to be done by those specializing in such work, thereby avoiding a small, inefficient maintenance operation. It should be possible to limit the investment by entering the market for a few city pairs only. Whether any new entrants into local service operations would be at a disadvantage compared to existing firms, however, is not a question of pressing importance. The local service carriers as a group have been unable to operate without direct public subsidy since the beginning of the industry. Since the local monopolies that they enjoy are mostly unprofitable, there is

5. Richard E. Caves, *Air Transport and Its Regulators,* Harvard University Press, 1962 (see Chapter 4).

little economic reason for potential rivals to scrutinize the barriers to entry into the common carrier business. As previously noted, there are large numbers of air-taxi operators.

The entry of existing common carriers into new markets is a different matter. The C.A.B. has been interested in the question of which carriers should be permitted to serve which specific routes; indeed, route authorizations have been one of its central concerns. Its policy has been much more flexible than with regard to entry of new firms into the ranks of the common carriers by air. The subject will be discussed below in the context of a general consideration of the Board.

Demand for Air Transport

In analyzing the airline industry it is useful to know the determinants of the demand for air transportation just as it is useful to know the determinants of the cost of air transportation. The industry is relatively new; technology is changing fast; investment in the new jet aircraft is large relative to the carriers' present resources; communities face vast outlays on air fields; pricing and services are still in an unsettled state. So it is important to understand demand and be able to predict it. Economists would like to know the price elasticity of demand and the probable response of the customers to changes in product policy and promotion policy. It would be useful to know the effect on air travel of forces outside the control of the airlines, including the income elasticity of demand, the effect of any changes in consumers' tastes or preferences, and the effect of action by other modes on air transportation. Competition among modes will be discussed in Chapter 19, including competition between air and rail.

It is easier, of course, to specify what it would be useful to know than to provide the information. Some information is available, however, concerning the nature of the demand for air transportation.

SEPARATION OF BUSINESS FROM NONBUSINESS TRAVEL—It is important, first, to divide the demand for air travel for private individuals into business travel, which is travel in connection with people's work, and nonbusiness travel. Most statistics on tickets sold or passengers carried, unfortunately, do not permit a breakdown between people traveling for business and people traveling for other reasons, but the distinction can be made in survey data. The distinction is necessary because the funds out of which business trips are paid for are different from the funds out of which nonbusiness trips are paid, and the price elasticity of demand and income elasticity of demand, therefore, must be investigated separately in two portions of the market. About 6 out of 10 passenger trips by domestic scheduled airlines are business trips.[6] It might very well be profitable for the airlines to charge higher prices for business than for nonbusiness trips. Price discrimination based directly on purpose of the trip, however, is not possible since it is not possible to keep the business and nonbusiness travelers separate.

LENGTH OF HAUL—It is also essential to consider separately the demand for air transportation in different geographic subdivisions of the total market. Individual markets have their peculiarities arising from such matters as the presence or absence of large bodies of water across the direct route between the cities in question. More generally, the competitive position of the different modes of travel varies systematically according to the distance to be covered. In short haul markets, where other modes offer service that is a close substitute for air in quality, the price elasticity of demand for air travel must be expected to be higher than in the long haul market where the competing service is relatively slow.

INCOME ELASTICITY—The relation between income and the demand for air travel can be approximated from sample surveys of the general population. The per cent of adults at different income levels who took one or more air trips in a period of twelve months was estimated in 1962 to be as follows:[7]

Family Income (dollars)	Per Cent Who Took At Least One Air Trip
Under 2000	3
2000–2999	5
3000–3999	5
4000–4999	6
5000–5999	6
6000–7499	8
7500–9999	13
10,000–14,999	25
15,000 or over	34
All incomes	11

6. See, for example, *Inflight Survey, New York's Domestic Air Travelers,* November 1955 through October 1956, and the subsequent survey, April to September 1963, by the Aviation Department of the Port of New York Authority.

7. J. B. Lansing and D. Blood, *The Changing Travel Market,* Institute for Social Research, 1964, p. 287.

Thus, only 3 per cent of the lowest income group took an air trip, 97 per cent not patronizing the airlines. These statistics make clear that air travel is common only among people in the upper part of the income distribution. They also suggest strongly that as the income distribution moves upward with the growth of the economy the demand for air transportation should increase.

PRICE ELASTICITY—The price elasticity of the demand for air travel is a topic in which there is much interest. It remains, however, a subject of controversy. Prices have had to be set in the absence of definite knowledge of what level would be most profitable for the industry. A review has been made by Bartlett of the positions on the question of price elasticity of different airlines and of the Civil Aeronautics Board in the period 1947–1962. There have been reasonably consistent advocates of a low price policy, who have argued that the future of the industry requires development of the market through reduced fares and promotional fares of different types. There have been also reasonably consistent advocates of a high fare policy, who argue that demand is inelastic and that the prosperity of the industry requires unchanged or increased fares. Bartlett also shows that there have been shifts in the position taken by different organizations.[8] It is possible, of course, that a shifting position is correct in that the price elasticity of the demand for air travel does change from time to time.

Why not vary the price, observe the results, and find out about price elasticity? Unfortunately, experiments with changes in fares are difficult and likely to be inconclusive. For example, reduced fares were introduced in August 1962 on the Chicago–Los Angeles route on an experimental basis. The reduction took the form of a new, no-frills service priced 20 per cent below the previous minimum. Four airlines participated. After four months of experience with the new plan, they disagreed about whether it should be continued. The problems include the following: (1) A change in fares made by introducing a new low priced class of service may merely pull customers out of other classes of service instead of attracting new fliers. (2) It may merely pull customers out of other markets instead of making a net addition to air travel (Take your vacation in California instead of Florida!). (3) The effect of changes may be gradual. Time may be required for people to learn about the changed fare and to adjust their plans. Vacation plans, for example, may be made well in advance. (4) The effect of the change may depend on the nature of the service by competing common carriers and on their response. (The coach rail service from Chicago to Los Angeles is un-

8. Hale C. Bartlett, *The Demand for Passenger Air Transportation, 1947–1962,* unpublished doctoral dissertation, University of Michigan, 1965.

usually good and inexpensive. The reduced air fare may pull people off the trains over a period of time. Or it may pull them off the roads. What happens in this market need not be the same as what would happen in another market where the competing modes have different characteristics.)

The discussions of price elasticity of the demand for air travel ordinarily proceed on the assumption that there is a single price elasticity in a single market. If, as seems probable, there are several submarkets with different elasticities, the situation is more complex. There is every indication that the market for long trips is different from that for short. Air enjoys a larger share of the longer markets by reasons of its basic advantage in speed. It is quite likely that the demand is less elastic in the markets, say, for trips to points 1,000 miles or more away. In a sense, the airlines exploit this situation by charging the same price per mile at all distances even though costs per mile fall with distance.

SEARCH FOR METHODS OF SPLITTING THE MARKET—Much of the history of airline promotional fares may be interpreted as an attempt to develop profitable price discrimination. (Compare the theoretical model of price discrimination discussed in Chapter 4.) There has been a search for a principle of classification by which to split the market. Type of accommodation is a traditional method of dividing the passenger travel market into one, two, or more classes. Service may also be divided according to the time of the flight, as in low rates for flights at inconvenient hours late at night. Groups may be charged special rates, but at the price of policing the definition of what constitutes a group for the purpose. Servicemen in uniform are recognizable, and have been charged special, low rates. Attempts to charge special, low rates for people without reservations who wait to see if a flight is full have been less successful. It is hard to be sure that the person who made a reservation and then cancelled it is entirely unconnected with the individual waiting at the gate.

One of the more promising methods is to charge low marginal rates for extra members of a family. This system will separate out one group of nonbusiness travelers since women with children are unlikely to be traveling on business. A reason for believing that the market for family travel may be relatively elastic with regard to price is that air travel is sold in the same market as auto travel. Auto costs do not rise according to the passenger capacity of the vehicle. Air costs rise, of course, according to the number of people who take the trip. (This point is further developed in Chapter 19 in the discussion of competition across modes.) It may be possible to handle family travel at low marginal cost by taking advantage of the fact that speed may be less important than price in family travel, so that families may be given financial inducement to travel on off-peak flights.

PRODUCT DIFFERENTIATION—With regard to shifts from one airline to another, there is little experience with the effect of price variation since it is C.A.B. policy not to permit such variation. Product variation also may be used to split the market, and the effects of product variation are better understood. Passengers are interested in the type of aircraft. Other things equal, they want a speedy, comfortable flight, and will select the airline most likely to give it to them. Thus, when the turbo-prop planes were introduced, piston aircraft were at a major disadvantage. Caves reports that Capital Airline's share of most of its markets more than doubled when the *Viscount* was first introduced. In the same way, the first of the jets operated at almost 100 per cent load factor at the expense of the propeller-driven aircraft in the same markets. There is, thus, vigorous competition among airlines with regard to the type of service sold. The variations in service offered, (number of flights, type of equipment, quality of meals, courtesy of hostesses, etc.) have direct and observable effects on competition among airlines. Effects of better service on competition between air and other common carriers and on the generation of new travel are much more difficult to observe.

Costs of Air Transport

Economists interested in the airline industry, like other industries, would like to know the level and shape of the short run and long run average cost curves, the cost of product differentiation. Economies of scale relate to the potential number of airlines; the level of average cost to intermodal competition; any important determinants of the level of costs are of interest. The shape of the relation of cost to length of haul, for example, is especially related to defining the place of air in the total market. The costs of air transportation are easier to study than the costs of other modes because all the carriers are regulated (in contrast to trucking) and because the output is primarily movement of one cargo, people (in contrast to the railroads).

RELATION OF OPERATING EXPENSES TO OTHER FINANCIAL MAGNI-TUDES—The financial position of the industry may be outlined by a breakdown of total operating revenues for a recent year for the consolidated United States scheduled airline industry:[9]

9. Air Transport Association, *American Aviation,* May 1965. Data for 1964.

Total operating revenues	100
Total operating expenses	89
Net operating income	11
Interest on long-term debt	2
Other non-operating income (net)	1
Income taxes	4
Net profit	5
Rate of return on investment (net income before interest and after taxes as per cent of net worth and long-term debt)	10.8

Operating expenses are about 89 per cent of operating revenues, leaving 11 per cent net operating income. After adjustment for interest, other income, and income tax, net profit in this year was about 5 per cent of revenue.

DISTRIBUTION OF OPERATING EXPENSES—The accounting information available for the industry permits a breakdown of operating expenses for the consolidated United States scheduled airlines industry, as follows:[10]

Operating Expense		Per Cent
Flying operations		27
Maintenance		20
General services administration		43
Passenger service	8	
Aircraft and traffic servicing	17	
Promotion and sales	13	
Administration	4	
Depreciation and amortization		10
Total		100

IMPORTANCE OF VARIABLE COSTS—Inspection of these categories suggests immediately that at typical levels of operation variable costs are a large part of the total. Fixed costs associated with the provision of the airways are absent from these calculations (in contrast to those for railroads) since the airways are provided by the government.

Caves has reported a study done by C.A.B. staff of the operations of one carrier during a strike in 1956. Costs in February 1956 were compared with the nonstrike month a year earlier. For this temporary shutdown operating expenses were quickly cut back by two-thirds.[11] Flying operations could be stopped almost completely and maintenance

10. Air Transport Association, *American Aviation*, May 1965. Detail will not add to subtotal owing to rounding. Based on preliminary data for 1964.
11. Caves, *op. cit.*, pp. 81–82.

was drastically reduced. Passenger service and promotion fell very sharply, and other items also declined. This study thus confirms the original impression that in this industry fixed costs are relatively small. The difference between average total cost and short run marginal cost is by no means so important as in the railroad industry, for example.

ECONOMIES OF SCALE—It also appears to be true, as noted in the discussion of entry, that a carrier with a fleet of half a dozen or more long range jet aircraft is not at a marked cost disadvantage compared with larger airlines. The long run cost curve for the industry, thus, seems to be fairly flat in the range of level of operation of the trunk carriers.

There are economies of scale in the use of larger aircraft, however. The following tabulation shows operating costs in cents per seat-mile for different types of jet aircraft in 1964 ranked by average seats per mile:[12]

Type of Jet	Average Seats Per Mile	Cost Per Seat-Mile
Caravelle	64	3.1¢
CV-880	94	1.9
CV-990	104	2.0
Boeing 720	111	1.5
DC-8	123	1.4
Boeing 707	124	1.4
DC-8	127	1.7

Factors other than seating capacity influence costs, but the above data show that there is a strong tendency for operating costs per seat-mile to be lower for larger aircraft even when attention is restricted to modern jet powered planes of considerable capacity.

REVENUE PASSENGER LOAD FACTOR—While airline costs can be reduced if service is reduced and are variable in that sense, for a given level of service costs do not vary with patronage. A usual starting point for the discussion of the costs of air transport, therefore, is the revenue passenger load factor. This factor is the percentage of the seat-miles flown in scheduled service which are sold. The cost of operating an aircraft between two points depends only to a very limited extent upon whether the aircraft is full or empty. The same terminal facilities must be provided, the crew will be the same, the expense for fuel for taxiing, for lifting the plane into the air, for moving it through the air and setting it down at the destination, all will be nearly the same regardless of whether the plane carries one passenger or a planeload. The load

12. Air Transport Association, *American Aviation,* May 1965, p. 41.

factor thus has an important relation to the cost per passenger carried.

The usefulness of load factor in understanding events in the industry may be illustrated by the following statistics, which show for the years 1960 to 1964 the revenue passenger load factor and the rate of return on invested capital of the domestic trunk carriers:[13]

	Passenger Load Factor	Rate of Return on Invested Capital[14]
1960	59.5	2.8
1961	56.2	1.5
1962	53.3	4.1
1963	53.8	4.2
1964	55.4	10.1 (approximate)

The load factor was 53.3 per cent in 1962 and rate of return 4.1 per cent. When the load factor rose to 55.4 per cent in 1964, the return rose to about 10 per cent on invested capital. Earlier the domestic trunks had earned 8.8 per cent in 1954–56 with load factor of 63 to 64 per cent. Not all the variation in rate of return can be explained by changes in load factor. The improvement 1960 to 1962 with deteriorating load factor, like much of the recent history of the industry, must be understood in terms of the effects of the introduction of the jets. But there is a definite relationship between load factor and rate of return.

Why don't the airlines get the load factor up to 70, 80, 90, or 100 per cent? A load factor of 100 per cent would be undesirable from the point of view of the traffic departments on the airlines. Their immediate reaction would be to increase the capacity of the flights on the ground that some customers are probably being turned away. Some reserve on most flights may be a useful cushion.[15] This consideration, however, accounts for only part of the problem. A basic difficulty in raising load factors is that traffic flows tend to be uneven with respect to direction. For example, there is a tendency for tourists to fly from the United States to Europe in June and July and to return in August and early September. If there were *no* traffic opposed to the heavy flow, the maximum load factor attainable would be 50 per cent, since the planes would have to return empty in order to take another load in the direction of the peak flow. Fluctuations in load over shorter periods, weekly, or even daily, tend to produce the same problem.

13. Air Transport Association, *American Aviation,* May 1965.

14. Net income before interest and after taxes as per cent of net worth and long term debt.

15. See the discussion by Stephen Wheatcroft, *The Economics of European Air Transport,* Manchester University Press, 1956. Wheatcroft was formerly Commercial Research and Tariffs Manager of British European Airlines.

There is a conflict between a high load factor and the economies of scale from the use of large planes. For a given size of traffic flow, the smaller the airplane the easier to increase the load factor. In the extreme, if the airlines flew such small planes that they carried only one passenger per plane, no doubt it would be possible to operate planes with 100 per cent load factor. This principle applies to events in the years 1958 to 1963. The introduction of large jet aircraft in 1958 and thereafter both tended to lower load factors and to reduce costs for a given load factor.

For a given size of aircraft, the problem of increasing load factor tends to be easier as the load between two points increases. For example, if there are 175 persons to be transported between two points at a given time, and the size of aircraft in use is such that it handles fifty persons, it would be possible to operate three full flights and one flight half full. If there were only seventy-five persons to be transported, there would be one full flight, and one flight half full.

UTILIZATION FACTOR—Another determinant of costs of operating an airline is the utilization rate of the aircraft owned by the airline. This rate is usually expressed in terms of the number of hours per year an aircraft is actually in use. An aircraft represents a substantial capital outlay. Clearly, the more hours of utilization per year that can be obtained from this outlay, the lower the costs per passenger mile.

In the early days of the industry, in the 1920s, utilization rates were on the order of 1,000 hours per year. At present, rates of over 3,000 hours are common. The chances are that a high utilization rate may be obtainable only at a low load factor. For example, if an aircraft is available for service on a particular route on which most of the traffic moves on six days in the week it may pay to operate the aircraft at a relatively low load factor on the seventh day rather than to let it stand idle. Whether operation on the last day will pay will depend on a comparison between the extra cost of operating the aircraft on the seventh day, and the extra revenue to be obtained from the extra flight.

ROUTE DENSITY—Just as there are fixed costs in the provision of an aircraft there are fixed costs involved in the operation of a station. Certain facilities must be provided whether one flight a week or one flight an hour is operated out of a particular station. They will depend at least partly on the number of people per flight. As the number of flights increases, the facilities will also increase but not in proportion. It is not easy to estimate the amount of cost required to maintain a station for a minimum volume of, say, one flight in and one flight out every day. Stations have been maintained for even lower volumes than that, especially on long international routes where it was necessary to provide intermediate stations and the volume of traffic justified less than one flight each way each day. In part the cost of providing scheduled air service will depend on whether the airport and terminal facilities would be maintained in large part for other purposes even if there were no scheduled air service, for example, for military flying, or for general aviation. A low route density, however, ordinarily will lead to high costs per passenger served.

ROUTE STRUCTURE—It is generally agreed that the route structure of an airline will have an important effect on its cost. Route structure is a determinant of load factor and utilization factor. There are four main types of route pattern which may be distinguished: radial pattern, circular, grid, and linear. The least efficient is probably the radial pattern, sometimes referred to as the "spoke pattern" because of the resemblance to the spokes of a wheel. It tends to lead to a high volume of traffic at the station at the center of the wheel but to poor station utilization at the stations at the end of the spokes. This pattern is characteristic of the operations of many European airlines which have a main terminal at the capital of their nation and radial lines leading out to other cities in Europe.[16]

Increasing attention has been given by airlines in recent years to problems of adaptation of their operations to their route patterns. Given a certain route pattern the problem is one of utilization of a given stock of aircraft, or minimization of the stock of aircraft needed. The problem is one which can be attacked by such methods as linear programming. The objective of the calculations for the private company is to determine the optimal scheduling of plane movements in order to maximize profits.

STAGE LENGTH—The operating costs of aircraft per mile operated are not constant but tend to vary with the distance operated. The relevant distance is the distance of the stage, that is the distance between the points where the aircraft takes-off and lands. (Stage length is not to be confused with trip length. Passengers [and planes] may make journeys involving more than one stage.) There is a tendency for the cost per mile of operating aircraft to fall as the distance increases from zero miles upwards. This decline in cost per mile arises from the fact that an aircraft must spend a certain amount of time and fuel in taxiing on the ground, in take-off, and in climbing to its cruising altitude. At the other end of the flight, similarly, time must be spent in landing and in

16. *Ibid.*, p. 46.

taxiing to the terminal gate. The cost of these operations represents a kind of fixed charge that can be distributed over a longer distance as the length of the trip increases.

As the length of flight continues to increase, there will be a tendency in the opposite direction arising from the need to carry additional fuel to fly the longer distance. There will come a point beyond which it will be necessary to replace some of the payload with fuel. More fuel must be substituted for payload as the distance increases beyond that minimum point. There will be some stage length beyond which the plane will not be operated.

A long-haul aircraft will be designed with substantial fuel capacity and limited cubic capacity of the compartments for carrying passengers or cargo. Such a plane *can* be used for short hauls but it will not be well adapted for short lengths. For such service the large fuel capacity will not be needed and the seating capacity is likely to prove inadequate. On a long-haul aircraft, also, the landing gear will be designed to absorb the impact of landing the plane after the weight of fuel has been reduced by the long flight. For a short-haul aircraft the landing gear will be designed to take the load of almost the full amount of weight the plane can take into the air at the start of the flight, since the reduction in weight from the consumption of fuel will be relatively small.[17]

From the point of view of the carriers, then, one of the basic characteristics of a new aircraft is the relation of cost per mile to stage length. At the time of the introduction of the *Boeing 727*, for example, the following estimates were publicized:[18]

Stage Length	Direct Operating Costs (dollars)	Cost Per Seat-Mile, Coach Configuration (cents)
400 miles	1.55	1.4
600 miles	1.40	1.25
1000 + miles	below 1.30	1.15

The decline in costs with distance is of special interest in connection with the fare structure of the industry, which as will be discussed below, contains little "taper."

17. Wheatcroft argued in 1956 that many of the operating problems of the airlines had arisen from the absence of a large, short-haul airplane. Since that date the most rapid technological developmnts have been in the long-range jets, and, more recently, the intermediate-range aircraft, rather than the type of plane he proposed.

18. William S. Reed, "Boeing Reveals Final 727 Design Details," *Aviation Week,* March 6, 1961, p. 60.

Public Agencies Concerned with Air Transportation

A policy of double subsidy to the airlines has a long history in the United States. Indirect subsidy is provided through the provision of terminals, airways and other services at less than cost. Direct federal subsidy to the airlines, which has existed since the first scheduled private air service in this country, continues but has diminished in importance. Of the public agencies concerned with the air transportation industry, the most important are the Civil Aeronautics Board, the Federal Aviation Agency, and the units of local government concerned with the construction and operation of airports. Each requires discussion.

CIVIL AERONAUTICS BOARD—Since 1938 the *Civil Aeronautics Act*, as amended, has been the fundamental legislation regulating the activities of the airlines. The *Act* provided for a Civil Aeronautics Board composed of five members appointed by the President of the United States with the usual provision for the advice and consent of the Senate. The Board was given broad regulatory powers over the airlines. Its functions include granting or denying of certificates of public convenience and necessity which amount to permits to engage in air transportation. The Board was given control over rates, and over the service offered by the carriers, which must be reasonable and adequate service to the public. The Board also acts as the grantor of subsidies to airlines. The Board has control over the fixing of the rate of compensation for airmail, which has been important because the traditional method of subsidy was through generous airmail payments. It may prescribe accounts and records to be kept by the carriers. Its responsibilities include approval of contracts and agreements among the air carriers, and approval of any consolidations, mergers, purchases, and the like. It also has responsibility for prevention of unfair or deceptive practices or unfair methods of competition in air transportation, and the approval or disapproval of applications for loans or financial aids to air carriers from the United States or any agency of the United States. Among the features of the *Act* of continuing importance was a declaration of transportation policy in the following terms:

Sec. 2. In the exercise and performance of its powers and duties under this Act, the Authority shall consider the following, among other things, as being in the public interest, and in accordance with the public convenience and necessity. . . .

(a) The encouragement and development of an air-transportation system properly adapted to the present and future needs of the foreign and domestic commerce of the United States, of the Postal Service, and of the national defense;

(b) The regulation of air transportation in such manner as to recognize and preserve the inherent advantages of, assure the highest degree of safety in, and foster sound economic conditions in, such transportation by air carriers; and to improve the relations between and coordinate transportation;

(c) The promotion of adequate, economical, and efficient service by air carriers at reasonable charges, without unjust discriminations, undue preferences or advantages, or unfair or destructive competitive practices;

(d) Competition to the extent necessary to assure the sound development of an air-transportation system properly adapted to the needs of the foreign and domestic commerce of the United States, of the Postal Service, and of the national defense;

(e) The regulation of air commerce in such manner as to best promote its development and safety; and . . .

(f) The encouragement and development of civil aeronautics.[19]

This statement of policy is to be taken into account by the Board in the specific economic decisions it is required to make under the terms of the *Act*. In a word, the Board enjoys and has enjoyed from its creation a complete arsenal of regulatory powers plus the power to grant subsidies within limits provided by Congress and it has a mandate to use its powers for a variety of public purposes with the emphasis on the stimulation of the growth of the industry. The policies of the Board will be considered briefly in the next section following a short account of other public agencies concerned with the aviation industry.

FEDERAL AVIATION AGENCY—Those activities of the federal government with respect to civil aviation that are not the responsibility of the C.A.B. have been assigned principally to the Federal Aviation Agency, which was constituted in its present form by the *Federal Aviation Act* of 1958. The F.A.A. is responsible for the construction and operation of the federal airways and of the air navigation facilities in terminal areas. It administers grants-in-aid for airports. It undertakes research and development in the field of aeronautics. In contrast to the C.A.B. it is not concerned with the economic regulation of the industry nor with direct subsidies to the airlines.

PROVISION OF AIRWAYS—It is technically possible to operate an aircraft with no ground facilities other than a runway from which it can take-off and on which it can land. The ability of aircraft to operate with a minimum of ground facilities is of importance in exploration of completely unknown areas or in the development of new territories such as the antarctic or northern Canada. Airlines in the United States, however,

19. See *Civil Aeronautics Act,* 52 Stat. 973.

operate in a completely different environment. Scheduled airlines do not take-off casually into an uncharted sky. The airways consist of designated lanes through the sky through which aircraft are guided. The guidance system has changed with changing characteristics of aircraft. The system includes air traffic control towers for guidance of aircraft near airports; route traffic control centers; and flight service stations for weather briefings, flight-following service, and search and rescue operations.[20]

Expenditures on the system of federal airways are increasing. The total for construction and maintenance, which was estimated at 107.9 million dollars in 1950 and 403.7 million dollars in 1960, was projected to be 950 million dollars in 1970.[21]

These facilities are by no means exclusively for the use of the scheduled airlines, and, in fact, some of the facilities are intended exclusively for the use of private fliers. A large part of the cost of operating the Federal Airways System should be allocated to civil aircraft other than the aircraft of the scheduled airlines. General aviation accounts for about two out of three flights reported by air traffic control towers of the F.A.A. Part of the cost of the system should properly be charged to the armed forces whose aircraft also make use of the airways.[22] Since the same system is used in these three types of operations, its cost must be regarded as a joint cost. Any allocation of this cost among the three classes of users will be in some degree arbitrary. It is clear, however, that the service provided by the federal government has been of substantial assistance to the commercial scheduled airlines.[23] Spokesmen for the railroads like to contrast this situation with their own complete responsibility to provide the railway—and pay real estate taxes on it.

PROVISION OF AIR TERMINALS—Air terminals, like airways, are provided by public agencies, and, also like airways, typically are used by military aircraft and general aviation as well by the airlines. Airports are expensive installations.

Information about the amount of federal money invested in airports is available though statistical information about the expenditures of the state and local governments is much less satisfactory. Federal aid to

20. For further detail see Federal Aviation Agency, *F.A.A. Statistical Handbook of Aviation.*
21. "Doyle report," *National Transportation Policy,* printed for the Committee on Interstate and Foreign Commerce, 87th Congress, 1st Session, January 1961, pp. 182–183.
22. The F.A.A. has estimated 40 per cent of the use is military. *Ibid.,* p. 168.
23. Wheatcroft states that in Europe a larger crew has been necessary on aircraft than in the United States because of the lack of complete coverage of radio navigational aids in Europe.

airports on any appreciable scale dates from the depression of the 1930s. The Civil Works Administration spent 11.5 million dollars on 585 small airports. Its successor, the Works Progress Administration, also spent substantial sums on airports from July 1935 onwards. The arrangement in that case was that half of the spending was by the federal government and half by local sponsors of the project. Substantial amounts of money were spent on airports for military purposes in the period immediately prior to and during World War II. Altogether federal aid to airports prior to the *Federal Airport Act* of 1946 amounted to 741 million dollars for airport construction. Of the 741 million dollars, 367 million dollars was involved in a defense landing area program.

The *Civil Aeronautics Act* had provided for a field survey of airports and such a survey was undertaken and brought up to date during World War II. It formed the basis for the *Federal Airport Act* of 1946. This legislation provided for sponsorship of an airport by any public agency, such as a state or local governmental agency, and the sponsor was to provide one-half of the total amount, matching the federal funds. In some situations the federal funds might be less than one-half of the cost of the construction of the airport.[24] From 1947 to 1964 federal aid funds for airports totalled about 798 million dollars to which were added 825 million dollars of funds from the local sponsors.[25] These sums are apart from the costs of operating airports, which are not easy to estimate for the country as a whole owing to the diversity of sponsorship.

ECONOMIC PROBLEMS OF AIRPORT CONSTRUCTION AND OPERATION— There are a series of economic problems associated with the provision of airports. Airports represent substantial capital outlays. The technical requirements of aircraft, translated into physical requirements for sites, work out to requirements for a large area, unobstructed, and nearly flat, with good load bearing properties and drainage in the soil, clear approaches, and good meteorological conditions. For major airports the economic problem is that such sites, located near large cities, and with good transportation facilities to the center of these cities, are desirable for purposes other than airports. There is a conflict, therefore, between the advantages of location near the center of a large city, that is, near the center of demand, and the desire to minimize the investment in valuable land.

There are several awkward problems in connection with the location and operation of airports. First, the benefit from the introduction of jet

24. This discussion is based on G. Lloyd Wilson and Leslie A. Bryan, *Air Transportation,* Prentice-Hall, 1949, pp. 103–104.
25. *F.A.A. Statistical Handbook,* 1964, p. 11.

aircraft in reduced operating costs and improvements in service has been accompanied by costs in the form of requirements for additional length of runways. These costs are incurred, at least in the first instance, not by the airlines but by the operators of airports. The cost to the airline operators of the introduction of the jet aircraft was less than the full social cost because of the added expense to the airport operators. The decision to introduce the jet aircraft no doubt was the correct decision, but it was not made on the basis of a correct calculation of total social costs. The organization of the industry in which separate organizations have responsibility for the aircraft and the terminals predisposed to incomplete calculation. Any system of organizing an industry which makes it unnecessary for those who make a decision to innovate to take the full cost of the innovation into their private assessment of costs necessarily stacks the cards in favor of innovation.

Second, airports have effects that extend beyond the boundaries of the fields. From the point of view of the operators of the airport and the airlines it is essential to prevent the construction of tall buildings in the approach paths to the airport and it may even be desirable to remove structures already in existence. From the point of view of persons living in the vicinity of an airport, the noise from the aircraft may constitute a serious nuisance, and accidents to aircraft may lead to damage to property or even loss of life on the part of persons living in the vicinity of the airport. Here also is a situation in which calculations that include only costs and benefits to the airlines and passengers on the airlines are incomplete. The tendency has been to have recourse to the courts and to the political processes to try to work out some solution of the conflicting interests. The problem threatens to become more serious with the prospective development of supersonic commercial aircraft that generate destructive sonic booms.

OTHER INDIRECT AIDS—A third main category of indirect aid has been research subsidized or paid for by the federal government. The state of the art of aeronautics has been advanced substantially by the development of military aircraft. The indirect benefits to civil aviation from the development of military planes have been substantial. The federal government has also aided research in this field through the National Advisory Committee for Aeronautics, which was established in 1915 to include representatives of several federal agencies and nonfederal participants as well. Currently large sums of money are being spent on the development of a supersonic air transport.

FINANCING—The provision of services to aviation by the government is not a matter of controversy though there are choices to be made about particular programs. The basic issue on which there is disagreement is whether the program of federal aid to aviation should continue to be paid for out of general funds. The Doyle report, for example, advocated that the program should be financed on a user charge basis. The proposal was to set up a basis for allocating a share of the joint costs to the military budget, and pay for everything else from a trust fund into which fees would be paid by users of the airways and other facilities. The scheme would be similar to the Highway Trust Fund. A system of user charges could cover the cost of terminals and airways even if the development of radically new ventures such as the supersonic transport were to be subsidized.

The Policy of the C.A.B. Toward Domestic Aviation

Perhaps the best starting place for a discussion of the policy of the C.A.B. is a description of some features of the situation in which that agency operates with special emphasis on those policies about which the C.A.B. has had no choice. In organizing its domestic air services a nation has essentially three choices:

(1) National monopoly. Many nations grant a monopoly or a near monopoly of domestic air services to a single organization.

(2) Regional monopoly. A nation may be divided into regions, each part of which is served by a single air carrier.

(3) Monopolistic competition. Competition may take two forms. (a) *competition through alternate routes:* Two or more possible routes may exist for service between two points, and these routes may be in the hands of separate organizations. (b) *direct competition:* Two or more carriers may operate service on the same route.

By the time the C.A.B. came into existence the American pattern had been set. On the main air routes it is one of direct competition by private carriers. The discretion of the Board extends only to the exact number of carriers to be allowed to operate on particular routes. On the thinly traveled routes, as already noted, the pattern is one of monopoly by private carriers subsidized by the C.A.B.

DIRECT SUBSIDIES—The normal procedure of the C.A.B. has been to use "closed rates" of subsidy, that is, to fix the absolute amount of the subsidy for an indefinite future period for a given carrier. The amount being fixed, with no provision for recapture by the government, the carrier has the normal incentive to minimize its costs in order to maximize its profits. The law provides for a return including subsidy to cover costs if they are incurred under "honest, economical, and efficient management." The Board, thus, has the power to disallow costs. This power has been exercised to disallow mileage flown which is regarded as excessive. The Board has used two round trips a day for local service as the normal amount. The Board has also on occasion disallowed costs for purchase of aircraft as excessive.[26] The Board in practice has not always been able to operate with closed rates of subsidy because of the slowness of the formal proceedings to set the rates.

Although the absolute amount of the subsidy paid has been larger in the postwar period than it was before World War II, its relative importance has declined. In 1938 the airmail subsidy amounted to 7 million dollars.[27] By 1956 all of the trunk carriers except Northeast Airlines had been removed from the subsidy list. In 1964 the subsidy to the local service carriers was 66 million dollars or about a quarter of their total revenue. Subsidy was also paid to other operators, notably 4 million dollars to operators of helicopter services. How long the direct subsidy should be continued is one of the issues of policy toward the industry.

RATE REGULATION—Any direct subsidies which it pays are inevitably a matter of concern to the Board. As long as the subsidy to the trunk lines continued the Board had a direct interest in minimizing their costs and maximizing their revenues. The Board's attitude toward entry of a new firm into a particular city-pair market reflected this concern. Any competition which on balance raised the subsidy bill was excess competition to the Board. Similarly, the optimal rate policy was that policy calculated to maximize the net revenue of the carriers or minimize their losses, in other words, the same level of rates that would have been set by a private monopoly. This philosophy had a reason in the rapid re-equipment of the industry with jet aircraft in the period immediately after the end of the subsidy. Financially part of the industry was doing badly, and the return of a need for subsidy was at least a risk. With the successful completion of the transition to the jets, the question arises, can the general level of rates be reduced?

With regard to the structure of rates the C.A.B., like other regulatory agencies in transportation, has raised no general objection to price discrimination as economists use the term but it has acted to prevent discrimination among persons not based on objective criteria. It is "unjust" discrimination that is forbidden by the law.

The actual history of the fare structure is that it evolved early into

26. See Caves, *op. cit.*, Chapter 11.
27. Doyle report, *op. cit.*, p. 182.

the approximate equivalent of a flat rate per mile. As previously observed, average costs show a tendency to decline with length of route segment. To an economist, therefore, a flat rate amounts to subtle but real price discrimination in favor of the short over the long route segments. "Taper" has been introduced very gradually into the fare structure starting with the addition of a small fixed charge per ticket, which slightly reduced the price per mile of long vs. short trips. Meanwhile the jets have increased still further the economy of serving the distant cities, so that it is an open question whether a close investigation would show much change in a measure of the degree of discrimination.

It is consistent with the whole approach of the board to the industry that it has prevented the development of price competition among the airlines. The industry has seen the introduction of a succession of new types of aircraft. A crucial point in the rate policy of the C.A.B. has been the refusal to allow an airline with old equipment to respond to an innovation by a competitor by lowering fares. The airline with the older aircraft is thus put in a position where it will be at a competitive disadvantage until it matches the rival's aircraft. The Board has allowed only limited price increases by the carriers with the new equipment in the form of special surcharges, for example, for jet travel.

PRODUCT RIVALRY AND PROGRESS—Has the oligopolistic industry under C.A.B. regulation behaved in the same manner as a private monopolist would have behaved without regulation? By no means! The policy of fixed prices plus free competition in service, given the sensitivity of demand to product improvement, has put a premium on rapid innovation. No airline can afford to lag very long or very far in the type of plane it flies. The penalty is immediate: rapid deterioration in its share of the market. The costs of the industry are such that low load factors and low aircraft utilization rates are almost certain to mean losses.

Airlines, therefore, are very actively interested in the procurement of new types of aircraft. They are under pressure to be first with a better plane. This pressure influences their behavior in the market for new aircraft. That market is one in which there is bilateral oligopoly: a small group of sellers, the manufacturers, face a limited number of buyers, the airlines. It is an international market since planes built in one country can be and are sold to airlines of another nationality.

Historically this market was one in which there were formal ties between particular manufacturers and particular airlines. These ties, however, were broken by federal policy in the 1930s.[28] At present there

28. See Caves, *op. cit.*, Chapter 5.

seems to be a tendency for large carriers to introduce new planes first, to their considerable competitive advantage. (In the international market, where Pan American is the dominant carrier, it placed the first order for jet transports. Trans World Airlines and Northwest, also international carriers, had to follow. Since they have also domestic routes, the effect was to start the rush for jets for domestic service.) The eagerness shown by the airlines to place orders for the supersonic transport years in advance of possible delivery illustrates the concern with being first.

Is the public interest well served by such intense product rivalry? There is no doubt that the effect is to speed up the process of introduction of new equipment. The industry must be given a high score for rapid product improvement. This improvement is generally in the public interest, and must weigh heavily in any overall judgment about the performance of the industry.

There is a body of opinion that holds that the rate of improvement has been in some respects too rapid. The airlines went through a very rapid succession of cycles of introduction of new equipment from the end of World War II to the introduction of the jets beginning in 1958. The last round of piston driven propeller aircraft is the one most often criticized. At the time, the jets were known to be a short period ahead. Yet new planes were introduced which pushed the old technology to its limits. They were more expensive to operate and only a little faster. The *Lockheed Super Constellation* and *DC-7* went into service in the fall of 1953. They flew 330 and 350 miles per hour, respectively. The improvement was not large over the *DC-6B*, introduced in 1951, which cruised at 300 m.p.h. The *Lockheed L-1649A*, introduced in June 1957, cruised at 340 m.p.h. The *Boeing 707-120*, the first turbo-jet, which cruised at 590 m.p.h., was introduced in October 1958.[29]

MATURITY AND ITS IMPLICATIONS—There is no unique measure of the maturity of an industry. If achievement of a reasonable level of profitability is a yardstick, the airline industry by 1964 to 1965 was about at the average rate of return on investment which the C.A.B. set as a standard in 1960, 10.5 per cent. This rate was proposed as a weighted average of a rate of 10.25 for the "Big Four" and 11.125 for the other trunks the C.A.B. believed would be necessary to maintain access to the capital market. The investment base on which the return was to be earned was depreciated assets. This average return thus is an average involving both debt and equity capital, and, given a lower interest rate on debt, implies a substantially higher rate of return on equity capital

29. C.A.B., *Handbook of Airline Statistics,* 1962, p. 502.

than 10 per cent.[30] An average of 10.5 per cent over a period of years implies, of course, that this rate of return will often be exceeded.

Growth is another indicator of maturity. The airlines have grown to the point where they as a group are easily the leading common carriers of passengers, having passed the railroads in 1957.

The maturity of an industry may also be considered in terms of the rate of change of technology. If a slower rate indicates maturity, what is required is a judgment about prospective changes in technology. It would appear that the rapid increase in speed observed in the past may continue for the long haul routes with the supersonic transport. For the shorter routes more air speed seems unlikely and even unnecessary. The bulk of travel time is now on the ground rather than in the air for trips of, say, 500 miles by medium range jet. Major innovations may come in the short haul markets with the much discussed vertical take-off or short take-off aircraft. Present indications are that these planes will have high power requirements, and, hence, will offer fast service at a premium price. For many markets the situation may move from one of a rapidly changing technology to one of exploitation of the market for a gradually developing technology.

Changes in policy that may be proposed as the industry becomes mature in these different ways are of several types. User charges to pay the cost of air terminals and airways have been mentioned. The indefinite continuation of cash subsidies also comes into question. The legislative statement of public objectives quoted at the beginning of the discussion of the C.A.B. is not a guide to when subsidy should end. Permanent subsidy to any part of the industry, however, such as the local service carriers, would require a strong case. In terms of speed the competition from automobiles becomes close when the autos are operating over the new Interstate System between points 100 miles apart, the average hop for the local service carriers. The gain in door-to-door speed from using planes on such routes is not likely to be large.

A further question arises as to whether some of the more restrictive regulatory practices of the C.A.B. will need to be continued indefinitely. With no further risk of subsidy, the Board might relax its controls over the entry of trunk carriers into new markets allowing freedom of adjustment of route structures. Maximum rate regulation may continue to be necessary, but more freedom for the carriers in setting rates may be considered. Most oligopolies in American industry do not require public regulation to prevent price warfare. Relaxation of restrictions on competition may even be carried far enough to permit major reliance on

30. Caves believes the Board set the rate too high. See Caves, *op. cit.*, Chapter 17.

competition rather than public-utility-type regulation to assure a high
level of economic performance by the industry. The crucial question will
be whether the industry grows rapidly enough so that there can be an
increasing number of competing firms of efficient size. Thus, there are
several areas in which the increasing maturity of the domestic airline
industry may be expected to lead to reconsideration of public policy.

International Air Transportation and the
Policy of the United States

International air transportation involves a mixture of economics and
politics, national profit and national prestige, which is potentially ex-
plosive. The interests and sensitivities of national states are involved
with the international airlines which serve them. The considerations of
national prestige hardly need emphasis: people take pride in the jet
airliners, which have become symbols of the modern age. For an empire
or any kind of international association of states the importance of
communications is obvious. Leaders can assemble by plane. International airlines are of direct usefulness in the foreign trade of a national
state. In view of the importance of the balance of payments to modern
nations, any advantage in the export trade is not to be taken lightly.
It is advantageous to a nation to have direct and frequent service from
its capital or commercial center to all parts of the world in which its
exporters hope to compete so that messages, people, and goods can move
quickly. An international airline under the control of a country will also
be of direct usefulness in the competition for tourist business. American
tourists who leave the United States on an English airliner will ordinarily be taken to London; on a French airliner, to Paris; on a Dutch
airliner, to Amsterdam; and so forth. They then automatically become
visitors to the country in which they land.

International air transport developed in the period after World War
I. The first stage was the development of local services on the continent of Europe and the continent of North America. By 1929 networks
existed in both of these areas. The second stage, between 1929 and the
outbreak of World War II, was the development of regular air services
from Europe to Eastern Asia and Australia and from Europe to South
Africa and South America. Services also developed from North America
to South America, and across the Pacific and the North Atlantic. By
1939 a complete world system existed in skeleton form. It was during
and immediately after World War II that the international agreements

were made which have determined the structure of international air transport.

Every principal European country early adopted a policy of the stimulation of its national airlines and every major European airline was heavily subsidized in its early days. There was extensive experimentation with different forms of subsidy. One system was a subsidy on a straight mileage basis. This method of subsidy put a premium on small, cheap aircraft. The British, for example, after a period of the use of subsidies on the basis of miles flown, substituted a policy of subsidy on the basis of the horsepower miles flown by the late 1920s.

An alternative form of subsidy which has been used fairly extensively in Europe is on the basis of specified route, schedule, and equipment. Under this system the government specifies exactly what it is going to get in exchange for the subsidy payment. The French at one time experimented with a system of awarding subsidies on a competitive bidding basis. The experience was not successful. By 1933 the French had set up a single air transport enterprise, Air France.

The present British policy dates from the British *Overseas Airway Act* of 1939. The predecessor of B.O.A.C. had been Imperial Airways, Ltd., which was a "chosen instrument" of government policy and was subsidized. The criticism of Imperial Airways was that it kept aircraft in service longer than was customary in other systems, and failed to give the government departments the cooperation they expected from a heavily subsidized company with important international and imperial contacts.[31] The result was a public corporation controlled by the government. It issues stock, but the stockholders have no voice in the management of the organization and are in effect government bondholders.

In spite of the heavy government involvement, in their dealings with foreign states international airlines have found it convenient to have at least the appearance of private enterprise. Expansion into new areas is made easier in some instances if the organization is not a direct arm of the national government. Nevertheless the connections between the international airlines and their governments are in most instances very close, even though some private capital may be involved.

The United States in the early period did not adopt a policy of government ownership but it has adopted the policy of government promotion of international air service by American air carriers. The early subsidies were of the same type as the subsidies to the domestic air-

31. See Oliver James Lissitzyn, *International Air Transport and National Policy,* Council on Foreign Relations, 1942.

lines, that is, they represented payments for the carriage of airmail in excess of any reasonable estimate of the cost of the service provided. The payments took the form of payment for space reserved for mail which in effect meant a guarantee of a minimum income to the air carrier. The Civil Aeronautics Board when it came into existence continued for a time the policy of subsidy through airmail contracts. This approach was the same as that adopted with regard to the airmail subsidies by the Board to the domestic airlines.

In the nature of international operations, agreements must be reached among the governments involved. From the early days of international air transport the principle has been recognized that every national state has sovereignty and jurisdiction over the air space above its territory, including its territorial waters, and has discretion as to the admission or non-admission of any aircraft to that air space. International air transportation is legally possible only if there is some kind of international agreement between the countries involved, or between a country and a private organization which desires to establish service to that country.

The attempt was made during World War II to establish freedom of air transport on a basis comparable to the freedom of the seas. The International Air Transport Agreement prepared in Chicago in 1944 was intended to establish Five Freedoms. These Five Freedoms, which have become famous, are the following:

1) To fly across territory;

2) To land for non-traffic purposes;

3) To put down a load taken on in the territory of the state of the nationality of the aircraft;

4) To take on a load destined to the state of nationality of the aircraft;

5) To take on or put down a load for or from any other contracting state.

General acceptance of the Five Freedoms would have meant that it would have been unnecessary for individual pairs of states to make bilateral agreements governing the air transportation between them. This effort was a failure. It proved to be impossible to secure general agreement among the powers concerned with air transportation along the lines specified in the Chicago agreement. The difference of opinion was particularly important between Great Britain, which was not prepared to sign the Five Freedoms Agreement and took the position that extensive regulation of international air transport was desirable, and the United States, which supported a policy of freedom of the air. The difference of opinion was not entirely ideological. The United States had emerged from World War II in a very strong competitive position.

Some settlement of the differences between Great Britain and the United States was essential to the development of the international air transport industry. A solution was achieved at the Bermuda Conference in 1946 resulting in the Anglo-American Air Agreement of 1946. A crucial part of this agreement was the establishment of a procedure for the determination of rates to be charged by airlines operating between points in the two countries. The arrangement was that the rates were to be developed through the International Air Transport Association, which had been established by representatives of the airlines of forty-two countries at a convention in Havana, Cuba in 1945. One important provision of the agreement was that the voting on rates was to be unanimous. Rates developed by the airlines through the International Air Transport Association were to be subject to review by the governments involved. For the United States, review has been by the Civil Aeronautics Board. The agreement also specified the routes and traffic points to be involved in the services offered by the airlines. Although it thus provides for rates fixed by agreement, the Bermuda Agreement does not place restrictions on capacity, number of flights, or "Fifth Freedom" traffic. The essential compromise reached at Bermuda was that the United States conceded that fares should be controlled while Great Britain conceded that capacity should not be controlled. The principles set forth in the Bermuda Agreement have been adopted by the United States also in other bilateral pacts. They govern the air traffic on the major international routes involving the United States, notably the North Atlantic route. Within Europe the situation is different. Stephen Wheatcroft estimated in 1956 that on only one-third of the international European routes was there no restriction with regard to capacity.[32]

How satisfactory has been the experience with this framework of agreements? There has been very rapid development of international air service. For example, the number of air passengers between the United States and Europe increased by a factor of ten from fiscal 1950 to 1964, from 297,000 to 3,084,000 in fourteen years. Calendar 1964 alone showed an increase over the previous year of one-fourth.

The level of fares has been a matter of concern to the United States. Payments by Americans to foreign airlines enter the international balance of payments. It is not surprising, therefore, to find the C.A.B. pressing for lower fares. The fare level maintained on interna-

32. See Wheatcroft, *op. cit.* Also see by the same author *Air Transport Policy*, M. Michael Joseph Ltd., 1964.

tional routes was very high in the early postwar years. Between 1950 and 1960, however, the average revenue per passenger-mile on flights of scheduled United States international carriers fell from .073 cents to .064 cents, declining further to .058 cents in 1963. For scheduled United States domestic operations there was an increase from .054 cents to .062 cents.[33] The costs per seat-mile on the long flights like that across the Atlantic probably should be less than for the short domestic route segments. The international rates, thus, may be higher than necessary to cover the cost of an efficient type of service even though the comparison to domestic American rates has become much more favorable. The North Atlantic market is too important and competitive to be typical. Other markets have diverse histories. The situation is one in which each national state holds a trump card in its right to refuse the Five Freedoms to the aircraft of other nations. The outcome is likely to depend at any time on bargaining skill and the general state of international relations.[34]

Air Freight

Air freight is of interest to the general student of transportation because of the problem of explaining its existence. It is not surprising that only on the order of magnitude of 1 per cent of all intercity ton-miles of domestic freight movement in the United States should be by air. Freight rates by air are on the average several times as high as by competing surface transportation. Average freight revenue per revenue ton-mile for scheduled air service in this country, as it happens, was exactly 22.69 cents in 1950 and again in 1962, and has shown a tendency to decline to lower levels only since that time, with an average of 10 cents per revenue ton-mile probably attainable with equipment being developed for the armed forces and expected in commercial use in the late 1960s.[35] Even that level is well above truck and rail rates.

REASONS FOR DEVELOPMENT OF AIR CARGO—If air freight is much more expensive than other types of freight, what commodities move by air, and why? An analysis of this question was published by Lewis,

33. F.A.A., *Statistical Handbook of Aviation*, 1964, pp. 122–123.

34. Not all trump cards are of equal value since some nations generate more air traffic than others and some landing places are more strategically placed than others.

35. The estimate of 10 cents is for the *Lockheed C-141A* developed for the Military Air Transport Service and is the manufacturer's estimate of a realistic commercial charge. See "Starlifter Goes Commercial," *American Aviation*, April 1965, p. 24.

Culliton, and Steele in 1956.[36] The basic answer to the question is that *total* costs are minimized by the use of air.

Lewis and Culliton suggest that users of air freight may be ranged on a continuum from those who use it only in case of emergency, at one end of the spectrum, to those who use it as a normal routine means of transportation, at the other end. An example of a commodity that will move by air freight but only in an emergency is a ship's propeller. If the propeller of a ship has been lost or damaged through some accident and the ship must wait in a foreign port until a new propeller arrives, it may pay to ship the propeller by air rather than tie up the ship indefinitely. Such shipments have actually been made. Under normal circumstances the propeller of a ship is the type of heavy object with low value in relation to its weight that would never move in air transport.

Emergencies of this type are not entirely unpredictable events from the viewpoint of the shipping company. From time to time it will happen that a ship will damage its propeller or some other vital part of its machinery and replacements will be needed. To prevent the necessity of shipping spare parts by air it would be necessary for the ship to carry a large number of spare parts all the time. It may be more efficient to plan on occasional shipment by air.

The same type of reasoning applies to a factory at some distance from a source of spare parts. It will be expensive to maintain a complete set of spare machinery, yet the breakdown of any one machine on an assembly line may tie up the whole factory for as long as it takes to repair the damage. In such situations air transport can be extremely valuable.

Emergencies of one kind or another continue to be important. In 1965 the magazine *Air Cargo* conducted a sample survey by mail of "commercial traffic executives." Those who used air freight were asked what percentage of their shipments by air they considered to be "of an emergency nature." Half of those replying indicated 75 per cent or more.[37]

A second type of situation in which air freight may be used is to provide for the distribution of some commodity directly from a central installation such as a main factory without the necessity of a regional system of depots or warehouse. Reserves may be pooled at a central location. The total reserves needed may thereby be reduced. If there is a probability of 1 out of 100 that a given item will be needed on any

36. Howard T. Lewis, James W. Culliton, Jack D. Steele, *The Role of Air Freight in Physical Distribution*, Graduate School of Business Administration, Harvard University, 1956.
37. *Air Cargo*, "1965 Air Freight Survey," June 1965.

day in any one region, a spare may be kept. Two regions would need two spares. If the reserves are pooled, the probability that both would need the item the same day is low, only .01 times .01 or .0001. One spare will still suffice, for a saving in size of needed inventory (in this example) of 50 per cent. Here the cost comparison would be between the cost of shipment by rail or by truck or by water plus the use of the warehouse system and the cost of the air freight.[38]

Among the commodities that move regularly by air freight there are some commodities that are perishable and would not move at all by any other method of transportation. Cut flowers may move from a warm or tropical climate to a market in centers such as New York during the winter months. Speed is essential in delivery of the flowers in attractive condition. Fresh fruits and vegetables present similar characteristics. Recently planeloads of ten-day-old calves have been shipped to Europe. By sea the mortality would be prohibitively high.

Information may be needed quickly. If it is not perishable, it may have a high rate of obsolescence. Daily newspapers fall in value with the passage of time at an alarming rate. Something of the kind may happen to other kinds of printed matter, such as advertising displays designed to be used in the context of a particular sales campaign.

Commodities may also move by air in areas where there is no existing service by land or sea, or where such service is extremely difficult. An example of this type of use of air freight is flying in construction machinery and supplies to sites in the northern Canadian wilderness, as was done in the development of the Labrador iron deposits.

Finally, air shipment may be less expensive because of costs directly associated with the shipment other than the direct payment to the carrier. Packing costs may be less, breakage and pilferage may be smaller. Insurance costs may be lower. It is total transfer costs that are relevant. There will be some saving in cost of carrying a stock of goods while in transit as the speed of movement is increased. All of these advantages of air freight derive from the general economic functions of transportation of Chapter 2.

IMPACT OF TECHNOLOGICAL CHANGE—The development of jet powered air transport in the 1960s is having a dramatic effect on air freight. The larger, faster, and more economical aircraft are lowering the cost of shipment. Over the decade the decline seems likely to be on the order of 50 per cent or more, from over 20 cents to perhaps as low as 10 cents per ton-mile.

38. For a discussion of the logic of pooled reserves see P. Sargant Florence, *The Logic of British and American Industry,* Routledge and K. Paul, 1953.

The movement of air cargo takes two forms. Large passenger jets can handle up to 20,000 pounds of freight in addition to passengers, roughly the equivalent of a truckload. The jet freighters handle up to 96,000 pounds, or 48 tons, roughly the equivalent of a freight car. The reduced rates associated with this equipment have been leading to large annual percentage increases in air cargo. How far this impetus will carry the industry is one of the interesting and difficult problems of forecasting developments in transportation.[39]

39. For an example of a forecast of air cargo see Stanley H. Brewer, *A Projection of Air Cargo Growth Rates for the Port of New York Authority Airports, 1960–1980,* Seattle, 1960.

17

Marine Transport

PUBLIC POLICY toward international ocean shipping involves both economic and military objectives, but traditionally the military considerations have been dominant. Twice in the twentieth century the United States has been engaged in world conflicts in which it became a matter of urgent necessity to construct and operate a large fleet of merchant ships. The country found that it needed not only ships, but trained personnel to operate the ships, and shipyards capable of the construction of additional vessels.

Economic objectives have never been entirely absent from discussions of American policy toward ocean shipping, however, and are increasingly stressed. The development of American shipping has been seen as leading to development of the foreign trade of the country. In recent years considerations of the balance of payments on international account have become important. It is an objective of American economic policy to reduce or eliminate the deficit that has emerged in the American balance of payments. The United States has been concerned also with assisting the economic development of the free world. Although less stress has been laid on the point in public discussion, there is a logical connection between the economic development of the free world and the development of shipping on the oceans which constitute the principal avenues of trade among nations lacking common boundaries.

American policy, as it has developed, has employed both promotional and regulatory methods to achieve its goals. The main effort, however, has been subsidies, which in the large have been directed toward military rather than economic objectives. The regulatory legislation has been of secondary importance.

There have been frequent expressions of general dissatisfaction with American policy toward ocean shipping in recent years from sources in the industry as well as from Congress and the executive branch of the government and also people in academic life. A general review both of the objectives of policy and of the instruments needed to achieve those objectives under modern conditions appears to be needed. The problems are difficult from the American point of view because of the international character of an industry that involves the vital interests of many nations. It is not possible to proceed as if the entire problem were one of the internal, domestic affairs of the nation. Furthermore, the American shipping industry is weak in contrast to the strong position of the American international air carriers.

The discussion that follows begins with an introductory description of the nature and costs of the marine transportation industry. The shipping conferences, international cartels which dominate ocean shipping, are then discussed. The final section of the chapter reviews the main features of American maritime policy.

Nature and Costs of Marine Transport

LINERS AND TRAMPS—Ocean-going merchant vessels fall into three broad categories: passenger vessels, under which head may be included combination passenger and cargo carriers; freighters; and tankers. Of these the most numerous and economically the most important are the freighters. Freighters may be divided, on the basis of the use to which they are put, into two categories, liners, that is, common carriers engaged in scheduled service, and tramps, which seek for cargoes wherever they can be found. The United States maintains in reserve a fleet of inactive ships left over from World War II. If these ships are left out of account, the active United States-flag merchant fleet engaged in foreign trade contains about 615 vessels distributed as follows:[1]

1. Quoted by Committee of American Steamship Lines, *Financial and Economic Data on the American Merchant Marine and the Shipping Fleets of Other Nations*, p. 4, based on data from the United States Department of Commerce, Maritime Administration, September 1963. As of December 31, 1964, the total United States fleet of ocean-going ships of 1,000 gross tons and over was 2,529 vessels of which 1,512 were in the reserve fleet. See United States Department of Commerce, Maritime Administration, *Merchant Fleets of the World*.

Type of Vessel	NUMBER OF SHIPS		GROSS TONNAGE (IN THOUSANDS)	
	Number	Per Cent	Number of Tons	Per Cent
Passenger and combination vessels	31	5	450	8
Freighters				
Liners	425	69	3550	61
Tramps	114	19	1100	19
Tankers	45	7	675	12
	615	100	5775	100

On a tonnage basis freighters account for about 80 per cent of the active United States-flag fleet, and about three out of four of these freighters are liners. The distribution of United States-flag vessels in international trade by type and employment is strongly influenced by public policy. For the world as a whole freighters account for about two-thirds of the number of all ocean-going ships.

FLAGS OF CONVENIENCE—The preceding statistics, it may be noted, refer to United States-flag vessels. There are substantial numbers of United States owned vessels that are operated under foreign flags, flags of convenience. Most of these ships are registered under the flags of Panama, Liberia, and Honduras. The Department of Defense has taken the view that these United States owned ships are actually under the effective control of the United States. Ships owned by United States nationals but registered under the flags of other N.A.T.O. powers are regarded as a secondary reserve. The use of the registry of the three small countries has been under pressure from labor unions and from the European maritime powers. The purpose of the arrangement from the owners' point of view has been to permit the use of foreign crews paid at foreign wage rates that may be on the order of one-fourth of the United States rates. Many ships in these fleets were United States vessels transferred or sometimes sold to foreign owners with the approval of the United States Government under restrictions intended to keep them under effective United States control in the event of a national emergency. Many of the ships were purchased from foreign builders whose costs are substantially below those in the United States. In the following discussion United States owned ships under foreign registry are not considered. From the point of view of American national interests these arrangements are at best a method of adaptation to a basically unsatisfactory situation.[2]

2. As of December 31, 1964, the Liberian fleet exceeded the United States active fleet and nearly equalled the fleet of the United Kingdom, the largest in the world, in cargo carrying capacity! *Merchant Fleets of the World*, pp. 4–5. Of course, the Liberian fleet is owned by nationals of many different nations.

S. S. Warrior STUDY AND THE COST OF OCEAN SHIPPING—The most satisfactory introduction to the cost of ocean shipping may be to report a detailed investigation of one actual voyage, an investigation which was undertaken by the Maritime Cargo Transportation Conference of the National Research Council and published in 1954.[3] The *S. S. Warrior* was a modified C-2 vessel under time charter to the Military Sea Transportation Service in March 1954. (Vessels may be hired for some special employment under a "charter-party." The agreement may be for a single voyage, or a period of time. It may be a bare boat charter that covers simply the vessel itself.) The *S. S. Warrior*, however, was being operated under a system by which the vessel and its crew were under time charter to the Military Sea Transportation Service.

The vessel was of a type in general use, and one which still is in general use, and the cargo was believed to be a general cargo reasonably representative of average mixed cargos in foreign trade. The *Warrior* is a five hatch ship with a rated load displacement of 14,950 tons. The light weight of the ship is 4,345 tons leaving a deadweight carrying capacity of 10,605 tons. The amount actually loaded on the ship was 5,015 long tons, or 11,200 measurement tons. A long ton is 2,240 pounds. Measurement tons require a more complex explanation. The capacity of a vessel is limited in cubic volume as well as in weight. A ship must be considered fully loaded either if the space available for cargo is filled or if the weight of the cargo is the maximum the ship can carry. The practice has developed of using as a basis for charging cargo tons that are defined in a manner specifying a relation between weight and volume. An underlying relationship is that one ton of sea water (2,240 lbs.) fills 35 cubic feet. On the East coast the practice is to equate 40 cubic feet of cargo to 2,240 pounds, on the West coast 40 cubic feet to 2,000 pounds, while in foreign ships the customary equivalence is between 35.3 cubic feet and 2,204.6 pounds or one cubic meter per metric ton. Freight quotations may provide that the ship has the option of charging freight on the weight or the measurement, vessel's choice. The statistics just shown indicate that the *Warrior* was carrying light-density cargo, that is, the number of measurement tons was more than twice the number of long tons of weight. (Railroads handle the same basic problem by varying freight rates rather than varying the system of counting tons.)

3. *The S. S. Warrior, An Analysis of an Export Transportation System from Shipper to Consignee,* November 30, 1954. The Maritime Cargo Conference, National Academy of Sciences, National Research Council, Publication 339.

The analysis of the movement divided the transportation of the cargo into seven segments.

1. *Domestic movement:* The assembly of the cargo of the *S. S. Warrior* involved some 1,156 shipments to cover the 5,015 long tons. A total of 2,231 long tons moved to the port by rail. Allowing 32 tons to the car, which was the 1952 national average, that amount of freight is the equivalent of 78 loaded rail cars. A total of 2,277 long tons moved to port by truck. That is equivalent to 252 truck loads at 9.01 tons to the truck, which is also an estimated 1952 national average. The remaining 507 tons were generated in warehouses within the port and moved to the ship either by lighters or by rail to lighters and from the lighters to the ship.

These statistics emphasize one of the main characteristics of ships. A ship is a large unit of operation, and transportation of a mixed cargo involves a substantial outlay for assembling the freight.

2. *Receipt and storage:* The assembly operation implies a warehousing operation in which the freight from these various sources was brought together and stored until the complete shipload could be assembled. This stage also involved the organization of much of the freight on pallets. This operation involves attaching the cartons or boxes or other individual pieces of freight to a small platform called a pallet. Freight and pallet can then be moved as a unit in subsequent operations.

3. *Loading:* The next stage in the operation was the loading of the cargo on its pallets into the ship. The in-shore cargo was entirely palletized. Some vehicles were loaded from lighters that came alongside the off-shore side of the ship, and these were not secured to pallets.

4. *Voyage:* The next stage in the movement was the voyage itself. The ship had a designed speed of 15.5 knots. The trip from New York to Germany actually took 10 days, 13 hours from berth to berth, for average speed of 14.6 knots. This time would vary somewhat for the same route from voyage to voyage depending on the weather conditions prevailing and on whether the vessel chose the optimum route through the weather configuration taking into account the ocean currents and the traffic rules governing the movement of ships.

5. *Discharging:* Discharge of 78 per cent of the cargo was to rail cars, which were brought directly alongside the ship at the berth in Germany or reached through the pier loading shed. The remainder was mostly stored in a pier shed for later forwarding. This phase of the movement was completed with the setting down of the cargo on the rail car or other vehicle or the pier.

6. *Receipt and handling:* This phase of the movement is the equiva-

lent in reverse of the receipt and storage stage, which is the second segment of the movement. It includes the cost of checkers to tally the cargo and the cost of the quayside gangs who received the cargo from the vessel.

7. *Delivery:* In this case delivery was almost entirely by rail. Some 99.4 per cent of the cargo of this ship moved to its final destination by rail in Europe.

A breakdown of the cost of movement into these seven segments is shown in the accompanying table:

System Segment	Total Cost (dollars)	Per Cent	Cost/Long Ton-Mile (dollars)	Cost/Long Ton (dollars)
1. Domestic movement	88,957	37	0.0670	—
2. Receipt and storage	14,827	6	—	3.16
3. Loading	41,292	18	—	8.23
4. Voyage	27,297	12	.001	—
5. Discharging	18,185	8	—	3.63
6. Receipt and handling	12,962	5	—	2.58
7. Delivery	34,057	14	0.0206	—
	237,577	100	.0098	47.37

The total cost was 237,577 dollars. Of that amount only 12 per cent represented cost of the voyage itself. The costs of the actual voyage were only about one-tenth of a cent per long ton-mile.

The cost of loading alone substantially exceeded the cost of the voyage proper, while the cost of discharging the cargo, though smaller, was equal to about two-thirds of the cost of the voyage. Omitting inland movement at both ends, the combined cost of receipt and storage, loading, discharging, and receipt and handling was more than three times the cost of the voyage. These costs represent an allocation of total costs. The cost of loading, for example, includes the cost of the vessel and crew while loading was taking place.

The cost of movement of the cargo within the United States prior to arrival at the dockside and of delivery of the cargo at the foreign destination is in part independent of the cost of the ocean transport. Nevertheless, it cannot be treated as entirely separate. The packaging of the cargo and the use of such devices as pallets and containers may affect the cost of these segments of the total transport system as well as the cost of stages two through six.

Another result of this study that deserves emphasis was the slowness of the movement. The weighted average time for the segments of cargo was estimated at 32.7 days from the domestic origin to the foreign destination of the individual shipments. The slowest time was 97 days.

These periods are much longer than the elapsed time of the voyage it-self, which, it will be recalled, was 10.5 days. The average shipment was three times as long in transit.

It was a main conclusion of the research project that the best chances for reductions in cost in the long run were in the "process" segments, that is, segments 2, 3, 5, and 6, especially "receipt and storage" and "loading." The results make clear the economic reasons for the development of containers and the rationalization and automa-tion of the handling of cargo. In addition, the data emphasize the im-portance of terminal costs in ocean transportation. Taking items 2, 3, 5, and 6, as terminal costs, and item 4 as line-haul cost, it appears that terminal costs were about three times line-haul costs on a voyage of over 3,000 miles. Even for railroads, which have heavy terminal costs, it will be recalled that a typical relationship would be terminal costs equal to line haul costs for a movement of roughly 300 miles.

The terminal costs obviously varied with the number of tons of cargo handled. The voyage costs, however, were not to any major extent a function of the type or quantity of cargo. These costs depend primarily on the type of vessel and the voyage to be made rather than upon how heavily laden the vessel may be.

ADDITIONAL OBSERVATIONS ABOUT COSTS—The fact that voyage costs are largely fixed independently of the cargo carried is of impor-tance for understanding the market for shipping services. Since the marginal cost of carrying extra cargo up to the capacity of the vessel is small, there will be economic pressure on the operators of a ship to accept extra cargo at any price in excess of the handling costs for the marginal cargo. This pressure may be expected to be felt in periods of excess capacity.

The industry does in fact suffer from chronic excess capacity in-terrupted by intervals of high demand. When demand shifts, capacity responds slowly. Increases require new construction. Reductions in capacity are especially slow because the lifetime of a ship is twenty years or perhaps even longer. There will be little immediate reduction in the supply of shipping in response to a reduction in shipping require-ments.

DEMAND FOR OCEAN SHIPPING—The demand for ocean shipping tends to fluctuate depending on political events. Wars and political crises tend to create sharp increases in the demand for shipping. Since the supply of vessels is inelastic in the short run, shortages of shipping are reflected in upward pressure on prices. The most sensitive prices are the rates for chartering vessels. During the Korean Crisis of 1951–1952, charter rates in the world market for dry cargo vessels reached a level more than twice that prevailing in 1949. The Suez Crisis in 1956 also led to a temporary jump in charter rates.

The long run trend in the demand for ocean shipping in periods when there is no crisis has been upward as the volume of international trade has increased.

The demand for ocean shipping is generally believed to be insensitive to price in the short run. The volume of goods available for export from a given port to another port is not likely to respond rapidly to changes in freight rates such as might result from the appearance of additional ships ready to take on cargo on the trade route in question.

Market Practices in Ocean Shipping

Market practices in the ocean shipping industry have developed around a system of shipping conferences. The following discussion concerns the nature of these conferences, restrictive practices in the market for ocean shipping, and the economic effects of the conferences.

NATURE OF SHIPPING CONFERENCES—As early as the latter part of the nineteenth century, shipping conferences developed in the ocean shipping industry.[4] The first conferences appeared in 1875 in the trade between India and the United Kingdom. The system is worldwide. A shipping conference is essentially an agreement among the shipping lines engaged in a particular trade. The conferences agree on rate schedules. They may allow "open" rates on some items on which there is no agreement. To make an agreement is not enough, however, the agreement must be enforced. The conferences, therefore, engage in restrictive practices designed to prevent entry of competitors into their respective trades.

RESTRICTIVE PRACTICES—There are three competitive practices that have developed out of the desire to enforce agreements and prevent rate cutting. "Fighting ships" are vessels used for the purpose of driving another carrier out of a particular trade. When a vessel of the firm under attack is loading for a particular voyage, the fighting ship is also announced as preparing to make that voyage, and as ready to accept cargo at ruinously low rates. The losses involved will then be distributed among the members of the conference.

The "deferred rebate" is a device to make it worthwhile for a shipper to be loyal to the conference. A rebate of, say, 5 to 10 per cent,

4. For a general discussion of the conferences, see Daniel Marx, Jr., *International Shipping Cartels,* Princeton University Press, 1953.

is allowed, on shipments over a certain number of months, say three, six, or twelve months. The rebate is not paid for three to six months after the period in question. If the shipper patronizes an outsider he loses the deferred rebate. He also accrues no rebate on any other shipments he may be making with conference ships in the interval. Thus, he is under heavy financial pressure not to do any bargain hunting for low rates. Special arrangements for individual voyages lose attractiveness to the shipper. Both of the above practices are illegal in United States trades, and have been illegal since the *Shipping Act* of 1916.

The third practice, the use of a dual rate system, has a more complex legal history. The practice is one by which a conference establishes rates at two levels, the lower of which is charged to merchants who agree to ship their cargoes on vessels of members of the conference only and the higher of which is charged to merchants who do not so agree. If dual rates were also forbidden, the position of the conferences would be greatly weakened. Congress in 1961 amended the *Shipping Act* of 1916 to permit dual rate contracts with spread of up to 15 per cent of the ordinary rate.[5] Thus, the conferences have Congressional approval.

ECONOMIC EFFECTS OF SHIPPING CONFERENCES—The shipping conferences traditionally have operated under conditions of secrecy, revealing no more about their operations than they have been legally required to make public. Until recently, much of what was known about their operations dated back to investigations conducted in Great Britain by a Royal Commission on Shipping Rings which reported in 1909; and to an investigation by a committee of the House of Representatives of this country known as the Alexander Committee in 1914.[6] Recently there has been renewed interest by committees of the Congress, notably the Joint Economic Committee under the chairmanship of Senator Paul Douglas.[7] The Joint Economic Committee has made a series of complaints about the conferences from the American point of view. First, the Committee charges that the international ocean freight rate structure has been weighted against United States exports. Exports rather than imports bear most of the cost of shipping. In substantiation of this statement the committee had extensive statistical studies conducted by government agencies. It found, for example, that on trade between the Pacific Coast of the United States and the Far East freight rates were higher outbound than inbound on 80 per cent of items sampled. For

5. The *Bonner Act*, 1961, 75 Stat. 762.

6. See Marx, *op. cit.*, for information about these investigations.

7. *Discriminatory Ocean Freight Rates and the Balance of Payments,* Report of the Joint Economic Committee, Congress of the United States, 89th Congress, 1st Session, Report No. 1, January 6, 1965.

example, on canned goods the outbound rate was $47.50 and the inbound rate $22.75.[8] These rates, however, are not necessarily those actually charged owing to the possibility of secret rebates, which were found by earlier Congressional investigations in 1962. Foreign-flag lines have resisted disclosing rates actually charged. The leading United States operator on the route from the United States North Atlantic coast to the Far East was found to be charging rates outbound almost high enough to permit him to return in ballast and not lose money.

The second complaint deals with what is known as "third-market discrimination." The Committee found evidence that it costs more to ship comparable products to markets in South America, Africa, and India from the United States than from Europe and Japan. A sample of rates were studied for forty export commodities. For these commodities, average rates per ton-mile were computed exclusive of cargo handling, which reportedly costs $12.88 per ton in New York compared to $5.67 in Rotterdam and only $2.50 in Yokohama. Net of these charges United States rates per ton-mile were 85 per cent higher than rates from Europe and 138 per cent higher than rates from Japan.[9] The effect on the competitive position of American exporters hardly needs emphasis.

Within the conferences the United States lines are not likely to be in a strong bargaining position. They carry only a small fraction of total United States trade, about one-tenth, and possess a correspondingly small fraction of the shipping capacity of the conferences. It was the Joint Committee's view that the American lines should withdraw from the conferences. This view as to American policy is also that taken in the most recent comprehensive economic monograph on the industry by Allen R. Ferguson and associates.[10] A comprehensive evaluation of the conferences from a world point of view is impossible without more information than is now available.

An impression of the importance of the issues involved may be gained from a comparison of ocean freight rates with tariffs. Ocean freight rates average 12 per cent of the value of United States exports and 10 per cent of imports. Tariffs average 7 per cent of the value of imports.[11] The freight rates on the average, thus, are the larger of the two.

8. *Discriminatory Ocean Freight Rates, op. cit.,* p. 14.

9. *Ibid.,* pp. 18–19.

10. Allen R. Ferguson, *et al., The Economic Value of the United States Merchant Marine,* Northwestern University, Transportation Center, 1961. Marx, writing in 1953, was more tolerant of the conferences.

11. *Discriminatory Ocean Freight Rates, op. cit.,* p. 9. Data for 1962.

American Maritime Policy

The great days of American shipping were the days of wooden ships and sail. The gradual disappearance of the American merchant marine from the seas had reached such a point during World War I that the country was forced to rely on foreign shipping at extremely high rates and to make an attempt to construct a merchant marine of its own in a hurry. The circumstances proved extremely difficult and led to the delivery of the ships, for the most part, after the conclusion of the conflict.

In an effort to avoid a repetition of this fiasco, modern American policy started afresh with new legislation in 1936. Although the policy of using public funds for the merchant marine had its origins in 1916, the modern system of direct cash subsidy dates from 1936. The declaration of policy in that legislation is still the official foundation of American maritime policy. It reads as follows:[12]

Title I–Declaration of Policy

It is necessary for the national defense and development of its foreign and domestic commerce that the United States shall have a merchant marine (a) sufficient to carry its domestic water-borne commerce and a substantial portion of the water-borne export and import foreign commerce of the United States and to provide shipping service on all routes essential for maintaining the flow of such domestic and foreign water-borne commerce at all times, (b) capable of serving as a naval and military auxiliary in time of war or national emergency, (c) owned and operated under the United States flag by citizens of the United States in so far as may be practicable, and (d) composed of the best-equipped, safest, and most suitable types of vessels, constructed in the United States and manned with a trained and efficient citizen personnel. It is hereby declared to be the policy of the United States to foster the development and encourage the maintenance of such a merchant marine.

The policy established under this act was notably successful in World War II. In large part as a result of the activities of the United States Maritime Commission, predecessor of the present organization, a total of ninety-five ships were delivered in 1941 immediately prior to American entry into the war. Those ships and the facilities developed to construct them proved invaluable. As a result in part of this preparation it was possible to deliver over 4,000 merchant ships in the course of World War II.

There has been a succession of public agencies concerned with mari-

12. 49 Stat. 1985, approved Je. 29, 1936.

time policy since the United States Shipping Board was set up in 1916. It was followed by the United States Maritime Commission in 1936. Currently, there are two federal agencies concerned with the subject, the Maritime Administration and the Federal Maritime Commission.

MARITIME ADMINISTRATION—The Maritime Administration was set up in 1950 in the Department of Commerce as one of the successor agencies to the United States Maritime Commission. Its responsibilities are essentially promotional. It is the agency which administers the program of subsidies to the merchant marine. It has custody of the inactive fleet of 1,500 ships maintained as the National Defense Reserve Fleet. It also has responsibility for a modest research and development program and is the owner of the famous nuclear-powered NS *Savannah*.

FEDERAL MARITIME COMMISSION—The Maritime Commission in its present form dates from a reorganization in 1961. Its responsibility is regulatory. The Commission is composed of five members appointed by the President of the United States with the usual provision for the consent of the Senate. Its areas of responsibility include regulation of common carriers by water engaged in the foreign commerce of the United States. It is the agency with which tariffs are filed by shipping conferences, and it has responsibility for investigation of discriminatory rates and practices as well as for regulation of rates. It is also the agency under attack by the Joint Economic Committee in the report cited in the previous section, in the course of which the Committee observed: "Although the Shipping Act, which provides for conference regulation, was adopted almost 50 years ago, the regulation of steamship conferences has never been carried out in the manner intended by Congress. . . . The statutory powers are ample and have been strengthened as recently as 1961, but their enforcement has been grossly inadequate."[13] Whatever the inadequacies of the Commission, it seems fair to add that the Congress itself has not been beyond criticism in the field of maritime policy, as will be developed below.

The discussion which follows will review the methods presently used by the United States to stimulate ocean transport. These methods include the reservation of the coastal trade, operating subsidies, construction subsidies, cargo preference laws, and other policies affecting marine transport.

RESERVATION OF THE COASTAL TRADE—The policy of cabotage, or reserving the coastal trade to American shipping, dates from as early as 1808. The restriction has been extended to the intercoastal trade and the

13. *Discriminatory Ocean Freight Rates, op. cit.,* p. 5.

trade to noncontiguous areas: Alaska, Hawaii, and Puerto Rico. In these trades the only competition the shipping companies have had to face has been from American operators of other modes of transportation.

There has been no active opposition to the policy of restricting the coastwise and intercoastal trades to American operators. There has been controversy, however, concerning the role of Canadian ships on the Great Lakes and concerning the treatment of the trades with noncontiguous areas. There have been complaints by the residents of those areas, especially of Puerto Rico, that the economy of the island is at a disadvantage because of the legal requirement of the use of unsubsidized, high cost American shipping. They argue that either there should be more subsidized service between the United States and the islands, or the islanders should be permitted to make use of the low cost foreign operators. (Subsidized ships do make a limited number of calls at Honolulu.) As matters now stand they feel that they are being called upon to bear the expense of a merchant marine that is intended not for their special benefit but for the general advantage of the United States, with special emphasis on military preparedness. Why should this part of the cost of national defense be borne disproportionately by the inhabitants of the outlying possessions? The most satisfactory answer to these complaints, of course, would be to reduce the cost of American shipping to a level competitive with other maritime nations. But to the extent that such cost reductions are not possible, there is a real question whether the policy of subsidy should not be extended to the trades with noncontiguous areas.

In recent years American operators have abandoned the package freight business on the Great Lakes. It is difficult to see how the reservation of this trade to American ships to the exclusion of the Canadians either promotes American shipping or serves the defense of the United States.[14]

OPERATING SUBSIDIES—Operating differential subsidies are intended to cover the difference between American and foreign costs of operation. Most importantly, the operating subsidies cover the difference in wages paid to ship personnel. The details of calculation are complex. The subsidy covers wages, subsistence, maintenance, and repairs, and insurance, but not fuel. Comparisons are made of monthly wage costs per ship for the American vessel with the weighted average of all foreign competitors on the route. Roughly speaking the subsidy has been estimated to amount to about 50 per cent of total operating costs on a domestic cost

14. See Daniel O. Fletcher, *A Study of Package Freight Carriers on the Great Lakes,* unpublished doctoral dissertation, University of Michigan, 1960.

basis over the period 1947 to 1961. The subsidies allow for profits that may average about 10 per cent of the "capital necessarily employed" by the operators. The law includes recapture rights if profits are excessive. Half of the excess may be recaptured by the government. There is also provision for re-recapture by the shipping companies if later earnings fall below 10 per cent.

How much money is involved? The estimation of the amount of subsidy is a confusing topic for investigation. The subsidy accrued is not the subsidy paid in any given period, there being a lag in payments, and the recapture and re-recapture provisions may lead to changes that are retroactive. The approximate amount of money involved in the subsidy is indicated by the fact that as of June 30, 1960 some 969 million dollars in net advance subsidy payments had been made through the period from 1947 through June 30, 1960. Since that time payments have been increasing and are around 200 million dollars a year.

Operating differential subsidies have been paid to 14–16 companies in recent years. Those eligible are only operators who are engaged in water borne commerce on designated essential trade routes. The essential routes seem to be selected primarily on the basis of the volume of trade that moves on the routes. Political considerations also may enter. The subsidized operators must provide regular service with a stated minimum and maximum number of sailings. They also must man the ships with United States citizens and meet secondary requirements such as repairing the ships in United States yards. Note that this policy denies operating subsidies to American tramp shipping companies. Tankers and ships in the coastal trades also are not included.

This system of subsidies has been criticized in several respects. First, it offers little incentive to the ship operators to economize on labor. In effect, they are able to buy labor at low foreign wage rates. The Maritime Administration alone stands to gain from reductions in the monthly wage bill resulting from automation.

In general, a system of subsidies with recapture and re-recapture reduces the incentive to reduce costs. Why should the operator work hard to cut costs when the government, not the operator, reaps most of the benefits? From this point of view a system of closed subsidies, such as that used by the C.A.B., appears much more likely to achieve its objective.

Also, the restriction of the subsidized operators to the designated essential trade routes has been criticized as unnecessarily rigid. The Joint Economic Committee has uncovered instances in which the volume of trade on a route has changed without corresponding adjustment of capacity. For example, one contract in 1957 provided for 150 sailings a year between United States North Atlantic ports and Venezuela. The volume of trade with Venezuela fell by 58 per cent after the contract was negotiated, but the contract was not changed until the situation was called to the attention of the Maritime Administration by a member of the Committee.[15]

Finally, objection has been made to the rule that *all* seamen must be citizens. From the point of view of national defense it is not necessary that all unskilled workers be Americans.[16]

CONSTRUCTION SUBSIDIES—The construction differential policy administered by the Federal Maritime Board at present allows for a subsidy up to as much as 60 per cent of the cost of a commercial vessel. The basis for estimating the amount of the subsidy is a comparison of the cost of construction in the United States and abroad—a difference which is not easy to estimate. The subsidy also covers national defense features included in the plans. The specifications must be approved by the Maritime Administration. The purpose is to provide the assistance necessary to assure the replacement of at least some of the obsolete ships in the American merchant marine with new and modern types of ships in such a manner as to maintain a minimum mobilization base of shipyard facilities including the necessary trained shipyard personnel.

The total amount of money involved in the construction differential subsidies is substantial. From 1947 to 1958 the total new construction under the provisions of the legislation came to 501 million dollars, of which 207 million dollars was met by the subsidy plus 32 million dollars allowance for national defense features in ship design. A major problem in American maritime policy in the 1960s has been the "block obsolescence" of the merchant fleet. Since a large number of ships were constructed during World War II, and the normal life of a ship is about twenty years, most of the fleet built in 1943–1945 had a presumptive retirement date of 1963–1965. The policy of the Maritime Administration has been to try to even out the replacement program. By allowing ships to remain in use for twenty-five years, thus stretching out the replacement period, the cost to the Administration has been held to the level of roughly 100 million dollars a year.[17] The aid given includes, in addition to the construction–differential subsidy, trade-in allowances on old ships, government guarantees of mortgage bonds covering up to

15. *Discriminatory Ocean Freight Rates, op. cit.,* p. 43.

16. See Ferguson, et al., *op. cit.*

17. For fiscal 1962 the cost of the construction differential was 141 million dollars; for 1963, 94 million dollars.

75 per cent of the cost to the operator, and certain special forms of tax relief to subsidized operators in connection with new ship construction.

The construction-differential subsidy is primarily of assistance to the shipyards. The ship operators in the absence of government intervention could purchase ships from foreign shipyards, presumably at the same prices as the prices they now pay net of the subsidy.

There are anomalies in the working of this program, as the two subsidies are taken together. It is to the interest of the operator of a subsidized ship to have the ship constructed to economize on fuel costs. Since the fuel is not included in the operating subsidy but the cost of construction is half borne by the government, there is pressure to over-design the ship to save fuel. The interests of the Maritime Administration and the operator also conflict in regard to automation as already noted. The subsidized operator has no reason to favor capital outlays designed to save wages.

In 1963 the Maritime Administration nevertheless announced a revision of its standards to encourage and even require automation. In the spring of 1964 the first vessel built under the new policy was launched; the *Mormacvega* is planned to carry a crew of thirty-four, in contrast to the fifty said to be needed on a nonautomated vessel of similar size.

Direct pressure is one way to achieve results. Indirect methods which would change the incentive system have also been proposed. One scheme, for example, would have the Government build the ships and retain title to them. It would then charter them to the operators under a system of competitive bidding. There would be no operating subsidy system. The Government, of course, would show a loss on the ships. Such a system, however, would be much simpler to administer than that now in use.[18]

CARGO PREFERENCE LAWS—The objective of the cargo preference legislation is to reserve to American ship operators half of the volume of shipments abroad under the foreign aid programs which have been adopted by the United States in the postwar period. The basic legislation concerning cargo preference is Public Law 664, August 26, 1954.[19] The law provides that at least 50 per cent of the shipments shall be transported on privately owned United States-flag commercial vessels. The total volume of trade effected is about 6 per cent of total United States trade. Thus, the net effect of the law is to reserve about 3 or 4

18. *Proposed Program for Maritime Administration Research,* Maritime Research Advisory Committee, National Academy of Sciences, National Research Council, 1960, p. 37.
19. 68 Stat. 832.

per cent of the total volume of American export trade to American vessels. A large part of this traffic moves in tramp vessels, which tend to specialize in bulk shipments, such as shipments of grain from American agricultural surpluses. This legislation has been the mainstay of American tramp vessels in recent years. It has been estimated that they are dependent on government cargoes for more than 80 per cent of their business. There seems little reason to doubt that American tramp shipping would disappear from the oceans without it, in the same manner in which American tramp shipping did disappear in the years subsequent to World War I.

It is the contention of the Joint Economic Committee that this policy carries with it the risk that the United States Government will find itself paying exorbitant rates. The matter came to national prominence in the Kennedy Administration when Soviet Russia objected to paying about 26 dollars per ton to move wheat to Russia when the rate on foreign vessels averaged under 15 dollars per ton. This situation illustrates again the difficulties which must continue to arise as long as the American merchant marine is not economically competitive.

NEED FOR NEW POLICIES—Maritime policy appears to be due for a thorough reconsideration. The range of basic choices of objectives is limited. Military considerations still seem to rule out complete withdrawal from the high seas. A possible minimum public commitment would be to determine military needs as closely as possible in light of the new technology of war, meet those needs as a part of the cost of defense, and make no public effort to develop the American merchant marine beyond that point. In view of the high costs both of construction in the United States and of operation of vessels using American crews, the result of such a policy would be a sharp reduction in commercial American shipping.

The position that this country should let other nations carry its overseas trade has had an attraction for many economists. They have argued that in the ocean shipping industry other nations have a comparative advantage. It is efficient, therefore, to allow them to specialize in this activity while the United States specializes in other economic activities in which it has a comparative advantage.

This argument, however, was more impressive in the period when the United States enjoyed a surplus in its balance of international payments. In a period of chronic deficits it is difficult to be quite so relaxed about turning over the carrying trade of the nation to others. The ocean shipping industry is important in the context of the balance of payments for two reasons. Direct payments for the carriage of freight and passengers, which result in dollar earnings of about 900 million dollars a year,[20] are only part of the story. As developed above, ocean freight rates can have an important effect on the competitive position of basic export industries.

An alternative policy is to make a determined effort to develop an American merchant marine which will be economically competitive. It has been urged by students of the industry that there is in the long run no satisfactory substitute for an economically competitive merchant marine, and that such a merchant marine is a realistic possibility.[21] The benefits from success in such a policy would be considerable. The first gain would be the annual saving in the cash subsidy. Further, it appears that the military requirements are primarily for improved quality of shipping and are reasonably compatible with the requirements of economic success. The military needs for rapid and efficient cargo handling are of this character. The military need for speed may be in excess of the economic need, at least in some types of ships, but higher speeds have commercial advantages.[22] Basic improvements in technology would have other advantages. From an international point of view improved transportation on the high seas offers an opportunity to stimulate international trade with associated benefits to world economic development. In a period when total world trade is expanding increased competition and expansion of the American merchant marine is not likely to lead to any special hardships for other maritime nations.

Effective American competition on the high seas is possible only as the result of a successful program of research and development. The general direction such an effort would have to take is known as a result of work already done. First, the only economically realistic solution to the problem of how to pay the high American wage rates and still compete effectively must be to increase the productivity of labor by automation. There seem to be no insuperable technical obstacles to automation. In fact, one extreme proposal has been sketched out for a vessel that would be entirely unmanned while on the high seas and would use pilots only while in harbors at either end of a voyage.[23] Second, there must be drastic improvements in cargo handling systems. The need for such improvements is shown, for example, by the study of the *S. S. Warrior* summarized above. Again, there do not appear to be insuperable

20. In 1962 all U.S.-flag operators earned $927 million in foreign exchange. See Committee of American Steamship Lines, *Financial and Economic Data on the American Merchant Marine and Ships of Other Nations*, 1964.

21. See especially *Proposed Program for Maritime Administration Research, op. cit.*

22. *Ibid.*, especially pp. 13–15.

23. *Ibid*, pp. 138 ff.

technical obstacles to the development of improved systems. Progress has been made in the direction of developing improved methods based on such methods as the use of containers for general cargo.

The political and administrative obstacles to progress, however, are formidable. Essentially what is required is the consent or, in some respects, the active cooperation of a variety of interest groups in addition to the necessary technical progress. The present institutional arrangements are not well adapted to obtaining that support. The international complications deserve special mention. Large, economical vessels can be used only if channel depths in foreign ports permit them to reach the terminals. Vessels designed to use modern cargo handling systems must make use of foreign terminals which must be compatible with those systems. Foreign customs regulations must permit clearance of goods in containers if containers are to be shipped direct to inland destinations overseas. Effective regulation of shipping conferences must be international. An extreme example of what can happen is in the strong negative reaction of foreign maritime powers to attempts to obtain information about the practices of shipping conferences. In July, 1964, the British Government adopted legislation forbidding British lines to obey American laws.[24] International cooperation in this field, it appears, will not be obtained easily.

24. *Discriminatory Ocean Freight Rates, op. cit.*, p. 32.

18

Transportation by Waterways and Pipelines

THIS CHAPTER is devoted to two important transport agencies: the waterways used for the domestic waterborne commerce of the United States, and oil pipelines. These two, with the railways, highways, and airways, complete the list of the five major transport agencies. Electric transmission lines and natural gas pipelines, which do not compete directly with the other transport agencies, are omitted from this volume.

The total volume of freight moved by inland waterway is about equal to that moved by oil pipeline, and, as noted in Chapter 12, the two together account for about one-third of the total volume of intercity freight traffic. When the deep sea domestic movements along the coasts and to the noncontiguous parts of the United States are also taken into account, which amounted to 313 billion ton-miles in 1962, the total movement by water becomes easily the larger of the two. Waterborne commerce is of broader importance in the markets for transportation than movements by pipeline although the technical feasibility of moving solids by pipeline has been demonstrated. The following discussion will treat of waterborne commerce at greater length.

Transportation by Waterways

The waterways that are used commercially for the movement of passengers and freight between points in the United States follow routes that are to be understood, of course, in the light of the geography of the nation. The system includes, in addition to the Great Lakes and the deep sea routes, a total of about 25,000 miles of navigable inland waterways. These waterways are maintained for the most part by the Corps of Engineers, United States Army. Of the 25,000 miles about 15,000 have a depth of nine feet or more, and 10,000, less than nine feet. The Gulf Intracoastal Waterway and Atlantic Intracoastal Waterway are considered to be parts of the system of inland waterways.[1]

A depth of nine feet is substantially less than is required by ocean-going vessels. The average depth of Atlantic and Gulf ports as of 1960, by way of comparison, was thirty-five feet, with greater depths in the major ports, while the St. Lawrence Seaway has a twenty-seven-foot channel.[2] The total of 25,000 miles of inland waterways may be contrasted with the network of over two and a half million miles of surfaced roads, the 41,000 miles of the Interstate System, the 227,000 miles of railway line in the United States, the 67,000 route miles operated by commercial airlines, or the 155,000 miles of pipelines. By comparison the total number of miles of inland commercial waterway is not large.

The total of 234 billion ton-miles of freight movement on the inland waterways in 1963 was distributed among the systems as follows:

Inland System	Per Cent of Ton-Miles
Atlantic and Gulf Coast waterways	21
Mississippi River System including the Ohio River and tributaries	35
Great Lakes system	41
Pacific coast waterways	3
Total	100

These statistics exclude movements on the oceans and the Gulf of Mexico but include any portion of the voyage of deep-sea vessels on inland rivers, canals, or connecting channels, or on the Great Lakes.

1. See for a description of the inland waterways The American Waterways Operators, Inc., *Big Load Afloat*, 1965, pp. 38–40, pp. 65–99.
2. Harry O. Locher, *Waterways of the United States*. Prepared by the National Association of River and Harbor Contractors, 1963.

The principal commodities carried by water in domestic commerce are as follows:[3]

Commodities	Per Cent of Tons Carried in Domestic Commerce
Petroleum and products	42.6
Coal and coke	18.1
Iron ore and iron and steel	8.6
Sand and gravel	11.9
Grains	2.0
Logs and lumber	3.4
Chemicals	2.8
Seashells	2.7
All other	8.0
Total	100.0

The total system of water transportation is divided by geography, by differences in the type of vessel appropriate under different conditions, and by differences in demand and the nature of competition into a series of separate industries. Vessels used on the Great Lakes differ from those on the oceans, and from those on the river systems. Economically it is important to distinguish private from common and contract carriers, and bulk carriers from those handling a wide range of commodities. (Passenger traffic by water is in general unimportant except on routes to islands and other points not easily accessible by land.) It is possible for traffic to decrease on the New York State Barge Canals at the same time traffic is doubling on the Mississippi River, as in fact happened between 1950 and 1961. What happens to the movement of petroleum from the Gulf ports to the Atlantic seaboard has no particular relation to the rate of development of traffic in iron ore from Labrador up the St. Lawrence River. The movement of grain on the Columbia River system involves yet another range of considerations. In total, however, the waterborne commerce of the United States has been increasing. Domestic waterborne commerce increased from 579 million tons moved in 1947 to 788 million tons moved in 1963, or an increase of 36 per cent over sixteen years.[4]

The issues of public policy related to water transportation fall into three categories. There are questions of investment policy having to do with how much public money to invest in the development of waterways

3. Detail will not add to total owing to rounding. Source: *Waterborne Commerce of the United States, Calendar Year 1963, Part 5, National Summaries*, p. 21, Department of the Army, Corps of Engineers. This report contains extensive data on shipments by water by commodity showing geographic detail.

4. *Ibid.*

and associated questions concerning outlay for maintenance. There are questions of financial policy concerned with how to meet the cost of these activities. And there are questions concerned with whether and in what respects operators of vessels should be subject to economic regulation. In no one of these areas is there a consensus of informed opinion that the basic framework of policy is well established.

INVESTMENT IN WATERWAYS—The total amounts invested in waterways are substantial though naturally much less than the sums invested, say, in roads. Historically, the Corps of Engineers over the period 1824 through June 30, 1959 spent about 5.5 billion dollars, of which 4.9 billion dollars was for work still in use at the close of the period. The latter total was divided about three-fifths for new work and two-fifths for operation and maintenance. The division by area was as follows:

Area	Per Cent
Inland waterways	57
Great Lakes	11
Seacoast harbors	32
Total	100

In a review of the subject in 1960 the Corps of Engineers projected annual expenditures for navigation improvements in the general neighborhood of 350 to 400 million dollars a year rising to 500 million dollars by 1975. (The other agency of the federal government making substantial expenditures relating both to domestic and foreign waterborne commerce is the United States Coast Guard, which in 1960 projected annual expenditures rising from the then current level of 234 million dollars to 412 million dollars by 1975.)[5]

At an abstract level the problem of evaluating proposed investments in waterways resembles the problem of evaluating investments in highways. The way is provided by the government in both instances, and the principal beneficiaries are private. There is the difference, however, that the major users of the waterways are the commercial users engaged in the movement of freight while the major users of highways are people driving their own cars. The requirements in terms of depth of channel and length and cross section of locks for commercial users of waterways are more demanding than those of the operators of small boats for recreation. As will be developed below, there are important economies of scale in the operation of large vessels or large numbers of barges in an integrated tow, and the extent to which these economies can be realized

5. "*Doyle Report,*" *National Transportation Policy,* printed for the Committee on Interstate and Foreign Commerce, 87th Congress, 1st session, January 1961, p. 175, p. 177.

depends on the character of the way. These gains are analytically similar to the reduction in fuel consumption and other costs of operation from better roads. In addition, water transportation can be extended only to those points to which waterways have been developed. The gains from the extension of a waterway to shippers who formerly used a more expensive method of transportation may be compared to the gains to shippers by highway from the opening of a more direct route. There has been in recent years a development of interest by economists in analysis of policy with regard to water resources. Reliance on rigorous analysis of gains and benefits has not been characteristic of investment policy in this field. Benefits and costs are computed, but the calculations may overstate benefits and understate costs. And the results of the calculations may influence but do not determine which projects will be authorized and financed by Congress.[6]

FINANCING WATERWAYS—By analogy to the system of highway finance one would expect a system of user charges to finance waterways. The argument in favor of such a system of finance is similar. Traditional practice, however, has been to make no charge and collect no toll for the use of navigable waterways of the United States. There are exceptions to this practice of which the most notable are the Panama Canal and the St. Lawrence Seaway. The latter will be discussed below.

There has been enthusiasm for the idea of a system of user charges for waterways among the representatives of the railroads, and most economists approve the principle. The waterways operators have been less receptive to the idea. They have pressed, however, for the improvement and extension of the system of commercial waterways. A resolution of the issues that has been proposed, notably in the late President Kennedy's *Message on Transportation,* would be to set up a waterway users trust fund to finance expenditures related to navigation by the federal government. The arrangement would be parallel to that already developed for highways.

If such a system is set up, should the primary reliance be on charges that apply over the entire nation such as fuel taxes or on toll charges or other imposts levied on the users of particular waterways? The system of highway finance relies in large part on levies by state and local governments that are spent in the jurisdictions in which they are collected. Even so, as discussed in Chapter 14, there are problems of cross-subsidization. A satisfactory system of user charges for waterways would

6. See the discussion in Clair Wilcox, *Public Policies Toward Business,* Richard D. Irwin, Inc., revised 1960, pp. 821–822.

have to include provisions to prevent a situation in which the users of some of the more important waterways were in effect taxed to provide for the construction of facilities that were of no use to them. A system of tolls would be one way to meet this requirement, but there may be other possibilities analogous to the annual registration fees required of the operators of motor vehicles.[7]

THE ST. LAWRENCE SEAWAY—A brief account of the Seaway may serve both to indicate the type of considerations that influenced a specific major investment in a waterway and to illustrate the financial discipline involved in calculations concerning the economic success of a project when the project is financed through tolls.

The Seaway, which was opened in 1959, consists essentially of a route from Lake Erie to Montreal with a twenty-seven foot channel developed jointly by Canada and the United States. The section of the route for which the United States is responsible is in the upper St. Lawrence River in the vicinity of the Thousand Islands. The St. Lawrence Seaway Development Corporation was set up by the United States to be self-liquidating. Funds were borrowed from the Secretary of the Treasury to be repaid with interest over a period of fifty years. By the end of 1963, when construction was complete and repairs needed in the early years of operation were also complete, the plant of the Corporation in service had a cost of 129 million dollars. Tolls are assessed and collected by the Canadian counterpart, the St. Lawrence Seaway Authority, and divided on an agreed basis that takes into account the unequal expenditures by the two countries, the Canadians receiving the larger share of the revenue.

Revenue has fallen short of expectations, especially revenue in the early years of the Seaway. The schedule of tolls was set up on the basis of a forecast, which may be compared with the actual tonnage as follows:[8]

TONNAGE OF CARGO,
ST. LAWRENCE RIVER SECTION

Calendar Year	Actual	Estimate
1959	20,300,000	25,000,000
1960	20,600,000	29,000,000
1961	23,400,000	33,000,000
1962	25,600,000	37,000,000
1963	30,900,000	41,000,000
1964	39,300,000	45,000,000

7. For one set of proposals see the *Doyle Report, op. cit.,* pp. 197ff.
8. See the *Annual Reports* of the St. Lawrence Seaway Development Corporation.

For the period of 1960 to 1963, thus, the volume of cargo moved through the St. Lawrence River Section, which is the section where tolls are levied, was on the order of nine to eleven million tons below the estimates. What was the reason for the miscalculation?

It is instructive that the difficulty could be foreseen in a volume published in 1959 by T. L. Hills. The book appeared in the year the Seaway opened, which was five years after the decision to construct it. The American legislation providing for the Seaway was dated May 13, 1954. The Seaway was built primarily for two purposes, to provide for the movement of iron ore from Quebec and Labrador to the Great Lakes, and to provide a more economical route for the movement of grain from the Great Lakes to the St. Lawrence. Movement of ocean-going vessels was not so crucial in the decision. Hills assembled estimates made prior to opening of the Seaway of the expected traffic, which are summarized in Table 18.1.[9]

Table 18.1—Advance Estimates of Seaway Traffic Made Prior to Completion
(thousands of tons)

Commodity	ST. LAWRENCE SEAWAY DEVELOPMENT CORP. 1959	1965	CANADIAN DEPARTMENT OF TRADE AND COMMERCE —[2]	GREAT LAKES ST. LAWRENCE ASSOCIATION —[2]	UNITED STATES DEPARTMENT OF COMMERCE Min.[2]	Max.[2]
Grain	12,100		8,200	10,000	6,500	11,500
Iron ore	10,500		20,000	20,000	30,000	37,500
General cargo	6,400		9,876	5,700	11,038	11,038
Other	7,500	—	6,456	10,000	10,240	24,240
Total	36,500	52,000	44,532[1]	45,700	57,778	84,278

1. By 1959 this estimate had been revised downward to 31 million as of April 15, 1965.
2. Hills reports that no precise future date is given for these estimates but 5 to 10 years after opening of the Seaway is implied, which would be 1964 to 1969.

The actual tonnage moved in 1964 was as follows.

Commodity	Tonnage of Cargo, St. Lawrence River Section, 1964 (millions of short tons)
Grain	15
Iron ore	12
General cargo	4
Other	8
Total	39

The estimates of movement of iron ore were much too high, in the range of twenty to thirty million tons as against twelve million. It appears that the projections of American needs for imported iron ore

9. T. L. Hills, *The St. Lawrence Seaway*, Methuen, 1959, p. 135.

grossly overstated the requirements. The decision relied in part upon estimates by the National Resources Board in 1950 of requirements for imported ore. They were influenced by the depletion of the deposits of high grade hematite ore in the Lake Superior region. The estimates were made in advance of successful commercial installations for the working of the extensive taconite ores in the Lake Superior region, and it appears that development was not correctly anticipated.

Note that this error in the estimation of the benefits from an investment in transportation was essentially a miscalculation of technical progress, not in transportation, but in the treatment of iron ore. From the point of view of methodology in investment forecasting, it is interesting to speculate as to what might have been done to make a more accurate forecast. Evidently the only possibility would have been for those making the forecasts to have obtained better information from people well informed about prospective developments in the processing of iron ore.

Fortunately for the economic future of the Seaway the estimates of grain movements were in error in the opposite direction. More accurate estimates of grain movements would have required more accurate analysis of long run developments in the world market for grain and the probable volume of supply of grain in that market from the American and Canadian Great Plains

REGULATION OF INLAND WATER TRANSPORTATION—Economic regulation of the inland waterways is limited in coverage. The basic legislation is the 1940 revision of the Interstate Commerce Act, Part III of which is devoted to carriers by water. Perhaps the most important feature of the legislation is the exclusions. Private carriers by water are exempt, just as private carriers by highway are exempt from regulation. Bulk carriers by water are also exempt. Other common and contract carriers are subject to regulation by the Interstate Commerce Commission. They are required to file rates with the Commission and adhere to the published rates. They are subject to maximum rate control but the Commission does not have power to fix minimum rates. The Commission also has control over entry in the regulated branch of the industry. Thus, since 1940 the I.C.C. has had extensive regulatory power over the common and contract carriers. (Prior to that date less complete regulatory powers were divided between the I.C.C. and the Maritime Commission, with the I.C.C. concerned especially with traffic by rail and water under common management and the Maritime Commission with coastal and intercoastal commerce.)

Why was the regulation of inland waterways extended in 1940? Part of the background of the legislation was a report in 1934 by the Federal Coordinator of Transportation which laid stress on the lack of prosperity of the industry, which he attributed to uncontrolled competition. By 1940 this reasoning was becoming dated as recovery from the depression of the 1930s proceeded. The waterway interests opposed the extension of regulation, evidently doubting that it would make them more prosperous. The more compelling arguments must have been those in favor of government regulation to control industry practices in the interests of shippers by setting maximum rates, preventing unjust discrimination, requiring that published rates be adhered to, and the like.[10]

Whether there is adequate justification for regulation of inland water transportation remains unsettled. There are at least two views of the question, one that regulation should be discontinued, and one that it should be made parallel to economic regulation of railroads since railroads compete with water transportation. Thus, in his *Transportation Message* the late President Kennedy took the position that either minimum rate regulation should apply to the water carriers generally, including bulk carriers, or that it should be discontinued for the railroads. These choices should be evaluated in the light of the economic characteristics of the industry. The reader will recall the position taken in Chapters 13 and 14 that minimum rate regulation is not now needed for the railroads. The question of minimum rate regulation for the waterways must be considered in the light of the economic characteristics of the industry and its place in the total market for transportation.

ECONOMIC CHARACTERISTICS OF INLAND WATER TRANSPORTATION— Economic information about inland water transportation is not easy to assemble. Much of what is available refers only to the part of the industry regulated by the I.C.C. The exception is statistics of output, which, as indicated above, are available in considerable detail by type of commodity and by port from the Corps of Engineers.

The I.C.C. regulates only a small fraction of the companies which operate vessels on inland waterways. In 1965 it was estimated by the American Waterways Operators, Inc., a trade association, that roughly 24 per cent of these companies are engaged in private carriage and 68 per cent in exempt for-hire carriage leaving only 8 per cent which are regulated.[11]

The I.C.C. receives annual reports from about 209 carriers of which about half are very small Class C carriers with annual operating reve-

10. See the discussion in Stuart Daggett, *Principles of Inland Transportation,* Harper & Brothers, fourth edition, 1955, Chapter 32.

11. *Big Load Afloat, op. cit.,* p. 60.

nues under 100,000 dollars. The Class A and B carriers are divided into areas as follows:[12]

Area	Number of Carriers
Atlantic and Gulf Coasts	37
Great Lakes area	14
Mississippi River and tributaries	22
Pacific Coast area	25
Intercoastal area	1
Total	99

It would be helpful to have detailed knowledge of the extent to which all carriers within an area are actually or potentially in competition. As a first approximation, it would appear that there are several moderate sized sellers in each economic market plus fringe competition. Many carriers may operate over the same waterway. In other words the situation is more like that in highway trucking than in the railroad industry. Entry, as previously noted, is controlled by the I.C.C.

There is evidence of important economies of scale in the industry in the size of the individual ship or the individual barge tow. It is less clear that there are important economies in the operation of several ships or several tows by the same carrier. Barge sizes have been standardized at $26' \times 175'$ and $35' \times 195'$, and tows are assembled in multiples which take into account the widths of the locks. (The terminology in the industry contains some curious anachronisms. A "towboat" provides the motive power for a "tow," but it pushes rather than pulls the assembled barges.) Barge tows with loads up to 40,000 tons are reported to be common; that load would be roughly equivalent to the load carried by ten freight trains each with seventy cars loaded to fifty-five tons.[13]

Engineering estimates are available of the cost of iron ore carriers of different capacities.[14] We may take the relationships as indicating the economies of scale in construction of ships for movement of commodities in bulk on the Great Lakes. The estimates assume, of course, a set of input prices and a particular type of design. Cost depends notably upon design speed as well as deadweight carrying capacity. Assuming a speed of sixteen knots, an ore carrier of 10,000 tons deadweight capacity

12. *Transport Statistics in the United States,* for the year ended December 31, 1961, *Part 5,* "Carriers by Water."

13. Locher, *op. cit.,* p. 131.

14. Harry Benford, et al, *Current Trends in the Design of Iron-Ore Ships.* Presented to the Society of Naval Architects and Design Engineers, June 1962.

was estimated to cost about 900 dollars per ton, and one of 80,000 tons, about 300 dollars per ton or 24 million dollars.

Another set of estimates from the same paper show required freight rates in dollars per ton for voyages of different lengths. (For ocean-going ships larger capacities are feasible and restrictions of depth of channel and lock capacity may be removed.) The required freight rate is the amount estimated as needed to cover full costs including operating costs, depreciation, and return on investment. For assumed voyages of 6,000 and 20,000 miles round trip distance, the estimates follow:

OPERATING DEADWEIGHT (TONS)	REQUIRED FREIGHT RATE (DOLLARS PER TON)	
	6000 miles	20,000 miles
20,000	10.00	34.00
100,000	4.00	12.00
180,000	2.50	9.00

The cost for moving a ton of ore 10,000 miles works out, at $9.00 per ton, to the remarkably low figure of $.0009 or just under one mill per ton-mile. Increasing the vessel from 20 to 180 thousand tons reduces costs by a factor of about four. These economies are impressive. They indicate that a small operator with one or more small vessels will be at a substantial disadvantage in situations in which large vessels can be used, while even large vessels are less economical than giant ships.

That economies of scale in size of vessel are important is also relevant to any attempt to understand the place of water transportation in the total transportation market. The full potential economy of water transport can be achieved only by shipments in very large quantities.

Average charges per ton-mile are available based on reports to the I.C.C. from the Class A and B regulated carriers, those with annual operating revenues in excess of 100,000 dollars. For 99 carriers average revenues per ton-mile are about four mills with average hauls of 532 miles. Average revenue varies among areas as follows:[15]

Area	Average Revenue Per Ton-Mile
Atlantic and Gulf Coasts	$.0079
Great Lakes	.0034
Mississippi River and tributaries	.0028
Pacific Coast	.0132
Intercoastal	.0045
All areas (average)	.0040

15. *Transport Economics*, July 1964, p. 7. Data are for the second half of 1963.

The average of four mills may be compared with the average for rail of about 1.4 cents per ton-mile. (Railroad rates would be well below 1.4 cents, of course, for like traffic.) The average length of haul of 530 miles compares with 464 miles in the same year for rail, 267 miles for Class I motor carriers, 314 miles for pipelines carrying crude petroleum, and 261 miles for pipelines carrying petroleum products. Water transport, on the average, is for the longest distances.

Data on the average speed of water transport has been published recently by the industry. From Pittsburgh to New Orleans, downstream, typical time in transit is said to be 8 days, 18 hours for 1852 miles, implying average speed of about 9 miles per hour. Upstream the time on this route is 14 days, 2 hours, implying about 5 miles per hour. From Minneapolis to New Orleans typical time in transit is 7 days, 22 hours for 1,731 miles, which also works out to about 9 miles per hour. Upstream takes 13 days, 12 hours, which implies 5 miles per hour.[16] These speeds illustrate the point that water transport is slow.

In summary we may say that the place in the total transportation market occupied by water transportation may be characterized in general by low cost associated with large volume movements. Water transport is slow, and on the average it is for long distances. And it is restricted to commercial waterways whose total length is much less than the route mileage operated by the other methods of transportation.

Information on the economic performance of the several branches of the industry is limited. As noted earlier, the overall trend in volume of freight movement by water has been upward, but not all areas show the same trend. Data on profits for the regulated sector of the industry are available. In 1962, for example, net income after income taxes of the Class A and B operators was 15,700,000 dollars, which amounted to 8 per cent on capital and surplus of 205,000,000 dollars. The following year was more profitable, with net income after taxes of 20,200,000 dollars, or 9 per cent of capital and surplus. Operators on the Mississippi River and tributaries did better than the average, earning 12 per cent, while those on the Atlantic and Gulf Coast earned only 4 per cent on the same basis.[17] These rates of return on the average indicate that the regulated industry as a whole has been in reasonably good financial condition. There does not seem to be in existence, however, any broad economic evaluation of the performance of carriers engaged in inland water transportation including comprehensive profit data, analysis of

16. *Big Load Afloat, op. cit.,* p. 15.
17. *Transport Statistics in the United States, Part 5,* "Carriers by Water," for the years ended December 31, 1962 and 1963.

trends in efficiency, and analysis of changes in the position of water transportation in the market for transportation as a whole.

DIRECTIONS OF PUBLIC POLICY—In conclusion, we may summarize the tentative conclusions reached in the three areas of public policy with which the discussion has been concerned. With regard to investment policy, decisions must be made separately about each specific proposal. There is a definite need for improved economic analysis of individual projects with better forecasting methodology. With regard to financial policy, there seems to be no adequate reason why a system of user charges should not be applied to waterway users. The system should be so developed as to prevent excessive cross subsidization among groups of users of waterways either geographically or as between commercial vessels and pleasure boats.

With regard to regulatory policy, a definitive study of competition in the industry remains to be written. Tentatively, it appears that there are a considerable number of sellers of water transportation in each area and that the economic barriers to entry are not so high as to inhibit new firms from appearing or small firms from expanding. Relaxation of regulation may be more appropriate than extension of regulation to cover minimum rates. There does not seem to be evidence of the use of temporary reductions in rates to drive out competition with the expectation of later monopoly returns. Nor does there seem to be evidence of inequity through reduction of rates on some classes of traffic between certain points to very low levels while exorbitant rates are charged elsewhere. The necessary degree of monopoly to make such practices possible does not seem to exist. Tentatively, then, it would appear that introduction of minimum rate regulation is not necessary. In the absence of compelling arguments in favor of regulation, it seems appropriate to apply the general presumption in favor of reliance on the normal workings of a competitive market with the usual requirement of compliance with antitrust legislation.

Pipelines

Pipelines built for the movement of petroleum and petroleum products are a highly specialized method of transportation. In the United States they are privately owned and operated, in this respect resembling the railroads rather than the highways, waterways, or airways.

There has been no anxiety as to whether the pipelines could pay their way such as there has been with regard to the railroads. Rather, from time to time there have been expressions of concern that pipelines have been making too much money and policies have been designed intended to impose a ceiling on the return from investment in them. The issues of public policy with regard to pipelines have had to do with the relation of the pipelines to the other stages in the production and marketing of petroleum and especially the competition between vertically integrated oil companies and those independent companies engaged only in refining or only in other specific stages in the productive process. In the early days of the industry the old Standard Oil Company prior to its dissolution in 1911 used control over transportation needed by its rivals to force its way to a monopoly position in the industry. In one remarkable incident, Standard obtained rebates from a railroad, not just on its own shipments, but on shipments made by a competitor. Under such circumstances the competitor might be expected to have difficulty in matching Standard's selling prices. This affair caught the public imagination and since then people have been sensitive to the possibilities of using transportation to obtain market power in the oil industry. If two firms both use a pipeline owned by one of them, high rates for use of the line could mean profits for one and losses for the other. Discussion of the actual importance of such situations leads into consideration of the geographic location of refineries in relation to sources of production and markets in the oil industry.

A second aspect of pipeline transportation of interest to the student of transportation is the place of pipelines in the total market for transportation. The problem may be viewed from the point of view of the petroleum industry, which may choose between shipment by pipeline, by water, or by other methods. From this point of view the costs of transportation by pipeline are of central interest.

The following discussion, then, will consider the cost of transportation by pipeline, the place of pipelines in the transportation market, and current public policy toward the pipeline industry. The question of general public policy toward the oil industry will not be discussed, the purpose being only to indicate how considerations of policy toward the industry have influenced policy toward pipelines.

ECONOMIES OF SCALE IN PIPELINE TRANSPORTATION—The most important determinant of the costs of pipeline transportation is the economies of scale associated with increasing the diameter of the pipe. The volume of a liquid that can be moved through a line depends upon the diameter of the pipe and the horsepower of the pumps installed along the line. Careful estimates of the cost relationships have been prepared by Leslie Cookenboo based essentially upon engineering cost studies.[18] The fundamental relationships involved depend upon the principles of geometry concerning the relation between the surface of a cylinder and its volume. At the simplest level, consider a circular cross-section of a pipe. Since, of course, the area of a circle is πr^2, the area of the circle will increase with the *square* of the radius. The circumference will increase only in proportion to the radius since the circumference is $2 \pi r$. The friction that must be overcome to move a fluid through a pipe is the friction between the fluid and the wall of the pipe. By an extension of this reasoning, increasing the diameter of a pipe will increase the volume of fluid in the pipe faster than it will increase the surface of the fluid in contact with the wall of the pipe. Hence, there are economies in the horsepower required in pumping from increasing the diameter of the pump. There are also economies in the cost of the pipe itself. Thus, for larger pipes the number of tons of quarter inch steel for casings per unit of pipeline capacity is less than for smaller pipes.

The same kind of relation between the area of the surface of a container and the volume of its contents also applies to other methods of transportation. It applies, for example, to railroad cars. Yet, as discussed in earlier chapters, the scale of railroad cars is limited by the gauge of the railroad as well as by the clearances in tunnels and elsewhere along the right of way. And in the case of railroads efficiency requires that the same gauge and the same cars be used throughout the system. Water transport and highway transport also face limitations on the size of the vehicles. Pipelines, however, can be built to whatever diameter is required. Furthermore, there is no problem in using one diameter of pipeline for a gathering line and another for long distance movements in bulk. The only effective limit on the diameter of a new pipeline comes from the demand side of the market. There is no sense in building pipelines of larger capacity than will be used.

The gains from scale are substantial. Under Cookenboo's assumptions, for example, the lowest cost per thousand miles for a throughput of 100,000 barrels per day in an 18-inch line would be about 16 cents per barrel. Yet 400,000 barrels per day in a 32-inch line would cost about 8 cents per barrel.[19]

The implications for the industry are important. It would be extremely wasteful, for example, for four competing refineries in a con-

18. Leslie Cookenboo, *Crude Oil Pipe Lines and Competition in the Oil Industry,* Harvard University Press, 1955.

19. *Ibid.* See graph, p. 26.

suming area each of which used crude oil from the same area of origin to build four pipelines. If, for example, each required 100,000 barrels per day, as just shown to build four parallel 18-inch pipelines instead of a single 32-inch pipeline would double the cost per barrel for transportation. Some system for joint use of the same line in such circumstances is essential. It also follows that costs for moving petroleum on a route that has a large pipeline will be much lower than on other routes not thus provided. There will be external economies in locating large refining capacity in the same area.

What is the level of cost of transporting oil by pipeline compared to other methods of transportation? On this point statistics of revenue per ton-mile are available from the Interstate Commerce Commission based on reports to it from regulated carriers. Revenue per ton-mile of oil pipelines has been stable from year to year in the neighborhood of 3.1 mills.[20] That level of revenue per ton-mile represents an average over a variety of conditions. It is in the general neighborhood of the cost of bulk movements by water.

PLACE OF PIPELINES IN THE TRANSPORTATION MARKET—The total movement of petroleum falls into two parts, the movement of crude petroleum and the movement of refined petroleum products. The share of the movement by pipeline is much larger in the transportation of crude. The statistics for crude, which are for tons rather than ton-miles for each method of transportation, are as follows:[21]

Method	Per Cent of Crude Oil Transported
Pipelines	76
Water carriers	18
Trucks	6
Total	100

The movement of refined products is distributed as follows:[22]

Method	Per Cent of Refined Petroleum Products
Pipelines	20
Water carriers	38
Trucks	36
Railroads	6
Total	100

20. Average revenue per ton-mile was 0.312 cents in 1942; 0.315 cents in 1960; 0.318 cents in 1963. See *Transport Economics*, July 1964, p. 1.
21. American Petroleum Institute, *Petroleum Facts and Figures*, 1959, p. 197.
22. *Ibid.*, p. 197.

The total movement of petroleum is very large. The pipelines alone account for about 17 per cent of the total volume of intercity freight ton-miles, as shown in Chapter 12. Petroleum also accounts for a substantial part of deep-sea domestic waterborne traffic, and for about 44 per cent of the total volume of world trade.[23]

The larger share of pipelines in movements of crude than in movements of products is reasonable in view of the special suitability of pipelines for very large movements. Flows of crude from major fields to refineries may have this character. Distribution of refined products to individual points of consumption requires smaller volumes.

There has been interest in the use of pipelines to transport solids. The movement of solids is accomplished by the use of a carrying fluid; for example, coal may be moved in water. A 108 mile pipeline has been constructed in Ohio and used to transport coal to a power plant near Cleveland. More ambitious schemes have been proposed such as moving Canadian wheat by pipeline to the Great Lakes. To date the economic feasibility of these proposals remains to be demonstrated.[24] The crucial comparison is likely to be with rail costs for bulk movements in specialized, integrated trains that move back and forth between the points in question.

PUBLIC POLICY TOWARD PIPELINES—The I.C.C. became concerned with the pipelines when the *Hepburn Act* (1906) added pipelines, except those carrying water and gas, to the list of carriers subject to its jurisdiction. The companies initially maintained that they transported only their own products and, hence, were not common carriers subject to the *Act*. When the Supreme Court held that they were common carriers,[25] they set very high minimum tender requirements and high rates, which effectively limited use of their lines by independent oil companies. Independent refiners located their facilities so as not to rely on the lines, for example, avoiding reliance on crude oil pipelines by locating refineries near the oil fields.

The Department of Justice brought suit under the *Elkins Act* in 1940 which charged that dividends paid by pipeline companies to their parent companies were unlawful rebates within the meaning of that Act. A consent decree in 1941 resulted. Under that decree the dividends the pipeline owning companies could receive have been limited to 7 per cent of the valuation of the pipeline. The effect was similar to regu-

23. *Ibid.*, p. 202.
24. For a technical discussion of the engineering problems see *The Transportation of Solids in Steel Pipelines*, Colorado School of Mines Research Foundation, Inc., 1963.
25. *The Pipe Line Cases*, 234 U.S. 548.

lation of the level of rates charged. There has been dispute as to the method of valuation of the property; a case brought by the Department of Justice was settled in favor of the companies in 1959 by the Supreme Court. The I.C.C. in 1940 proposed a minimum tender requirement of 10,000 barrels, which has been accepted. The effect of these developments has been to move the pipelines gradually in the direction of becoming common carriers in fact instead of plant facilities for the vertically integrated companies. Proposals have been made from time to time for divorcement of the pipelines from the companies but to date the usual arrangement is for the pipelines to be owned and operated by vertically integrated enterprises.

19

Competition among Methods of Transportation

For purposes of exposition it is convenient to discuss separately the different methods of transportation. Similarly, the determinants of the location of economic activity, the policy of the Interstate Commerce Commission, and technological changes in transportation and in transportation-using industries are logically separate topics. Yet aspects of all of these topics may be important in a single actual situation in the competition between methods of transportation. The first section of this chapter is devoted to the movement of grain, a type of service in which competition has been keen, and is intended to illustrate in this field the interplay of economic forces related to competition in transportation. General discussion of the issues involved in the allocation of freight traffic among the modes of transportation is postponed to Chapter 20.

The second section of this chapter is concerned with the competition among different methods of transportation for intercity passenger business. The purpose of this section will be to analyze the place in the total market for passenger transportation of each of the four principal modes of passenger travel, auto, air, rail, and bus. Competition in the passenger

374

market will be found to offer both similarities and differences from competition in the movement of freight such as grain.

Competition in the Movement of Grain

TRADITIONAL PATTERN OF GRAIN MARKETING—What is now described as the traditional pattern of marketing of grain developed in the years of railroad dominance in transportation. Grain moved from the farm at harvest to country elevators located on the railroads. Since local transportation was expensive the elevators tended to be spaced so that farmers would not have far to haul the grain, under six miles, one writer suggests, but the maximum distance for movement to the country elevator no doubt varied from one part of the country to another.[1] Storage capacity typically was limited both on farms and at country elevators, so that there was a pronounced seasonal peak in rail movements at harvest from the producing areas to consuming areas. Most of the grain moved in standard boxcars adapted to the purpose with minor modifications such as installation of a grain door.

The railroad rate structure for grain movements included special features, especially transit privileges, which were intended to "hold the grain to the rails." Transit privileges permit shippers to pay the through rate for a shipment of grain between two locations even though the actual movement may be interrupted once, or more than once, while the grain is milled into flour, or stored, cleaned, or blended. The railroad, in effect, absorbs the terminal costs involved in halting the movement and unloading the grain and subsequently loading it again and assembling the loaded cars into another train proceeding in the same general direction. In effect shippers are offered special inducement not to transfer to water transport at intermediate halts.

Railroad rates for grain were not typically mileage rates. The New York Central, for example, and other roads in the same geographic area, moved grain on rates based on a group rate system known as the McGraham Formula. This system grouped together large numbers of points of origin and destination. For grain movements from the West, for example, all of New England was a single area of destination. The railroad rate structures, thus, departed widely from a system of charges based on cost.

1. See Richard H. Steiner, "Development of the New York Central Grain Mileage rates," *Papers, Fifth Annual Meeting Transportation Research Forum,* 1964. Also see *An Analysis of Grain Transportation in the Northwest,* United States Department of Agriculture, Economic Research Service, E.R.S. 200, December 1964.

CHANGES IN THE MARKET—A variety of changes in the market have taken place. The development of trucking plus the construction of high quality rural roads has broadened the market area for the local, country elevators. In the Pacific Northwest in response to a questionnaire developed by the Economic Research Service of the Department of Agriculture, elevator operators indicated on the average that they served local areas with radius of eighteen miles, and half the operators sometimes received shipments from outside their normal buying radius, from distances ranging up to one hundred miles. At the same time there has been a tendency toward construction of additional storage capacity for grain in the producing areas both on farms and at the country elevators. The flow of grain to the consuming areas thus tends to become more even during the year. As a consequence it has become possible to develop specialized railroad equipment designed to be used year round for the movement of grain. The railroads are employing increasingly for grain movements covered aluminum hopper cars of 100-ton capacity.

In some parts of the country improvements in the inland waterway system have taken place in recent years or are now under construction that facilitate barge movements of grain. Improvements are in progress on the Columbia River. Navigation on the Tennessee River was improved by the T.V.A., and the system of dams and locks completed in 1945 permits barge traffic as far as Knoxville.

Trucks have entered into the movement of grain in other ways than as local transportation to the country elevator. Trucks may be used to move grain from the country elevator. They may make the haul all the way to a terminal elevator, or they may be used in conjunction with barge service so that the grain moves from the country elevator to the consuming area by a combination of truck and water service. Or the grain may move direct from the farm to the terminal elevator or processor without ever being elevated at a country elevator. This practice seems to be highly developed in Montana and southern Idaho, where elevators located in what are considered to be terminal market areas report about one-third of their truck receipts come from farmers directly.

The long hauls by truck usually are backhauls. Trucks returning to their base of operations can legally carry grain under the agricultural exemption (see Chapter 14). If no other loads are available, it will pay them to carry grain at low rates rather than to return home empty.

RAILROAD RATE POLICY IN THE NORTHWEST—The combined effect of these developments may be observed in the recent history of railroad rates in the Northwest. In the twelve years from 1946 to 1958 there were a series of railroad rate increases. The effects of these rates on methods of shipping grain were felt gradually. The operators of country elevators in this period did begin to ship more grain by truck and barge. Of eighty-seven operators, fifty-eight responded to the Department of Agriculture survey that they had shifted some traffic from the rails in this period because of the higher rates. One reason that the shift was gradual was that trucks might not be available, and rail facilities were in existence. For grain intended for export, transit rates were not a consideration beyond the terminal in the port area. Transit rates did play a part, however, as they were designed to do, in inducing terminal elevator operators to send on by rail to inland destinations grain which came to them by rail.

Gradually, the railroads felt the pressure of the competition, and they introduced a series of rate reductions beginning in May 1958 intended to be competitive with truck and barge rates. By 1960 the rail rates had been reduced by as much as 40 to 50 per cent of their value in 1958 in Washington, northern Idaho, and eastern Oregon. The reduced rates involved curtailment of the traditional transit privileges. These reductions, as might be expected, have led many of the country elevators to increase again their shipments by rail.

It is, perhaps, not surprising that the reduced rail rates have been protested by the water carriers. The rates have remained in effect while the case has been contested. The water carriers have maintained that they have been forced to reduce their rates below full cost because of the reduced rail rates. The I.C.C. has argued that the truck-barge combination was the lowest cost method on the basis of full costs and, hence, should be allowed to carry the traffic. The railroads should not be allowed to lower their rates even though the reduced rates were in excess of out-of-pocket costs.

This line of reasoning seems to have influenced the Commission more than it influences most economists. From society's point of view it is the incremental costs which are relevant, the extra resources used by carrying the grain by one method rather than another. If the railroads can add the grain to their other traffic at a social cost less than the social cost of moving the grain by barge, the railroads should move the grain. It is cases such as this one which bring into question the desirability of continuing the Commission's power over minimum rates.[2]

The legal controversy should not distract attention from the effects of competitive pressure. The competition among trucks, combined truck-

2. See the discussion in Chapter 13. For a discussion of this case see James C. Nelson, "Competitive Issues in Grain Transport in the Pacific Northwest," *Papers, Fifth Annual Meeting Transportation Research Forum,* 1964, pp. 10–20. See also 319 I.C.C. 534, decided August 26, 1963.

barge service, and railroads has brought about substantial reductions in rates. It has forced reconsideration of the railroad rate structure with regard to transit, and is putting pressure on the railroads to introduce more modern equipment.

GRAIN RATES IN OTHER AREAS—Similar economic forces are at work in other areas in the grain trade. The events in the Southeast illustrate additional factors in the situation. Since World War II there has been a shift in the location of economic activity in poultry and live-stock feeding. Perhaps the most dramatic has been an increase in broiler production in Georgia, where proceeds from sale of broilers is the largest single item in agricultural gross revenue while even the sale of eggs and other revenue from poultry equal or exceed cotton.[3] This minor agricultural revolution, as Lemly describes it, has been based on an increased flow of grain into the South, which always has imported grain, but recently imports much more. The grain has moved in large part by barge on the Tennessee River, taking advantage of the nine foot channel. Tonnage of grain on the river increased by twelve times from 1950 to 1960!

The railroad response to this development has included elements similar to those in the Northwest: revision of a traditional rate structure under pressure and introduction of modern equipment (the well-known Big John aluminum hopper cars of the Southern Railway). There has also been controversy before the I.C.C. A feature in the Southeast that has not been introduced as yet in the Pacific Northwest is the use of multiple car rates. Reduced rail rates are quoted for shipments of five carloads, 450 ton minimum shipment, in the aluminum cars with individual capacities of 100 tons or more. The direct effect of the reduced rail rates has been to increase movement of grain by rail. There are also indirect effects on both shippers and buyers of grain who may be re-grouped into larger units in order to take advantage of the reduced rates associated with large shipments.

Developments in the northeastern part of the country have followed a similar sequence. Reduced rates without transit rights have been introduced, calculated on a mileage basis without reference to the McGraham Formula.

It is instructive to note how behind the entire development two changes which have nothing to do directly with railroads have made possible gains in railroad efficiency. The development of storage capacity in the grain producing areas plus the development of trucking which permits country elevators to serve broader areas have concentrated the

3. See James H. Lemly, "Regional Factors in Grain Rate Adjustment in the South," *Papers, Fifth Annual Meeting, Transportation Research Forum,* 1964, pp. 21–26.

grain in increased volume at the points of shipment and reduced the seasonal peaks. The railroads have been able to take advantage of this situation to reduce costs of shipment. They have been under pressure to introduce innovations in equipment and in rates because of competition from trucks and barges and from the two operating jointly.

Competition in the Market for Intercity Passenger Transportation

Competition exists in the market for passenger transportation both for local and for long distance travel. Transportation of people within urban areas has been discussed in Chapter 15. The following material concerns intercity travel. In the transportation of grain and other bulk commodities the price charged for the service is of central importance and the preceding discussion has reflected that fact. In the market for passenger transportation, however, qualities of service other than price are of crucial importance. The following discussion, therefore, begins with a basic description of the nature of product differentiation in the market for passenger travel. There follows a discussion of common carrier pricing and automobile competition. The analytical framework thus developed is applied to the decline of railroad passenger business in the 1950s. The discussion relies upon sample surveys as well as upon aggregate statistics based on counts of passengers.[4]

DIFFERENTIATION OF SERVICE IN THE TRAVEL MARKET—The starting point for the analysis of the total travel market must be the recognition of the difference in point of view of the sellers of transportation and the buyers. From the point of view of the sellers of transportation the problem is one of the ways in which the transportation service they offer is differentiated or may be differentiated from the service offered by other carriers. From the point of view of the buyer the problem is one of the principles on which he may make his selection of the method of transportation he will use.

Buyers and sellers interact in markets that are geographically defined. The analyst, who cannot think in terms of all the thousands of pairs of points of origin and destination, must seek to group together geographically distinct markets into groups of markets that are as homogeneous as possible.

4. For examples of surveys taken among passengers while en route, see the series conducted by the Aviation Department of the Port of New York Authority in cooperation with the airlines. *The Census of Passenger Transportation, 1963* by the Census Bureau is based on a cross section survey that includes nontravelers. See also the surveys conducted by the Survey Research Center, which are summarized in John B. Lansing and Dwight M. Blood, *The Changing Travel Market,* Institute for Social Research, 1964.

Buyers distinguish the service offered by sellers of transportation in a market on the basis of its speed, its price, and other characteristics whose consideration may be postponed for a moment. Both speed and price require discussion.

The relative speed of different methods of transportation varies with distance. For example, it is faster to travel across the continent by air than by auto, but for trips between most pairs of points 100 miles apart auto travel is faster than air. It is door-to-door speed that counts, not the maximum rate of speed attained at any moment of time while en route. There is an analogy between time and money spent on a trip. Just as, in considering cost of freight movement, it is useful to separate terminal cost from line-haul cost, in considering cost in time of passenger movement it is useful to separate fixed cost in time to get to the terminal and get started from time spent between terminals. Auto travel involves very low "terminal cost" in time to get started and to reach the final destination. For common carriers the "terminal cost" in time is higher. It will vary depending on the exact location of the terminals and their accessibility from the exact points of origin and destination. Relative speed of the competing modes, therefore, is a function of distance, and their competitive position also becomes a function of distance.

The relation between air and ground travel time has been investigated for the fifty most heavily traveled city pairs as of 1960. The assumed actual points of origin and destination are the city centers, and ground time is estimated to include time to check and recover baggage at the airport as well as driving time. The estimates follow:[5]

Between Airport Mileage Range (miles)	Mean Flight Time, Non-Stop (minutes)	Ground Travel Time (minutes)
0 – 250	53	99
251 – 500	83	98
501 – 1000	119	116
1001 and over	246	114

As these statistics show, the ground travel time at the two ends of an air trip is somewhere between 1.5 and 2 hours for trips from city center to city center. If anything, ground time probably is even longer for other trips. Flight time exceeds average ground time only for long trips.

The importance of speed is not the same to all travelers. In general, business travelers place a premium on speed. They typically wish to

5. Based on *Air Transportation; A Study of Transportation Means Between Airports and the Metropolitan Areas They Serve,* prepared for the Federal Aviation Agency by Human Sciences Research, Inc., February 1961. See Table I-1.

reach their destination, transact their business, and get back to their point of departure as soon as possible. For people on vacation, however, often "getting there is half the fun." Even when they would prefer to arrive promptly, they may not feel strongly about it. In effect, they may place a low value on saving time. Hence, choice of mode for business travel is likely to be more responsive to changes in speed than for nonbusiness travel.

Consideration of price also leads to the division of the market according to purpose. Business travel is paid for out of business funds. Increases in consumers' incomes are not increases in the funds available for business travel. The calculation of costs made by a business organization in deciding whether to pay for a particular trip by a particular individual differs from the calculation of costs for nonbusiness trips. The total cost of the business trip will include the remuneration of the traveler while en route plus his expenses. The fare will be a fraction of the total cost. A change of, say, 10 per cent in the fare will be less than a 10 per cent change in the cost of the trip. Hence, choice of mode for business travel is likely to be less responsive to changes in price than choice of mode for nonbusiness trips.

DISTANCE TO DESTINATION AND PURPOSE OF TRIP AS DETERMINANTS OF CHOICE OF MODE—It is possible using survey data to compare modes actually used for recent trips. The comparison is shown in Table 19.1. The differences in mode choice associated with these two

Table 19.1—Use of Air, Rail, Bus, Auto, and Mixed Modes on Most Recent Business and Nonbusiness Trips, by Distance, 1962 (percentage distribution of trips by purpose and distance)

Mode Used	BUSINESS			NONBUSINESS		
	100–499 Miles	500–999 Miles	1000 Miles and Over	100–499 Miles	500–999 Miles	1000 Miles and Over
Air	21	42	67	3	15	30
Rail	5	8	2	4	5	11
Bus	9	4	1	9	9	6
Auto	62	42	26	81	65	45
Two or more modes	3	4	4	3	6	8
Total	100	100	100	100	100	100
Number of trips	302	91	93	1459	239	291

Source: The Changing Travel Market, op. cit., p. 245.

variables, distance and purpose, are very large. Of the trips studied in 1962 taken for business reasons to places 1,000 miles or more away, two out of three were by air. Of business trips from 100 to 499 miles away, only 21 per cent were by air. Of nonbusiness trips of 1,000 or more miles, 30 per cent were by air; on nonbusiness trips of 100 to 499 miles, only 3 per cent were by air.

COMMON CARRIER PRICING AND AUTOMOBILE COMPETITION—The influence of price on choice of mode of transportation is especially important in the competition between the common carriers and private automobiles. The common carriers, it should not be forgotten, sell their services in a market dominated by private automobiles, which account for 80 to 90 per cent of all intercity passenger travel. To simplify discussion, consider a situation where a common carrier allows no family plan or other discount for a party. The fare for the party then will increase in direct proportion to the number of passengers. If the operating cost for travel by auto is 4 cents per mile and a common carrier also charges 4 cents, for one person the cost of travel by auto and by common carrier will be the same. For a party of two people, however, the common carrier will charge 8 cents while the cost of operating the car is still 4 cents. For three, four, or five people the comparison becomes still less favorable to the common carrier. For six people, it is 24 cents against 4 cents. Under such circumstances it would be reasonable to expect a larger proportion of parties of one to travel by common carrier than of parties of two or more. The accompanying table confirms this expectation.

Table 19.2—Use of Air, Rail, Bus, Auto, and Mixed Modes on Most Recent Nonbusiness Trips, by Distance and Whether Traveled Alone, 1962
(percentage distribution of most recent nonbusiness trips)

| | Distance | | | | | |
| Mode Used | 100–499 MILES | | 500–999 MILES | | 1000 MILES OR MORE | |
	Went Alone	Not Alone	Went Alone	Not Alone	Went Alone	Not Alone
Air	12	1	36	6	51	18
Rail	11	3	14	2	15	8
Bus	30	5	20	5	10	4
Auto	41	89	24	81	10	66
Two or more modes	6	2	6	6	14	4
Total	100	100	100	100	100	100
Number of trips	239	1198	70	162	99	182

Source: *The Changing Travel Market, op. cit.,* p. 249.

On nonbusiness trips 1000 miles away, of those who went alone 51 per cent went by air, but of those who went in a party of two or more, only 18 per cent went by air.[6] The common carriers were very largely priced out of the market for family travel.

OTHER ELEMENTS IN THE MARKET—In a brief account it is not

6. For a multivariate statistical analysis of choice of mode see John B. Lansing and Dwight M. Blood, *Mode Choice in Intercity Travel,* Institute for Social Research, 1964.

possible to do justice to the considerations other than speed and price which influence the market for passenger transportation. They include comfort, safety, attractiveness of the scenery, flexibility of route, and the convenience of having a car after arrival at the destination. People differ according to their personal feelings about the different methods of transportation, and these feelings influence their behavior. Some people like to drive, while others find it tiresome; some enjoy trains, while others prefer planes. The carriers seek to influence and to build upon these attitudes and preferences in their efforts at promotion and in the details of the service which they provide.

THE DECLINE OF RAILROAD PASSENGER SERVICE—One of the most important developments in the passenger market has been the decline of railroad passenger service. The method of looking at the passenger travel market just outlined may be used to analyze that decline. The questions at issue concern why the decline occurred, and whether it could have been slowed down, or even prevented.

To summarize the main facts: as noted in Chapter 13, the peace-time peak year for railroad passenger service in the United States was 1920 and the trend from then until 1952 was as follows:[7]

Year	Passenger-Miles by Railroad (including commutation) (Billions of passenger-miles)
1920	47.4
1930	26.9
1940	23.8
1945	91.8
1950	31.8
1951	34.6
1952	34.0

After a decline from 1920 to 1940 and a peak in World War II, there was a postwar decline. In 1951 or 1952 it would have been possible, however, from a study of the series to argue that the decline from the wartime peak was over, and that the trend would now continue to be upward as it was from 1950 to 1951. The present analysis will focus on the ten years, 1951 through 1961, during which in fact the number of railroad passenger miles fell by almost 50 per cent. The trends in inter-city common carrier service over that decade were as follows:[8]

7. Source: United States Bureau of the Census, *Historical Statistics of the United States, Colonial Times to 1957*, 1960, p. 430.
8. Source: I.C.C. See *Annual Reports*.

Passenger-Miles by Common Carriers
(excluding commutation)
(Billions of passenger-miles)

Year	Rail	Air	Bus	Water	Total
1951	31	11	24	1	67
1956	24	23	22	1	70
1961	16	32	20	2	70

Over this period total travel by common carrier increased slightly, and bus travel fell slightly. The main changes were in rail and air, which reversed their positions. Auto travel is not shown in the table, partly because the estimates of total auto travel are of uncertain reliability, but there is no question that auto ownership and travel increased.[9]

Aggregate statistics also make it possible to separate trends for first class and rail coach service. Coach travel fell over the years 1951 to 1961 from 20 billion to 13 billion passenger-miles, while first class rail travel fell from 10.5 to 3 billion. The decline, thus, was much more pronounced in first class travel.

CAUSES OF THE DECLINE—The causes of the decline may be sought by considering the place of rail in the total market as defined by the characteristics of the service: its speed, price, comfort, availability, and people's attitudes toward it in comparison to different modes. As far as speed is concerned, rail travel can hardly compete with air for long distances. For short trips travel by auto is ordinarily faster than rail. Rail travel can claim an advantage in speed only in limited circumstances. Speed is at a premium for business travel. Therefore, one would expect rail to be weak in competition for business travel. It seems safe to conclude that during this decade rail lost business travelers to air and auto. The rapid decline in first class travel is consistent with this interpretation of what happened. Survey data also show a decline in the proportion of all adults taking business trips by rail.[10]

If speed is important for business travel, price is important for nonbusiness travel. Since the automobile dominates the nonbusiness travel market, price competition is especially important as between autos and rail. If the relative price of rail and auto is important, rail should do better in competing for travel by single people than by families. Survey data support this interpretation. In 1962 rail trips were taken

9. See Dwight M. Blood, "Some Inconsistencies in Statistics of Intercity Automobile Travel," *Papers, Fourth Annual Meeting, Transportation Research Forum,* December 1963, pp. 85–91.

10. See *The Changing Travel Market, op. cit.,* pp. 128. From 1955 to 1962 the decline is from 2 to 1 per cent.

by 7 per cent of the entire adult population but by 12 per cent of the single people under forty-five years of age and 10 per cent of the single people over that age (including the widowed and divorced).[11] The families were more likely to drive.

Would a policy of radical reductions in fares for families have helped to stem the decline in rail travel by winning customers from the automobiles? More precisely, would the change in revenue from introducing such a policy have exceeded increased costs? The prerequisites for a successful policy of price discrimination were stated in Chapter 4. The railroads did have the necessary degree of control over their prices to change their fare structure for families, subject to I.C.C. approval. There is no practical problem about dividing the market: families are easy to tell from other passengers. It has just been argued that the demand for travel by families is more price elastic than the demand for travel by single individuals because of the peculiar character of the cost per person of travel by auto. There remains uncertainty, however, as to just how responsive family travel would have been to drastically reduced rail fares. The marginal cost of additional passengers by rail must have been very low during this period since there was excess capacity resulting from declining sales.

The actual policy of most of the railroads is indicated by the trend in revenue per passenger-mile, which was as follows:[12]

Year	Average Revenue Per Passenger-Mile, Line-Haul Railroads
1952	2.665¢
1956	2.685¢
1961	3.082¢
1962	3.113¢

The railroads raised their fares, on the average, especially in the second part of the decade. The increase is understated by the above tabulation since in the later years an increasing fraction of the service was coach rather than first class. (If fares had been constant, average revenue would have fallen owing to increasing use of the less expensive service.) To raise fares in the time of falling demand implies a policy of minimizing losses while withdrawing from the market.[13]

11. Source: John B. Lansing, William Ladd, Nancy Barth, *The Travel Market 1961–1962*, p. 55.

12. I.C.C., *Annual Report,* 1963, p. 225.

13. For a more extensive discussion of railroad pricing see John B. Lansing and Herbert E. Neil, Jr., "An Analysis of Non-Business Rail Travel," *Land Economics,* May 1959, pp. 139–148.

Other characteristics of the service also played a part in the decline of railroad passenger service. In a survey in 1955 it was found that comfort was the leading advantage of rail travel in popular estimation. People, however, were of two minds as to how comfortable rail service actually was, with favorable comments about the clean, roomy, comfortable ride offset by unfavorable observations about noise, dirt, fatigue, and the like. The railroads did not succeed in establishing a reputation as the most comfortable way to travel.

Once the downward trend was well started it tended to reinforce itself. In geographic terms by 1962 the relative position of rail travel was weak in the rural areas, which can be served flexibly by auto and bus, and relatively stronger in the towns and cities. Yet the larger cities are especially well served by the airlines. In this sense also the railroads were in the middle under pressure from two directions. The relative availability of rail was greatest in the small to moderate sized towns and cities. The percentage of all adults who took at least one rail trip in 1962 was 9 per cent in places with population of 2,500 to 49,999 and 10 per cent in cities of 50,000 to 1,500,000 compared to 7 per cent in the country as a whole.[14] In the market as a whole, however, declining patronage led to less frequent and, therefore, less satisfactory service.

There is a psychological factor that tended to reinforce the downward pressure on rail transportation. As rail lost out increasingly to air, people came to think of rail service as slow and old-fashioned. Busy, modern, efficient people would be more likely to fly. Businessmen sensitive to the impression they would make had some reason to travel by plane.

There are three overlapping subgroups of the population who constitute a kind of residual market for the railroads: people who own no cars; the aged, who may be unwilling or unable to travel by other means; and people in the lower income groups. Of these groups only one is increasing in size. There are more old people as time goes on, but fewer poor, and fewer without cars.

Viewed as a whole, the analysis leads to the conclusion that the railroads were in a weakening competitive position in the period 1951–1961 in terms of the speed and quality of the service offered. Price policy might have been used more aggressively at least to slow the decline of the railroads in one part of the market—the market for family travel. There does not appear to have been any strategy short of a

14. Source: Lansing, Ladd, Barth, *op. cit.*, p. 59.

revolutionary change in technology that would have prevented the loss of the bulk of business travel to competing methods of transportation. The history of railroad passenger service in this period thus illustrates the complex interplay in the market for passenger transportation of considerations of price and of the characteristics of the service offered.

20

Issues of Economic Policy in Transportation

To FORMULATE THE MAJOR ISSUES of public policy toward transportation it is essential to view the transportation system as a whole. In this chapter we shall review the economic characteristics of the transportation system and in this context summarize the broad problems of economic policy in the field.

Economic Characteristics of Transportation

CHARACTERISTICS OF THE MARKET FOR TRANSPORTATION—Transportation as an industry has a combination of special features that distinguishes it from other industries. Transportation is not sold in a single national or international market. It is sold in a complex system of interrelated markets and submarkets. These markets are divided both geographically and according to what is being moved from place to place. The markets for transportation are further characterized by a high degree of differentiation of service. The two basic principles of differentiation of service are speed and reliability. The contrast in speed

388

between air freight and barge shipments may illustrate differences in speed; the contrast between sailing vessels and steamships illustrates differences in reliability of arrival at the expected time at the expected destination. Other principles of differentiation of service are also important depending on the market. For movement of people, safety, comfort, and such special features as the convenience of a car on arrival are important as well as speed and reliability. For movement of fragile freight, packaging requirements and breakage rates are important. For some bulk commodities, contamination is important; for valuable objects, risk of theft. Differentiation is important within modes of transportation as well as across modes. Not all planes are alike, nor all railroad service.

The sellers in these numerous and highly differentiated markets have sharply different cost characteristics. The relative importance of terminal costs and line-haul costs varies, and plays a major part in determining which sellers can offer the lowest cost service in which market. Sellers with low terminal costs and high line-haul costs compete most effectively in the short-haul markets. Sellers with high terminal costs are more competitive for long hauls. For example, trucks have low terminal costs and compete effectively for short hauls. Economies of scale are important to sellers' market positions, the crucial economies being those associated with the size of the unit of service. For example, large ore carriers are more economical per ton-mile than moderate-sized or small ships. Sellers' costs differ, finally, according to whether they own the way over which their vehicles move and, if not, how it is paid for.

As a consequence of the wide variations in the nature of the service and in costs, wide differences exist in price. The price per ton-mile for freight movement varies by as much as a factor of 100 from bulk movements by water to small, special shipments by air freight.

RELATION OF TRANSPORTATION TO THE ECONOMY—Transportation is in a special position with regard to the rest of the economy. Transportation is essential to a modern economy; the division of labor rests upon it. Both geographic specialization based on dissimilar natural resources and the internal specialization and use of machinery characteristic of mass production rest on transport. Improvements in transportation can have major indirect results. Competition often takes place between transportation and nontransportation activities. The transportation company that improves the speed and reliability of service competes with the warehouse, the storage facility, or the small plant as much as with other sellers of transportation. The indirect effects of improved transportation may be highly visible especially when a special service is provided. A company decides to rely on air freight and close a warehouse. When what is improved is not the final service but the way, as the highway or the waterway, the consequences are indirect, they may be delayed, and, hence, they are inherently difficult to observe. A decision in the 1930s to improve navigation on the Tennessee River helped to revolutionize the poultry industry in Georgia in the 1950s.

Since the whole organization of production rests on transport facilities, there is a special public interest in them. This interest takes the form both of a concern with their development and with preventing any distortion of their use. Control of the transportation system of an area by a private monopoly, if unchecked, would carry potential control of the economic life of that area.

Problems of Transportation Policy

GENERAL PUBLIC GOALS FOR TRANSPORTATION—The general public goals against which the performance of the transportation industry can be evaluated are plural: they concern primarily efficiency, economic progress, equity, and political strength and unity. Emphasis may differ among these objectives, and differences in emphasis lead to different recommendations for policy. Conflicting private and local interests may be involved in transportation policy, of course, as well as the general interest that is under discussion. Consideration of the goals of economic policy leads to the development of criteria that can be applied to the evaluation of any specific policy. The disagreement that may appear when a given policy appears successful by one yardstick and unsuccessful by another yardstick should not be interpreted to mean that no yardsticks exist. Although there are areas in which there are conflicting judgments, some policies appear desirable by any reasonable yardstick and others, equally undesirable.

NEED FOR PUBLIC INTERVENTION—The principal reliance in the American economy is on the market mechanism for the control of economic activity. The market mechanism alone, however, is not adequate in the field of transportation to achieve a satisfactory level of performance evaluated in terms of the general goals just enumerated. As a consequence a variety of forms of public intervention have developed which are used in different circumstances to supplement or correct the market mechanism. Subsidy is used to supplement the market mechanism where it fails to take into account socially important values.

Economic regulation is used to restrain monopoly with the objective of improving the allocation of resources in production or promoting equity in the distribution of resources. Public agencies assume responsibility for the provision of transportation facilities which are necessary but which private agencies are unwilling to provide or which it is judged inappropriate to leave in private hands. The need for public intervention is well established, as is the usefulness of each of the major forms of intervention. There is a margin of controversy, however, concerning the extent of public intervention which is required and the form which it should take.

MORE REGULATION OR LESS?—A basic current question of public policy is presented by the increased variety of means of transportation that has been associated with progress in the industry. The question is one of the extent to which it is becoming increasingly possible to rely on the forces of competition in the market for transportation instead of upon economic regulation. In the economy as a whole the principal reliance is upon competition as a regulator. To what extent is such reliance possible in transportation?

A related set of questions arises out of the history of the regulation of some forms of transportation. Some of that regulation was introduced to produce "order" in some branch of transportation and to prevent what were seen as the consequences of excesses of competition. The evils observed, however, were not so much the result of excesses of competition as of deficiencies of aggregate demand in the economy. The cure of deficiencies of aggregate demand was often sought in the 1930s by policies aimed at restricting or eliminating competition. This remedy is regarded by most of the economics profession in the 1960s as an anachronism. Our ability to prevent another major depression is a matter of fiscal and monetary policy, not of our ability to revive the cartel policies of the N.R.A.

The area of transportation policy where a re-evaluation of the need for regulation seems most urgently required is the regulation of motor trucks. Restrictions intended to limit competition by motor trucks may not now be necessary, especially controls on entry and restrictions as to the commodities a trucking firm may carry and the routes over which it may carry them.

The economic questions presented by such proposals require a judgment as to the probable course of events in markets in which economic forces are allowed freedom of action. The problem must be understood, of course, in the institutional framework that would exist, including especially in the United States the antitrust laws.

The view taken here is that the development of competition has reached an advanced stage. The effectiveness of competition by truck improves steadily as the national highway system is developed. The effectiveness of competition by water improves with improvements in navigation. There are no major economic barriers to entry in the trucking industry. The time seems to have come to relax if not to remove entirely minimum rate regulation for freight movements. Such a policy should be associated with other policies designed to insure that competition will be effective including the relaxation of controls on entry into trucking.

Complete removal of economic regulation over the railroads, trucks, pipelines and water carriers is not seriously proposed by any substantial body of opinion among students of transportation policy. The original reasons for the development of railroad regulation still apply. There remain markets and submarkets within which monopoly power persists, which should remain subject to the control of maximum rate regulation. There remains a public interest in a system of common carriage with published rates to which the carriers are bound to adhere refraining from secret concessions to favored parties. The protection involved remains, as it has always been, protection for the carriers against pressure from large buyers of transportation as well as protection to the public.

User Charges and the Allocation of Traffic Among Competing Methods of Transportation—Efficient use of resources requires rational allocation of shipments among competing carriers and competing methods of transportation. To secure rational allocation the basic reliance in a market economy is upon the self-interest of the customers, who may be expected to purchase transportation in such a manner as to minimize their costs. Businessmen will select the lowest cost method of transportation available to them, assuming no differences in quality of service. If quality of service differs, the purchasers' choices must consider more than the prices, but the same basic reliance on purchasers' desires to minimize their costs should lead to efficient allocation of resources. The managers of public enterprises, like their private counterparts, should behave in such a manner as to minimize costs.

The shippers will make their decisions based on the rates quoted to them, however, and their decisions will not be efficient if the charges do not reflect the cost to society of the service. The users should make decisions in the light of prices that reflect social costs, including the cost of any part of the transport system provided by a public agency. The user charge principle rests on this requirement. The principle states that the cost of any form of transportation should be paid by the users.

Application of this principle is not without difficulties and complications. Whenever joint or common costs are incurred in the provision of transportation, the cost of any particular service can only be approximated. For example, when a way is used by a variety of users, the cost of provision of the way must be allocated among them, whether a railway, airway, waterway, or highway is under consideration. Some element of judgment enters the allocation. Reasonable allocations, however, can be devised. The same type of problem arises when a facility is used for transportation and nontransportation purposes. Waterways present the problem in cases of multiple purpose projects. Again, reasonable allocations are possible.

There is not much controversy among transportation economists about the general proposition that highway users as a group should pay the cost of highways except where there is special reason for an exception to the rule, and that users of railways, airways, and waterways should do the same. Railroad transportation is in fact paid for by railroad users in the United States almost entirely, and, as a first approximation, the costs of highways are paid by highway users. However, there is no national airways trust fund and no waterways trust fund. Application of the user charge principle would require that such funds be established or that equivalent arrangements be made. This action was proposed in a report entitled *Federal Transportation Policy and Program* dated March 1960 and signed by Frederick H. Mueller, then Secretary of Commerce, and transmitted by President Eisenhower to the Congress. This report represents the views of the Eisenhower administration regarding transportation as closely as any single document represents them. Two years later, in April 1962, the late President Kennedy transmitted to Congress a "Message on Transportation" setting forth the views of his administration. The position he took on user charges is essentially the same: he proposed introduction of such a system both for waterways and airways.

A qualification to the principle of user charges must be entered when there are substantial benefits to non-users from increased service. Extra service provided in whole or in part for the benefit of non-users should be paid for. The benefits provided by the American merchant marine for the common defense are a leading example. A further qualification to the user charge principle must be entered when the purpose of public policy is to promote progress in transportation or stimulate development of the economy, as discussed in the next section.

The requirement of efficiency leads to an unambiguous price policy only under certain conditions. The preceding paragraphs assume that a price system that will meet the problem of financing a transportation system will also provide for the efficient operation of an existing system. A price system based on average costs will meet the financing problem. Obviously if the full cost of a service is divided among the users of the service, and they pay accordingly, the full cost will be covered. Essentially, a user cost system is a system based on that objective. A price system based on average cost, however, can be the same as a price system based on marginal cost only when average and marginal cost are the same. Further, a price system based on short run marginal cost can be the same as a price system based on long run marginal cost only when these costs coincide. These discrepancies can lead to discrepancies in policy proposals, especially when the discussion concerns the component parts of a total transportation system. For example, some economists argue for price equal to short-run marginal cost for a facility with excess capacity, such as the Mackinac Bridge, in the full knowledge that price would be less than average cost, including principal and interest on the bonds whose sale provided funds to finance construction of the Bridge. The losses might be absorbed within the framework of a general system of user charges. The position taken here is that the merits of each such proposal must be weighed individually. It is a question of how much loss of efficiency can be prevented by a proposed change in price policy, and how much unfairness in distribution of charges will result.

INVESTMENT POLICY—The most numerous problems of transportation policy that are related to the objective of economic progress are problems of investment policy. For public agencies the choices concern the amounts to be invested in public facilities; private agencies face similar decisions. How much public money to invest in basic transportation facilities involves a choice between transportation and all uses of funds including private uses as well as education, public health, national defense, and all the uses of public funds. Economic analysis can make important contributions to this choice by illuminating the costs and gains of particular proposed projects, but the choice itself is properly made through the political process.

It is apparent, however, that it will be necessary to continue to invest large sums in basic transportation facilities. The most obvious needs for large amounts of money are in the construction of highways and in urban transportation by all modes of transport. The needs for roads will not be met by the scheduled completion of the Interstate System. No program yet adopted will meet the transportation needs in most large metropolitan areas. In the next decade it seems probable that proposals will be made for the expenditure of many billions of dollars for the reconstruction of urban areas with a large fraction of the outlay on transportation facilities.

The analysis of proposed investments in transportation has received the attention of economists. The theory of investment decisions has been worked out and practical methods are in use by which the decisions are made. Progress can be expected by the refinement of the practical methods. Progress will involve the improvement of the techniques of measurement of the costs associated with projected investments and, more especially, improvement of the techniques of measuring and of forecasting the gains. Forecasting is inherently difficult but it is also an inherent necessity in any investment planning. It is especially important and especially difficult when the investment will have a long useful life, as is commonly the expectation for basic transportation facilities.

Techniques of forecasting have become most elaborate in the field of urban transportation planning. Further development and refinement of these techniques is needed. Their closer integration with general urban planning is to be expected in view of the interlocking provisions of the *Housing Act* of 1961 for comprehensive planning for urban development including coordinated transportation systems, the requirements of the *Federal-Aid Highway Act* of 1962 for cooperative planning by the states and local communities as a precondition for projects in urban areas of over 50,000 population, and the parallel requirements for planning in the *Urban Mass Transportation Act* of 1964. The effect of these requirements for planning, it is to be hoped, will include increased attention to the study of the demand for urban transportation and of the effects of transportation systems upon urban development.

SUBSIDIES—There is a public interest in the development of new systems of transportation which may justify subsidy in the early stages. The argument is analogous to the infant industry argument for tariffs. The justification is that, given a period of public support, the new system will be able to develop to the point where it can earn its own way. The indirect benefits of the existence of the new transportation system justify special attention to its growth beyond that normally given to new industries through such devices as the patent system.

The general public support of aviation illustrates the type of support which may be given. The question now at issue is whether the time has come to discontinue that support. As discussed in Chapter 16 direct subsidies no longer are paid to the trunk lines. A specific question is whether subsidies to local service carriers should be withdrawn. No

Congressman is likely to be enthusiastic about a reduction in air service in his district. But the infant industry argument implies that at some point the infant industry must become self-supporting and adjust the level of service to what the market will support. Market forces should ultimately determine the place of each transport agency.

Continuing subsidies require justification, which most commonly is found in the requirements of the national defense, as in the subsidy to the merchant marine. There are other political reasons for continuing subsidy, such as the need for a particular transportation service in the interests of national unity. It is also possible to develop an economic case for continuing subsidy in some special situation. An argument along these lines has been used in urging subsidy to urban mass transportation used by members of low income groups. In general, the burden of proof properly rests on the shoulders of those who propose the permanent subsidy.

A second level of questions concerns methods to be used for the provision of subsidies where subsidies are found to be warranted. The most successful systems of subsidy are those which include an incentive to the operators of the system to reduce their costs. The closed rate subsidies of the Civil Aeronautics Board are of this type. It may not be easy, however, to set fixed subsidies which preserve the incentive to efficiency and yet are neither so high as to provide a bonanza to the operators nor so low as to lead to losses for the operators and the withdrawal of service. The system of subsidies in ocean transportation may claim the doubtful distinction of being worst adapted to the public interest of any now in use. When the public interest requires rapid technological progress, the subsidy system fails to provide adequate rewards to the shipping companies for making the required advances.

THE THREE-FOLD NATURE OF PROGRESS IN TRANSPORTATION— Viewed in the context of the characteristics of transportation developed in the first part of this chapter, economic progress in transportation may take several forms. Progress may consist, in the first place, in the development of new types of service. Improvement may be in speed, in reliability, or in other dimensions of the quality of service. For example, jet aircraft offered a sharp increase in speed over piston aircraft, just as railroads had offered an increase in speed over inland water transportation a century before. Progress may consist, in the second place, in the extension of known types of service to additional routes. The St. Lawrence Seaway did not represent introduction of new transportation but the extension of existing methods to new routes. Progress also may consist, not in the development or extension of improved service, but in the reduction of the cost of existing service. Frequently, but, of course, not always, improved quality of service is accompanied by lower costs.

When public policy toward transportation is intended to bring about economic progress in transportation, it is appropriate to measure the success of the policy against the progress which results. Economic progress has three dimensions, as just noted, and a policy may be intended to bring about the development of new technology that will make possible faster, more reliable, or otherwise improved service; it may be intended to bring about the extension of improved methods to new routes or increased frequency of service on existing routes; or it may be intended to reduce costs. It is appropriate, then, to ask for any proposed program, what type of progress is intended? Is the gain likely to be worth the cost? Are there alternative possibilities that are more promising? When the program has been carried out further questions should be raised, what progress was achieved, if any? Was the public intervention worth the cost?

TECHNOLOGICAL INNOVATION—In the field of the development and first demonstrations of new technology there are choices to be made as to public intervention. There are choices to be made as to the total effort to be devoted to these purposes, and as to which projects to select of all possible projects. The problems of evaluation are essentially problems of forecasting costs to achieve a desired result and forecasting the benefits to the public that will be achieved by the new technology. Formally, the problem is similar to forecasting the costs and gains of an investment, but there is likely to be a large margin of error in the forecasts. In the aviation industry, for example, there is a choice between using federal money to develop a supersonic transport or a very large subsonic plane, or both, or neither. The supersonic transport is intended to produce faster service on certain routes, the long stages. The large subsonic aircraft is intended to reduce costs on certain routes, those which can support a large volume of traffic. Evaluation in each case requires estimates of the extent of the improvement and of its probable cost.

After the event it is easier to make at least rough judgments as to the success of particular ventures. For example, the first nuclear merchant vessel, the *Savannah,* has not been followed quickly by many more such vessels. There has been to date no improvement in the service available to shippers, nor has any reduction taken place in the cost of shipping, or in the burden of subsidy from the public treasury. It seems probable that equal expenditure on other projects would have been more productive, whatever the ultimate developments in nuclear powered ocean-going vessels.

What are the areas within transportation where new technology is most needed at present? The question is one for which opinions may be expected to differ. The field of ocean transport, however, is likely to be high on any list. From an American point of view the continued subsidy of an inadequate merchant marine into the indefinite future is not an appealing prospect. From an international point of view general improvement in world economic capabilities would be likely to follow from improved transport which was faster from the shipper in one country to the consignee in another, more reliable, and more economical.

A second area where technical innovation would be extremely valuable is in the movement of people overland in densely populated urban areas. Automotive transportation has been brilliantly successful in providing flexibility of service between specific origins and destinations. The collection and distribution functions of a transportation system are thus well performed. But there is no satisfactory solution to the problem of limited urban highway capacity, and the resulting congestion is all too familiar. The accident rate on urban highways is much too high. A method or combination of methods is needed that can move vehicles in large numbers rapidly and safely down main routes while retaining flexibility of local movement. Perhaps automatic control devices will be required, the use of special vehicles, the development of systems of tunnels or elevated pathways, or some entirely different arrangements.

The public benefit to be gained from innovations in transportation is so very large that increased public effort to stimulate research and development of new technology would seem worth the outlay. The sums involved in investment in transportation are so large that substantial gains can hardly fail to result from any innovations that improve the usefulness of the facilities or reduce the required outlays for fixed facilities, not to mention the indirect benefits of improved service. What is here urged is systematic effort to develop new and substantially improved systems of transportation. Past efforts have been much more successful in the refinement of existing systems and parts of systems. In the field of highway transportation the research efforts of the manufacturers of vehicles have been devoted primarily to the improvement of the vehicles considered separately, while the research effort of the Highway Research Board and Bureau of Public Roads has been concerned primarily with the planning and construction of highways. Joint consideration of what might be done if both vehicle and way were to be varied has been a relatively neglected direction of inquiry. In this respect the railroads have an advantage since both vehicle and way are under their control, a fact which no doubt accounts in part for the railroads' respectable record of technical progress in the movement of freight. Consideration of dramatically new technology, however, which might involve abandoning existing roadbeds, changing the 4', 8.5" gauge, or perhaps even substituting other guidance devices for rails, seems to have required direct intervention by the Federal government in its study of transportation in the Northeast Corridor.

EXTENSION OF TRANSPORTATION SYSTEMS—The second stage in direct public intervention after the first use of new technology involves efforts to extend transportation systems into new areas. This stage may or may not require public support. Such support frequently has been given to new transportation systems, as, for example, in continuing public subsidy to airlines. As discussed above, the basic choices have to do with when to introduce such support, how extensive the support should be, and when the support should be stopped. Since gains and costs can be forecast only with difficulty, there is here an area for controversy.

RATIONALIZATION AND IMPROVED ORGANIZATION—Public intervention to stimulate progress in transportation may involve neither the development nor the introduction of new technology. Some forms of intervention are concerned with the rationalization or improved organization of methods of transportation using existing technology. Under this heading are programs intended to lead to standardization of facilities. The British commission on railway gauges worked in this field over a century ago. Modern efforts of critical importance are concerned with such matters as standardization of containers. Public intervention also may seek to improve the organization of the flow of people and goods by the development of terminals and systems of access to terminals and markets. The bus terminal constructed by the Port of New York Authority near the Manhattan entrance to the Lincoln Tunnel is an example of such an activity.

DISORDERLY PROGRESS—Viewed as a whole, there is a disorderly, one might say an unkempt, character to American transportation policy. There is a clear need for rationalization in several areas. The user charge principle should be pushed farther in the interests of efficient allocation of resources. The organization of regulatory activities should be made more consistent with increased reliance upon market forces. There are particular branches of transportation in which a basic reconsideration of policy is needed, more conspicuously in the maritime industry.

Yet in another sense American transportation policy has to its credit a record of many successes. Although the transportation of the country has not developed without waste and inefficiencies, the system as a whole has become complex yet flexible. It provides to the economy a widening choice among a variety of transportation services. Progress has indeed occurred toward the goal set down in the National Transportation Policy in 1940: ". . . the end of developing, coordinating, and preserving a national transportation system by water, highway, and rail, as well as other means, adequate to meet the needs of the commerce of the United States, of the Postal Service, and of the national defense."

Index

Index